On the Edges of Development

Routledge Studies in Development and Society

1. Searching for Security
Women's Responses to Economic Transformations
Edited by Isa Baud and Ines Smyth

2. The Life Region
The Social and Cultural Ecology of Sustainable Development
Edited by Per Råberg

3. Dams as Aid
Anne Usher

4. Politics of Development Cooperation
NGOs, Gender and Partnership in Kenya
Lisa Aubrey

5. Psychology of Aid
A Motivational Perspective
Stuart Carr, Eilish McAuliffe and Malcolm MacLachlan

6. Gender, Ethnicity and Place
Women and Identity in Guyana
Linda Peake and D. Alissa Trotz

7. Housing and Finance in Developing Countries
Edited by Kavita Datta and Gareth Jones

8. Peasants and Religion
A Socioeconomic Study of Dios Olivorio and the Palma Sola Religion in the Dominican Republic
Jan Lundius and Mats Lundahl

9. Environment and Development in the Straits of Malacca
Mark Cleary and Goh Kim Chuan

10. Technical Knowledge and Development
Observing Aid Projects and Processes
Thomas Grammig

11. World Bank and Urban Development
From Projects to Policy
Edward Ramsamy

12. Poverty Orientated Agricultural and Rural Development
Hartmut Brandt and Uwe Otzen

13. Political Conflict and Development in East Asia and Latin America
Edited by Richard Boyd, Benno Galjart and Tak-Wing Ngo

14. Marine Natural Resources and Technological Development
An Economic Analysis of the Wealth from the Oceans
Marco Colazingari

15. Global Migration and Development
Edited by Ton Van Naerssen, Ernst Spaan, and Annelies Zoomers

16. Children, Structure and Agency
Realities Across the Developing World
G.K. Lieten

17. Understanding the Social Dimension of Sustainability
Edited by Jesse Dillard, Veronica Dujon and Mary C. King

18. On the Edges of Development
Cultural Interventions
Edited by Kum-Kum Bhavnani, John Foran, Priya A. Kurian and Debashish Munshi

First published 2009
by Routledge
711 Third Avenue, New York, NY 10017

Simultaneously published in the UK
by Routledge
2 Park Square, Milton Park, Abingdon, Oxon OX14 4RN

Routledge is an imprint of the Taylor & Francis Group, an informa business

First published in paperback 2012

Library of Congress Cataloging in Publication Data

On the edges of development : cultural interventions / edited by Kum-Kum Bhavnani . . . [et al.].
p. cm.—(Routledge studies in development and society ; 18)
Includes bibliographical references and index.
1. Economic development projects—Social aspects—Developing countries.
2. Women in development. 3. Community development—Developing countries—Citizen participation. I. Bhavnani, Kum-Kum.
HD75.8.O6 2009
306.309172'4—dc22
2008041161

ISBN10: 0-415-95621-8 (hbk)
ISBN10: 0-203-88044-7 (ebk)

ISBN13: 978-0-415-95621-5 (hbk)
ISBN13: 978-0-203-88044-9 (ebk)
ISBN 13: 978-0-415-65053-3 (pbk)

On the Edges of Development

Cultural Interventions

Edited by Kum-Kum Bhavnani, John Foran, Priya A. Kurian, and Debashish Munshi

Routledge
Taylor & Francis Group
New York London

Contents

Part II: Emergent Discourses of Development

Part III: Fictions of Development

Diagrams and Figures

DIAGRAMS

FIGURES

Acknowledgments

It has taken the cultural interventions of not just the editors and the chapter authors but several women and men around the world, some cited and many uncited, to pull together a collective effort to craft an alternative approach to development. We are grateful to each of our contributors as well as every one of those who provided insights that shaped our arguments, commented constructively on drafts of chapters, or quite simply engaged us in conversations around issues of development.

The genesis of this volume was in an interdisciplinary conference *On the Edges of Development* organized at the University of California at Santa Barbara (UCSB) in October 2004. The presentations at the conference brought together scholars and activists from around the globe to talk about the fictions of development, the visions of development, and Third World Cultural Studies, and sparked the idea of putting together an innovative volume that would look at development through fresh lenses.

We would like to thank all those who participated in and helped organize this conference, especially the members of the conference committee. A special word of gratitude goes out to the UCSB Chancellor, Henry Yang, for his support and his introductory address at the conference. We also thank the many UCSB-based sponsors of the conference including the Institute on Global Conflict and Cooperation, the Institute for Social, Behavioral, and Economic Research (ISBER), the Global and International Studies Program, the Deans and Provost of Letters and Science, the College of Creative Studies, the Hull Chair in Women's Studies, the Interdisciplinary Humanities Center, the Office of International Students and Scholars, the Center for Black Studies, the Department of History of Art and Architecture, the Latin American and Iberian Studies Program, the Multicultural Center, the Women's Center, the Women's Studies Program, and the Department of Sociology. We also thank Aparna Sindhoor for her conference finale performance of *Agua-Thanneer-Water*, an evening of dance, theater, and music that brought alive people's stories about their struggles over water, a theme we touch upon in our introduction as well as in other chapters.

Halfway around the world, in the southern hemisphere, we thank the Faculty of Arts and Social Sciences and the Waikato Management School at the University of Waikato in Hamilton, New Zealand, for their support to this project. We are also grateful to the University of Waikato's Cultural Committee, the New Zealand Federation of Graduate Women (Waikato Chapter), the Departments of Political Science and Public Policy; Geography, Tourism and Environmental Planning; Societies and Cultures; and Continuing Education for their support in helping bring Kum-Kum Bhavnani to Waikato to deliver the Vice Chancellor's Lecture in 2007. Thanks also to the many colleagues on campus, especially Patrick Barrett, Rachel Simon-Kumar, Jeanette Wright, and several others in the Department of Management Communication and in the Department of Political Science and Public Policy, for their active engagement with the ideas thrown up in the volume.

In terms of logistical support, we thank Ben Holtzman and his team at Routledge for working so patiently and diligently with us and Krista Bywater and Molly Talcott for formatting and proofreading of manuscripts.

Parts of this volume have appeared previously in the following books, whose publishers we thank for permission to reprint the following material:

We thank Duke University Press for permission to use parts of María Josefina Saldaña-Portillo's "Development and Revolution: Narratives of Liberation and Regimes of Subjectivity in the Postwar Period," pp. 17–59 of her *The Revolutionary Imagination in the Americas and the Age of Development* (Durham: Duke University Press, 2003).

We thank Zed Press for permission to use parts of Françoise Lionnet's "'She Breastfed Reluctance into Me': Hunger Artists in the Global Economy," pp. 214–234 in Susan Perry and Celeste Schenck, editors, *Eye to Eye: Women Practising Development across Cultures* (London: Zed Press, 2002).

We thank Taylor and Francis for permission to use parts of John Foran's "New Political Cultures of Opposition: What Future for Revolutions?" pp. 236–251 in John Foran, David Lane, and Andreja Zivkovic, editors, *Revolution in the Making of the Modern World: Social Identities, Globalization, and Modernity* (London: Routledge, 2007).

Kum-Kum and John thank Reena Bhavnani, our sister and sister-in-law, whose struggle has taught us so much about the power of love, compassion, and imagination in making the world a richer place.

Priya and Debashish say a special thank-you to Akanksha Khwaish and Alya Laaeqa for the questions they raise, the energy they pump into our lives, and the perspectives they provide for what it takes to build a sustainable future.

Introduction

From the Edges of Development

Kum-Kum Bhavnani, John Foran, Priya A. Kurian, and Debashish Munshi

After some six decades of circulation, *development* continues to be a contested term, referring both to the ideal of improvement in people's well-being and to a far more dystopian reality on the ground. Because of our commitment to a noneconomistic development as an important way to ameliorate poverty, we start from the premise that the post-1940s development project has clearly "failed the Third World" (Bhavnani, Foran, and Kurian, 2003b, 2). In the contemporary neocolonial age, the nexus of big business, financial institutions, and capitalist regimes have wreaked havoc on the Third World in the name of development, usually making the word a euphemism for the exploitation of the world's natural resources to benefit minuscule transnational elites located in all sections of the world.

Flames of death and destruction, fueled by the desire of the United States, the United Kingdom, and their allies to control the cash-rich resource of oil, have engulfed large parts of the world, most visibly in the Middle East, from Iraq to Lebanon, but also in places such as Sudan and Venezuela, which are firmly in the media gaze but whose oil resources are often not discussed at length. The battles to control water—the other vital resource—have had no less devastating consequences (see, for example, Bhavnani and Bywater, Chapter 4, this volume). Much of the strife in the Middle East has been about Israel's relentless push for a development that is based on a disproportionate control of water systems that has left Palestinians with scarce access to a vital resource. In fact, as Vandana Shiva (2002) points out in *Water Wars*, some of the most important conflicts of our time revolve around contested needs for resources that are crucial for being seen as part of this apparently modern, technologically advanced, and strongly scientific era. So obsessed have neoliberal governments and market libertarians become with their need to control water that they have systematically promoted the privatization of a resource that every living being ought to take for granted, an obsession that has had tragic consequences for the poor in regions as diverse as Bolivia, South Africa, and India. Development-driven projects funded by the World Bank in South Africa that redrew water distribution networks on commercially viable lines sparked cholera epidemics in the poorest regions of the country (Bond 2001; see also Conca 2006).

State terror was unleashed on the residents of the Bolivian city of Cochabamba to quell protests against the exorbitant prices of water set by Aguas del Tunari, a subsidiary of the transnational corporation Bechtel (Shultz 2005b). The government annulled the contract only after sustained public protests and rebellion (Olivera 2004).

That these regions were predominantly populated by Black people would come as no surprise to those who have followed the development agenda in much of the world. In most cases, the worst impacts are felt by Third World subaltern publics who are at the receiving end of the environmental havoc and social upheaval caused by an endless quest for resources on their lands (Munshi and Kurian 2005, 2007). Some of these Third World publics include the Adivasis[1] in India (see, for example, Kurian 2000; Baviskar 2003), the Ogoni peoples who bore the brunt of multinational oil exploration in Nigeria (Rowell 1996), the Kayapo in Brazil (Turner 1999), and the Meratus Dayaks of Indonesia (Tsing 1993, 2005).

In each of these cases, development as a project that centers growth as its main goal has failed the most vulnerable people of the Third World because of a misplaced emphasis on varieties of top-down, elite-devised "modernization" strategies, a lack of attention to the central contributions of women and people of color, and a disregard for culture. For this form of development project, the Third World has been used as space for the creation of new "resource frontiers . . . made possible by Cold War militarization of the Third World and the growing power of corporate transnationalism" (Tsing 2005, 28). As Anna Tsing (2005, 28) points out, these "resource frontiers" were places where business and the military joined hands to "disengage nature from local ecologies and livelihoods" and rebrand natural resources as commodities for trade and profit. As Tsing (2005) shows, through a powerful study of the South East Kalimantan region of Indonesia, the relentless pursuit of resources to fire the engine of development has devastated local populations not just economically but also culturally, as local ways of living and being give way to the profit-and-loss logic of capitalism. This is not totally new of course. Retelling what is a familiar story, the ravages of colonialism meant that European colonizers had embarked on what they saw as a mission to "civilize" the colonies but, as Frantz Fanon says, we now "know with what sufferings humanity has paid for every one of their triumphs of the mind" (1965, 252). This link between the civilizing mission of colonialism and the modernization project of development is rarely discussed within mainstream publications on development. As a result, much of conventional development is founded upon a set of fictional narratives that overlook many of its exploitative practices—fictions which might suggest some reasons for its failure for the peoples of the Third World.

There is another face to development, however. For us, this is an apt moment to insistently interrogate the dominant paradigm of development that has—along with the rather different approaches in Harry S. Truman's 1949 inaugural presidential address and at the 1955 Bandung Conference—

served to produce the idea of the Third World (Hadjor 1992; Prashad 2007). Truman, in his 1949 inaugural presidential address said: "We must embark on a bold new programme for making the benefits of our scientific advances and industrial progress available for the improvement and growth of underdeveloped areas. The old imperialism—exploitation for foreign profit—has no place in our plans. What we envisage is a programme of development based on the concepts of democratic fair dealing" (quoted in Sachs 1992, 6).

As Wolfgang Sachs says, "Two billion people became underdeveloped on that day," and, we would argue, despite Truman's insistence otherwise, that it provided a legitimation to continue the colonial relationship albeit in a more modern guise. Truman's way of thinking about development is in contrast to, for example, the notion put forward at the 1955 Bandung Conference when Third World countries emphasized the importance of Third World nations relying on each other for scientific technical assistance and expertise, rather than relying on, and thus becoming dependent on, First World nations for such knowledge. Although the thinking about development at Bandung was top-down, nonetheless, those at that conference envisioned development as having the potential to be mutually supportive through a reciprocal exchange of scientific and technological expertise. In other words, development, at Bandung, was not viewed merely as a site for the entry of capitalism.

In our interrogations, we also seek to show how a critical element of development is about access to resources by the poorest and most marginalized populations and, as Mike Keefe-Feldman says, this access is "a struggle that is at once cultural, political, and ideological" (2006). The struggles over life-sustaining "goods" such as water, land, and forests epitomize not only the ongoing process of commodification of such resources but also a reframing of essential resources, within the antiprivatization movement, "from public good to human right" (Conca 2006, 215, 246). In this way, new concepts of development—from below, democratically engaged, and seeking empowerment by those most affected—are constantly bubbling up. It is this refusal of globalization, with its many entangled and complex dimensions, as well as the refusal of an economistic development-from-above, that are explored in this volume.

POST-DEVELOPMENT AND ITS CHALLENGES

Wide-ranging critiques of the modern development project from a variety of perspectives have been present at least since the 1970s. Perhaps the most radical of these critiques are those that have emerged since the 1990s over the rejection of the development project itself—sometimes grouped together under the umbrella term of *post-development*, *alternative development*, or *neo/populist development*, to name the most prominent (see, among others, Escobar 1992, 1995; Rahnema 1997; Esteva 1992, 2006). Post-development perspectives scrutinize the narrow rationalist thinking upon which mainstream development—its institutions and practitioners—rely. The philosophical basis for the failure of development is this rationalist approach founded on a belief in a unilinear notion of progress and the conviction that the Third World is deficient in both knowledge and information (McFarlane 2006; Ziai 2004). The struggles "between global capital and biotechnology interests, on the one hand, and local communities and organizations, on the other, constitute the most advanced stage in which the meanings over development and postdevelopment are being fought over" (Escobar 1995, 19).

Arturo Escobar's post-development argument, drawing from Foucauldian thinking, identifies three major discourses—democracy, (cultural) difference, and antidevelopment—which could serve as the basis for envisioning new struggles and expanding "anti-imperialist, anti-capitalist, anti-productivist, and anti-market struggles to new terrains" (1992, 431). Through this emphasis on discursive analyses, as well as the significance it gives local and indigenous knowledges, post-development offers a move away from "the centring of economic relations" (Brigg 2002, 421), which characterize mainstream development studies. Indeed, Foucauldian notions of discourse and power have been central to the efforts of many post-development authors in focusing on the discourses of rationality that drive mainstream development institutions and development practices (see also, for example, Ferguson 1994; Escobar 1995; Kothari 2001).

The post-development critique of development dovetails with feminist, indigenous, and environmentalist critiques of the development project (see, for example, Fernandes and Menon 1987; Sen and Grown 1987; Shiva 1988; Marchand and Parpart 1995; Spivak 1999; Kurian 2000; Bhavnani, Foran, and Kurian 2003a). Each of these critical trajectories has demonstrated, in varying detail, the flaws, absences, and the explicitly destructive nature of modern economistic development.[2] There are, also, however, many who question this modern development project and simultaneously take issue with the writings of those sympathetic to post-development, who appear to simplify and homogenize mainstream development and underestimate its appeal for Third World states (see, for example, Pieterse 1998). Thus, in his comments on post-development, Piers Blaikie calls for "a more politically astute and practical reconstruction of certain aspects of 'development,' particularly in the neopopulist mode of developmentalism" (2000, 1033). Further, he criticizes what he considers to be a "romanticised notion of the local," the failure to question problematic "social agendas that appear at the local sites of power" (Blaikie 2000, 1038–1039), and, alongside others, the absence of credible alternatives offered by post-development work (Blaikie 2000; Pieterse 1998, 2000; Schuurman 2000; Matthews 2004). A number of other analysts have attempted to moderate post-development's argument that development is one form of colonization and have argued that such a notion not only stems from a misinterpretation of Foucauldian notions of power, but is also "a hyperbolic rhetorical device" (Brigg 2002, 422; see also Rossi 2004). Indeed, as Aram Ziai succinctly states, the "ambivalence of post-development" lends itself to either a "reactionary neo-populism" or an emancipatory radical democracy (Ziai 2004, 1045, 1058).

Against this background, Sally Matthews (2004, 380) offers the argument that the African context "with its rich variety of ways of understanding and being" is a source that "can provide the seeds for thought for all those . . . who question the PWWII [post–World War II] development project." In contrast to the lamenting of the loss of African values that some argue occur in the wake of mainstream development (Etounga-Manguelle, 2000), there are others such as Jean-Marc Ela (1998), whose argument we embrace, albeit critically, in this volume:

> Africa is not against development. It dreams of other things than the expansion of a culture of death or an alienating modernity that destroys the fundamental values so dear to Africans. . . . Africa sees further than an all-embracing world of material things and the dictatorship of the here and now, that insists on trying to persuade us that the only valid motto is "I sell, therefore I am." In a world often devoid of meaning, Africa is a reminder that there are other ways of being. (Ela 1998)

This eloquent statement offers much food for thought, despite the fact that it homogenizes "Africa," a homogenization that is a little too close for our comfort to how colonizers and Eurocentric perspectives view the continent.

FROM THE EDGES OF DEVELOPMENT

In this volume, we as editors, along with the chapter contributors, take account of the contributions of the post-development scholarship. We are mindful that some of the critiques of post-development scholarship stem partly from the desire for answers—for alternatives to existing paradigms and practices of development. Our volume does not offer prescriptions or "how-to" formulae for doing development. The primary goal of this volume is to reenvision development through a rigorous yet imaginative exploration of how alternative conceptualizations—many of which emerge from the edges of development—can recenter the myriad refusals to contemporary mainstream development policy and thought. These conceptualizations draw on a variety of approaches from the realms of cultural studies, postcolonial studies, critical geography, and literary criticism. Most specifically, we adopt a Third World Cultural Studies perspective that represents "a political approach to culture, and a cultural approach to politics, focusing on how political discourses circulate and compete" (Foran 2002, 3). Our approach in this volume builds on the Women, Culture, Development

(WCD) paradigm, which rearticulates development by centering women and viewing culture as lived experience, thereby making visible the agency of subaltern women and men in the facilitation of social change and transformation in the Third World (see Bhavnani, Foran, and Kurian 2003a).

Mapping these cultural, political, and ideological fault lines is a major step in demystifying development. We put forward our cartography as a way to demonstrate how the articulation of the labor, cultures, and histories of women and men outside the mainstream frame of development offers more helpful insights to ameliorate injustice and inequality, the ultimate goal for all forms of development. The subaltern women and men centered in our approach are not seen, first and foremost, as victims in a system of cruel and unjust inequalities, but rather, as leading agents of change. This emphasis on racialization, ethnicization, and gender includes, by definition, a discussion of indigenous modes of agency. That we base our thinking on cultural studies approaches means that paradigms of development can be propelled toward an active engagement with subaltern agency. This, in turn, decenters the top-down approach to development we have critiqued previously.

A special aim of our volume is to shift development from its Eurocentric focal points much as the subaltern historians (see Chakrabarty 2000) "provincialized" Europe by positioning European art, history, literature, and philosophy as simply one of many strands of intellectual thought rather than the primary one. In line with the idea that Europe is "an imaginary figure that remains deeply embedded in clichéd and shorthand forms in some everyday habits of thought" (Chakrabarty 2000, 4), we argue that mainstream development is largely elitist, functionalist, and inclined to privilege First World ways of being. From this it is possible to see that this unilinear or progressivist concept of development is entrenched in policymakers' and practitioners' minds along with top-down science and technology. We address this unilinearity through a series of critical interrogations. This only becomes possible when drawing on multidisciplinary perspectives which emanate beyond the borders of the mainstream development literature. In our insistence that we closely examine the edges of development rather than an epistemological core, we put forward an idea of development that focuses on the realities of people's lives in the Third World. What this means is that, in this volume, we turn the spotlight onto the lived experiences of the largely unsung but key protagonists of the South such as "peasants, tribals, semi- or unskilled industrial workers in non-Western cities, men and women from the subordinate social groups—in short, the subaltern classes of the third world" (Chakrabarty 2000, 8). It is this multidisciplinary approach—one that peels away the fictions of development, that centers refusals to development, and that understands the significance of science and technology as being crucial in creating greater equality as long as it is not under the control of those whose only motivation is to create greater and greater profits—that we offer here. That is, we privilege an analysis of ways in which development has been, and continues to be, refused. In so doing, this collection focuses our critical gaze on the discourses that create an inferiorized Third World and which quickly translate into forms of development that are inherently oppressive (see Bayoumi, Chapter 1, and Munshi and Kurian, Chapter 7, this volume).

In the quest to articulate this new conception, we have organized the volume to address three questions: (1) How is mainstream development "refused," and how can such a refusal suggest ways toward a more equitable and livable development? (2) How are emergent discourses around science, sexuality, and gendered economies challenging dominant approaches to development? (3) How do fictions and other cultural productions help us to analyze mainstream development as well as envision alternatives?

ORGANIZATION AND CONTENTS

In Part I, we look at the notion of "refusing" development as being both a utopian ideal and a necessary aspect of many struggles from below which aim to alter the terms of globalization from above. To "refuse" development is to show its devastating consequences as it is propounded by governments, global financial institutions and trade agreements, and transnational capital. Refusing development simultaneously redefines cultural symbols and political agents in ways that point toward effective opposition and credible alternatives. This part of the volume juxtaposes past and present, and draws its materials from a rejection of the all-consuming hegemonic paradigm of *Westernity*. Molefi Asante (Chapter 5) engages with this term while Moustafa Bayoumi (Chapter 1) reminds readers of the struggles for Algerian independence as played out in Paris in 1961. Hume Johnson (Chapter 2) analyzes this refusal through her examination of the creative strategies of struggle carried out by women street vendors in Jamaica, and Ara Wilson (Chapter 3) shows how the contested sexual geography and varied layers of the economy of Bangkok form a significant part of Thai women's daily political and cultural practices. Finally, Kum-Kum Bhavnani and Krista Bywater (Chapter 4) show how the challenges to the privatization of water in India lead to a refusal that gives succor to social justice movements around the world. Each chapter, in its own way, thus traces pathways toward alternatives to current regimes of development.

In Part II, we look at the emergent discourses of development. Discourses—the ways in which we talk about the world—play an important role in shaping that world, for better or for worse. Our use of discourse also connotes the lived experiences of people, how identities are constructed, particularly political ones, how cultural meanings are transmitted and interpreted, and how individuals, groups, communities, and nations relate to each other in ways that inevitably include cultural processes. Four areas that have assumed increasing visibility in this contestation between visions of development are the struggles over political discourses of liberation, science, sexuality, and the ways that economies are gendered. The contributors to Part II take up these ideas. María Josefina Saldaña-Portillo (Chapter 6) reflects on anticolonial liberation narratives from across the Third World, and Debashish Munshi and Priya Kurian (Chapter 7) inform us of the ways in which genetic bioengineering and immigration play out in complementary tension in New Zealand. John Foran (Chapter 10) presents a theory of the new languages of revolution through the conceptual lens of political cultures of opposition. Magdalena Villarreal (Chapter 9) analyzes the impact of the rural development policies of the Mexican state and capital on women, while Ming-Yan Lai (Chapter 8) narrates the many stories of Filipino/a overseas workers in Hong Kong. Collectively, these chapters suggest the force of culture in development and social change and link discourse to social structures in a variety of ways.

The final part of the book, Part III, explores the idea that development is, in many senses, made up of a number of fictions. The failure of the half century of development since the end of World War II to deliver much in the way of a better life for the 80 percent of the planet's population that make up the Third World—the *majority* world—is one way to think about how the grandiose and desirable goals of development have become fictions. Another way to see the fictions of development is to comprehend that the very idea of development is a construction, or rather, a series of constructions, in people's minds, be they planners, government officials, international lenders, or members of nongovernmental organizations (NGOs) and civil society. A yet deeper layer to fictions of development lies in cultural production, particularly novels and myths, which, ironically, are sometimes able to tell the stories of development more realistically, and certainly more vividly, than scholarly production. Tera Maxwell (Chapter 13) discusses the ways in which Filipina discursive reappropriations of a mythic past counter contemporary modernist arguments, while Kennedy et al. (Chapter 12) discuss Paule Marshall's unsurpassed classic set on a fictional island in the Caribbean, *The Chosen Place, the Timeless People*. Films, both documentary and features, constitute another set of fictions around development with lessons about how development might be imagined differently. Lena Khor (Chapter 11) looks at the Mama Benz phenomenon in West Africa, while Françoise Lionnet (Chapter 14) moves us to the southwestern Indian Ocean and explores the insights afforded by thematizing development as a fiction.

It is our hope that a central focus on how culture shapes development, the wide interdisciplinarity we present, the broad and diversely situated regions of the world that are brought into contact with it, the themes we have organized the volume around, the connections between scholarship and social change, and the juxtapositions of the past with the present and future will constitute unique and significant contributions of this volume. The tracing of development as an ever-new possibility that lies at the intersection of feminist, cultural, and Third World studies promises glimpses of a new world on the horizons of the new century. We urgently need such glimpses.

As we send this book to press in November 2008, Barack Obama has just been elected President of the United States. In scenes reminiscent of the first democratic election in South Africa in 1994, queue upon queue of voters, many black, were determined to cast their (sometimes first) vote to indicate their desire for a new future in the U.S. Hope and optimism are peeking from the edges of development. But it is a hope tempered by the ravages of unbridled capitalist mechanisms of development manifest in global crises ranging from the collapse of money markets and an economic recession in the West to the human catastrophes in places as far flung as the Democratic Republic of Congo, Iraq, and Afghanistan caused by rampant exploitation of natural resources under the guise of "conflicts" and wars. We welcome any change, large or small, that offers a chance for women and men in the Third and First Worlds to move forward together to create a world free of inequality and injustice. *¡Sí se puede!*

NOTES

1. *Adivasi* literally means "original dwellers" and is a widely accepted term in India to refer to indigenous or tribal peoples.
2. See, for example, the review of WID (Women in Development), WAD (Women and Development), and GAD (Gender and Development) approaches in Bhavnani, Foran, and Kurian (2003b), and a discussion of the marginalization of environmental issues in mainstream development in Kurian (2000).

Part I

Refusing Representations of Development

1 October 17, 1961

Moustafa Bayoumi

The failures of development are self-evident everywhere you look. Global justice remains elusive and basic needs such as water and health care are increasingly privatized out of the reach of far too many people. Across the planet, warfare is ascendant, corruption rules, and poverty expands. Clearly the time is long past to examine the idea of Third World development and its relationship to European imperialism. New paradigms are urgently called for, formations of thinking that can mine the truth of how various peoples across the global south (and in the pockets of the global south found in the industrialized north) actually live. In this chapter, I propose that Third World Cultural Studies (TWCS) contains the possibility to break from modernization theory's colonial past (and present) due to its sensitivities to the historic and lived experiences of subject populations and to the varieties of colonial violence. An engaged TWCS, moreover, seeks to historicize our contemporary condition and to recover lost and hidden histories that remain obscured by the dominant representations of our era. A historical sensibility is essential to the success of TWCS. Amnesia is characteristic of power, which forever seeks to forget all that is inconvenient for its execution, but there can be no justice without memory. To that end, I explore in this chapter the concept of TWCS by turning to one incident, a forgotten moment more than forty years ago when colonial violence invaded the city of Paris.

It was one of those crisp October mornings in Paris, the kind that bring people out in overcoats and hats onto the river bridges. On this day, while the water lapped gently beneath them, several hundred people assembled on the Saint-Michel bridge in the fourth arrondissement, steps away from the Préfecture de Police and the Palais de Justice. They were as still as night, observing a minute of silence in mourning for a group of Algerian dead. Among the crowd this morning was the mayor of Paris and several other elected officials, though the president of the republic was notable by his absence only. Meanwhile, on the other side of the bridge, their access blocked by the police, protesters had amassed noisily and were holding up a sign marked in bold block letters that read "Shame to the FLN collaborators." This group of the extreme right, stranded on the left bank, bellowed familiar slogans like "Proud to be French!" and "Algérie Française!" (*Agence France-Press*, October 17, 2001), their belligerent voices easily transported over the diamond waters of the Seine. But there was no violence this time, and the brief ceremony seemed over before it all began. The feelings it embodied, however, felt like they had never ceased.

The day in question was October 17, 1961, a date that had long been forgotten by many in Paris, but the ceremony just described took place forty years later to the day. This time, in 2001, the police protected the protestors, who in turn were not Algerians but French. Forty years earlier, the scene looked quite different. A massive and peaceful demonstration had been planned for that night by the Fédération de France of the FLN (Front de Libération Nationale). Twelve days earlier, on October 5, 1961, the prefect of police, Maurice Papon, now infamous for sending 1,560 Jews off to concentration camps during the Vichy years, had decreed an ethnic-specific curfew on the Algerian population alone: all Algerians, or "Muslim French of Algeria" as they were called, were to be off the streets between the hours of 8:30 p.m. and 5:30 a.m. Cafés were to close at 7 p.m. and, as a police circular stated, "it is highly recommended to the Muslim French to circulate separately, small groups being likely to appear suspect with the rounds and patrols of the police" (Le Cour Grandmaison 2001, 204).

The Algerian war, begun in 1954, had come home to roost in important ways. So much so that Michel Debré, then prime minister, had written in 1958 that the FLN's capital was Paris (Einaudi 1991, 25). The same year General Raoul Salan stated, "The Mediterranean runs through France as the Seine runs through Paris" (quoted in Vidal-Naquet 1963, 107). (Salan, it should be remembered, became a founding member of the far right OAS—the Secret Army Organization—and was a leader in the failed putsch to assassinate President de Gaulle.) In fact, Debré and Salan's chronology is slightly off. Thousands of Algerians had been in the French capital as laborers since the beginning of the century, but as the war went on, the center of its conflict increasingly enveloped Paris. Police violence against Algerians in Paris, however, predates the Algerian war. In 1953, police opened fire on a group of peaceful demonstrators from the PPA (Parti Populaire Algérien, a precursor to the MNA, the Mouvement Nationale Algérien) during a demonstration on Bastille Day, killing seven and wounding thirty (Stora 2001, 60). But with the liberation war, the levels of violence escalated dramatically. By the late 1950s, the "café wars" had broken out between two rival national liberation groups, the MNA and the FLN, and this bloody fratricidal conflict between the two groups claimed almost 5,000 lives and 10,000 (overwhelmingly Algerian) wounded, a large number in Paris and its suburbs (Einaudi 1991, 20–21).

By 1960, the FLN emerged victorious, only to face off with a new enemy, a police department heavily populated with former Algerian administrators and deeply infiltrated with OAS sympathizers. Papon himself, who was made prefect in 1958, had served two years in the Algerian city of Constantine before accepting his latest appointment. During extensive operations of surveillance and detention, police systematically arrested and tortured hundreds of Algerians in known locations in Paris. Thousands were detained in four different internment camps set up in France or were removed to camps in Algeria. The FLN responded by firebombing police installations, and the two groups often confronted each other on the street. On June 8, 1961, Papon then issued his police force a pass to carry out whatever repression they felt was necessary. He told them to "take care of your business regarding the Algerians. When it comes [down to it], you will be covered" (Péju 2000, 176). The war between the two groups intensified, and Papon stated publicly on October 2, 1961, that the police force's "resolution to suppress terrorism [was] unshakeable. For every blow received, we will carry out ten" (Péju 2000, 182). Three days later, he imposed the broad-brushed curfew on the 150,000 Algerians living in and around the city of light, a dark decree of collective punishment and humiliation delivered in the sanctified name of security.

To protest the curfew and its racism, some 30,000 Algerians—men, women, and children—heeded a call by the FLN to organize and began assembling in the heart of the city, knowing they would be challenging the law. By 8 p.m., they had arrived from the *bidonvilles* and poor neighborhoods of the city, places like Belleville, Montmartre, and Barbès, and from the surrounding suburbs or *banlieues*, namely Nanterre, Gennevilliers, and St. Denis. Following the FLN's recommendations, they were wearing their best clothes and were armed only with their collective power. Exactly what happened next is finally in little dispute, but its implications certainly are. The police responded with overwhelming brutality, bludgeoning the demonstrators with batons as they emerged from the metro stations, shooting others, seizing over 11,000 (the police admitted to arresting 11,538 people), carting them away in ready vans to the Palais de Sports, where they endured further torture for days. Later, they would be moved to an internment camp at Vincennes, as the Palais des Sports had to be quickly "disinfected" for a Ray Charles concert on October 20 (Le Cour Grandmaison 2001, 214).

For days, the killing continued, some reportedly at police headquarters itself and under the watchful eye of Papon, and Algerians would continue to be found dead in the nearby woods, hanging from trees. Dozens more were found later floating on the top of the river, their bodies plump with water, their hands bound behind their backs (Vidal-Naquet 1963, 116; Péju 2000, 159).

The massacre of scores—and probably hundreds—of peaceful Algerian demonstrators in the heart of the city, at the hands of the police, and under the half-closed eyes of the Parisians is a horrific event in its own right, but what heaped injury upon even death was what followed in the French public sphere. The massacre was suppressed from the official record as the police began systematically seizing documentary evidence of the evening's carnage, and politicians aped official denials. Eugène Claudius-Petit, a member of the National Assembly, had demanded an inquiry from the government on October 30, to which Roger Frey, minister of the interior, responded by saying there was not even "a sign of the appearance of a shadow of proof" (Vidal-Naquet 1963, 117). In the municipal council, a vote was put forward for an inquiry, the results being 43 to 39 against such a course of action (Einaudi 2001, 255). Instead, the council adopted a resolution "addressed to the Parisian police expressing our confidence and gratitude" (Einaudi 2001, 247).

Meanwhile, the publisher François Maspero witnessed the event traveling around the city that night. From his bookstore, La Joie de lire, on 40, rue Saint-Severin, he saw what he described as a "neighborhood under siege." He wrote:

> The blows of the nightsticks were taken on the head, then, when the victim fell to the ground, surrounded by several men, the beating continued. The men who were doing the beating did not just have fortified nightsticks but all different types of arms, bludgeons made out of rubber or riding crops. There was no resistance. What made the greatest impression [on me] was the muffled sound of the blows to the skull. (Maspero 1999)

While some French passersby cheered the police, Maspero and a group of others assisted a handful of victims into a nearby pharmacy. Over the next few weeks, Maspero worked on a pamphlet with several other people in order to publish an account of the events. Paulette Péju edited the testimony of dozens of witnesses, and Maspero combined this with six photographs taken by the photographer Elie Kagan that night. The printer refused to print the pamphlet, and the police seized the galley sheets. Jacques Panijel, an amateur filmmaker who witnessed some of the black events of the night, produced a docudrama detailing the demonstration, along with scenes from the difficult daily life of Algerian laborers, the torture room used by the police in 28, rue de la Goutte d'Or, and the ensuing massacre (Panijel 1961). After its initial showing in October 1962, it too was seized. The journalist Pierre Vidal-Naquet published a book in 1963 titled *Torture: Cancer of Democracy*, in which he details not just the incidents of October 17, 1961, but also the torture chambers found in Algeria and around France during the war years. The book, banned in France, would be published in that country only in 1972. No one, it appeared, wanted to remember. This amnesia pertains not just to that night but basically to the whole of the Algerian war. Let bygones be bygones, the feeling went, for what good would it do? After all, "the essence of a nation is that all individuals have many things in common, and also that they have forgotten many things," wrote Ernest Renan in 1882 (Renan 1990, 11).

Slowly and resolutely, however, the events of the night of October 17 did come forward, and burning away the fog of collective amnesia is one hopeful aspect of this story. For four decades, there had been no official recognition of these events, until, after years of effort by historians (such as Jean-Luc Einaudi and Mohammed Harbi), novelists (like Leila Sebbar and Didier Daeninckx), and activists (who formed the organization, 17 octobre 1961: Contre l'oubli), the city finally installed the plaque on the Saint-Michel bridge in 2001. It bears the simple inscription: "To the memory of the numerous Algerians killed by the bloody repression during the peaceful demonstration of 17 October 1961," with its text facing in the direction of the police station. Recognition might bring acceptance, one might believe, but the scene witnessed in 2001—with the familiar refrain of Algérie française—felt rather like regression. If this was about coming to terms with the past, then "What does coming to terms with the past mean?" as T. W. Adorno, in another context, once asked. Answering his own question, Adorno writes: "We will not have come to terms with the past until the causes of what happened then are no longer active. Only because these causes live on does the spell of the past remain, to this very day, unbroken" (Adorno 1986, 29).

Indeed, the October massacre casts its spell over a host of issues, many of which are germane to the chapters in this volume. Why, for example, is a just reckoning of the past repeatedly fought—and worth fighting—for? Why is the contest for memory so important for forging a workable future? And why is it that colonialism's structures of feeling continue to thrive in a world that has ostensibly recognized the failures of conquest and overseas rule? If we investigate the October massacre and its subsequent history, we may find that the answer to these questions lies in the simple fact that we live in an increasingly single and organized humanity, and that the denial of one's past equates not just to a blindness, but to the expulsion of one's place in that very same humanity. There will be more said about this shortly, but there is also something else that we are bound to discover via the October massacre, namely a notion involving the specific configurations of power that made up (in part) 1960s France and that is perhaps frighteningly relevant to our contemporary (globalizing, unipolar, and violent) world.

Fifty years ago, Hannah Arendt raised a provocative question, inquiring into the precise relationship between imperialism and totalitarianism. For her, imperialism was the first act for the subsequent tragedy of World War II and the Holocaust. It was, in her words, "a preparatory stage for coming catastrophes" (Arendt 1968, 123). Combining race-thinking with mob violence, imperialism unleashed a new species of men, colonial administrators, whom she labels "functionaries of violence" (Arendt 1968, 137) and who were given "more latitude than in any Western country" to "create new realities" through violent means (Arendt 1968, 136–137). Joseph Conrad's Kurtz, from *Heart of Darkness* ([1902] 1990), is paradigmatic of the lawless and violent colonial administrator for Arendt. The lawlessness and aloofness of colonial rule, along with its brute violence, may have emancipated the bourgeoisie from the economic and moral limitations of the European state, but it also infected the project of living together beneficially in a social polity. "African colonial possessions," she argues, became the most fertile soil for the flowering of what later was to become the Nazi elite. Here they had seen with their own eyes how people could be converted into races and how . . . one might push one's own people into the position of the master race" (Arendt 1968, 206). Everyone else is, at any appointed time, merely superfluous.

In Arendt's narrative, imperialism "boomerangs" back to the metropole when the same species of violence that is used on the natives abroad repatriates itself at home (Arendt 1968, 206). The army becomes a police force, domestically and internationally, and the liberal nation ossifies into totalitarian terror. Arendt was not the only one to make this claim. Aimé Césaire labels Nazism a "boomerang effect" of colonialism (Césaire [1955] 2000, 36) and, prior to Hitler, J. A. Hobson worried about how "the arts and crafts of tyranny, acquired and exercised in Empire, should be turned against our liberties at home" (Hobson [1938] 1965, 152).

There are ample reasons why this story makes even more sense in 1960s France, and they are not limited to the brazen fact that the police chief at the time, Maurice Papon, was later convicted for his Nazi collaboration. Since Papon was also a colonial police official in Algeria before assuming his metropolitan post, we ought to examine the police in Algeria closely to see how the boomerang effect flew through the sky and landed on the Île-de-France. From early on the police assumed a military stance in Algeria and that role was transferred to the metropole. We should be less than surprised at this confusion and co-mingling between local and colonial policing, for after all, what else could we expect in a war that wasn't even labeled a war until 1992, before then being known only as a police action "to maintain law and order"?

The creep of totalitarian violence occurred early in the war, when the Algerian colonial police force, which was "armed with powers unknown to the police in France," in the words of Vidal-Naquet (1963, 31), was accused of carrying out vicious acts of torture. The French government responded by attempting to "integrate" the Algerian colonial police with the French police. "The intention [here] was to 'metropolitanize' the Algerian police," writes Vidal-Naquet, "but was there not a risk of 'Algerianizing' the French police? . . . This forecast proved all too true," he explains, "for the police officers who were transferred from Algeria to France formed 'activist' groups which became torture cells" (Vidal-Naquet 1963, 33). This is of course the same policing that the demonstrators met that night in October.

Rather than continuing this argument in detail, we can instead consider that what we call globalization today is the successor to European colonialism. If that is the case, then there may be many reasons to consider certain totalitarian arrangements of power as the inheritors of imperialism, which carries with it consequences for understanding our present political order. But instead of following this question through, I wish instead to feed off of it, for I am more interested, in this chapter, in investigating that most surprising element of the October massacre—not that it happened, but that it happened in Paris.

The October massacre is an incidence of colonial violence that has exceeded the geography of the colony and has disrupted the supposed sanctity of metropolitan space. Our very security in the First World, we must note, has long been premised upon exporting a violent anarchy to the Third World. "We're fighting the terrorists abroad so we do not have to face them here at home" (*Federal News Service,* November 1, 2004) yaps President Bush in nonsense, but there is history to his nonsense. If development discourse all too often feeds off of a kind of fictive anterior time, then the October massacre illustrates a First World division of the world according not to time (say, developed and developing worlds), but to space, particularly as it relates to the varieties of violent experiences. Consider what Carl Siger, in his 1907 *Essai sur la colonization*, says: "The new countries offer a vast field for individual, violent activities which, in the metropolitan countries, would run up against certain prejudices, against a sober and orderly conception of life, and which, in the colonies, have greater freedom to develop and, consequently, to affirm their worth. Thus to a certain extent the colonies can serve as a safety valve for modern society. Even if this were their only value, it would be immense" (quoted in Césaire 2000, 41–42).

What I am suggesting is that we investigate the varieties of violence more closely and interrogate cultural responses to various forms of violence carefully. Only then can we hope to identify the peculiar arrangements of power and the particular players involved, all in the hopes, really, of averting further catastrophe. In this regard, we ought to question whether colonial violence ever left us, and if it remains an overseas affair. Furthermore, in the spirit of a TWCS approach, which aims to examine the lived experiences and politics of Third World peoples in their totality, we also ought to ask about the cultural components to colonial violence. On its bloody face, colonial violence appears irrational and sadistic in the extreme. Colonial violence after all always aims to "teach a lesson" to a group, so it addresses not just a subject but also a people through its brutality, and by doing so, it becomes not just an individually harmful but also a people-destroying force. But we may be excusing its own excesses by considering it irrational. Rather, we ought to view colonial violence, wherever or whenever it flares, as always rational, calculated, and culturally coded. In colonialism's own vernacular, pogroms are not acts of terror but, in the bland words of J. A. Cathill, are "administrative massacres" (quoted in Arendt 1968, 216).

Colonial violence then is demonically bicultural with the aim of establishing a pacified and compliant monoculturalism (disguised by a feeble biculturalism comprised of native and ruler cultures). In the Algerian war, that was certainly the case. Cultural inquiry played a large, rational, and calculated role in driving an oppressive, not a liberatory, spirit. The anthropologist Jean Servier, for example, was instrumental in setting up Les Harkis, an Algerian auxiliary military force of more than 100,000 people that was established to be a native enforcer of the natives (Horne 1987, 254–256). After the war, France abandoned the enforcers and many of them were tragically murdered in Algeria. The *pied noir* police force in France, furthermore, was listened to because it argued that it had a better sense of Algerian culture and thus knew how to inflict the right kind of pain.

More recently, we witnessed something similar with the Abu Ghraib torture scandal in Iraq, where humiliation and horror were dispensed in deliberately cultural ways. "They forced me to eat pork and they put liquor in my mouth," reports Ameen Sa'eed Al-Sheikh, an Iraqi detainee at Abu Ghraib. He continues:

> The guard started to hit me on my broken leg several times with a solid plastic stick . . . They stripped me naked. One of them told me he would rape me. He drew a picture of a woman to my back and makes me stand in shameful positions holding my buttocks. Someone else asked me, "Do you believe in anything?" I said to him, "I believe in Allah." So he said, "But I believe in torture and I will torture you. . . ." Then they handcuffed me and hung me to my bed. They ordered me to curse Islam and because they started to hit my broken leg, I cursed my religion. They ordered me to thank Jesus that I'm alive. And I did what they ordered me. This is against my belief. (Sworn Statements 2005)

To where, precisely, have we traveled when someone in a uniform can aver that torture is his religion? Where in the world is this hellish space? In a time when a kind of TWCS has become an instrument of conquest, what precisely is our role, as critical intellectuals? In other words, what is the task of a TWCS today, where the world may increasingly be organized into a single humanity but where those who don't qualify are not relegated to a kind of second-class global citizenship but instead are increasingly expelled from humanity altogether, cast out as refugees, displaced persons, the *sans papiers*, the disappeared, the forgotten, or homeless Muslims lost in the carceral wilderness of Guantánamo Bay?

There is an urgency to the work ahead of us if we want to reclaim TWCS from its imperial past and terrifying present. That work, it seems to me, must reside in specific acts of recovery and connection in both local and global dimensions. Recovery happens by exhuming hitherto hidden pasts, such as the October 1961 massacre, histories that illustrate both the human costs of domination and the bureaucratic administration of power. This can only happen by sensitivity to the full complexity of lived experience in any one place, the kind of work that cultural studies is best suited for. Connection resides in electing affinities with other oppressed peoples around the world, learning the grammar of their struggles, and beginning to speak a common language of resistance out of a desire to produce an authentic global society made to the full measure of humanity.

There is an example of this found in the literature surrounding the October massacre. In 1963, the African American novelist William Gardner Smith published *The Stone Face*, a brilliant novel about a black American, Simeon Brown, escaping American racism by fleeing to Paris, only to discover that the blacks in Paris are the Algerians, who wear the same "baggy pants, worn shoes and shabby shirts" and have the "sullen, unhappy, angry eyes" that Brown recognizes from the streets of Harlem (Smith 1963, 4). This little-known novel is a triumph in transcultural empathy, a way of feeling one's connection in the world through a shared experience with another "Other." By the end of the novel, Brown is caught up in the October massacre and he witnesses the police's ferocity directly: "A few dozen yards away from him a policeman was swinging his club over a woman who was holding a baby. She fell to her knees, bent forward to protect the infant, and the police club kept flying up and down, up and down. Simeon stared, realizing that he was weeping, *feeling those blows against his own body*" (Smith 1963, 182). It with this "feeling these blows against his own body" where I will end, for if there is future to a Third World Cultural Studies, it resides not just in the ability to describe the lived realities of various Third World peoples fully. Rather, the promise lies in creating work that expresses its truth so clearly that one not only feels like one is there, but also feels the need to act.

2 Ode to "Quasheba"

Resistance Rituals among Higgler Women in Jamaica

Hume N. Johnson

INTRODUCTION

Resistance is no stranger to Jamaica. Neither is "refusing development," particularly that purported by hegemonic groups, from colonizers to globalizers. Rooted in a historical tradition of struggle against British slavery, colonialism, and the plantation system, this small island-nation, the largest in the English-speaking Caribbean, is now permanent resident to openly violent opposition as well as "hidden transcripts," embodied in "everyday forms of peasant resistance" (see J. C. Scott 1985, 1990). Emerging historical studies aimed at rethinking Afro-Caribbean politics of resistance during and after slavery are increasingly recognizing women as having played a critical foundational role in slave resistance, the labor movement, diffuse community mobilizations and organization as well as various modes of contemporary cultural resistance. This innovative historico-theoretical recasting powerfully illustrates how despite extraordinary sexism and racism, aimed at silencing and excluding them from the "bourgeois" public sphere, Afro-Caribbean women catapulted themselves to the foreground of collective struggles and cultures of resistance by turning everyday activities into sites of resistance and ordinary spaces into theaters for collective action (Reddock 1995; Shepherd, Brereton, and Bailey 1995; Wilmot 1995; Momsen 1996; Sheller 1997).

It is the ferocity of the popular struggles often performed by these women that have come to embody and awaken the essence of Quasheba. The name *Quasheba* recalls the popular nineteenth-century colonial stereotype and caricature of the Afro-Jamaican slave woman. Quasheba was synonymous with "warrior woman" or "queen of the rebels," and was used to describe an independent, outspoken, feisty female slave; a noisy and aggressive troublemaker. But beyond literary satire, Quasheba was the public voice of female leadership and a pillar of active resistance in the Jamaican slave community (see Sheller 1997). It is therefore through a theoretical resurrection of the symbolism of Quasheba during the slavery and post-emancipation periods that we may be able to gain a better understanding of the political economy, continuities, manifestations, and symbolic meaning of contemporary women's activism in Jamaica, particularly the disguised and overt forms of popular protest carried out by higgler women in the informal economy.

Any theoretical discussion of the remarkable narratives of slave women's activism and resistance in Jamaica cannot be divorced from the political site at which such resistance took place. I therefore take as my point of departure the situational and analytic paradigm of street-based entrepreneurship and the sociopolitical context of informalism within which Afro-Caribbean slaves were heavily involved during and after slavery. I emphasize the centrality of the street (surrounding market centers) as this was the amphitheater of economic, sociocultural and, significantly, political activity for both enslaved and free Afro-Jamaican women.

Significantly, it was street/market context which facilitated the materialization of "Quasheba" and her transformation as a central actor in both historical and contemporary cultures of peasant resistance. This is because the street in the contemporary period is home to an expanding informal (or "hustle") economy which has emerged in peripheral countries such as Jamaica. This economy finds its bases and is contextualized by modern capitalism, globalization, and transnational trade as well as the failed development experiments of structural adjustment[1] and economic liberalization. The fallout from structural adjustment was enormous—fiscal deficit; debt; massive unemployment; impoverishment; inequality; drastic deteriorations in health, education, and a range of other social services; generalized urban maldevelopment; garrisonization;[2] and criminality and violence (Domínguez, Pastor, and Worrell 1993; Grant-Wisdom 1994; Le Franc 1994; Gordon, Anderson, and Robotham 1997).

Like many Third World governments, Jamaica still finds it virtually impossible to grow its economy, create jobs, stem unemployment, drive down inflationary pressures, improve standards of living, and offer its poor any kind of meaningful life. The poor, including vast networks of women, thus became the major casualties of global recession and austerity policies. Informalization has been an almost organic response to chronic joblessness, growing destitution, and a way out of misery for massive numbers of poor in the urban slums who were driven to rely on their own devices and to seek imaginative ways to eke out an existence.[3] This street-turned-economic space became dominated by hordes of sidewalk vendors, higglers, mobile hawkers, peddlers, and hustlers determined to stitch together a livelihood and confront/resist their marginal status.

Women predominated in this arena. While some women opt for casual jobs in the domestic services as household helpers, washerwomen, babysitters (nannies), or forbidden ("service" and "distribution") industries such as prostitution and drug trafficking, a large majority are engaged in daily rituals of radical, creative entrepreneurship such as higglering,[4] street vending, and itinerant hustling.[5] Their principal goal is to reshape their economic vulnerability and improve their lives to attain "moral/social honour" (Gray 2004) and middle-class "respectability" (Freeman 2005; Hope

2005) within the limits of a highly stratified, status-oriented, and patriarchal postcolonial Jamaican society. The crucial presence of contemporary higgler women in informal and imaginative economic pursuits is the subject of recent academic research (see Freeman 2001, 2005). However, their (inherited) audacity as feminized powerbrokers in this domain is yet to be comprehensively accounted for.

Based on my ongoing empirical research on Jamaican popular protest, this chapter tackles this theoretical and empirical deficit by foregrounding the popular political struggles undertaken by disadvantaged, urbanized "higglers," street vendors, and peddlers to safeguard their way of life. Using as my situational and analytical frame the "hustle" economy, I illustrate the ways in which gender, social class, and economic status intersect and collaborate to structure these women's interest and participation in popular political action and establish/project their identity as feminized powerholders in this economic public sphere. Without romanticizing these struggles (or abstracting them from their counterpoint to the quest for "law and order" by the Jamaican state), I examine the combination of circumstances which drive inner-city women from a focus on their routinized economic activities to become "disorderly" figures at the forefront of spontaneous and episodic protestations and collective action.

For these poor women, resistance is a must against what they see as the encroachment of the modern capitalist state, big business, and other superordinate groups on their livelihood. The development orchestrated by the state has failed them, by not serving their interests and by not taking account of their struggles. But rather than succumbing as victims of inequity and marginalization, these subaltern women have "refused" development. In so doing, they expose its flaws and calamitous effects on the poor and revise the terms dictated by globalization and effect development on their own terms and at their own convenience. Indeed, rather than necessarily "buying into" the trappings of modern capitalism by merely selling consumer goods, they see it as an inescapable, requisite aspect of the struggle to survive poverty and improve their lives. By resisting efforts by the Jamaican state to streamline their operations and remove them from the street, these women unconsciously reimagine development. They demand that it become more equitable and livable.

THE STREET AS ECONOMIC SPACE: HISTORICAL BEGINNINGS FOR QUASHEBA

The antecedent to the modern informal economy in Jamaica was the plantation market culture which emerged during slavery. The market and the street, for example, acquired prominence during the transitional apprenticeship (period of "half-freedom" between 1834 and 1838 aimed at preparing slaves for "full freedom") and post-emancipation phases. British planters and estate owners, aiming to escape the enormous costs and burden of feeding a massive slave population, allotted both male and female slaves plots of land (later called "provision grounds") on which to cultivate their own crops, on their own time, for their own consumption. Both male and female slaves sold the surplus from their provision grounds at weekend markets (French 1995; Momsen 1996; Sherlock and Bennett 1998).[6] It was, however, women who dominated marketing and effectively claimed ownership of this economic domain. Although many worked in the urban domestic services as nannies, cooks, and washerwomen, a large majority became involved in higglering and hawking goods about the streets almost exclusively for profit. Indeed, as early as 1672 in Jamaica, slave women were involved in buying and selling the surplus production from their provision grounds on Sunday mornings in public markets (French 1995; Momsen 1996; Sherlock and Bennett 1998).

The very exercise of planting, harvesting, and selling their own crops transformed the (still estate-owned and -controlled) provision grounds into an arena of independence and material betterment as well as a source of personhood. In other words, the mostly *illiterate* slave women had officially entered the money economy as *skilled* (my emphases) entrepreneurs and autonomous financial brokers (French 1995; Sherlock and Bennett 1998).[7] So important had the Sunday market become that the otherwise stringent laws restricting the mobility of the slaves were relaxed during the apprenticeship years (1834–1838), at least where marketing activities were concerned (Momsen 1996).

According to Mimi Sheller (1997), the presence of the vast and highly visible networks of women facilitated a crucial flow of information between town centers and the countryside and between markets and fields; this flow of information enabled the slaves to orchestrate and execute collective action. Indeed, given their numerical dominance in urban public spaces, it was also women who filled the streets and squares during popular mobilizations or demonstrations and played impressive roles in some of the most violent public disturbances and riots. The historical record reveals the heavy involvement of women in popular petitioning, court-based contestations, as well as open and violent rebellions and demand-making urban riots over social, economic, and political rights. The bulk of the popular protestations and collective struggles focused on the rights of the free peoples to practice their indigenous religions. However, in the main, the issues over which women protested include low wages, unfair terms of unemployment, growing destitution, and a deep sense that justice was unavailable through the courts (Wilmot 1995, 284–287; see also Reddock 1995; Mintz 1996; Momsen 1996; Sheller 1997).

Significantly, however, it was this arena of small-scale entrepreneurship, marketization, and informalism, dominated by a ready and active network of women exhibiting elements of civic engagement and social capital, which ultimately created an enabling environment for organized slave resistance in Jamaica. Recent historical scholarship on slave resistance, particularly those "engendering [Caribbean] history" (Reddock 1995; Shepherd, Brereton, and Bailey 1995; Wilmot 1995; Beckles and Shepherd 1996; Mintz 1996; Momsen 1996; Sheller 1997) is awash with evidentiary transcripts of the impact of Quasheba in this domain during and after slavery. Together, these analyses confirm that it was the near-permanent presence of black women in the public spaces of towns, and notably, their monopolization of the public spaces of the markets which played an important role in the ultimate development of a politically active Afro-Jamaican public.

Given that many women were largely dependent on the informal economy (for their livelihood and to feed their families) and hence vulnerable to economic recessions, urban women became involved in violent clashes and rioting as much as or more than men (Wilmot 1995). Indeed, "many examples of 'violent language' recorded in British records were spoken by women, whether during slavery and apprenticeship, or in later court-house scuffles and riots; when violence occurred, working class women were often at the forefront, brandishing not only insults and provocation but quite often weapons as well" (Sheller 1997, 9). Swithen Wilmot's (1995) account of the Morant Bay rebellion of 1865 confirms the active participation of women in violent assaults, with women not only directing the attack on the authorities but raiding police stations for "guns, bayonets and swords" and "marching like soldiers" to the courthouse, the site of the landmark rebellion (Wilmot 1995, 290–292; see also Sheller 1997). It is clear that by bonding together through common loyalties and affective ties (and by laying claim to market space through their efforts to better themselves), Afro-Jamaican women had managed to promulgate an urban political culture of collective direct action, including liberal use of violent strategies.

It was, however, this kind of aggressive, unruly, and "unladylike" behavior which, on the one hand, fashioned the image of Quasheba as independent, self-confident, and a (physically and mentally) powerful (read as "masculine") force to be reckoned with in the popular public action, and on the other hand, consolidated/underlined the emerging perception that lower-class women suffer the lack of (white/British/middle-class/feminine) "respectability"[8] and gentility.

THE HIGGLER WOMAN—THE MODERN REINCARNATION OF QUASHEBA

For theoretical and analytic purposes, I wish to provide a political sketch of the higgler and, significantly, underscore her historical mutation from a rural peasant woman, buying small-scale agricultural goods/produce for sale in both rural and urban markets to a "big time" (refers to her reputation as successful and socially mobile) urbanized entrepreneur. For nearly two centuries, the Jamaican higgler has also come to embody a figure of black Afro-Caribbean womanhood in which strength, size, autonomy, physical movement, travel, and business acumen are defining characteristics—a powerful counterpoint to the more middle-class European model of “respectability” (Freeman 2001). No longer the colorful country higgler who traditionally wore a head tie (scarf) and printed skirts, the urbanized higgler is a dark-skinned (or light-skinned), overweight, Afro-Jamaican woman dressed in tight, revealing, and/or garish costumes with large amounts of gold jewelry and elaborate hairstyles, immediately negating the traditional conventions of Eurocentric beauty that obtain in Jamaica (Hope 2004, 2005).

Her style of banter and modes of economic and political negotiation, embodied in demanding postures and crass statements, are forceful and volcanic. This image of femininity is considered to be obscene, loud, vulgar, and “unladylike” (Hope 2004; Freeman 2005). That she is defined less by “Victorian” demure and more by vivacity and “local-ness” means that the higgler is ranked at the base of the race/class/color/gender hierarchy in the Eurocentric organizing frame of the Jamaican society. But what she has lost in “respectability,” she has gained in “reputation.” Since the 1980s, Afro-Jamaican “higglers” have been the promulgators of a new brand of female entrepreneurship; they have managed to expand, significantly, their traditional roles as local “market intermediaries” of ground provisions to becoming medium and large regional and international retailers.

Higglers metamorphosed their self-made domestic operations by becoming active participants in a set of informal export/import activities whereby networks of women travel together to neighboring Caribbean islands (including Curaçao, Panama, Bermuda) to purchase foreign goods for resale in the markets and shopping arcades across urban Jamaica. Many of these women traders, who eventually obtain nonimmigrant visas to the United States, successfully extend their trading activities beyond the rural/urban locality to a more global context by traveling to US metropolitan areas such as Miami and New York to purchase food, the latest clothing, fashion accessories, and other consumer goods for resale to wholesalers, retailers, and individuals in Jamaica (cf. Freeman 2005 for a focus on Barbados).

The overwhelming material and symbolic success of this “neo-higgler” was, paradoxically, officially recognized by the Jamaican government during the 1980s, by the levying of customs duties and prescribed taxes on their activities and the reclassification of the titleship “higglers” to their new branding as “informal commercial importers” (ICIs). These higglers sought alternate sources of income and symbolic empowerment within the economic structures of transnational marketization and global free market capitalism, thus resurrecting the economic and creative genius of their traditional agricultural counterparts.

Although I use the terms *higglers*, *peddlers*, and *street vendors* interchangeably, alongside these “successful” higglers are also scores of women who do not necessarily fit into the “ICI” or “neo-higgler” classification.

They do not wear elaborate jewelry or the latest fashions. They are unable to travel on commercial airlines to large North American cities to buy goods for resale on the local market. Instead, they are engaged in similarly autonomous but much smaller-scale or petty subsistence activities. Most are itinerant street vendors who can be seen teeming the streets and markets of major Jamaican towns (May Pen, Mandeville, Santa Cruz, Lucea to St. Ann's Bay, and Linstead) peddling (at much cheaper rates) a variety of consumer items, including toiletries, cosmetics, cigarettes, rags, hats, and belts.

Many can also be found selling cold beverages, soups, and snack items (peanuts, chips, and lollipops) at public events. Given the historical model of Caribbean livelihood, defined more by flux and movement than by stasis and sedentarism (Freeman 2005), it is the public space of markets and streets in which the higgler also operates. Indeed, the urban poor often see the sidewalks, street pavements, bus stops, street intersections, shopping piazzas, and storefronts as well as public parks as providing the most favorable business opportunities. Downtown Kingston in Jamaica is a prime location. Not unlike many cities across the developing world, downtown Kingston is the definition of bustling commercialism and capitalistic enterprise, Jamaica's endowment to the (economic) globalization project and the quintessential space for inventive economic entrepreneurship, cultural reproduction, and contentious politics. Located below the gated, middle-class communities of Upper St. Andrew and sprawled along the Kingston waterfront, this area plays host to "big business"—large manufacturing and distribution companies, financial corporations, retail and service industries, as well as the mushrooming street-based entrepreneurship dominated by higglers and peddlers.

The shopping places of the latter are to be found on King, Princess, Pechon, Tower, Barry, Beckford, and Orange Streets. As a participant-observer through this bustling commercial district as a college student in the 1990s, and in 2004 during fieldwork for my doctoral study, I saw huge tarpaulins hung across the road, creating ceilings for makeshift streetside shops, a plethora of either wooden or "plastic bag" stalls sprawled on almost every corner, handcarts and "mobile stalls" being pushed around to maximize sales, and overstocked stationary kiosks parked in open spaces or perched on the flanks of and/or inside the St. William Grant Park. Crowds of women, men, and child vendors line the pavements, some with carton boxes with assorted items tagged to the sides or open suitcases revealing the latest jeans and shoes; others carry huge bags loaded with goods, buckets (with juice, water) on their heads or in their hands, which allows for roving to and from different trading spaces. It is also customary to see the "alleyways between shop buildings on Princess Street filled with brightly coloured brassieres and shirts on hangers" (*Jamaica Gleaner,* December 6, 2001). No doubt, the streets and sidewalks of urban Jamaica have been transformed into exciting and vibrant shopping places as well as sites of political resistance.

The street thus carries crucial analytic currency as it is the locus of collective struggle and expression for the urban poor and the political platform upon which they mount popular resistance against the encroachment of the Jamaican state. Like their historical slave counterparts, this Habermasian public space is where Afro-Jamaican higglers assemble, make friends, earn a living, spend their leisure, and express their discontent. That the street as a public place possesses this intrinsic social/civic engagement feature makes it possible for women traders in this instance to mobilize without having an active network. It is however the potential for this kind of active political engagement and social camaraderie which exposes the streets of urban Jamaica as a hub of conflict and chaos and renders higglering and street vending, in all its forms, a vexing illegal mode of entrepreneurship, which the Jamaican state can scarcely tolerate.[9]

Like many governments across the Third World, the Jamaican government has waged war on street vendors as part of its response to public pressure to "clean up" this shopping area and "remove higglers and vendors from the streets" (*Jamaica Gleaner,* September 6, 2002; *Jamaica Gleaner,* September 1a, 2000).[10] Unquestionably, many of the streets in the downtown Kingston business district are so extraordinarily choked with informal business activity as to render them impassable to even emergency vehicles (police, ambulance), delivery trucks taking goods to (officially authorized) businesses, and, ironically, to the thousands of pedestrian-shoppers who converge on this area daily. With the severe congestion and crime (extortion, drug-dealing, pilfering) associated with downtown Kingston, state authorities refuse to abide such a precarious counterculture, albeit a vibrant and active use of the urban space. Indeed, a *Jamaica Gleaner* editorial of December 2, 2003, bluntly expressed the growing public distaste for street vending:

> Illegal vending is a subset of squatting, which, for political reasons, has been allowed to get out of hand. . . . Like all other businesses, they [vendors] must play by the rules of commerce including where and when they can set up shop. They must pay reasonable fees for the *privilege* (not the *right*) to ply their trade. . . . Their wholesale capturing of the streets of Downtown Kingston is an affront to law and order and a stop must be put to it once and for all. This will call for a mix of force and tact but unless the authorities prevail the city will fall victim to incremental chaos. (*Jamaica Gleaner,* December 2, 2003; emphasis mine)

Bowing to intense public pressure from business and civil society interests, the Jamaican state has thus waged a protracted war of attrition against street vendors. Large-scale merchants, whose storefronts are littered every day by hordes of street peddlers who jeopardize profits, typically endorse the state's vendor removal plan (see *Jamaica Gleaner,* September 6, 2002; November 5, 2002). In many countries of the periphery where informal street trading is a way of life, large-scale merchants and entrepreneurs "whose opportunity costs and favourable business environment had been appropriated by street vendors joined the authorities in their clampdown" (Bayat 1997, 54; *Jamaica Gleaner*, November 20b, 2001).

In the face of the great fortune being made by the surrounding businesses even while they suffer deep and persistent poverty, the increasingly demeaned but empowered Jamaican street traders are therefore likely to interpret any action by the government to coercively remove them from the streets not only as a threat to their subsistence security and livelihood but as a state siding with "big business," which is not insignificantly composed of white/brown, middle-class, "respectable" entrepreneurs or immigrant Chinese merchants. In other words, endemic poverty, restricted economic opportunity, and polarized class relations have set the broad terms of the class conflict that constantly reproduces itself in Kingston's commercial district. It is therefore no wonder that public order efforts on the part of the government, however rational or beneficial, so menace crucial elements of (informal) people's subsistence routines (J. C. Scott 1976) and so offend the lower classes that intense resistance, including "hidden transcripts" and/or open explosions of rage and anger from the members of this marginal sector, are the predictable responses.

HIGGLER WOMEN: BETWEEN SURVIVALISM AND RESISTANCE

For close to fifteen years, armies of small-scale vendors, hustlers, and "higglers" have acted in defiance of efforts by the Jamaican state to remove them from streets, sidewalks, intersections, piazzas, and storefronts or urban areas into what many believe to be unsafe, decrepit, unlucrative selling arcades. Using "everyday," low-profile, silent, and concealed protestation narratives and practices as well as open collective disturbances, a powerful network of informal women traders (supported by a large contingent of the male constituents of this poor and marginalized sector) have united in popular resistance to defend their way of life against the encroachments of superordinate groups, including the Jamaican state. By employing the impressively inventive and effective tools of "anancyism,"[11] and/or "cat and mouse games," Afro-Jamaican street vendors and higglers have managed to persistently outwit or outmaneuver the state authorities—the police and Metropolitan Parks and Markets (MPM)—marshaled to drive them off the streets.

For example, determined to cash in on the lucrative market of the street but wanting to feign compliance by appearing to obey removal orders, vendors would obediently clear off the streets and abandon trading on piazzas and storefronts, in accordance with instructions from the local political body, Kingston and St. Andrew Corporation, but return the next day to sneakily peddle their goods and continue with business as usual. Rather than compete with each other for profit opportunities, sellers also network with each other to devise even more clever ways of deceiving the authorities.

Many itinerant traders, for instance, artfully store their goods in the passageways that run between large retail stores and buildings and peddle them in small portions on the streets. It is worth noting that consumers, particularly keen shoppers and bargain hunters, also understand the language and politics of illegal vending and are themselves unwittingly absorbed as active participants and facilitators in these counterhegemonic practices of resistance. A news report published in the *Jamaica Gleaner* in 2001 reveals that "costumers of shoe and belt vendors who are willing, lounge beside the more expensive stores, while their correct sizes are quickly sought by eager sellers in an alley a few metres away. [In order to avoid being caught], watchmen are employed to shout when the authorities, usually clad in blue approach. Cries of 'MPM, MPM' [Metropolitan Parks and Markets] elicit swift movement and the crowded streets are cleared in minutes" (*Jamaica Gleaner,* December 6, 2001).

These resistance strategies of "false compliance" and/or "passive non-compliance" (J. C. Scott 1985) mean that Jamaican male and female vendors have developed the empowering capacity to "call the bluff" of the authorities and escape penalty. Through this collective resistance-response tactic, they thereby reinforce their dominance of the street and underline their customary rights and usage of this public space while weakening the ability of the state to enforce its removal policy and invoke its "rule of law." Of course, the persistent disregard for warnings and orders to clear the streets often attract harsh penalties such as the seizure of goods, which itself costs a prohibitive or subsistence-reducing J$500 to reclaim (*Jamaica Gleaner,* December 6, 2001) and lost profits on account of a state-imposed trading stoppage.

However, despite the employment of coercive strategies as well as political techniques (refurbishing of vending arcades in the market district—installing improved sanitary facilities and ready-made stalls), many street and pavement vendors are reluctant to reposition their businesses. This is due, in part, to declining security in the commercial district and a genuine fear of predatory criminality in the trading areas to which they are being relocated. Despite their majority status, women traders are especially susceptible to crime—physical violence, extortion, robbery, and the upheavals of gang warfare which tend play out in the downtown Kingston market district (see *Jamaica Gleaner,* September 1b, 2000). The following quotations by female vendors expose the gravity of their vulnerability and explain, in part, their resistance to relocation:

> "We nah go 'shooting valley' [referring to the Oxford Mall]." (*Jamaica Gleaner,* November 20a, 2001)

> "If police are running from Oxford Mall, why should we go there?" (*Jamaica Gleaner*, November 20a, 2001)
>
> "When we sell round there, dem [thieves] take up wi [our] goods and we can't do nothing bout it. When we sell here so [referring to the street], we more safer. We can't go round so go sell, dem will kill we off." (*Jamaica Gleaner,* November 5, 2002)

The predominant factor conditioning their defiance, however, is that most of the nearly 15,000 vendors, who ply their wares in downtown Kingston, simply prefer to sell on the sidewalks and streets on account of their being lucrative economic trading spaces. Higglers especially rely heavily on maximizing profits at specific times such as weekends (Fridays, Saturdays), "Back to School" (July, August), and during peak shopping periods such as Christmas and (although less so) New Year's, Valentine's Day, and Easter (*Jamaica Gleaner,* December 6, 2001). While shoppers *do* patronize the arcades to which they are to be resettled, many small-scale vendors and hustlers fear the intense competition from big businesses and, in instances even from their arcade-based counterparts—the more established ICIs or neo-higglers.

Given that, at present, the streets and sidewalks prove to be the most lucrative spaces to earn their livelihood and "move up in a life" (better their lives; become socially mobile), Afro-Jamaican women traders, like their historical counterpart, Quasheba, tend to become involved in more militant resistance campaigns, explicitly combative and violent. These include mounting hostile street demonstrations and administering a succession of "shut downs" of the downtown Kingston commercial district. For example, in 1999, vendors (both male and female) collectively defied the police and officers from the MPM who were enforcing the government's "Vendor Removal Action Plan" by physically hauling down the shutters of some competitor stores in the business district. "If we cyaan [cannot] sell, then no body will sell" was their rallying cry (*Jamaica Gleaner,* December 22, 1999).

Again in 2001, following the refusal of authorities to allow vendors to off-load their goods for sale in prohibited areas, hundreds of angry street vendors, led by mostly female traders, prompted the closure of several businesses through aggressive demonstrations, which effectively ground to a halt all commercial activity in the city. Spurred on by a powerful network of higglers, these empowered "informals" bore placards and chanted "no seller, no store." In symbolic assertion of their right to "justice" and, in recognition of their "moral economy" vis-à-vis these very streets on which they earn their food, they marched in procession on Beckford Street, strutting past members of the security forces as in ritualized challenge to their authority (see *Jamaica Gleaner,* November 20a, 2001).

The differentiated roles (and distinctive impact) of male and female vendors in these kinds of social protests are worth noting. Jamaican higgler women, for example, raise the visibility of their concerns about their political marginalization and inequalities in access to resources by participating in showy displays vis-à-vis the media. From the singing of chants, walking, marching, and bearing placards, it is higgler women who invest emotion and meaning in the movement to "refuse development." This is because they are often the most vocal and spirited at protest and tend to deploy perhaps the most gendered "weapons of the weak"—sexual manipulation, verbal assault, including expletives. For example, it is higgler women who are likely to employ techniques and strategies otherwise deemed "inappropriate" and "uncivil." In aggressive vendor demonstrations, they are the ones who swear at business owners who choose to remain open, the ones most willing to openly and fearlessly challenge the authorities, the ones to boldly demand "justice" and, in instances, publicly undress (usually remove underwear to expose their rear ends and genitalia) with a view to intimidate and enervate their opponents.[12]

Although both male and female street vendors often join forces in protest, it has therefore been politically strategic for higgler women to position themselves at the forefront of the protest action, especially when it involves issues of victimization such as police manhandling and unfair seizure of goods within the context of subsistence and (female) impoverishment. It is also here that female vendors exert the most extraordinary power. Through their seemingly natural ability to express deep emotional anguish—bawling, screaming—women in this context prove to be effortless champions at tugging at the heart strings of removal officers and via the media, solicit public empathy.

On the other hand, it is the men, giving emphasis to their resistance, who generally engage in physically aggressive and confrontational tactics such as "strong-arming" the shutters of businesses, forcing them closed, burning tires (and in instances, market stalls), blocking roads with boulders and debris, and engaging the police in combative physical clashes and gun warfare (*Jamaica Gleaner*, December 22, 1999; *Jamaica Gleaner*, November 20b, 2001; *Jamaica Gleaner*, September 24, 1998). Of course, it is to be acknowledged that although higgler women, for the most part, play the *mummalashi* (Jamaican vernacular, meaning "verbal assault") role, this does not mean that they do not also engage in the some of the same kinds of physical rebellion ordinarily aligned to their male counterparts. Next, I examine what these popular struggles mean for the female traders involved and the negotiation of power relations in this highly classist and status-oriented postcolonial society.

PROTEST PARTICIPATION BY WOMEN HIGGLERS—MEANINGS AND LESSONS

There is widespread agreement that "participation in social protests raises the political consciousness of women, sometimes, but not always contributing to a revised view of their subordinate status in society" (West and

Blumberg 1990, 31). It is unquestionable that the cultural and political dimensions of the informal processes described in this chapter hold potentially transformative effects for those engaged in them. In the first place, it is important to acknowledge that the informal economy, as an economic site, in a context of capitalism and the free market, facilitates small-scale entrepreneurship and thus provides a thriving source of income and a better way of life for a vast number of women, many of whom, based on their social identities as members of Jamaica's disadvantaged and marginalized underclass, are unable to claim real access to resources through the formalized, recognized channels of the society. Through free enterprise, higgler women are offered a range of social and political resources which allows them to realize some "success" and "social betterment" within the otherwise confining socioeconomic structures of the Jamaican society.

But beyond street entrepreneurship, the informal economy is also a space of political negotiation and resistance as well as social and cultural engagement, and thus provides the enabling environment for protest participation and performance. Here, the power of the street demonstration offers higglers real weapons by which to "refuse development," as defined by their counterparts in the formal economy, as well as to launch a counterwar against the encroachments of the Jamaican state and other superordinate groups and structures. Therefore, while higgler women retain an interdependency with global capitalism in their quest to survive poverty and improve their social standing, they simultaneously utilize the political/cultural arena of the street to physically, materially, and symbolically struggle against the efforts to deny them this way of life.

At the same time, the higglering and vending class are left with limited options. For example, they can continue to resist the moves of the state to remove them from the streets and invite the seizure of their goods and hefty fines. They can relocate to the allotted vending areas and face a loss in profit or, although unlikely, they can cease operating informal trading altogether. Clearly, imitating large-scale merchants and store owners whose businesses are defined by status is not an option for masses of higglers who operate more roaming enterprises. It also goes against the interests of these informal folks whose lives often demand flexibility, innovativeness, and constant change (of places and priorities). Interminable mobilization may seem unrealistic but based on the empirical evidence, there seems to be general agreement among the higglering sector that disruptive, confrontational tactics cannot be abandoned.

These deliberately offensive challenges illustrate the higglers' physical and moral dominance over the street as public sphere and assert or consolidate their right to inclusion and voice participation here. At the very least, it forces the state to rethink its position, change its objectives and consider alternate and subordinate voices in decision making. Within this process of struggle, Afro-Jamaican higglers, like their traditional Quasheba counterparts, are learning the importance and potency of unity. This means networking, supporting each other, and acting together in opposition to a common enemy—the Jamaican state as embodied in the police and removal officers of the MPM. Rather than passive victims, they are increasingly recognized as empowered actors. Their confidence and esteem has also increased enormously as they realize the power of (violent) protest. Many are increasingly unafraid to defy the law, challenge the police, and, in instances, accept the assistance and commanding influence of extralegal actors, such as criminal gangs and dons (see Johnson 2005). Based on the argument presented in this chapter, it is clear that Jamaican women have always challenged traditional views of poverty. For centuries, higglers and street vendors have been mobilizing hundreds of their colleagues in the streets in popular collective struggles aimed at resisting encroachments on their livelihood by superordinate groups led by the Jamaican state. The reasons for their persistence and contemporary success are manifold.

Perhaps most fundamental is that the vendor protests are operating at a time when the Jamaican political climate is overwhelmingly tolerant of protests. For the massive numbers of higglers and vendors, this means that the momentum of resistance can be maintained even in the face of sporadic state clampdown. Secondly, there is no disillusionment among higglers regarding their ability to maintain long-term invisibility on the streets and guarantee the continued existence of this way of life. This resolve is based on their increasing awareness, not only of their own subordination and lack of rights but also that it is the state which is the source of their oppression. The attempt by the Jamaican state to introduce renovated market areas does not therefore reduce the incentives for protest and the vendors' commitment to defend their means of livelihood. Thirdly, public opinion, while at times highly critical, has largely been in the favor of the need of disadvantaged classes to survive poverty and better their lives.

NOTES

1. The development experiment of structural adjustment, advanced by developed societies but led and supervised by the United States vis-à-vis the International Monetary Fund/World Bank, imposed on lesser developed countries, required a deregulation of the economy. This included installing a competitive exchange rate, encouraging foreign direct investment flows, privatizing state-owned enterprises, massively reducing government expenditure, and liberalizing trade by removing barriers and relying on market forces in line with global trends (Grant-Wisdom 1994; Le Franc 1994).
2. The term *garrisonization* is derived from the notion "garrison." Fashioned during the political party "civil wars" over (electoral) turf in Kingston during the 1960s and 1970s, a garrison in this context is seen as a political stronghold completely controlled by a political party such that any significant social, political, economic, or cultural development within the garrison can only take place with the tacit approval of the leadership (whether national or local) of the dominant party. The garrisons have morphed into politically homogenous communities run by local area leaders called "dons"

and where residents vote en bloc for the same political party. Garrisons are also increasingly linked to positional gun warfare and the illegal drug trade, thereby rendering them whole communities which operate beyond the state and the law. For a full account of the garrison phenomenon, see Chevannes 1992; Figueroa 1995; Figueroa and Sives 2003.

3. Many informals also see "informalization" as having positive consequences such as "flexible" working hours, freedom from management codes and regulations, as well as financial independence.
4. *Higglering* in Jamaican parlance means selling or vending, usually on the street. The *higgler* (said to be derived from the English word *haggler*) was traditionally used to classify rural women who peddle agricultural goods in the open markets of the city of Kingston and other town centers. In contemporary references, the term *higgler* is also used to refer to an "informal commercial importer" as a result of their transnational trade in cosmopolitan products (name-brand clothes, shoes, and cosmetics).
5. Like higglering, *hustling*, in Jamaican jargon, is used to refer to the practice of selling on the street. The term also describes any creative and imaginative means (legal or extralegal) employed by the poor to earn a living. In this case, an itinerant hustler is a street peddler who moves about selling a variety of goods usually in an effort to maximize total sales per day.
6. Not surprisingly, women benefited from equal access in the land allocation process. Chattel slavery, after all, operated a common system of oppression and exploitation. Slaves were, regardless of gender, slaves and, for all intents and purposes, the "property" of their masters and "equal under the whip." Paradoxically, this was despite occupational inequalities on the estates where women dominated field work and men the skilled occupations. For a more complete discussion of the gendered aspects of plantation life and higglering, see French 1995; Momsen 1996; Sherlock and Bennett 1998.
7. This conclusion is measured against the range of skills required for higglering. The higgler, for instance, had to develop not only counting and change-making skills but profit-making techniques. One of her first tasks in the market was to identify, establish, and maintain her own selling spot, a system maintained by mutual recognition of each other's right to that space. An urgent priority is also to secure and maintain a staunch customer base as well as keep track of money, barter, and distinguish between and maintain a balance of overhead costs and profits (see Sherlock and Bennett 1998, Chapter 15: "Pens, Provision Grounds and Higglers").
8. The Eurocentric notion of "respectability" is rooted in colonialism, where racial/class/gender/color hierarchies are upheld and reproduced in the institutions of marriage and education as well as codes of conduct. Respectability is then pitted against the African-derived and creolized version of "reputation," as a sort of countercultural response to colonial domination and the elusiveness of respectability. In a literal sense, reputation is aligned with anti-establishment activities, lower-classness, and promiscuity. See Besson 1993 and Freeman 2005 for fascinating explications of the "respectability/reputation" dialectic. The former attempts to "engender" the respectability/reputation debate by challenging the original male orientation. The latter focuses on its contemporary outgrowths in the Caribbean.
9. The streets also provide host to individuals involved in other types of street industries and services such as cleaning windshields; parking, "guarding," or washing (customer's) vehicles; begging; and illicit activities including thievery (picking pockets, shoplifting, snatching handbags, and jewelry), extortion, and "murder for hire." It is this acknowledged reality of deteriorating conditions in downtown Kingston—congestion, underdevelopment, its control by

"dons" who traffic in illicit activities such as extortion, drug-dealing, contraband, stolen goods, and generalized lawlessness—that threatens the lives and livelihood of those who live, work, or operate businesses in the community. In fact, consensus exists among the business sector that Kingston has evolved into an unplanned, unmanaged, and increasingly lawless manner, and its central business district downtown has become a model example of social decay, public disorder, and a total lack of effective municipal leadership. For a more explicit discussion of this development, see Johnson 2005.

10. The world of the higgler has historically been a hard one. The colonial authorities, for instance, despised marketing activities. One report, quoted by Sherlock and Bennett (1998, 174), noted that the authorities in Spanish Town in 1822 complained about the streets being greatly infested by a set of hawkers and peddlers from Kingston to the great injury of the trading part of the community and in the very eye of the police. Street vendors were frequently apprehended, and the main newspapers published regular reports on the penalties imposed for peddling goods through the streets (see Sherlock and Bennett 1998).
11. "Anancy" is a colorful and imposing character in Jamaican mythology and folklore. Caricatured as an insect identical to the spider, Anancy symbolizes trickery and is celebrated for his gimmicks, cunning, and ingenuity in finding loopholes in or "beating" (dodging, skirting, eluding) the system.
12. Donna Hope extends this politics of feminized empowerment to the Jamaican dancehall music culture, where she argues persuasively that "many ICIs operate simultaneously in the space of the dancehall as independent women who have attained significant economic wealth through their own enterprise and who are able to flaunt and display their bodies in the erotic postures that have become popularized as one site of female empowerment in the dancehall [as well as in the wider society]": Hope 2004, 106.

3 Plural Economies and the Conditions for Refusal

Gendered Developments in Bangkok

Ara Wilson

URBAN PLURALISM

Bangkok is a remarkably commercial city. Its sprawling metropolis is a patchwork of markets, with high-rise shopping malls alongside vernacular bazaars; a renowned sex industry; and all manner of hawking, vending, and small-time trade. Residents of the capital city thoroughly inhabit the market economy. This commercial character has made Bangkok an emblem of globalization in the global south or Third World.

Yet the frontier of capitalist development in Thailand contains a diversity of economic forms and meanings. Such plurality, this chapter proposes, is critical to how and when ordinary people refuse the project of development and modernization. Bangkok residents engage in work, exchange, and consumption that are *not* capitalist—spiritual offerings, gift giving, bartering, and the wide range of labor and resources that are so central to kinship and family.[1] Even so commodified a space as a shopping mall contains a variety of economic activities. Gifts are given, favors done, laborers paid. Most stores, shops, and stalls have some fashion of spirit shrine, with a transnational pantheon of sacralized objects drawn from animist, Hindu, Mahayana Buddhist, Theravada Buddhist, and nationalist traditions. Shopkeepers make offerings to the shop's shrine, while numerous workers and passersby place garlands, drinks, fruits, and symbolic figures on the popular shrines outside of shopping complexes. Spiritual offerings, friendly exchanges, small-time trade, corporate retail, and wage labor represent different economic activities.

In the midst of capitalist development in the global south, one finds not just one economy but multiple economic systems: not just a capitalist market economy, but a variety of markets and nonmarket economies as well. Viewing economic systems as a regulated pattern of production, distribution, and consumption rather than as supply and demand on an idealized market allows us to see economic modes that differ from capitalist (or planned socialist) economies. These have been called folk economies, kin economies, economies of affection, or moral economies. Some versions also approximate what Marxists and political economists have described as precapitalist, peasant mode of production, semifeudal, or petty commodity production.

Bangkok may seem an odd choice for a critical evaluation of development, which so often conjures images of elaborately planned, expertly managed projects in rural areas. Development in Thailand includes the projects of a large body of nongovernmental organizations (NGOs) and UnitedNations-related activities, foreign government aid (for example, Japan), as well as state-driven development schemes. In this chapter, I focus generally on capitalist development, that is, the growth of the market economy particularly in relation to global markets. This process is encouraged by the Thai government,[2] multilateral agencies like the International Monetary Fund (IMF), most foreign advisors, and directly or indirectly by some NGOs, for example, those oriented to income-generating activities. From the 1970s until 1997, Thailand's economy grew at rapid rates that attracted the eager attention of global investors and which intensified processes of changes under way. What observations of Bangkok show is that, even at the frontier of capitalist commerce, the market economy does not enter a vacuum but interacts with other economic modes, capitalist and noncapitalist. For those in megacities, growing suburbs, and hard-pressed countryside, the interacting economies are the grounds for daily life and for understanding development. Just as development "is a series of constructions" (Introduction, this volume), so too are moral economies. Such series of constructions about the divide between modern and tradition, Thai and foreign, market and nonmarket, inform how people refuse or accommodate the forces of developmental modernity.

In this chapter, I review different interpretations of the relationship between capitalism and local economies, examining as well how these models involve gender and sexuality in conjunction with ethnicity, race, and class, an intersectional project that is sympathetic with efforts to "queer development" (Lind and Share 2003). I consider modernization theory's interpretation of capitalism penetrating and supplanting economies of intimacy; the critical view of moral economies as grounds for resistance to capitalism; the ways that the folk economy engages and accommodates capitalism, through consumption; and finally, the way that the differences between capitalist and noncapitalist realms are conceptualized. I argue that the interaction of capitalist and alternative economies, and the way this interaction is interpreted, shapes conditions for resistance to development and other modes of capitalist modernity.

My discussion draws on this literature and comparative scholarship in Southeast Asia, adding observations from long-term fieldwork in Bangkok spanning more than a decade.[3] Because the aim is conceptual, there is less attention to individual Thai voices than some readers might desire and more emphasis on collective representations. Nonetheless, my discussion is guided by efforts to advance post-Orientalist feminist scholarship on the global south (informed by postcolonial theory) that "provincializes Europe"

(Chakrabarty 2000) by recognizing the differential modernity of Asia and the place of Asian actors in creating and resisting globalization. My approach also builds on critical attempts to address the articulation or mutual constitution of culture and political economy in historical processes.[4]

MODERNIZATION

What is the relationship of these alternate economies to capitalist economies? What can be made of the "economic difference" found in Bangkok—of different modes of capitalism, markets, labor, exchange, and consumption? And what does this plurality of economies have to do with social change? These questions have animated theories of modernization and development and their critics.

Writing about African development, Goran Hyden proposed the phrase "economies of affection" to describe this mix of kin and informal economies (Hyden 1983). The economy of affection and moral economy differ from capitalist economies by being enmeshed in local relationships. They are "guided by principles of reciprocity embedded in customary rules rather than universal and abstract laws from above" (Hyden 1987, 117–118, cited in C. Scott 1995, 51). Economies of kinship are not oriented to extracting and accumulating profit (although families may accumulate great wealth) but to social reproduction. Labor and exchange within this alternate economic system recreate and elaborate social worlds, not only the earthly here and now but also sacred, past, and future realms. Economies of affection have been recognized as an important resource for survival—as a crucial safety net catching the fallout from capitalist crises. Indeed, this role has been taken for granted by the engineers of capitalist development (but in ways that naturalize and exploit household labor). With privatization and cutbacks in government services that have characterized development policies for decades, the work of caring for the sick, the elderly, and children, and the general well-being of families and communities has fallen disproportionately to women. This is one example of how these alternative economies are gendered.

These local economies are profoundly gendered at material, symbolic, and everyday levels. As feminist anthropologists have shown, kinship economies construct sexual and gender identities through the sexual division of labor and marriage systems (Rubin 1975). Economies of affection disproportionately involve women's labor in the home, on family farms, and in small-scale trade—that is, in major parts of what is allocated to the informal economy. In Thailand, women's labor in growing rice, trading goods, hawking food, and selling sexual services adds up to significant circuits in the domestic economy.

These economic activities are typically ignored in conventional economic measurements of gross domestic product (GDP), for example, and in development policies. Yet the significant role of women in the informal economy has been a staple in conventional and feminist discussion of economic development in Thailand and elsewhere. What have been less addressed are the interactions of multiple economic systems and meanings and how these interactions involve and affect gender. The feminist geographers J. K. Gibson-Graham (the pen name of Katherine Gibson and Julie Graham) have suggested that recognizing "a plurality and heterogeneity of economic forms" provides "the possibility of theorizing economic difference" (1996a, 11).[5] Investigating local economies in dynamic interaction with capitalist systems will enrich our understanding of how development, modernity, and globalization impact gender transformations in the global south.

The dominant interpretation of the "plurality and heterogeneity of economic forms" (Gibson-Graham 1996a, 11) in the global south follows a temporal logic of progress. In this model, the strength of noncapitalist economies represents a holdover from the past, in the way that a spirit shrine attached to a modern shopping complex is seen as an anachronism. The expectation is that capitalism will "penetrate" local economies and will disaggregate co-mingled practices and values into different spheres. Wage labor and monetary trade will be the province of the formal market economy that counts as the public realm (ideally separated from the "public" of government), while activities associated with kin and community will be relegated to the domestic realm of households, a "private" domain whose ideal economic roles are confined to savings and consumption.

For modernization theorists like Hyden, the actually existing, chaotic alternate economy embedded in kin and community presents a problem, an obstacle to take-off and development in Africa. Catherine Scott (1995, 89) notes that theories of development such as Hyden's rely on a dichotomous distinction between "the rationalized, efficient sphere of capitalism with the stagnant precapitalist social formation." Modernization and development theories are ideologies, and their conceptions of economic value, social spheres, temporal progress, and modern subjectivity are shaped by gendered and imperial logics. As C. Scott (1995) and María Josefina Saldaña-Portillo (2003) have shown, the conceptualization of the underdeveloped economies of the Third World is itself gendered. It constructs an opposition between timeless, feminine local tradition, and dynamic, agentful, masculine modernity.

Even critics of modernization theory link the economy of affection with female spaces, practices, and values (C. Scott 1995, 55–57). Theorists of the global power arrangements that underdeveloped the Third World, such as the proponents of dependency theory, accept core tenets of modernization theory (see, for example, C. Scott 1995, 87–104, on Immanuel Wallerstein 1979, and Saldaña-Portillo 2003, 52–54, on the work of Andre Gunder Frank 1967). They consider existing local economies "unproductive" sectors characterized by problematic traditions. These portrayals echo the image of the Third World woman as victim that characterizes progressive feminist imagery about the global south (Ong 1988; Mohanty 1991). In radical theories of development, the radical agents who will transform Third World societies are envisioned in masculine terms (C. Scott 1995; Saldaña-Portillo 2003). This gender-biased theory misses local gender oppression (because women's subordination is considered mainly in relation to capitalism) and misunderstands local-global and gendered dynamics involved in development and modernization.

Clearly, the modernization thesis that economies of affection would subordinate themselves to capitalist development has not been borne out. Noncapitalist economies continue to exist side by side with capitalist development. Their vibrant presence in daily life suggests that these economic modes are not mere survivals, archaic relics of the past. Interpreting older cultural forms as anachronisms reflects ethnocentric Western understandings of social space and time (Chakrabarty 2000). A postcolonial feminist approach builds an analysis from the coexistence of different cultural logics rather than viewing the non-Western modes as either quaint or dysfunctional relics from a receding past.

Folk economies do more than endure as custom or as a safety net for modern Thais. Pockets of alternate economies even flourish with capitalist development. "Crony capitalism" and "corruption" are examples of the problematic place of economies of affection in development. Nepotism reflects the place of close ethnic and family networks in business, while graft represents locally calibrated expectations of exchange. But here, the model of economic interaction is illuminating: crony capitalism and routine graft are generated through local codes interacting with, and being distorted by, capitalism, specifically by global finance (Pasuk and Baker 1998).[6]

MORAL ECONOMIES

Perspectives that apply a critical lens to capitalist development take a different approach to the interaction between capitalist and noncapitalist economies. This approach sees economies of affection as a vital source of resistance to capitalist development. Where modernization theorists speak of local traditions posing obstacles to development, it is not hard to reinterpret these interferences as strategic "weapons of the weak" that sabotage official plans for remaking the economy (J. C. Scott 1985). Aihwa Ong (1991) provides an interpretive reading of the outbursts of spirit possessions in Southeast Asian factories as "cultural struggles"—an embodied critique of the dehumanized relations of industrial manufacturing.

Here the concept of the "moral economy" is helpful for thinking about grounds for resistance. Noted English historian E. P. Thompson (1971) coined the term to describe eighteenth-century English markets that were governed, or at least constrained, by community values and expectations. James Scott (1976) used moral economy to explain the fluctuating peasant resistance in Malaysia. He argued that peasant uprisings did not simply result from objective hardship but also from elites' failure to meet established expectations. That is, revolt does not just come from the empty belly (the material level) but from symbolic, subjective, and cultural sources, from customary relations and local codes. The concept of moral economy is historical, suggesting that norms and the conditions for resistance are produced in particular conjunctures, and change over time.

The erosion of the moral economy invites resistance as people reassert the legitimacy of precapitalist values within capitalist spheres. In recent years, Thai peasants have formed an Assembly of the Poor that has marched on the capital demanding responsive government policies to address the needs of farmers and rural society. We find this expression of moral economic values not only in the revolts of factory workers and farmers, but among middle classes as well. When I worked at a large information technology conglomerate, my colleagues in marketing valued creative labor and human relations and faulted management for not recognizing the importance of these domains (Wilson 2004, Chapter 4). As Ong (1991) and others have shown, one also finds economic critique in spiritual practices. The renaissance of Buddhist meditation or ascetic values among middle classes in Thailand can be read as an effort to create a distance from materialist values that suffuse a rapidly developing society.

There is widespread understanding that capitalist development is affecting Thai society. But how do industrial manufacturing, corporate structures, and commodified exchange affect Thai customs, patterns of relationships, and identities? One answer can be found in the operations of the plural economy, at the intertwined levels of material system, symbolism and ideology, and everyday experience. Capitalist economies have altered economies of affection, changed the borders between market and nonmarket, and weakened the moral economy.

INTERACTING ECONOMIES

The moral economy provides important grounds for resistance, yet at the same time, we need to be careful not to romanticize it. Economies of affection are not free from inequalities, as feminists have shown. Emphasizing only the oppression of capitalist or imperialist forces can mean overlooking local inequalities, such as patriarchal arrangements (C. Scott 1995).

The variegated character of Bangkok's urban landscape revises the image of where resistance comes from. While it predates capitalism, the moral economy is not *pre*capitalist, in the sense of being replaced by capitalism (it continues to coexist, although it can also be weakened by modernization). In Bangkok, the moral economy does not provide a space *apart* from capitalist development. Rather, daily life transpires across and within a range of economic practices and norms. Following the views of postcolonial theory and cultural political economy, we should not expect social transformation to come from authentic locales outside capitalist modernity. Nor do we need to expect radical agents to be either authentic natives or wholly remade revolutionaries (typically gendered masculine) who have cast off the constraints of tradition (C. Scott 1995; Saldaña-Portillo 2003).[7]

Moreover, local economies do not necessarily always provide norms, spaces, and identities that underwrite radical resistance to capitalist modernity. The fact that there are multiple economies in Bangkok suggests that there are also multiple interactions between capitalist economies and economies of affection. A grounded examination of the dynamic interactions between capitalism and noncapitalism suggests that they are not discrete spaces organized temporally on a neat path to modernization or revolution. At particular junctures, the interaction of economic fields can promote or diminish conditions for resistance. In Thailand, the resistance to capitalist development remains surprisingly constrained when compared to other sites in the region, for example, the Philippines. Certainly some of this constraint is due to repressive legacies of the Cold War. But repression does not explain comparative differences in resistance. I argue that interactions of capitalist and folk economies generate conditions that restrain gendered resistance to capitalist modernity in Bangkok.

In the rest of this chapter, I sketch two modes of interaction between capitalist and alternate economies that diminish the conditions for resistance by enlisting Thais in capitalist practices and ideologies. First, examining Bangkok's thriving consumer economy, I propose that people use commodified consumption to reproduce local social relations, or the folk economy. Next, I consider how people interpret the border between folk economies and capitalism, or between what is often read as tradition and modernity. These interpretations reflect capitalist ideologies about tradition and modernity that erase local economic histories and erode potential countervailing pressures of the moral economy.

CONSUMER ECONOMIES OF AFFECTION

For more than a hundred years, capitalist growth has already been altering life in the countryside and city. Major transformations were long under way through the effects first of international trade[8] and then industrialization programs and state development schemes, as, for example, movies and then radio broadcasts were brought into the countryside by traveling salesmen. This has had specific gendered impacts, for example, in the great numbers of young women migrating from the provinces to urban areas to work in factories, private homes, or massage parlors. As I will show, the conceptions of development also involve notions about sexuality and gender.

Women factory workers, wanting to partake of the offerings of modernity, buy consumer goods at department stores (Mills 1999). Tomboys (or its derivative *tom,* which means lesbian, butch, masculine female, or female-to-male transgendered person) frequent shopping malls (Wilson 2004). Since the 1980s, Thais have saved less and spent more, particularly on food and leisure, in cross-class cosmopolitan consumerism.

Consumerism is thought to reflect individual desires, rising materialism, and ruptures with tradition. But as historical and critical studies of the consumer economy have shown, practices of consumption need to be understood socially. Following anthropologist Daniel Miller (1998), among others, I consider how commodities are integrated into ongoing practices and used to perpetuate relationships.

Modern manufactures circulate within economies of affection in Thailand. The marriage gift that a groom's family gives to the bride's family now includes consumer items and cash as well as the more traditional gold and livestock. Offerings to spirits include soda or imported whiskey. In creole Chinese-Thai (Sino-Thai) communities, paper models of cars, televisions, and other consumer goods are burned as votive offerings for recently deceased relatives. Spiritual offerings, support for parents, and gifts to friends: all these exchanges rely on the products of retail. Consumer markets not only meet but also shape demand. Department stores construct a calendar for giving, providing packaged New Year's gift baskets, Chinese moon cakes, or saffron-wrapped temple donations. Consumption should thus be read socially, as part of what is called social reproduction. The purpose of these purchases is to perpetuate relationships, communities, and values and thereby recreate social worlds. In this way, the recreation of folk economies uses capitalist economies.

As Thorstein Veblen ([1899] 1973) made clear with his concept of conspicuous consumption, and as Pierre Bourdieu (1984) showed in French concepts of taste, people consume to position themselves in hierarchies of status. The power of consumer goods to negotiate social position is heightened in the social terrain of Thailand after three decades of economic growth and the 1997 Asian economic crisis, which began in Bangkok. Rural families are often criticized for how they spend remittances from their youth who have migrated to the cities for work. This money typically goes to consumer goods rather than productive items—to a television or refrigerator instead of a water buffalo or more land. These purchases are motivated by codes of social standing in their communities and the modernizing nation. People enlist in the opportunities and resources connected with globalization because of emerging class systems but also because of enduring status hierarchies associated with rank, region, age, ethnicity, and kinship. Social inequality motivates consumption.[9] As these examples show, people's engagement with the global market economy does not merely represent capital penetration in a unidirectional, top-down fashion, but represents an intersection between capitalism and folk economies that are not inherently egalitarian nor fixed in time. Their dynamic interaction illuminates the success of a consumer economy.

Gendered consumption offers a telling example of the ways local practices motivate people to engage with global modernity. There is a premium on attractive and respectable appearance for both men and women in Thailand, but with different intensities and different scales according to gender. Contemporary femininity relies on grooming, comportment, and consumption. The ideals of femininity guiding consumption are not purely foreign, but rather are the result of the interaction of local and global. In Thailand, a ferocious shampoo market reveals a long-standing emphasis on women's hair (although only in the modern period did long styles become the norm). The gendered aesthetics of body appearance reflect a combination of elite aristocratic ideals and an emerging pan-Asian image inflected with Western, Chinese, and Japanese values.[10] Transnational influences, urbanization, and class transformations have intensified and redefined an already strong emphasis on bodies and appearance in femininity.

The analysis I am putting forth differs from common representations of the consumer economy seducing hapless victims, a portrayal that feminist cultural critic Meaghan Morris (1988) points out is gendered. Instead, my analysis sees consumption as systemic, as a historically situated interaction of plural economic fields. Thais engage the consumer economy because of commitments to *local* (albeit changing) patterns of exchange and identity. The increasing reliance on consumption to fulfill these commitments mutes critiques of capitalist modernity.

IMMATERIAL ECONOMIES

This chapter has suggested that how people respond to the forces of development crucially involves interpretations, constructions, and experiences of the economic. In daily life and in public discourse, people inhabit and navigate different economic registers. They also interpret the fluctuations of plural economies.[11] How Thais make sense of the dynamic interaction of plural economies informs their experiences of globalization and their responses to it. The interpretation of the economic registers of their everyday lives, as well as the understandings of what counts as "tradition" and "modernity," shape how people respond to development: whether, when, and how they refuse it.

The separation of capitalist from noncapitalist values is undeniably important in Thai worldviews. In Thailand, the shifting border between capitalist and noncapitalist economies causes palpable public and individual anxiety. One example is the prevalent discourses about young people's orientation to consumption—their penchant for shopping malls (especially during school time), focus on consumer goods, and diminished feelings of obligations towards parents. Another commonly voiced concern is over religion, over people's marketized relationship to temples, merit, and spirituality. People work to establish—or to reclaim—the border between the market sphere and nation, kinship, community, or culture, which are considered apart from market logic.

While there *are* material and systemic differences between capitalist markets and local economic systems, as I have discussed, more often it is the *imagined* border that forms the conflict zone. The distinction between these realms is not only material but is also symbolic: the border is emotionally resonant and is interpreted and experienced in public discourses, political contests, and everyday life. The perceived difference between capitalist and noncapitalist realms informs evaluations of Thai society, particularly sexual and gender identities.

One illustration of these imagined borders can be found in generalized representations of traditional Thailand. When Thai people wanted to teach me about traditional Thailand, they most often pointed to commonplace notions about Buddhism, peasant ways, the olden days (*samai kon*), and colorful court rituals. State, commercial, and such conventional images of traditional Thailand produce a composite portrait that minimizes economic dimensions. As I have suggested, such constructions of the traditional and the economic have gendered, ethnic, and class dimensions.

In this composite portrait of tradition, Thai market women become icons of the cultural landscape rather than recognized as motors of the nation's economy. (For decades, foreign experts bemoaned the lack of "Thai" entrepreneurial spirit, by which they meant Thai men.) Chinese Thais have been seen as an alien presence for over a century. Even as they became Thai citizens or partnered with Thais, they were represented as outside Thai history and culture. The consolidated representations present a de-materialized vision of Thai tradition that places Thai and Chinese women outside of the economic history of the country. This discourse downplays the centrality of markets that were embedded in social communities, thereby erasing the presence of moral economies in Thai society. What results is a false juxtaposition between noneconomic Thai culture and capitalist modernity that obscures the ongoing interactions of dynamic local and capitalist economies.

Moreover, capitalist development defines what counts as modern and traditional. Modernity is associated with things urban, industrial, digital, associated with Western and Japanese origin. Capitalist development has also projected images and definitions about presumed tradition. Mass media presents images of the "traditional" past—in tourist campaigns and nostalgic imagery romanticizing court life or peasant life. The décor of the most upscale hotels quotes Thai traditions in the costumes of bell hops, antique displays, and even references to traditional rural hospitality of the sort that modernization itself eroded, such as displays of the water bowl and ladle available for passersby at the edge of rural compounds. The government has also worked to define Thai tradition as a public relations tool. After the 1997 Asian economic crisis, for example, the government's "Amazing Thailand" campaign, designed to prop Thailand's image, included advertising of Thailand's wares as well as promotions of what it defined as "Amazing Thai culture" (Wilson 1999). What state and commercial discourses represent as authentic Thai tradition are often invented or recently borrowed (many craft techniques are recent imports from Burma, for instance) and are always highly selective. Thus, we need to recognize that often what counts as modernity and tradition is shaped by capitalist development itself. Such a recognition offers a caution to locating resistance to sources of local values that are defined as old "traditions" in opposition to development.

The division between capitalist and noncapitalist realms plays a role in defining "Thai" identity. When I worked at the information technology company, I found the professionals who were utterly immersed in globalization would say, "I'm 100 percent Thai" or "I'm a true Thai" (*Thai-tae*) even when they had Chinese or Vietnamese ancestry. Beyond simply citizenship, *Thai* has come to signify an identity that contrasts with a denationalized cosmopolitan and as a nationalist affiliation formulated on an uneven global stage dominated by the West and white racism. But the meaning of Thai also refers to a mode of being and an affective state. The worldly professionals' conception of Thainess invoked a mode of relation characterized by generosity, not by accumulation. This definition of Thai identity is bound up with folk economies in contrast to rational and accumulative capitalist economies.

Borders between what counts as tradition and what counts as modernity are often symbolized through gender, ethnicity, and sexuality (Narayan 1997). The same selective representation applies to the symbolic divide between moral economies and capitalism. The schism between tradition and modernity can be read not only temporally, as past and present, but also as coterminous economic fields. A cardinal example of the gendered investments in the border between market and nonmarket relations is found in attitudes towards prostitution, particularly in the pervasive judgment of the sex worker. The sex worker, who blurs the divide between commerce and intimate life, embodies the transgression of this boundary. Thus, sex workers are stigmatized not only because they have sex with many men, but also because they violate this divide (Wilson 2004). Elite or middle-class Thais often represent sex workers as lazy and greedy, particularly when they do not come from the poorest economic region of the Northeast. Sex workers have to be adept at fluently navigating intimate and commercial exchanges in their work and have to manage the stigma for doing so.

Other gendered and sexual economic symbols are found in queer identities. In Thailand, there is a category for sexual and gender deviance, *kathoey*.[12] This term has come to describe the male-to-female transgendered person or feminine gay man. As gay has become an identity available to urban cosmopolitan men, *kathoey* has also become more class inflected, associated with working-class and rural forms of sex/gender crossings. There is increasing public recognition of toms, with their heightened presence often explained as a "fashion." Associating tom with fashion presents deviation from female sexual and gendered norms as a phase; the assumption is that the young women will grow out of it. The association with fashion, as well as Western derivation of such words as *tom*, the word for toms' feminine partners (*dee*, from "lady"), or gay, links these forms of sex/gender transgression to modernity. As a result, these identities are attributed to rising materialism and the erosion of values among contemporary Thai youth (Sinnott 2004; Wilson 2004).

The association of *tom*, *dee*, and gay with modernity reinforces an ideological distinction between modern queerness and traditional heterosexuality. Heterosexual relations have transformed markedly in relation to twentieth-century political economic forces.[13] Yet whatever these modern transformations, heterosexuality is rendered as authentic and traditional. *Kathoey* is an older Thai identity than is heterosexual, yet is not heralded as a part of Thai "tradition." Instead, queerness is located as modern, which renders it less authentic, less "Thai," and links it with materialist values linked with capitalist modernity: selfishness and a lack of control. Material and symbolic boundaries between capitalist and moral economies underwrite the evaluations not only of sexual deviants like sex workers or toms, but a range of social identities and relationships in Thailand.

This symbolic border between different economic modes is constructed, strategic, and ideological. The prevailing understanding of the separation between the economic world and local realms is a by-product of capitalist modernity itself. Commercial culture—advertisements, television, tourist marketing, and so forth—convey powerful concepts of tradition and culture. Nostalgic and anachronistic representations of Thai society juxtapose modern markets with noneconomic tradition. In so doing, capitalist (and state) discourses minimize the historical and ongoing linkages between Thai social life and economic operations.

How people understand the difference between commercial values and what they see as their values—where the line is between capitalism and the rest?—is linked to how they conceptualize the problems of developing Thai society. These interpretations inform their conceptions of power, unfairness, and resistance. Hence, understanding how people see the interaction between capitalist and noncapitalist realms, or more generally, how they conceptualize the interaction between modernity and tradition, illuminates the conditions for critiques of development. The ideology of Thai society has gendered ramifications for the evaluation of identities and resistance. The imagined divide between capitalist modernity and Thai tradition mitigates against resistances by redirecting public criticism away from powerful systems of capitalism or the accommodating state to other targets: the materialism of today's youth, sex workers, queers, or irritation at the chaos of street markets, that province of poor women.

The pulsing plurality of Bangkok's public life shows how globalization is realized in everyday life. People navigate and interpret these fluctuating economies in their day-to-day lives and in political and cultural struggles.

Economies of affection do not reflect the past or a lower stage along a linear path to modernization, but are part of modernity itself. Taking economic pluralism as a starting point, this chapter has sketched varying interactions of coexisting economic fields, systemically, morally, and ideologically. These interactions shape the material, symbolic, and subjective conditions for refusing or accommodating development.

NOTES

1. One way that kinship can be seen as economic lies in the centrality of exchange, whether material, symbolical, or metaphorical. In Thailand, many relationships are interpreted in terms of exchange: parent-child, senior-junior, laity-monk, and human-spirit. All children are born indebted to their parents. However, gender shapes the repayment of that debt. Young men can apply the merit from a brief ordination in the monkhood to dispatch their major obligations, while women must use increasingly monetary and material means throughout their parents' life (Wilson 2004, 11–15).
2. The Thai government, influenced by multilateral agencies, began five-year plans for economic development in 1961. Overall, the plans, or their realization, have prioritized private, foreign trade, and exchange liberalization and, whatever the rhetoric about rural development, have favored cities—above all the capital, Bangkok, and industrial zones, over the countryside. Thailand's first five-year plan (1961–1966) focused on increasing farm, industry, and power production. The second development plan (1967–1971) focused on infrastructure. These early development plans coincided with the US presence in Thailand during the Indochina wars. The third development plan (1972–1976) endorsed privatizing state-owned enterprises and sought growth in financial and commercial sectors, including commercial agriculture and import-substitution manufacturing. Responding to the overwhelming growth of Bangkok, the fourth economic plan (1977–1981) called for decentralizing manufacturing zones and promoted export-oriented production.
3. My fieldwork in Thailand spans 1988 to 2005, including continuous stay from December 1992 to January 1995. See Wilson (2004) for an overview of the major research.
4. For more on post-Orientalist scholarship, see, for example, Chakrabarty (2000). My approach could be called *cultural political economy*, a term favored by the Institute for Advanced Studies in Social and Management Sciences at the University of Lancaster. For frameworks forging a historically grounded analysis of political economy that sees material and symbolic dimensions as intertwined, see, for example, Polanyi (1957); Ong (1991); Miller (1998); Villareal (2001); and Bhavnani, Foran, and Kurian (2003b).
5. Gibson-Graham critiques the understanding of a "hierarchical relation of capitalism to noncapitalism" (Gibson-Graham 1996a, 11) in order to deconstruct notions of global capitalism. While recognizing the plurality of economic fields, including the diversity of capitalist forms, I still rely on a concept of capitalism as an imperial economic system, and thereby depart from Gibson-Graham's emphases.
6. It is also worth remembering the corrupt operations of heralded corporations within the United States, memorably Enron and WorldCom, among other infamous examples.

7. The argument that we not seek transformation from agents and spaces beyond or before the current social order has famously been made by Donna Haraway (1985) in her work on cyborgs and repeated in Antonio Negri and Michael Hardt (2004). See also Ong's (1991) arguments about cultural struggles in postmodern labor conditions).
8. Given that Thailand was never formally colonized (although it has not escaped occupation or imperialist forces), trade and investment have played a greater role in "modernizing" Thai society than has colonial restructuring.
9. People do not only engage with capitalism as consumers, of course, but as workers. Their labor in transnational venues can also be understood as efforts to negotiate status and power in their family, community, and in the eyes of the nation. Mary Beth Mills (1999) explores how female factory workers use their work to juggle and realize the claims of urban modernity and the rural communities. Similarly, I have argued that Thai distributors of Avon, Amway, or other direct selling corporations value an affiliation with an American global system as a way to establish an identity that is both modern and fulfilling the requirements of fiscally responsible adulthood (Wilson 2004, Chapter 5).
10. Chulanee Thianthai (2005) found that the ideal body types and styles for Thai young men and women reflected Chinese and Western styles, with an increasing emphasis on slimness for women in particular.
11. Maribel Alvarez (2003) and Magdalena Villarreal (2001) have explored the meanings of money and work in Mexico. Angus Cameron and Ronen Palan (2004) take a radical constructionist stance, arguing that globalization is more about "imagined economies" than real material processes.
12. *Kathoey* is pronounced more like "gatoy" in American English.
13. Heterosexual relations have altered over the twentieth century: migration from China to Siam-Thailand changed from mainly single male sojourners to married couples; the bride gift from a groom to the bride and family underwent enormous inflation; courtship became more erotic and oriented to dating couples; and the suburban nuclear family has become an emblem of modern citizenship. Even with these significant transformations, modern modes of heterosexuality are interpreted as reflecting tradition or nature (Wilson 2004, Chapter 3).

4 Dancing on the Edge

Women, Culture, and a Passion for Change

Kum-Kum Bhavnani and Krista Bywater

> You must understand the whole of life, not just one little part of it. That is why you must read, that is why you must look at the skies, that is why you must sing and dance, and write poems and suffer and understand, for all that is life.
>
> Krishnamurti

We have failed to make the world a better planet. This failure, exacerbated by the end of the Cold War and the rise of projects of capitalist/neoliberal economic globalization has meant that poverty has become increasingly feminized even as women work in formal and informal economies to a greater extent than ever before. Environmental degradation and resource depletion continue at an alarming pace, and conditions for peace and security remain elusive. It is widely accepted that a misplaced emphasis on the positive impacts of globalization, a disregard for culture, and a lack of attention to gender inequalities have contributed to this failure.

Alternative forms of development are necessary to revitalize the potential of development to ameliorate poverty and improve the lives of people throughout the Third World. Focusing on women's lives, experiences, and culture, in development projects and discourse reveals how people from the margins of society can transform globalization. People are not solely victims of the plans, conscious or not, propagated by transnational elites. Rather, they are simultaneously agents who configure innovative ways of surviving, protesting, demanding social justice, and improving their lives. In our search for new ways of conceptualizing development we look to women's agency and people's movements to inspire us.

"Woman" is a category that is commonly used across the academy. Although it refers to women, more often, it implies gender. What this means is that the category "woman" is not only about the relationship between "women" and "men," but, in addition, that inequalities of power and of access to resources are embedded within this category and these relationships. That is, the category of woman is not neutral: it is a category saturated with inequalities.

The commonsense agreement about inequalities between women and men needs more refinement—we need to ask which women's lives are actually noted; in which parts of the world; which aspects of their lives; which women's voices are heard; who is telling the stories; and, are there any continuities for women across class, region, nation, sexuality, and "race"/ethnicity? In other words, are there any issues common to all women's lives that might help us work out why we still draw on the category "woman" as if it were a unitary category, when we are aware of its limitations and possibilities for masking power inequalities among women?

There is, of course, a global public acknowledgment for protecting *all* women's rights and an often unquestioned acceptance that women must, at the very least, be treated as equal to men. The *New Zealand Herald* reported, on March 4, 2007, that New Zealand is seventh among the top 10 countries which have narrowed the "gender gap," following the Scandinavian countries, with the United Kingdom coming ninth, Australia fifteenth, and the United States twenty-third. While this is good news, it is also information that we would like to interrogate. A number of scholars argue that many of the public discourses about feminism/women's rights rest on a particular understanding of how to eliminate inequalities, which holds that if women are regarded in the same way as men—for example, given equal pay for equal work—women's rights will be improved, and, eventually, achieved. The problem with this argument is that the structural *causes* of inequality—capitalism, patriarchy, racism, and heterosexism to pick a few—are not examined, and, indeed, left untouched in this approach. In other words, these statistics do not tell us, for example, what the differences are between white women, Maori women, and other women of color in New Zealand, regarding wages, political representation, and professional rank, let alone the consequences of, and resistances to, racism, both material and psychological.

The previous paragraphs glide quickly over the meanings of "woman," "power inequalities between women," and "race/ethnicity and women," all of which often lead to intense debates. The usual way to move through these discussions is to engage with the intersectionality of the category "woman"; that is, woman is defined as a category that is intersected by axes of inequality other than gender—such as race, sexuality, nationality, wealth—which all cut across woman and each other at different angles.

We prefer the term *configurations* to *intersectionality*. To configure connotes more movement and fluidity than lies in the notion of intersection. It is closer to our metaphor of dancing as we pick our way through this tangle of power and inequalities, without tripping up, and yet being confident in our sure-footedness. *Configuration* also connotes agency, offering a way of thinking about how inequalities such as "race," gender, nation, sexuality, and wealth work with and against each other. The idea of configurations suggests activity and graceful movement with a consequent attribution of agency to the subjects of the configurations. Intersectionality is too static, too close to losing sight of agency. It is too angular, suggesting sharp and rigid boundaries that leave little room for negotiation.

These discussions about "woman" and "intersectionality" may also be better comprehended in the context of the past two decades of globalization. Neoliberal economic globalization is often characterized by the easy movement of money and goods facilitated by a decrease of state controls, an increase in privatization, extensive use of the new information and communication technologies, flexibility in production, and a lack of accountability on the part of political and economic elites (see, for example, McMichael 2003). All these characteristics are now taken for granted, and, one might say, naturalized in the current era: that is, they are seen as inevitable.

WATER

A close examination of the world's water problems reveals the negative impacts of economic globalization and also reveals that people can challenge and alter the course of globalization for their betterment. Over the past two decades, international financial institutions such as the World Bank and International Monetary Fund (IMF) have promoted water privatization through structural adjustment programs. As conditions of loans, countries from Bolivia to India have been pressured to turn over their cities' water utilities to transnational corporations such as Vivendi, Bechtel, and Suez. Privatizing water and managing it through the free market transforms it from a common resource and human right to a commodity and ensures that companies profit by controlling a raw material necessary for human survival—water.

To address countries' water problems, water privatization or marketization is the solution most often endorsed by transnational corporations, development agencies, financial institutions, and governments. How we choose to manage water resources will become increasingly important because, as is now commonplace knowledge, we face a global water crisis that will only worsen with time. According to the 2006 United Nations Human Development Report, 1.1 billion people do not have access to enough clean water, and 2.5 million live without adequate sanitation services (Ross-Larson, de Conquereaumont, and Trott 2006, 5). Half of the world's hospital beds are occupied by patients with water-borne diseases, and almost 5,000 children die every day from preventable water-borne illnesses such as diarrhea and cholera (Ross-Larson et al. 2006, 6). People in the Third World suffer the most from water scarcity and pollution, especially the poorest among them—typically women and children. Two in three people who do not have enough clean water live on less than $2 a day, and one in three survive on less than $1 a day (Ross-Larson et al. 2006, 7). These facts reveal the severity of the global water crisis which disproportionately affects the world's poorest populations. Clearly, development cannot be successful without drastically increasing the number of people who can access greater quantities of safe drinking water.

The failure of water privatization projects around the world illustrates that this is not the single best answer to countries' water problems. The water sector is one of the last public infrastructures to be privatized, and investors see its potential to reap enormous private profits (Postel 1992; De Villiers 2000; Barlow and Clark 2002; Finger and Allouche 2002; Shiva 2002; McDonald and Jehl 2003). Most countries have experienced the privatization of numerous public services and utilities and the reduction of state sovereignty and democratic oversight; water is one of the remaining utilities whose privatization is being challenged with a strength that makes it important to analyze. Most are aware that people and governments can ill afford to lose control of water sources and distribution systems. Lack of safe water jeopardizes the public health, and as a consequence, limits human potential and decreases human productivity. As a result of water shortages, women, who are primarily responsible for managing water for their families, must travel farther distances (sometimes up to six kilometers), abandon income-generating activities, use more of the household money, or take girl children out of school to fetch safe water (see Coles and Wallace 2005).

Most transnational institutions that support development projects argue that privatization of water systems is the best way to solve countries' water crises. These institutions contend corporations are more efficient than governments at providing services, including water distribution. It is suggested that by removing subsidies, users will pay the full cost of water and it is this price increase that will deter consumer wastage. Thus, market principles form the underpinnings for protection of the environment and management of natural resources. This logic does not consider that those suffering from water scarcity already use the least amount of water: the majority survive on as little as five liters a day (Ross-Larson et al. 2006, 5). Every time an American flushes the toilet he or she uses the same amount of water a poor woman in India might use all day.

From our reading and research, a capitalist economy is an inadequate mechanism to manage water resources because it does not guarantee conservation or efficient use of water. People who can afford to pay for water will continue to use the resource often with little regard for its conservation. Economic principles are also inadequate to manage water resources because the poorest people in the world already pay the most and use the least amount of water. For instance, slum residents in Jakarta, Indonesia; Nairobi, Kenya; and Manila, the Philippines already spend five to ten times more on water than people in New York and London (Ross-Larson et al. 2006, 7). High-income residents in cities such as Mumbai, India and Dar es Salam, Tanzania use fifteen times more water than poor households (Ross-Larson et al. 2006, 7).

When water utilities are privatized, they are run for profit and not as a public service. As a result people who cannot afford to pay their water bills, or those who cannot get formal water connections because they are homeless or live in informal settlements or slums, cannot access sufficient amounts of clean water. When people cannot afford to purchase potable water, they are forced to use contaminated water or obtain clean water illegally. Furthermore, proponents of water privatization do not account for the cultural significance of water. Some cultures regard water as sacred, believe it is the responsibility of all people to ensure it is used sustainably, and promote traditions that encourage sharing of water supplies (Shiva 2002; Olivera and Lewis 2004). For example, Vandana Shiva writes that water in India is "a sacred common heritage . . . to be worshiped, preserved and shared collectively, sustainably used and equitably distributed" (2002).

Millions throughout the world have resisted water privatization promoted in the name of development. Because of citizens' protests and corporations' poor performance, governments have been forced to end water privatization schemes in more than a dozen countries, among them Tanzania, Gambia, Ghana, Sierra Leone, Chad, Mali, Belize, Bolivia, Argentina, Brazil, Guyana, Trinidad and Tobago, and Malaysia. Examining these cases reveals the problems of neoliberal globalization, as well as offering a glimpse into people's ability to resist, and the need to create alternative frameworks for development. At the beginning of the twenty-first century, the events in Cochabamba, Bolivia, demonstrated how the world's most marginalized people, especially women, are affected by and contest top-down development schemes that promote privatization at the expense of people's livelihoods and human rights.

From January to April of 2000, protests raged in Cochabamba, Bolivia, as a broad base of coalitions joined under *La Coordinadora de Defensa del Agua y de la Vida* (The Coalition in Defense of Water and Life; Finnegan 2002; Olivera and Lewis 2004; Shultz 2005b). La Coordinadora demanded the Bolivian government end its contract with *Aquas del Tunari*, a consortium of corporations including Abenoga of Spain, four Bolivian companies, and International Water, a subsidiary of Bechtel that held the majority interest in the company. On September 3, 1999, the Bolivian government signed a forty-year contract with the only bidder for its water sector, *Aquas del Tunari*, giving the company complete control of Cochabamba's water resources and supply. The details of the contract with Aquas del Tunari were not made public until November 1, 1999, after the Bolivian government had passed a new pro-privatization law, Law 2029 (Olivera and Lewis 2004). The new policy was designed to safeguard the corporation's investment in Cochabamba's water system. It eliminated the guarantee that water would be supplied to rural areas, made private and community water collection systems illegal, required people to obtain permission to build water tanks to collect rain, and set prices against the US dollar. If the *boliviano* decreased in value, the contractor who won the water bid would be protected from currency fluctuations as people's bills would increase to reflect the equivalent price in US dollars (Olivera and Lewis 2004, 9–11).

Through Law 2029 the Bolivian government, in order to promote privatization, eradicated citizens' *rights* to water to guarantee profits for the transnational corporation. Since 1985, Bolivia, in its bid to obtain loans from the World Bank, has been a strong follower of the bank's structural adjustment policies and has privatized many national industries and utilities, including its railways, telephone system, and tin mines. The World Bank, in its 1999 *Bolivia Public Expenditure Review,* encouraged private investments in the country's water services and recommended all subsidies for water be removed in Cochabamba (Antonio Gonzalez and McCarthy 1999). Following the World Bank's suggestions, Bolivia's contract with Aquas del Tunari allowed the company to charge people the full cost of water, thereby eliminating water subsidies for the poor. The corporation also benefited from the mandates of Law 2029, and Bolivia's government guaranteed Aquas del Tunari a sixteen percent annual profit irrespective of the company's performance (Olveria 2004, 9–11).

After Aquas del Tunari took control of Cochabamba's water system, people saw their water bills increase by as much as 300 percent (Olivera and Lewis 2004, 10). People earning $100 a month, which is more than the minimum wage in Cochabamba, were suddenly forced to spend a fifth of their earnings on water. When women went to community wells, which they had built and maintained for generations with their own money and labor, Bolivian soldiers denied them access. Law 2029 allowed the water company to take control of all community water sources and removed the right of people and communities to have access to clean water (Peredo Beltrán 2004). In response to soaring water prices, women reduced household water usage by limiting baths, washing, and cleaning and by prioritizing water for cooking (Peredo Beltrán 2004); these measures were not enough. Unable to afford the price increases, people refused to pay their water bills and soon marched in the city's streets in protest.

An aspect of Cochabamba's history that receives less attention is women's involvement in the movement. Women, from diverse backgrounds and groups, were important in the mobilizations against the water privatization project. Rural women from irrigator groups were some of the first protestors to enter the city to oppose the government's contract with Aquas del Tunari. Among the poorest people in Cochabamba, rural women and men could no longer afford to irrigate their crops because of the privatization. Women were active participants from the beginning of the movement and took to the streets to build support for the opposition to the company.

Women from the countryside networked with and were joined by lower-, middle-, and some upper-class, urban women and men; youth; factory workers; and people from neighborhood associations and peasant cooperatives. They formed a broad coalition—La Coordinadora—that represented diverse segments of society. To save its deal with Aquas del Tunari, Bolivia's former president, Hugo Banzer, declared a state of emergency on April 8, 2000. Afterwards, protests intensified and women continued to participate in the movement against the privatization. Women often took charge of the protesters' blockades, stood at the front line despite police violence, distributed items such as rags and vinegar to protect people from tear gas, collected food, and made meals for protesters. Their actions enabled hundreds of other protesters to continue their struggle against the police. Women organized committees and visited media outlets to inform them about the resistance on the streets. They took it upon themselves to close down *chiche* (an alcoholic beverage) bars to prevent their *compañeros* from drinking and to stem violence. However, women were not afraid to use force against police and on occasion threw stones and used sticks during confrontations (Peredo Beltrán 2004). Women's organizing and work at the grassroots level enabled the protests to continue and showed the government that the people of Cochabamba would not stop until their water rights were restored.

Police used force to regain control of the city, killing one teenager, Víctor Hugo Daza, and injuring hundreds of demonstrators (Finnegan 2002; Shultz 2005b). With dozens of La Coordinadora leaders arrested and people's rights curtailed, such as freedom of movement and freedom of the press, the state of emergency was deployed to straightjacket democracy in the interest of global capital. Women were jailed along with men and were among those injured in demonstrations and confrontations with police. Despite the state's efforts to quell the public opposition, the government was forced to end its contract with Aquas del Tunari and to modify Law 2029. The Bolivian people, many of them women, succeeded in taking back their water utility, but not without much human suffering and political strife.

After leaving the country, the Bechtel Corporation, which held the majority interest in Aquas del Tunari, filed a lawsuit at the International Centre for Settlement of Investment Disputes (ICSID), a body of the World Bank, the same institution that had encouraged Bolivia's government to privatize Cochabamba's water sector in the first place. Bechtel sought $25 million in restitution from the Bolivian government for breaking their contract. In 2006 Bechtel withdrew its claim against the Bolivian government, acknowledging that the contract ended because of the country's civil unrest and the state of emergency (Bechtel Corporation 2006).

The actions of people in Cochabamba demonstrate that globalization from above—capitalist globalization—is not inevitable. People on the edge of society can shape the direction and nature of globalization. Women are key actors often overlooked in such struggles: they build social networks and also do the reproductive work that literally and figuratively feeds the movement. Not only did we see people successfully take back their water sector in Cochabamba, but the more recent events in the southern Indian state of Kerala show how people can challenge the forces of globalization, and, often it is the people with seemingly the least amount of power and resources. The most politically, economically, and culturally marginalized peoples like the Adivasi (original inhabitants also known as Tribals or indigenous peoples) in India demonstrate it is possible to dispute globalization with movements from the margins of society.

In 2002, people in the hamlet of Plachimada, Kerala awaited the opening of the Coca-Cola bottling plant. They hoped the new factory would provide permanent jobs for the agricultural workers, both men and women, who had worked on the 35 acres of land on which the factory was built. Jobs did not materialize for the majority of displaced laborers. Local politicians worked with factory managers to distribute jobs to party supporters and denied most Adivasis employment, on the pretext of the Adivasis' lack of formal education. Consequently dozens of villagers in Plachimada who had worked in the fields of landowning families were forced to travel six kilometers or more each day to neighboring villages in search of work. These changes presaged that the industrial development of the village would not bring the anticipated economic prosperity and social stability.

Six months after Coca-Cola's plant began its production, women in the village noticed the decreasing level of the water in local wells. They also noted that the water was becoming salty and hard, making it unfit for drinking, cooking, or washing clothes. Talking among themselves, the women realized the problem was not isolated to a few wells, but affected the entire community. They shared the news of the community's water problems with other villagers. At about the same time, villagers observed the company dumping its waste, a sludge, outside the factory compound and later selling it to local farmers as fertilizer (Bijoy 2006). When people handled the sludge, it caused rashes and skin irritations. Animals that came in contact with the sludge became ill.

Realizing Coca-Cola's excessive pumping of groundwater was depleting the resource and changing its quality, Adivasis in Plachimada organized a campaign against the company. On Earth Day, April 22, 2002, the *Coca-Cola Virudha Janakeeya Samara Samithy* (Anti-Coca-Cola People's Struggle Committee) inaugurated the struggle with 1,500 people blocking the factory gates, preventing Coca-Cola from transporting its products. They demanded the plant be shut down and the company be held criminally responsible for destroying the groundwater and people's livelihoods. The committee asserted Coca-Cola's unregulated use of groundwater was a form of water privatization as the company was using a public resource for its own profit.

The Adivasis faced opposition from police, the Coca-Cola Corporation, political parties, and even the *panchayat* (local village council), responsible for representing the interests of its constituents. With little outside support and sparse attention from the Indian media, the villagers continued their struggle, and Adivasi women, who are most directly affected by the water problems, formed the backbone of the movement (Shiva 2005, Bijoy 2006). In 2003, the movement finally gained international recognition when the

British Broadcasting Corporation (BBC) radio program *Face the Facts* reported on the people's struggle in Plachimada. The BBC sent samples of the local groundwater, as well as some of the sludge from the factory, to the University of Exeter. There, scientists found high levels of the minerals sodium and chloride and the toxic metals cadmium and lead. Numerous independent and government agencies, such as the Indian Central Pollution Control Board, confirmed the groundwater in Plachimada is not fit for drinking, bathing, or even washing clothes (Bijoy 2006).

In May, 2003, more than a year after the movement started, the panchayat decided to cancel Coca-Cola's bottling license to protect the groundwater resources for the good of the public (Bijoy 2006, 13). Kerala's State Pollution Control Board ordered the company to dispose of its sludge according to India's hazardous waste guidelines and to provide villagers with safe drinking water. Since 2003 the Coca-Cola Corporation, the panchayat, and government agencies have engaged in a series of disputes and legal battles to determine if the panchayat has the legal authority to set the conditions for the factory's operation and cancel its license. The plant stopped production in March, 2004, but is not permanently closed. The Anti-Coca-Cola Struggle Committee and its supporters declare they will not allow the company to reopen and will continue their opposition to the company, demanding criminal charges be filed and compensation paid for the pollution of the groundwater. Villagers still cannot drink the groundwater in Plachimada. Three or four times a week women must carry their pots and wait at the side of the road for the government-supplied water tankers to arrive and distribute water. Women also line up at public taps, which are turned on for a few hours on alternate days to collect water (Bywater fieldwork 2007).

The Adivasis who began the movement in Plachimada have inspired many people's movements throughout India, where people continue to fight for control of local resources and against unsustainable development. People's movements against Coca-Cola have begun in other villages in India (Mehndiganj, Ballia, Shivaganga, and Kaladera), where residents face similar problems because of the company's indiscriminate use of groundwater and unchecked pollution. The women and men of Plachimada demonstrate that by working collectively, people can challenge the most powerful global actors.

DEVELOPMENT

The actions of the Adivasi women conjure up what Mahbub ul Haq, the creator of the UN Human Development Index, said in 1989: "The basic purpose of development is to create an enabling environment for people to enjoy long, healthy, creative lives. This simple but powerful truth is too often forgotten in the pursuit of material and financial wealth" (quoted in

UNDP 1999, 1). The women of Plachimada were determined to create an environment for people to enjoy long, healthy, and creative lives.

There are, of course, other examples. Thai peasants plant organic vegetables on overirrigated golf courses (Klein 2002), and the forests have been regenerated in gender-specific ways so that *women* obtained rights to the land on which the trees were planted (Rowbotham and Linkogle 2001). Women in Senegal work to eliminate female genital mutilation in their villages through their public declarations, bringing together hundreds of villagers, while also taking care of the women whose job it as to conduct such cutting. Women who tap for rubber in western Brazil have created organizations that increase literacy and challenge the domestic violence in their lives. These examples of development are actions that can resist the apparent juggernaut of capitalist globalization in its pursuit of material and financial wealth for the few.

What the Plachimada women did, and thousands of other people are continuing to do, is development in ul Haq's sense. In other words, it is development as planned social transformation and development as redistribution that underlies their actions. And, therefore, it is development that could make globalization—"life as profit" as Arundhati Roy defines it—"un-natural" and "not-inevitable" (2004).

So far we have argued that although projects of capitalist globalization cannot decrease the inequalities of power they create around the world, some forms of development offer the conditions for resisting greater poverty, and that it is often women who might be in the best position to do this. One can see that it is the *peoples* of the Third World—the *subaltern*, or the *poor* are other terms to denote these mainly nonwhite constituencies—whose labor and work ensure the success of the profit imperative and, yet, who also form the cornerstone of the potential to offer resistance to globalization: development.

WOMEN, CULTURE, AND DEVELOPMENT

The devastating destruction of people, environments, and democracy has propelled us towards a synthesis of the theoretical, empirical, cultural, and political interconnections of women, culture, and Third World development. In the past few years we, along with coauthors Priya A. Kurian, John Foran, Debashish Munshi, Peter Chua, and Molly Talcott, have been working on a new paradigm we call Women, Culture, and Development(WCD; see Chua, Bhavnani, and Foran 2000; Bhavnani, Foran, and Kurian 2003b; Bhavnani, Foran, and Talcott 2005). This paradigm focuses on women in the Third World and was initiated from our research, teaching, and writing about development.

WCD argues that it is crucial in the twenty-first century to attend to how Third World development, since the 1950s, has failed in its goals of ameliorating poverty (at the time of writing, 2.7 billion people live on less than $2 per day. We argue that this failure of development is due to overly economistic assumptions on the part of development theories and policies. Further, we demonstrate that this failure lies in the exclusion of women from projects of development, or by viewing women *either* as wives and mothers *or* as laborers, thus not integrating women's reproductive and productive contributions. We argue, therefore, that it is not that development policies, projects, and theories make women invisible, but, rather, that the ways women are visible within development do not shed light on their lives—our lives—in all of its wonderful complexity. Some of the elements that come together to configure this complexity are: production and reproduction, lived experiences and cultures, and agency. WCD is able to retain the economic as a key means of grappling with the subordination of poor women in the Third World, yet does not privilege the economic above other aspects of people's everyday lives.

We focus on women not to exclude men, but because women are a foundation from which we can illuminate the circumstances of *all* people's lives, including men's lives. To focus on women within development in this way offers prospects for seeing the lives of people as more tangled and therefore as richer than has hitherto been suggested. Thus, the WCD paradigm applies to both women and men.

Culture is an important element in these discussions. What is culture? We do not think of culture as "high" culture or "low" culture. To our minds, culture emerges from the ways people live their lives—we live our lives. It is not a static property that resides within people or groups, but, rather, it is formed through relationships, often relationships of inequality. Culture is constantly shifting—the people of Plachimada show that as they develop their ideas about access to water, about how best to lead creative lives, and so do the women who oppose, for example, female genital mutilation around the world. Culture emerges from our *lived experiences*. So, culture is inherent in all relationships and offers a non-economistic, yet still material, way to produce knowledge and to present different strategies for making struggle and social change. In sum, a WCD approach to development studies places women at the center, culture on a par with political economy, and keeps a focus on practices and movements for justice.

There are numerous organizations that epitomize what we mean by WCD. Here, we examine four of them, chosen to provide maximum diversity in terms of region and issues. Each can be categorized as an example of development, for each works in a planned manner to achieve social, economic, political, and cultural change. Yet none of the organizations privileges the economic above other domains, and all work with a notion of culture as lived experience. Each has been initiated by women for women and all four have an established history of working primarily with women. Each organization is distinct from the others, although all four make links across reproduction and production. Yet all have been successful in their goals, cutting edge in their approach, and integrate all three elements of WCD to create new ideas about development.

The Self-Employed Women's Association, Ahmedabad, India

The Self-Employed Women's Association (SEWA) was founded in 1971 as a trade union for women working in the informal sector in Ahmedabad, Gujarat, India. The self-employed, informal sector constitutes over 90 percent of the economy in India (Srinivas 1997), and many have documented the importance of informal economic activities as a survival strategy for poor women (see, for example, Okine 1993). The organization began with women textile freight workers who had seen a trade union lawyer, Ela Bhatt, assist men textile workers to set up a union. Eventually, twenty-four women came together, set up SEWA, charged membership dues, and demanded that their wages be regularized. They were joined by used-clothes vendors and vegetable sellers who needed protection from police brutality and extortion. Following this, Muslim women who stitched quilts in the home and agricultural workers came for support, as did women who had been victimized when asking for legal wages in the tobacco processing plants (Rose 1992). SEWA took the issue of the harassment of the vegetable sellers to court, and the Indian Supreme Court ruled that the women had a right, as workers in the informal sector, to have a separate place to sell their goods. Since that success, SEWA has set up a bank for microcredit (each of its members is a shareholder), provides child care and access to health care for its members, and offers classes for literacy and other skill development. The organization also advises women on how best to create cooperatives. SEWA is seen as a role model for many organizations in India (M. A. Singamma Sreenivasan Foundation 1993) and has over 700,000 members, 181 producer groups, and 84 cooperatives (Namrati Bali, personal communication, 2003; Srinivas 1997; SEWA 2008). The main theme of SEWA is empowerment for poor women (Bhowmik and Jhabvala 1996), full employment, and self-reliance.

Women's Group of Xapuri, Brazil

Women's relationship to the environment has been widely discussed and continues to be so (see, for example, Dankelman and Davidson 1988; Jackson 1993; Mies and Shiva 1993; Agarwal 1998; Kurian 2000; Carruyo 2008). However, less has been written about women's role in defending forests in Brazil. While the now assassinated rubber-tappers' union president, Chico Mendes, is well known for having mobilized local populations to prevent clearing of the forests in the state of Acre in western Brazil, very little scholarly work has attended to the women of Xapuri, Acre, who were part of that union (see Campbell 1995 for an exception), even though almost two-thirds of the women in Acre have tapped for rubber at least once (Kainer and Duryea 1992, cited in Campbell 1995). This invisibility of the woman rubber tapper (*mulher seringueira*) is surprising, for women rubber tappers have long been active in defense of the forest (Campbell 1995). Demonstrators routinely used the *empate,* in which adults and children gathered at a forest clearing, to challenge the destruction of the trees by the cattle ranchers, often talking directly with the laborers themselves. In a few significant empates, it was women and children who "formed the front line of defense" (Campbell 1995, 30), and then "went back to the kitchen" (Campbell 1995, 46). The Xapuri Women's Group has been meeting since 1987 to support women's rights, provide literacy and skills education, and to challenge domestic violence.

Women in Black (Israel/Palestine)

Women in Black was started in January 1988 by Jewish women protesting the war in Israel/Palestine (after the start of the *intifada* against Israeli occupation of the West Bank and Gaza Strip). For five years, this peace group held weekly, silent vigils throughout Israel of women wearing black clothes until October 1993, when the Israeli-Palestinian peace accord was signed in Oslo. "The black clothing symbolizes the tragedy of both people, the Israeli and Palestinian" (Women in Black 1993). The actions of Women in Black opened a space for other organizations such as the Women's Organization for Women Political Prisoners (WOFPP) and SHANI, also known as Israeli Women Against the Occupation. These groups demonstrated regularly in solidarity with Palestinians in the West Bank and Gaza Strip and emphasized connections between violence against Palestinians and the increase in violence against women in Israel (Sharoni 1995).

It has been suggested that the group is gaining more in Israel (Peterson and Runyan 1999). There are presently Women in Black peace groups in many countries (including Bosnia and Herzegovina, Croatia, Germany, Hungary, India, Israel, Kosovo, Montenegro, Palestine, Serbia, Slovenia, United States), and there are also networks that exist via e-mail communication, art exhibits, as well as an annual peace conference (Cockburn 1999).

Tostan: Against Female Genital Mutilation in Senegal

Female genital mutilation (FGM) affects between eight and ten million women and girls per year in Africa (Sarkis 1995). It is also an issue that leads to heated discussions about cultural practices, their role in the subordination of women, and calls to change such practices. FGM is practiced mainly in Africa and the Middle East. The practice is protested by local and international women's organizations on the grounds of health concerns for women (the cutting is often conducted in unsanitary conditions and the women's sexual health is also at risk), as the violation of a woman's basic human right to enjoy sexual relations, and as a form of institutionalized violence against women (Kassindja and Bashir 1998). FGM was confirmed as being legally permissible in Egypt in June 1997 (*New York Times*, June 26, 1997). Due to the protests of women across the world, by January 1999, the practice was banned in Burkina Faso, the Central African Republic, Djibouti, Guinea, Senegal, and Togo and was being challenged by women in Kenya and the Sudan in April 1999.

Since then, both Kenya and Sudan have passed some legislation prohibiting FGM (Daileader 2001). In order to ensure the practice is eliminated, Muslim religious leaders in northern Kenya have spoken out against it (Irin 2007), and RAINBO, an NGO, held workshops in 2006 and 2007 to help participants work for the abandonment of FGM (RAINBO 2008).

Tostan is a nongovernmental organization (NGO) in Senegal that has worked with rural peoples for some time in a basic education program. In 1996, some of the women who had come together through Tostan established the "Malicounda Commitment," a series of pledges that FGM should be ceased (Mackie 1998). Tostan spearheaded a widespread grassroots opposition to FGM, and the practice was declared illegal by the Senegalese government in January 1999 (*New York Times*, January 18, 1999).

We see these four organizations as prime exemplars of our WCD paradigm because each integrates production with reproduction, foregrounds women's agency, and bases its ideas for change on culture as lived experience. In this way they integrate all three elements of WCD in bringing about meaningful social change (http://www.theshapeofwatermovie.com).

CONCLUSION

> *There is no people without culture. But what is often lost sight of is the quite natural link which I am bound to mention for the sake of frankness, between the political and the cultural.*
>
> Alioune Diop, quoted at an exhibit on Africa and decolonization at the P.S. 1 Museum in Queens, New York

At a time when the present era marks a period of realignments in the cultural and political economies of the world, when protests against the World Trade Organization, the World Bank, and the IMF have both brought together many constituencies that were previously quite distinct, as well as forced the supporters of neoliberalism to show the extent of state violence they will use to ensure global capitalism is not interrupted, it is clear that current times are marked by contradictions and realignments. Christian fundamentalists in the United States and Hindu fundamentalists in India traffic in images of female piety yet use women to recruit other women to their cause, while often drawing on limited notions of female rights and autonomy. Elective plastic surgery for women has increased in the past decade in the United States and Europe. Genital cutting has been banned by Senegal due to the efforts of women's organizations, but reconfirmed as a legitimate cultural practice elsewhere. In rural Bangladesh, women's economic independence appears to be possible only through obtaining bank loans that require them to make handicrafts to sell to tourists, thus reinscribing Euro-Western conceptions of Third World women's traditionalism. Lesbian and gay groups are subject to increasing legal restrictions and monitoring in Latin America, yet more people are prepared to engage in open protest against these measures. In Southeast Asia, throughout the Americas as well as in Europe, sex work has become a site for discussions about the interconnections among types of women's work, and about women's agency in making the decision to do this work, tourism, militarism, migration, and masculinity.

Janet Walker tells us that this is a period when satellite telephones are handed out by Red Cross workers, when websites are built by US college students to help unite Albanian families separated in the tragedy of Kosovo, when the greatest representation of East Asian women on the Internet is as subjects of pornographic websites. It is clear that contestation, tension, and contradiction organize our lives. In light of these inconsistencies, what forms of politics can move us towards a more just world?

This is why we close our chapter with the metaphor of dancing on the edges. Martha Graham said: *Dance is the hidden language of the soul. Think of the magic of that foot, comparatively small, upon which your whole weight rests.* Dancing, like everyday life, is hard work, it is painful yet full of joy, has no "value" in itself yet nourishes us, it is the way by which we all learn subtle moves and thoughts. It is demanding, and it is passionate. *Dance is for everybody. I believe that the dance came from the people and that it should always be delivered back to the people* (Alvin Ailey). Is it possible to dance the passionate dance of development, and in so doing, turn development into a means for social justice?

ACKNOWLEDGMENTS

Parts of this chapter were first presented by Kum-Kum Bhavnani at the Vice-Chancellorial Inaugural Lecture, University of Waikato, New Zealand, March 20, 2007.

5 Resisting Westernity and Refusing Development

Molefi Kete Asante

Development as a theoretical and practical concept has been dying for a long time, yet its revival is always threatened (Chinweizu 1975; Sachs 1993). This is due largely to the totalizing capacity of the West, based on its control of media sources and resources; academic journals; web-based and print; and its would-be ability to reduce almost every human achievement or behavior to the particular experience of the West (Huntington 1993).

In some ways development is an appendage of *Westernity*, a concept that encompasses many of the values that parade as modernity, postmodernity, and globalization. In fact, *Westernity is a paradigmatic insistence that portrays values of the Euro-American culture as culturally dominant and naturally conquering*. Attended to by the calling cards of aggressive individualism, chauvinistic rationalism, and ruthless culturalism, Westernity also follows a monstrous theology of white racial domination in regions of Asia, Africa, South America, and the Pacific. One should be clear that it is not necessary for Westerners to be present in a political or social area for Westernity to exist; in many instances it is prosecuted by locals with commitments to Western triumphalist ambitions. Thus, it is in the recovery of a multiplicity of discourses that we entangle the Western assertion of dominance and complicate its insistence on a rogue monopoly voice. This means for me, of course, that we cannot speak of "non-Western discourses" because in the very statement of such "non-Westernity" we have given a privileged position to the West. In transforming privileged rhetoric into discourses for the majority, we execute a revolutionary plan that challenges the style and the content of Western dominance. A part of this challenge is embedded in the idea of refusing development that confronts the definitions and resists a model of "development" that insidiously works to remove a people from its own contextual terms.

MOVING FROM WESTERN PARTICULARISM TO AFROCENTRICITY

The opinion makers and theorists of the West have taken some of the most revolutionary concepts of Africans and Asians and turned them into something supportive of Western hegemony (Cummings 2005). Like a black hole, nothing valuable seems to escape the grasp of Western intellectualism, including even the idea of building theories and ideas discussing Western hegemony. What is at stake in the refusal of development is the integrity of a people's values, community, and vision of itself. Struggling to maintain this integrity against a powerful *particularism* operating as if it is universal is a crucial moment in human history. Each nation must challenge the assertion, must confront the definitions, and must resist the development model that parades as one thing but ultimately is meant to remove a people from its own terms. For example, when the Kenyan government refuses to seat parliamentarians who wear African clothes but accepts those who wear European clothes, one sees the massive reach of Westernity. Similarly, in Asia it is typical in some nations for Western art to fetch greater prices than their own classical art! Whenever there is a discourse that operates as if there are no other discourses or voices in the world, you will find particularism. Thus, the ultimate example of this reduction to European particularism is when concepts derived from the historical experiences of Africans or Asians are interpreted in the context of one European movement or another. One can see this same process working in South America, Oceania, and among Native Peoples in several countries. Clearly when the Native American Apache spiritual leader Geronimo sought to protect his people from the encroachment of the white settlers in the American Southwest, he was victimized by the particularism of Europeans who could only see him as a terrorist (Adams 1990, 23–25). It was through the eyes of whites, not through the eyes of the Apache people, that this interpretation was made.

In effect, what is produced in the literature is an imperialistic iconography dedicated to the Europeanization of human ideas. In the United States the great voices against this hegemonic attitude have been those of the Afrocentrists who seek a level playing field not based on a hierarchy of color, race, gender, or class. Leading Afrocentrists such as Ama Mazama (2003), Maulana Karenga (2006), and Mekada Graham (2002) have challenged the cultural adventurism of Western particularism. Of course, my own work in Afrocentricity has been at the forefront of the movement to reorient thinking in the West about Africa and African people.

Afrocentricity, for example, is often referred to as philosophically part of the Hegelian notion of ideas when, in fact, it is much more rooted and grounded in the practical conceptualizations of the Yoruba philosophers of the Orisha Age (Asante 1998). The conceptualizers of the *Ifa* documents and the creators of the concepts of *Iwa, Shango, Ogun, Yemanja, Obatala, Eshu, Oshun,* and so forth are more directly related to Afrocentricity as an intellectual idea than Hegel.[1] The idea behind Afrocentricity is that people of African heritage and culture must define their own reality and speak from their own sense of agency. All intellectual ideas are acquirable by serious scholars. Of course, non-Africans can adopt an Afrocentric orientation to data about

Africans. However, the marginalization of Africans within their own histories is a direct result of Europe's writing of Africa's history to the extent that a single European, for example, David Livingstone, or Albert Schweitzer, is used to define an entire region of the continent. The European's experience in Africa may be useful in European history but it cannot define African history. During the past five hundred years, Europeans have attempted to move Africans and other people off of their own terms, but a strong contingent of African scholars have now rejected that assertion and have reestablished their own voice in the African narrative. Yet Eurocentric totalizers, those who speak as if Europe is the norm for the world, and their African or Asian interpreters, who always seem to know more about Europe than they do their own traditions, still insist in casting Afrocentricity, or any African or Asian idea, as a subset of some European ideal. I know that there are some who would see a separation between the white American ideal and the European ideal, but the American ideal, in effect, is an extension of the European cultural motif perhaps in its most naked form. If we say the West, then, we are referring to both the American and the European forms of domination as one. When an idea is seen as challenging the imperializing forms of Western thought, then an entire cadre of writers is brought out to attempt to destroy the idea. It is a militaristic response, or perhaps, a military configuration on the linguistic battlefield that activates European globalization.

COLONIALISM, GLOBALIZATION, AND DEVELOPMENT

Although the totalizing experience of Europe as a phenomenon has become more aggressive in this era, it has been a characteristic of Western political and social life for more than several hundred years. Let's take the specific example of Africa. When the German Chancellor Otto Von Bismarck held a conference in Berlin in 1884–1885 with fourteen European nations to divide up the African continent among them, the political bulldog had been unleashed. Europe saw Africa as a magnificent cake to be eaten. Europe's arrogance was not only something that would activate Europe against Africa; it would, by virtue of the authority Europe claimed, make Asia vulnerable to the same aggression. Three imperialistic doctrines with accompanying discourses came into being alongside this aggression against Africa. One was the rhetoric of *spheres of influence*, which meant that each European nation involved in the "scramble" for Africa could exercise its rights over a part of the African territory if it had a trading post on the coastline. The second one was called *effective occupation*, which meant that if Europeans had traded, lived in an African village, they could assume ownership. The third doctrine was called the *protection of European agents*, which meant that no African people or nation could prevent mercenaries, merchants, or missionaries from entering their territory without being punished by Europe. Before long, African states were engaged in wars against the merchants, missionaries, and militaries of these Europeans whose idea of capital privilege was also the grounds for imperialism (Chinweizu 1975).

Clearly, the three imperialistic doctrines were a precursor to the logic of a globalized development that is designed to catapult African, South American, and Asian/Oceanic nations into the Western circle. We know what it means for the corporations of the West who will reap the financial benefits of a much larger consumer base. But what does this mean for much of the Third World that faces the prospect of becoming the feeder nations to the informational, industrial, military complex of the West? The three characteristics of this trend are found in (1) the desperation brought about by capitalism and statism, (2) the rise of differentiated movements of alienated classes and groups in the West, and (3) the technological revolution in the field of information. These characteristics are manifested in varying ways: the political influence and reach of the unipolar United States; the new division of labor that integrates local economies through trade; the rapid flow of people, resources, and money transnationally; the elimination of time-space dichotomies in terms of information; and the increased transcontinental and transnational characteristics of markets.

None of these trends promises any significant changes for the people in the Third World except that these trends suck several categories of people into a world system that is ideologically, perceptually, and culturally far removed from their own contexts. The locus of control is no longer visible and, like the invisibility of Asian/Oceanic, South American, and African history for students in the West, we are placed on the outskirts of our own knowledge and information.

The advantages that might derive from integrative connections in terms of health, trade, education, and culture must be examined in the context of the unilateral flow of information. If the flow of information does anything, it often unsettles weak economies, destroys nascent languages, creates beggar populations, and thrusts cultures to the trash heap of history. The totalizing capacity of the West seeks to project itself informationally and militarily to overwhelm the sociocultural space of the smaller nations.

It is obvious that when history becomes the undifferentiated subject of the European perspective on everything in North America or the Pacific, the European triumphalist explanation of the conquests of the indigenous people of New Zealand and Australia, or the Eurocentric interpretation of all political and cultural phenomena become the preferred history of the land. In effect, the conquest of the land is also a conquest of communication about the history of the land.

Clearly a rhetoric of globalization promoted by Western interests is not a discourse; it is a monotonous monologue. Therefore, we must challenge this odd construction of reality to reveal its dirty underside as a hierarchical calculation of white supremacy. There can be no transhistorical religion of Westernity that suits the entire world. There can only be imposition.

There will only be the death of culture, the elimination of languages, the destruction of ways of life, the assault on information about societies, and the attempt to equate modernization, urbanization, art, education, or architecture with Westernization.

The European idea takes the concept of the center and the margin and plays with it in a different way than is construed by those who see culture as important in every human cultural community. The West's idea becomes binary, us against them, alterns and subalterns, we and the others, in an antagonistic position of one culture to another (Huntington 1996). Such an attitude creates, inter alia, individuals who believe that it is their right to direct, guide, or advise non-Europeans on the form, structure, and practice of government, society, and community. Arrogance born of the acquiescence or military defeat of Asians and Africans during the forming imperial age of Europe from the fifteenth to the nineteenth century still lingers in the construction of knowledge. In effect, it is a construction for good and evil, superiority and inferiority in the minds of Europeans. As one of the leading proponents of this ideology, Samuel Huntington, claims, it is a clash of civilizations and the aim is for the West to win (1996). I see in this construction something quite disturbing because in effect it is not so much a clash of civilizations that creates the problems of culture and language but rather a civilization of clashes.

THE GREAT REFUSAL

Globalization institutes the conditions for clashes. The paradoxes of globalization in its Western guise create contradictions based on transcontinental economies and transnational corporations. Since few African, Asian, Pacific, and Latin American nations are able to curtail the assertion of this global phenomenon, there will be numerous clashes simply because people naturally resist all forms of oppression. Inasmuch as the assertions and penetrations reduce other cultures to local phenomena, these local cultures will react with violent responses to the assault. Whatever form the idea of a globalizing development takes, it will constitute an imposition if it assumes that the European-American particularism is superior. What this amounts to is a form of warfare on the cultures of the world (Ani 1994; Federici 2005). No ancient culture will accept such imposition without struggle and violence. Ultimately, even those dislocated Africans and Asians or South Americans who argue the position of the Eurocentric assertion will challenge the idea of their marginalization within their own cultural contexts. What must be challenged is the implicit idea that the Eurocentric form of globalization will eliminate poverty, create wealth, and make poor nations wealthy so long as they follow the advice and the market predictions of the development experts from the West. Thus, they will seek to diminish all local institutions, cultures, norms, values, and traditions in order to enthrone a Eurocentric model of interpretation and meaning for the world. Globalization produces an Americanization-Europeanization of other people unless they participate in the great refusal. One sees this quite readily in the popular arts and culture where American music videos have become the fare for young people throughout the world.

The great refusal comes about when it is necessary for radically new intellectuals to speak of centeredness as a way people own or assume agency within their own contexts, thereby fulfilling their roles as legitimate partners in human discourse, something constructed together. Such an idea is fundamentally more about humanity than materialism, winning, and domination. Westernity, if it is about anything social, is about the culture of selling, which implies in many instances the notion of promotion. A centered position is one that seeks a mature relationship to other cultures, neither imposing nor seeking to advance its own material advantage. It is more about a culture's own sense of centering, that is, not marginalizing one's own culture, but claiming it as a valuable part of humanity. Only in the sharing of cultures can we have multicultural discourses. A globalization that seeks to have Chinese adopt French architecture as better or superior, Japanese believe that European renaissance art is more important than Japanese classics, English music is more "classical" than African music, and that Italian dance is more "classical" than Indian dance, and so forth, remains a bad idea. I do not have anything against cultural exchange and the idea of learning from other cultures, but I am fundamentally opposed to the idea that one culture is superior to another. Actually, the imposition of this bad idea does not lead to discourse, but to dis-ease, where the ultimate objective becomes not dialogue, but control, prediction, and subjection. To paraphrase a British colonial official speaking of the British role in India in the nineteenth century, the idea behind globalization is to make of all people Europeans in taste, desires, opinions, expressions, attitudes, behaviors, dress, while maintaining only the outer shell of their own origins.

To a large extent the Asian and African worlds have participated in this dramatic phenomenon because it is impossible for others to force an imposition without some acceptance on the part of the elites. This is the expectation of the globalizing ideology. The only method of resistance is through the assertion of our own agency as political and economic actors. As Afrocentrists have long claimed, we cannot be mere spectators to European history and culture when our own history remains invisible. The Africans who built the pyramids, invented writing, erected hundreds of stone cities in Southern Africa, and gave the world geometry did not wait for the Greeks or the British (Obenga 1989; Hilliard 2002; Asante and Mazama 2002).

Let there be a vast celebration of the beautiful and varied cultures of the world, and indeed, let new ones be born every day without ever giving up any. As creators of our own societies, we have valuable experiences to share, not to impose, which might be examined and adapted in a spirit of sharing and dialogue. This is the real meaning of multicultural interaction; otherwise we have a monocultural projection of Europe and European culture as the only acceptable discourse. Our intellectual acquiescence is much of the problem because our intellectuals have often granted Europe the right to assert itself without challenge.

NOTES

1. These are concepts and ideas that derive from the Yoruba philosophy. *Iwa* may be translated in English as "character." *Shango, Ogun, Yemanja, Obatala, Eshu, Oshun* refer to power, creativity, depth, generation, complexity, and beauty.

Part II

Emergent Discourses of Development

6 From Roosevelt in Germany to Bush in Iraq

Development's Discourse of Liberation, Democracy, and Free Trade

María Josefina Saldaña-Portillo

From the perspective of the cultural critic of the field of development studies, it was somewhat inevitable that the George W. Bush administration would turn to an emancipatory narrative of "national development" to justify its actions in Iraq once the stated grounds for invasion vanished. Iraqi stores of weapons of mass destruction (WMDs) were nowhere to be found, while intelligence reports on Al Qaeda links with Saddam Hussein proved to be doctored. The Bush administration lost no time in taking up a familiar Cold War stance—that of deposing tyrannical authority, on one hand, and of installing democratically elected governments, on the other—as the imprimaturs for a war of occupation. For Latin American scholars, this stance was regrettably familiar. Since the United States gained colonial possession of Puerto Rico, the Philippines, and Guam following the 1898 Spanish-American war, it assigned itself the tutelary mission of nation building in the Americas, which required repeated military intervention and the overthrow of (often democratically elected) governments deemed unsuitable. With the onset of the Cold War, this "nation building" took on the particular discursive form of development, juxtaposing the "freedom" of capitalist economic development with the "tyranny" of socialist forms of ownership. Indeed, Bush was relying on the power of this Cold War discourse of development when he sounded the trumpet for democracy and economic growth in Iraq, counting on a public so familiar with the cultural meaning of this discourse as to be transfixed by it. He wanted a simple equation to materialize in the patriot's mind: today's terrorist is yesterday's communist. This stance proved successful, at least until the situation in Iraq dissolved into an ethnic civil war that could not possibly be mapped onto the vectors of a Marxist war of national liberation. The war of occupation, Bush repeatedly told us in 2003 through 2006, would produce a Cold War dream: Iraq's national sovereignty and world peace at once.

It is a central argument of this chapter that national development, and its academic corollary, the field of development studies, emerged as a discursive formation immediately following World War II, for the purposes of managing decolonization globally and a crisis in capitalist overproduction for the

United States locally. The Bush administration diverges from this script in so far as "development" has become, in the last instance, an explicit justification for the United States' most bald imperial venture since 1898. Thus, at least one set of questions emerges for anti-imperialists to answer while confronting the debacle of the United States' re-imperialized foreign policy and the daily suffering of hundreds of thousands of Iraqis. How is it that an originally *anticolonial* discursive formation such as national development mutates into a doctrine for a direct act of colonization under the Bush administration? Is it simply a question of hypocritical wordplay on the part of this administration, or is there something in the discursive parameters of the narrative that allows for such a redirection? Furthermore, what work does this latest iteration of the national development narrative do for the United States locally and globally? What is the crisis in the United States' own cultural and economic development that this reconfigured narrative of liberation is managing? I am hopeful that revisiting the development of this emancipatory narrative of development may lend some insight into the United States' latest imperialist adventure.

The emergence of the discursive formation called "national development" captured the imagination not only of First World economists and politicians, but of nationalist and revolutionary leaders in the Third World as well. Development has occurred throughout history and across civilizations, certainly, but its formal, self-conscious articulation as a necessary and self-evident social process is of fairly recent elaboration, dating back to classical economists' theories of "progress," and to Marx and Engel's theory of the development of social classes and productive forces (Larrain 1989, 1–2).[1] The elaboration of the concept of "development-as-progress" in the late eighteenth through mid-nineteenth centuries, however, is distinct from the twentieth-century concern with the engineered economic development of entire "peripheral" and "semi-peripheral" areas. Development's contemporary usage to indicate the modernization of national economies dates back only to the beginning of the twentieth century and emerges, significantly, in *opposition* to imperialism. Immanuel Wallerstein places the origin of the idea of "national development" at 1917, in the "great ideological antinomy of the twentieth century, Wilsonianism vs. Leninism" (Wallerstein 1995, 108–109). Both the United States and the Union of Soviet Socialist Republics (USSR) expressed their desire for the liquidation of European empires on the basis of the right to self-determination of peoples. Indeed, this early coupling, by competing ideologies, of the right to self-determination with the need for political and economic integration of the periphery into the fraternity of sovereign nations, permanently wed nationalism to development and, in turn, national development to anticolonial struggle.

The historical record bears out Wallerstein's assertion. Roosevelt's purported condition for entering World War II on behalf of the Allied forces was the dismantling of empires following the war. He demanded the guarantee of equality of peoples and of free trade among them. In his memoir of his father, *As He Saw It*, Elliot Roosevelt writes that the president made this demand explicit to Churchill during their historic meeting in August 1941, which resulted in the Atlantic Charter. According to his son, President Roosevelt made the postwar abrogation of special trade agreements between the British Empire and its colonies a condition for US assistance (George and Sabelli 1994, 23).[2] Roosevelt attributed the cause of the war to monopolistic colonial relations, territorial rivalries, and currency devaluations associated with colonial competition; a position shared by US government officials, political pundits, and economists of the period.

Even before the war was formally over, the United States spearheaded the implementation of Roosevelt's conditions by hosting the United Nations Monetary and Financial Conference, more commonly known as the Bretton Woods conference. This conference was a preparatory meeting for the foundation of the International Monetary Fund and the World Bank. In the documents produced in preparation for, and in the aftermath of, the Bretton Woods conference, Roosevelt's "free trade among free nations" was repeatedly cited as the blueprint for peace and prosperity in a postwar era.[3] The Bretton Woods conference created structures that would put this principle into practice. It was the birthplace of modern development as social engineering on a global scale.

This new commitment to the right of sovereignty for colonized nations in the periphery dovetailed nicely, of course, with the economic interests of the United States. Government officials rightly perceived a looming crisis in US capitalist expansion, as the booming war-economy would need to find new outlets for its greatly expanded productive capacity (George and Sabelli 1994, 23). Roosevelt's administration saw no contradiction between undertaking the humanitarian mission of assisting in the development of decolonizing spaces and expanding the United States' network of trade.

In a US Treasury Department document explaining the Bretton Woods Accord to the public, a section on the International Bank for Reconstruction and Development (IBRD) states simply:

> The need for developmental loans is perhaps less urgent [than loans for reconstruction], though equally important from the standpoint of promoting trade expansion. The underdeveloped countries offer immense stores of raw materials that the more advanced countries, including the United States, need to supplement their own exhaustible resources. They also offer the prospect of a substantial market for manufactured goods. Their first need, however, is for machinery, tools, and heavy equipment, all of which will have to be imported and largely paid for with borrowed funds. (US Treasury Department 1945, 16)[4]

The point here is not that the United States was simply or only operating out of the ulterior motive of solidifying its neocolonial power, for benevolent intentions and self-serving economic interests are hopelessly intertwined.

Rather, my purpose is to illustrate that, at its inception, development was inextricably linked to managing a crisis in capitalist production precipitated equally by the exhaustion of colonial capitalism's expansive capacities and by the greatly expanded productive capacity of the US postwar economy. As a globalizing system, capitalism has always relied on supplementary discourses for its perpetuation and extension. Development, as it took shape in the fields of diplomacy and political economy, under the auspices of the United Nations, the International Monetary Fund, the IBRD/World Bank, and the US Treasury Department, began as precisely such a supplementary discourse. Development replaced the "civilizing mission" of the age of colonialism with the imperatives of self-determination, independence, free trade, industrialization, and economic growth in a postcolonial era.

It was John Maynard Keynes, as chairman of the commission for the establishment of the World Bank, who explicitly introduced the word *development* into the bank's title and into articles of its constitution. Keynes had in mind a much broader vision of the bank's mandate than the reconstruction of Europe, as his closing remarks at the conference make clear. He implored the members of Bretton Woods to look beyond the Bank's initial mandate for the reconstruction of Europe:

> [T]he field of reconstruction from the consequences of war will mainly occupy the proposed Bank in its early days. But as soon as possible, and with increasing emphasis as time goes on, there is a second primary duty laid upon it, namely to develop the resources and productive capacity of the world, with special attention to the less developed countries, to raising the standard of life and the conditions of labour everywhere, to make the resources of the world more fully available to all mankind. (quoted in George and Sabelli 1994, 34)

Development as a "primary duty" of this international agency has supplanted what British imperial theorist J. A. Hobson identified as England's "public duty" during the Great Age of Empire (Hobson [1938] 1965, 231). Indeed, the British empire is dwarfed in comparison with the bank's proposed purview as described by Keynes : "to make the resources of the world more fully available to all mankind." And yet the bank's purpose is not so far removed from the purpose of British imperial reason in Hobson's worldview: "It is the great practical business of the country to explore and develop, by every method which science can devise, the hidden natural and human resources of the globe" (Hobson [1938] 1965, 229). The social Darwinism invoked by Hobson's humanist imperialism, however, which characterized British colonial subjects as belonging to the "lower races," has been banished in Keynes's estimation of the bank's mandate; gone are the references to the "indolence and torpor of character" of tropical populations (Hobson [1938] 1965, 227). In their stead we have a nonbiological, evolutionary sociology of "less developed countries," and a universalized "productive capacity" of all world citizens. Development has also banished compulsory labor under colonial administrations, replacing it with free wage labor and a concern for "raising the standard of life and the conditions of labour everywhere."

It might be tempting to think of development as little more than warmed over colonialism, given its role in managing a crisis in capitalist production; or to think of it as a complete break from colonialism, given its putative claim to deliver on liberal democracy's promise of liberty and prosperity for all. However, it is important to see development's *difference from* colonialism, rooted in its action as a vehicle for facilitating decolonization, and its *links to* colonialism rooted in its redeployment of colonialism's logics and structures. For on the one hand, it is indeed quite stunning that suddenly, at least for a brief moment, all nations in the First World and the Third World—those destroyed by war in Europe and those "hindered" by a lesser development in decolonized and decolonizing spaces—existed on the equal footing of "aid recipient," standing within a single "*everywhere*" in need of improved conditions of labor and living. But, on the other hand, even as "development" emerged in concert with the universal right to national self-determination, it nonetheless carried within it the traces of imperial reason, of an evolutionary hierarchy and racialized subordination. Thus, on the one hand, development reformulates a racialized theory of human perfectibility and progress. Even as it dispenses with references to the "lower races" and genetically determined indolence, the traces of these categories remain in its concept of "less developed countries" with impaired productive capacities. Perhaps more significantly, though, what lingers almost imperceptibly is the categorical imperative, the divinely ordained nature of the civilizing mission. As the passive construction of Keynes's phrase "[a] primary duty is laid upon it" implies, the bank's duty to develop the world is mandated by a higher principle or power than mere economic interest, and it requires the fervor of faith to implement this principle. This trace of religious mission also inhabits development's liberatory promise to deliver "mankind" from need. On the other hand, developmentalism far exceeds the scope of colonialism, bringing the entire world under the surveillance of a few international agencies. Indeed, colonialism is rendered anachronistic by development. For it is precisely the marriage of development and decolonization that discursively legitimates the extraction of resources and productive capacity in a way the civilizing mission of colonialism never could.

Development's emergence is marked, then, by the articulation of a set of discursive signifiers (*equality of peoples, self-determination, less developed countries, free trade, limited productive capacity, prosperity, need, freedom*) with a new set of "neutral" filial institutions (the International Monetary Fund and the World Bank) dedicated, in turn, to the financing of trade and of national development geared toward trade. Development's discursive emergence was thus, paradoxically, *both* a liberatory strategy for decolonizing the world, *and* a neutral re-articulation of racialized colonial categories as national differences. Development rendered formal colonialism obsolete, but it also gave imperial knowledge production a new lease on life. And just as European colonialism sought access to the native's interiority, indeed to restructure interiority, for the purposes of soul-making, as Gayatri Spivak (1986) has suggested, development also seeks access to interiority, to restructure the interiority for the purposes of production. Thus, the interiority of the colonized Other is renewed in the form of the Third World subject in need of a culture of development.

If we look to these tropes, and to the set of discursive signifiers through which development mobilizes, then we see that by Truman's 1949 inaugural address, this discursive deployment of development had become hegemonic. Rehashing the 1947 "Truman Doctrine," the president's inaugural address proposed, as an alternative to "[t]hat false philosophy of Communism," a four-point program for increasing the prosperity of the United States and the rest of the world in tandem. After outlining the three points of his program pertaining to the domestic sphere, the Marshall Plan, and the foundation of NATO (North Atlantic Treaty Organization), Truman turned his attention to the world outside of Europe and the United States. In his fourth point, he insisted the United States "must embark on a bold new program for making the benefits of our scientific advances and industrial progress available for the improvement and growth of underdeveloped areas." He lamented that half of the world's population lived in such areas, often "in conditions approaching misery. Their food is inadequate. They are victims of disease. Their economic life is primitive and stagnant. Their poverty is a handicap and a threat both to them and to more prosperous areas. For the first time in history humanity possesses the knowledge and the skill to relieve the suffering of these people" (Truman 1994, 293, 296). What is remarkable, as Arturo Escobar points out, is not that Truman made such a statement, but that such statements "made perfect sense" to domestic and international audiences alike (Escobar 1995, 4). From former colonizing elites to independence leaders in Africa and Asia, from liberal economists in the United States to revolutionary leaders in Latin America, all had come to understand in a span of a few short years the southern hemisphere and its inhabitants as existing in a condition of "underdevelopment."[5] More remarkable still, many of these same leaders believed the proper application of development aid in the fields of "scientific advances" and "industrial progress" would rapidly remake the world in the image of the United States.

Truman's inaugural address re/cognizes half the world's population as "primitive" and "stagnant" "victims of disease," but more crucially for the purposes of this project, it also rhetorically reconfigures the interior space of the individual subjects living in these "underdeveloped areas."[6] Truman's speech thus registers a swerve in development discourse toward subjectivity, a move we can see clearly in his closing remarks, which shift the target of development from national economies to individuated subjectivities:

> The old imperialism—exploitation for foreign profit—has no place in our plans. What we envisage is a program of development based on the concepts of democratic fair dealing. . . . Only by helping the least fortunate of its members to help themselves can the human family achieve the decent, satisfying life that is the right of all people. Democracy alone can supply the vitalizing force to stir the peoples of the world into triumphant action, not only against their human oppressors, but also against their ancient enemies—hunger, misery, and despair. . . . Slowly but surely we are weaving a world fabric of international and growing prosperity. We are aided by all who wish to live in freedom from fear—even by those who live today in fear under their own governments. We are aided by all who want relief from the lies of propaganda—who desire truth and sincerity. We are aided by all who desire self-government and a voice in their own affairs. We are aided by all who long for economic security—for the security and abundance that men in free societies can enjoy. We are aided by all who desire freedom of speech, freedom of religion, and freedom to live their own lives for useful ends. (Truman 1994, 297)

Aiding the "underdeveloped areas" of the world becomes completely intertwined with fighting communism here, as US development aid to the "least fortunate" of the "human family" is aided, in turn, by those who oppose unnamed tyrannical governments and the "lies of propaganda." Certainly these closing remarks are aimed at the citizens of the USSR. They are also, however, directed at all those involved in revolutionary struggles "against their ancient enemies—hunger, misery, and despair," those who might be inspired by communism in this pursuit.

What is noteworthy beyond this imbrication of development, anticolonialism, and anticommunism, however, is the new terrain on which the battle both *for* development and *against* communism will be fought. Whereas Keynes was concerned with national "standards of living" and indexes of "productive capacity," with industrialization and infrastructure in "less developed" economies, Truman is concerned with a set of *attitudes*, including an attitude toward freedom from want: development is aided by "all who *long* for economic security—for . . . security and abundance." With Truman's speech, the desire for development-as-freedom is implanted within (underdeveloped) subjectivity, evinced by "wishes," "desires," "voice," "longing," and, ultimately, choice. It is no longer simply the "less developed countries" that may or may not embrace national development, it is now the millions of "despair[ing]" individuals who *desire* development, who would willingly choose it as the means for making "useful ends" of their own lives. The target of development is no longer only the "less developed countries," but now also the less developed subjects of the "human family."

That the Point Four Program was principally concerned with the desired/desiring subject of (under)development is underscored by the type of aid dispensed under its auspices. On June 5, 1950, Congress implemented Truman's Point Four Program by passing the Act for International Development, allocating 35 million dollars in direct foreign aid for such projects as adult literacy in India, education on disease prevention in children in Burma, and a vocational school in Libya (Lott 1994, 297). Compared to the lending capacity of the IBRD and the US Export-Import Bank, which in 1951 jointly extended more than one billion dollars in loans to "developing" nations, the sum allotted for implementation of the Point Four Program seems miniscule (Hayes 1951, 12). Arguably, the discrepancy in funding suggests that the Point Four Program was largely symbolic, part of a US Cold War propaganda campaign abroad. However, I would argue that the direction of the funding points us toward a significant *augmentation* in the discourse of development. While IBRD loans, especially those made in the early years, were directed toward national *economies*, toward building appropriate communication, transportation, and energy infrastructures at the national level, the Point Four Program made the target of aid the national *citizen*. Its aid was directed at constructing appropriate subjects for national development, at reforming the illiterate Indian, the diseased Burmese, the unskilled Libyan. Because its development was ideological more than economic, because its addressees were individual subjects more than national economies, the Point Four Program, with its micro funding for small-scale programs, made *individuals* available for development.[7]

Like Truman before him, John F. Kennedy responded to revolutionary movements in the Third World with a dual strategy of military intervention and development aid. Indeed, Kennedy's "covert" involvement in Cuba and Vietnam strategically, tactically, and geographically mirrors Truman's involvement in Korea and Guatemala. Nevertheless, under Kennedy's administration, development aid became a far more prominent aspect of US foreign policy than in the two previous administrations, especially with regard to Latin America (Kennedy 1962). Over a billion dollars in development aid and loans were extended to Latin America in the program's first year.[8] Devised under the advice of economic historian W. W. Rostow, the Alliance for Progress was a response to communist-inspired, national liberation movements.[9] Rostow saw himself as a member of an intellectual vanguard of economic historians and theorists in the battle to contain communism. His *Stages of Economic Growth: A Non-Communist Manifesto* (1971) is both an explicitly anti-Communist treatise on national liberation (as the title attests) and a foundational text in "modernization theory."

For Rostow and other modernization theorists, the path to national development was beautiful in its linear simplicity. Rostow's *Stages of Growth* (1971) distills from the histories of Europe, the United States, Russia, China, and Japan, five universal stages of development for all societies en route to becoming modern, secular nations: traditional society, preconditions for takeoff, takeoff, the drive to maturity, and high mass consumption. However, this "how to" book on modernization is less a study of national economics than a study of the culture of free will. Though he periodically discusses overhead capital investment, investment-to-income ratios, or industrial sectors conducive to compounded growth, Rostow inevitably returns to culture as the true indicator of whether or not modernization will take root in a society: "In surveying now the broad contours of each stage-of-growth we are examining, then, not merely the sectoral structures of economies, as they transformed themselves for growth, and grew; we are also examining a succession of *strategic choices made* by various societies concerning the disposition of their resources which include *but transcend* the income and price-elasticities of demand" (Rostow 1971, 16; emphasis mine). In this way, Rostow emphatically *disassociates* his inherently economic project from the economic ("which include *but transcend*"), and it is in this disassociation that subjectivity as the terrain of development enters the scene of modernization. It is within these "broad contours of each stage-of-growth" that we spot a manifest Subject of development.

When Rostow theorizes the economic growth of presumed modern nations as the consequence of a series of "strategic choices made" at transitional points in history, he displaces development onto a question of freely executing the proper will. He universalizes the uneven and heterogeneous Euro-American trajectories of development across "various societies," deriving *all* trajectories from a *collective, social disposition* for making the right choices, free of any imaginable material or historical constraints. Indeed, such a collective culture of free will transcends even the base motivations of profitability and competition, as "income" and "demand" are dispensed within the collective calculus of what to do with "resources."

The content of the collective culture of free will he describes is curiously bifurcated though in the chapter titled "The Preconditions for Take-Off" in a way that enables the individuation of the subjects of development to occur. Rostow once again locates the preconditions for increased rates of investments in industrial development in attitudes evinced by men:

> But to get the rate of investment up some men in the society must be able to manipulate and apply . . . modern science and useful cost-reducing inventions. Some other men in the society must be prepared to undergo the strain and risks of leadership in bringing the flow of available invention productively into the capital stock. Some other men in the society must be prepared to lend their money on long term, at high risk, to back the innovating entrepreneurs . . . in modern industry. Some other men in the society must be prepared to accept training for—and then operate—an economic system whose methods are subject to regular change, and one which also increasingly *confines* the individual in large, disciplined organizations allocating to him specialized *narrow, recurrent* tasks. (Rostow 1971, 20, emphasis added)

On the one hand, Rostow's phrase "must be prepared," which he repeats three times in the previous extract, suggests that, before compounded growth can occur, men must be ready either to assume leadership in industry and in banking, or to take their place on the factory floor. Once again, modernization depends on a certain shift in cultural attitude: on a society of men *at the ready*, asserting themselves as free agents making responsible choices at pivotal historical conjunctures. *Stages of Economic Growth*, however, is also a "how to" treatise on development. Thus, on the other hand, "must be prepared" can also be read imperatively: men must be made ready to be ready, in an Althusserian sense. The development imperative once again aims for the interiority of subjectivity: some men must be made ready to be ready to become the risk-taking, innovating subjects of capital, while others must be made ready to be ready to become the disciplined subjects of monotonous wage-labor. The imperative of development is also a regime of "subjection"—that "process of becoming subordinated by power as well as the process of becoming a subject"—aimed at making "underdeveloped" populations available to capital as never before (Butler 1997, 2). The vast majority of the men of these "traditional societies" in transition "must be prepared" to accept the routinized, narrow, and confining "conditions and methods of work" offered by industrial specialization. Development aid must be geared toward precipitating this transition in subjectivity at a national scale, thereby "making ready" the laboring population of an entire underdeveloped country for capital investment.

Not surprisingly, while Rostow's "stage theory" renders development "universal," indeed as an omni-historical process for all nations who will succeed the West, Rostow imbues this universal with a very particularistic content. Rostow repeatedly prescribes a Protestant "set of values" for the emerging bourgeoisie in developing countries:

> The income above minimum levels of consumption, largely concentrated in the hands of those who own land, must be shifted into the hands of those who will spend it on roads and railroads, schools and factories rather than on country houses and servants, personal ornaments and temples . . . surplus income derived from ownership of land must, somehow, be transferred out of the hands of those who would sterilize it in prodigal living into the hands of the productive men who will invest it in the modern sector and then regularly plough back their profits as output and productivity rise. (Rostow 1971, 24)

Given Rostow's rhetoric, this set of values is not simply Protestant but almost puritanical.

In Rostow's transhistorical analysis, the *ancien régimes* of Japan, China, Russia, France ("country houses and servants"), as well as the economies of present-day indigenous cultures ("ornaments and temples"), are rendered equally "sterile" before the vigor of the universal "productive men" of nineteenth-century Britain, the United States, and Canada. Indeed, Rostow specifies the four countries in the world that were singularly "born free" of the constraints of traditional society: the United States, Australia, New Zealand, and Canada. According to Rostow, the nonconformists of these new worlds, like their British ancestors, are uniquely unencumbered by the prejudices of caste or clan, of superstition or intuition, afflicting the rest of Europe and the world.

Rostow runs through the gamut of attitudes in a traditional society that must be transformed in order for sustained development to occur—those toward clan and region, children, work, and nature. Rostow insists these cultural factors are more important than the economic factors. And yet, toward the end of the chapter, Rostow observes that even these changes in societal values remain insufficient for bringing about the preconditions for takeoff:

> While in no way denying the significance of some such changes in attitude, value, social structure and expectations, we would emphasize, in addition, the role of the political process and of political motive in the transition.
>
> As a matter of historical fact a reactive nationalism—reacting against intrusion from more advanced nations—has been a most important and powerful motive force in the transition from traditional to modern societies, at least as important as the profit motive. Men holding effective authority or influence have been willing to uproot traditional societies not, primarily, to make more money but because the traditional society failed—or threatened to fail—to protect them from humiliation by foreigners. (Rostow 1971, 26–27)

Rostow illustrates the positive effect of this reactive nationalism with the examples of nineteenth-century Germany, Russia, Japan, and China. However, European imperialism and postwar nationalist liberation movements are also clearly invoked by this passage.

Significantly, Rostow's description of reactive nationalism is homoerotically gendered. Nationalism reacts to an "intrusion," to a penetration by a more powerful nation. As such, traditional society is feminized, rendered incapable of resisting this penetration. "Men holding effective authority" over these traditional societies nevertheless renounce them because of this emasculation, because they were incapable of warding off "humiliation by foreigners." As such, reactive nationalism in Rostow's account is implicitly a condition of aggrieved masculinity. Given Rostow's schema, in which most transitions to modernity are the effect of this reactive nationalism, only a chosen few countries exist in a condition of unaggrieved masculinity. European countries that constitute the "advanced nations" perpetrating the intrusion (Britain, France, and the Netherlands), and those few countries "born free," are the sole purveyors of a fully masculine modern nationalism. Far from renouncing the decolonizing, revolutionary nationalisms fueling postwar, communist-inspired liberation struggles, Rostow's development theory embraces them as *the* determinant factor in the transition to modernity by folding them into a hierarchical structure of gendered nationalisms.

However, as a consequence of this homoeroticized desire for the Other's full masculinity present in revolutionary nationalisms, colonialism is rendered a benign initiation into modernity. While imperial policies "did not always optimize the development of the preconditions for take-off," they did transform "thought, knowledge, institutions and the supply of social overhead capital which moved the colonial society along the transitional path . . . the reality of the *effective power* that went with *an ability to wield modern technology* was demonstrated and *the more thoughtful local people drew appropriate conclusions* . . . and a concept of nationalism, *transcending the old ties to clan or region*, inevitably crystallized around an accumulating resentment of colonial rule" (Rostow 1971, 27–28, emphasis mine). The manly "effective power" of the colonizer teaches "thoughtful" local people to *desire* it—to desire "an ability to wield modern technology," to emulate the father's knowledge/power.

With the use of phallic language like "intrusion," "humiliation," "effective power," and "to wield," Rostow figures colonialism as, at best, an unsolicited seduction, or at worst, an auspicious rape. In either case, development of the nation is once again metaphorized through the interiority of subjectivity, with colonialism figured as a constitutive trauma initiating adulthood for the underdeveloped subject. Furthermore, this trauma individuates the subject, forcing him to reject vertical ties of a multigenerational "clan" in favor of the horizontal ties of the presumably abstract and egalitarian national community. If colonialism initiates the development of the underdeveloped, then the development process itself is necessarily inscribed by a "dual demonstration effect" of colonial gendering. Nations of the developed northern hemisphere are gendered as demonstrative of full masculinity. Meanwhile, the emulative underdeveloped nations are gendered as demonstrative of aggrieved masculinity: "without the affront to human and national dignity caused by the intrusion of more advanced powers, the rate of modernization of traditional societies . . . would have been much slower than, in fact it has been" (Rostow 1971, 28).[10]

Rostow's *Stages of Economic Growth* illustrates the age of development's new discursive regime of subjection for formerly colonized and neocolonized areas of the world. This new set of metaphors, themes, and tropes for the formation of modern subjectivity is deeply nationalist and vehemently egalitarian, as we have seen. Indeed, it is a prior sovereignty of the nation and dignity of all individuals that is presumably aroused by the violation of colonialism in Rostow's account of reactive nationalism. As a response to postwar national liberation movements, this new regime of modern subjectivity must register the political affront of colonialism. Consequently, development promises to the periphery an alternative mode of integration, one that is predicated on national sovereignty and respects human equality—one that promises full masculinity to underdeveloped subjects.

But even as modernization theory advocated political sovereignty for the colonial world, it provided an alibi for European colonialism. Under the new discursive regime of development, gendered sexuality has been allegorized through a hierarchy of nationalisms. The aggrieved masculinity of reactive nationalisms was subordinated to, and yet oddly enabled by, the full masculinity of the original nationalisms. Thus, we have left behind the social Darwinism of British and Anglo-American colonialism, in which evolution is determined by one's proximity to an appropriately potent whiteness, without fully abandoning its racial legacy. In its stead we have a model of development in which modernity was determined by one's proximity to this risk-taking, decision-making, frugal, nonornamental (i.e. elemental), productive, fully masculine, national Subject. At the opposite end of the continuum of equally human subjects was the rule-bound, doctrine-led, adorned (i.e. supplemental), profligate, emasculated, clannish subject of the underdeveloped traditional societies.

In conclusion, I would like to touch upon some of the questions I raised about the war in Iraq. Does this discursive analysis of development shed any light on the justifications for war and continued occupation? It appears to have been the all too successful national development of Iraq, made evident in its scientific capacity to produce WMDs, that initially provided the grounds for an invasion. It is precisely Iraq's *success* as the most industrialized country in the Middle East which has been articulated as a threat to US security. Iraq possessed a dangerous equality to the US in its scientific ability and in the ability of a few of its risk-taking, decision-making, productive, and fully masculine national subjects in the Baathist party. I am not defending Saddam Hussein or the Baathist party, but rather I am interested in discerning the threat Iraq represented to an administration which knew full well there was no link between Al Qaeda and Saddam Hussein's regime. As it is never simply an economic interest which leads a hegemonic power into such a chaotic and chimerical adventure, I suggest that a "demonstration effect" was intended in the "shock and awe" campaign of the second Gulf War. "Shock and awe" as a form of modern warfare is meant to overwhelm the opponent with the recognition of the aggressor's superiority, to reassert a hierarchy of nations, while rendering its targets "senseless"—without sense or reason—in the face of the devastation it reeks. Indeed, even the United States' reconstruction effort has been overwhelmed by the success of "shock and awe" in destroying the country's infrastructure. The US military has bombed Iraq into a condition of underdevelopment which, in turn, compels development and the United States' guiding hand in it. Even the most antiwar and anti-imperialist among us, those who believe US troops should be withdrawn immediately, nevertheless recognize, in an echoing of Keynes's speech at the Bretton Woods conference, that a "primary duty" has been "laid upon" the United States and the international community to assist in the economic reconstruction of Iraq. There are economic profits to be reaped, of course, by Bechtel and Halliburton, but again, economic benefit and moral obligation are beautifully entangled in the development imperative. This development imperative even provides an implicit alibi for the brute show of force displayed in what is an imperialist and illegal war waged by US military on behalf of the George W. Bush administration. For even President Bush will happily acknowledge for the Iraqi people that "they don't like being occupied, who does?" In the development narrative, the occupation, though morally abhorrent to some, or necessary to others, in either case provides an incitement to subjectivity, an incitement for the proper masculine subjects to come forward and to properly develop the nation. Thus, it is crucial that the resistance fighters, like the nineteen Saudis who flew the planes into the World Trade Center and the Pentagon on September 11, 2001, be repeatedly represented in homoerotic terms. They are repeatedly represented in the US media as either cowardly in their pursuit of "perverted" tactics of guerrilla warfare, such as suicide bombings, or as inappropriately homosocial in their peripheralization of women, fueled by their fundamentalist Islamic beliefs. Thus, it is the Christian West's burden once again to show Muslims how to be properly heterosexual men by showing them how to "fight fair" and recognize the equality of women.

An alternate, more hopeful reading of our imperialist folly through the development narrative occurs to me. What if the Bush administration is but the manifestation of a prodigal *ancien régime*, squandering its "profit" on the "ornaments and temples" of war, rather than plowing it back into productive expenditures, such as health care and education? If we punch through our own shock and awe at the US capacity for destruction, is it perhaps we who are rendered sterile before the vigor of those universally productive men and women, the Chinese and Mexicans, working diligently in booming maquiladora industries in order to satiate our gluttonous capacity for consumption on credit? Is this war perhaps the last gasp of our hegemonic position in the world, a last, but profligate display of our decadent power on our way to becoming some future empire's periphery?

NOTES

1. Jorge Larrain, an intellectual historian of development, elaborates on this "birthplace" of all theories of development, and their inherent relationship to social contradictions in capitalist processes:

   > This relationship between the concept of development and historically determined social processes (which is only a particular formulation of the more general principle of the social determination of knowledge) can be applied to the subsequent development of political economy and

indeed to the general evolution of theories of development. Marx was the first to propose such a connection in the case of political economy when he argued that "the development of political economy and of the opposition to which it gives rise keeps pace with the *real* development of the social contradictions and class conflicts inherent in capitalist production." (Marx quoted in Larrain 1989, 2)

2. Certainly Churchill recognized Roosevelt's proposition of free trade conducted among free peoples as a call for the end of empire: "Mr. President, I think you want to abolish the British empire . . . everything you have said confirms it. But in spite of that, we know you are our only hope. You know that we know it. You know that we know that without America, the British empire cannot hold out" (quoted in George and Sabelli 1994, who, in turn cite it from Georges Valence 1992, 24–26).
3. See, for example, *First Steps Toward World Economic Peace* (Alfred 1943) and *The Bretton Woods Accord: Why It's Necessary* (Alfred 1944). These pamphlets are the published reports of the proceedings of public conferences hosted by the Citizens Conference on International Union in Washington, D.C. In speech after speech from the proceedings of the Bretton Woods Accords Conference, US Senators, State and Treasury Department officials, economics professors, and representatives from the agricultural and industrial sectors, repeatedly reference the need for dismantling colonial relations, associating free trade with the key to peace and security. For example, the inaugural speech of the Bretton Woods Accord conference, delivered by the Conference Chairman Louis Heaton Pink, begins:

   Bretton Woods should give us courage and hope. The proposed International Monetary Fund and Bank for Reconstruction and Development should serve as the keystone of future peace and security. These economic bodies, plus an international tariff agency, a lowering of tariffs and the removal of competitive trade barriers, are all essential to a firm foundation for the future. The most important objective to international cooperation is undoubtedly a large volume of trade. . . . If there were a free flow of trade between all commercial nations there would be no reason for major wars. The interchange of goods and ideas, not only eliminates to a very considerable extent the underlying causes of war, but would help materially to increase world-wide production and minimize unemployment. (Alfred 1944, 5)

4. In the Hearings of the House Special Committee on Postwar Policy and Planning in 1944, Assistant Secretary of State Dean Acheson was more direct about the United States' singular interest in ensuring access to new markets, not bothering to cloak this priority in the humanitarian language of development. He said, "No group which has studied this problem has ever believed that our domestic markets could absorb our entire production under our present system . . . we need those markets [abroad] for the output of the United States . . . we cannot have full employment and prosperity in the United States without the foreign markets" (Acheson 1944). Acheson is quite clear on whose peace and prosperity is primarily at stake.
5. Indeed, as Akhil Gupta demonstrates in his *Postcolonial Developments*, even subaltern populations around the globe came to recognize themselves as "underdeveloped" and to refer to themselves as such (1988, 39–42).
6. In *Encountering Development*, Escobar (1995) analyzes how development became the "common sense" of an era, and how this discourse recreated the world into "developed," "developing," and "underdeveloped" components. Escobar investigates how the discourse of development reorganized knowledge, creating new fields of vision and systems of speech, "creat[ing] a space

in which only certain things could be said [or] even imagined" (1995, 39). Combining historical, anthropological, and discursive analysis, Escobar suggests that new techniques in comparative economic indexing were combined with newly minted international "aid" programs to invent the subjects/clients of "development:" "the poor;" "the hungry;" "the peasant;" "women;" and "the environment." Escobar's study provides an excellent genealogy of how these broad categories of subjects were "discovered" by the discourse of development, how each subject/client was elicited by its own particular type of development knowledge/aid in "food," "health," "agriculture," "population control," and "sustainability." However, while Escobar's analysis of the subject-populations and knowledge-categories produced by development is exhaustive, he does not specifically focus on the (under)developed subjectivity or consciousness implied by development discourse, which is the focus of my project.

7. Making "underdeveloped" subjects available for capital investment is also the subject of an address delivered by Samuel P. Hayes, Jr., the Special Assistant to the Assistant Secretary of State for Economic Affairs, on January 26, 1950 (Hayes 1951). During this speech in defense of the Point Four Program before the League of Women Voters in Cambridge, Massachusetts, Hayes responded to criticism that the program was underfunded, especially in comparison with funding for the Marshall Plan. He explained the discrepancy in funding thusly:

   > In Europe, the preconditions for economic recovery were, in 1947, already present. The people were healthy, enterprising, literate, and skilled. . . . This [aid] was a kind of blood transfusion from one developed body to another developed but wounded body. Before capital and modern technology can be fully utilized in an underdeveloped one, there is usually a lot of groundwork to be done. The people in that area must be ready to receive technical knowledge and to make efficient use of capital, and the early stages of economic development in many areas must, therefore be concerned with improvements in basic education, health and sanitation, and food supply. (Hayes 1951, 12)

   The metaphor employed by Hayes, of a "blood transfusion" from one "developed body" to another again registers this mapping of the discourse of development onto individuated bodies with subjectivities. Thus, by extension, the implicit "underdeveloped" body must "be made ready" to receive transfusions of capital. The Point Four Program was understood by the State Department as working in tandem with national development loans, as aid aimed at remaking human subjectivities in preparation for remaking their national economies in the image of the United States.

8. These loans were supposedly contingent upon Latin American countries instituting land and tax reforms, as well as presenting the Kennedy administration with specific development projects. Tying aid disbursement to land reform once again highlights the dialectical relationship between development aid and revolutionary movements in Latin America. The Kennedy administration was compelled to articulate its aid program in the language of revolution, though in practice Latin American countries received aid regardless of whether or not reforms were effectively introduced and enforced. Hence, *New York Times* reporter Tad Szulcz represents the Alliance for Progress in revolutionary rhetoric, "It must be noted that the Alliance proposes a fundamental and drastic change in centuries-old patterns throughout [the] region" (Szulcz 1962, 12).

9. Rostow saw communism as an unfortunate by-product of the difficult transition periods between predictable stages of national economic growth. Ros-

tow's pre-Bolshevik Russia, as his prime example, already well on its way to modernization, with the Russian revolution portrayed a violent interruption in that nation's transition from a traditional to a democratic society. He held it was imperative to accelerate modernization processes all over the Third World and to ease transition periods with plentiful development aid (1971, 162–164).

10. Here Rostow shares Karl Marx's view of colonialism as a messianic revolutionary force in the history of colonized nations. From Marx's second article for the *New York Daily Tribune*: "England has to fulfill a double mission in India: one destructive, the other regenerating—the annihilation of old Asiatic society, and the laying of the material foundations of Western society in Asia" (Marx 1978, 659).

7 Migrants, Genes, and Socioscientific Phobias

Charting the Fear of the "Third World" Tag in Discourses of Development in New Zealand

Debashish Munshi and Priya A. Kurian

What is New Zealand doing in a book on development? After all, it sees itself as a First World nation. Its status as a member of the Organisation for Economic Co-operation and Development (OECD) is a source of both pride and anxiety—pride that it once was ranked close to the top of the OECD, anxiety at its current placement in the bottom third.[1] New Zealand might well appear as close to that mythical status of a developed state as possible. Yet, this identity of being a part of the First World is a profoundly shaky one. It is an identity that is constantly being bolstered and reinforced by an often strident rejection of the Third World within—be it in the shape (or color) of immigrants from the Third World, the presence of "Third World diseases" such as meningitis, or the inadequate pursuit of such markers of development as biotechnology (including genetic modification) or other forms of new technologies.

In this chapter, we examine how the ideologically constituted category of "New Zealand" is informed by particular notions of the Third World and how these play out in the dominant discourses around two of the most contentious issues in recent times: immigration and genetic modification. Although apparently very different, the discourses around the two issues share common anxieties about the protection and breaching of national, cultural, political, and genetic boundaries, epitomizing struggles over the politics of recognition and redistribution (see Kurian and Munshi 2006). These anxieties feed into New Zealand's fear of the Third World and its constant desire to make sure that it is never bracketed with the Third World in any context. We argue in this chapter that the obsession with the Third World in New Zealand is shaped in part by the forces of neocolonialism that underpin the global "capitalics" system (Munshi and Kurian 2005). Understanding how the Third World is a necessary construct for the continued flourishing of the First World can offer insights for critical intervention in the discourses around development, a project of which this volume is a part.

We acknowledge Gayatri Spivak's (1996, 27) concern that the issue of "Third World people in the First World claiming that title has to be treated with some caution . . . even because, in the very locus of their struggle, they have an interest in dominant global capitalism." The Third World "Other" in New Zealand is not part of a homogenous group. And we certainly do not claim an automatic marginality for immigrants who are often among the most privileged in their home countries. Yet, what the plight of large numbers of Third World immigrants in New Zealand brings to light is the contradiction between the skilled labor they represent and offer, on the one hand, and the monocultural vision/fantasy of nation and national identity that holds the country in thrall, on the other.[2]

Our analysis of the construction of the Third World seeks to examine the ways in which such a construction discursively positions the Third World as inferior and perpetuates the hegemonic idea of the West's superiority: "The deployment of this discourse in a world system in which the West has a certain dominance over the Third World has profound political, economic, and cultural effects" (Escobar 1995, 9). If the very idea of what it is to be New Zealand is shaped by what it is not—an inferiorized Third World—then what does it tell us about the goal, process, and focus of "good" development projects and policies of achieving development? How are such desires for development and fear of the alien driven by the forces of (political, economic, and cultural) globalization? Are there lessons to be learned in the unpacking of the discursive phobia of the Third World that marks New Zealand?

In this chapter, we draw on Third World Cultural Studies (TWCS) approaches to examine the discourses of immigration and genetic modification, as seen in the microcosm of New Zealand, to unravel the ways in which race, culture, and identity are deeply implicated in these discourses. Our discussion is informed by a study of media discourses, interviews, government documents, and secondary literature that forms the basis of a larger study of the discourses of immigration and genetic engineering in New Zealand. We conducted forty-two in-depth, semistructured interviews between 2003 and 2005 with a cross-section of the New Zealand public, policymakers, policy analysts, and members of nongovernmental organizations, of Maori, Pakeha (European), Asian, and other ethnicities, both New Zealanders and first-generation immigrants, to inform our discussion. In what follows, we use excerpts from interviews, public documents, and media reports to illuminate the contours of the analysis.[3]

We extend John Foran's (2002, 1) definition of TWCS as a representation of a "political approach to culture and a cultural approach to politics" to show how marking territories of culture and identity in the so-called developed world influences broader conceptions of development. TWCS draws on insights from postcolonial studies, subaltern studies, and Marxist literary criticism to offer a critical perspective on First World cultural practices (Foran 2000). It is precisely this critical perspective which allows us to see how cultural and political discourses in the First World position the Third World/er as what postcolonial scholars call an "Other" or as a "gendered subaltern" who is "epistemically violated by longstanding cultural formations" (Spivak 1999, 102). The TWCS lens we use in looking at the discourses of immigration and genetic modification in New Zealand incorporates feminist and postcolonial perspectives in exploring, scrutinizing, interrogating, and resisting masculinist, racist, and neocolonialist institutions of power vested in the dominant configurations in the two discourses. The integration of feminist and postcolonial perspectives is important because it allows a sharp focus on notions of *difference* within the larger discussions on development in a rapidly globalizing world where the proliferation of new technologies and the predominance of the logic of an all-powerful market have given rise to what we call *capitalics*—a politics fueled by global capital (Munshi and Kurian 2005).

THE CAPITALICS SYSTEM

The capitalics phenomenon ignores national or hemispheric, latitudinal or longitudinal boundaries. Instead, it divides the world into two semispheres. One is a bottom-line obsessed, and largely monocultural, "developed" space. And the other is the Third World, an ideological, if amorphous, space that seeks to resist the politically, economically, and culturally dominant structures of the developed world. This ideological division, we argue, is central to the ongoing struggles over issues of identity.

In the world of capitalics, the Third World, regardless of geographical location, is seen as not only the antithesis of what development stands for but also as a body of beings, institutions, and practices that are seen to be un- or underdeveloped, antiquated, and primitive. This labeling is most prominent in two emergent perspectives. One of these perspectives positions much of the Third World as in need of developmental aid, philanthropy, and goodwill from the developed world which adopted the slogan "Make Poverty History" (Make Poverty History 2005).[4] The other perspective looks at the poor of the Third World as the new capital and *The Fortune at the Bottom of the Pyramid* (Prahalad 2005). Both these perspectives look at the Third World as the Other—a social, cultural, economic, and political entity that needs protection, benevolence, and a blueprint for progress that is drawn up by the dominant, largely Western sphere of the world that sees itself as developed.

Driven by a conceptual notion of development as money, markets, and management, C. Krishna Rao Prahalad declares that the "poor must become active, informed, and involved consumers" in a poverty-reduction program that co-creates "a market around the needs of the poor" (2005, xii). This unabashedly capitalist approach talks of improving the lives of the poor in the Third World but does not hide the fact that it is motivated by the assumption that "there is money at the BOP" (bottom of the pyramid) and that "by virtue of their numbers, the poor represent a significant latent purchasing power that must be unlocked" (Prahalad 2005, 10–11). What this approach does not talk about, however, is the political agenda that goes hand in hand with the business agenda.

The collaboration of politics and business underlined in the capitalics phenomenon marks the Othering of the Third World by legitimizing a two-tiered process of globalization where Western transnational corporations and nations can allow the unfettered flow of global capital to create Third World markets and maximize profits but at the same time retain tight control over human migration and the use of new technologies to maintain a divide between the developed world and the Third World Other. Nowhere is this desire to maintain a raced dividing line more evident than in the dominant discourses around immigration and genetic modification. Immigration and genetic modification have long been seen as part of the dominant mainstream concerns of "sustaining development"—the former to provide "legal aliens" to feed the expanding production lines and the latter to foster high-yielding designer foods for the world's supermarkets. The emphasis in both discourses is on economic benefits through productivity and exploitation of human and natural resources.

Examined through a TWCS lens, however, these discourses reveal a wall between the First World "haves" and the Third World "have-nots" which, in the process, perpetuates the dominance of the capitalics world order. A TWCS perspective provides a vision for resistance, and much of this resistance comes through a critical reading against the grain of the seemingly benevolent discourses of a globalized polity. Discourses around immigration and genetic modification reproduce dominant masculinist and (at least latent) raced ideologies. Policy developments and public discourses around immigration and genetic modification do not occur in isolation; they tie into forces of economic globalization and neoimperialism within which are embedded issues of race, culture, and nature. That juxtaposition of race and nature is evident in the way the ghosts of their "recombinant mutations" continue to "haunt the cultural politics of identity and difference," according to Donald Moore, Jake Kosek, and Anand Pandian (2003, 1). If immigration brings out anxieties about the threat to social and cultural identities, genetic modification triggers fears about the threat to the integrity of species and organisms.

What adds complexity to the discourses of immigration and genetic modification in New Zealand is that the dominant voices in both discourses take seemingly contradictory positions. The dominant voices in the immigration discourse want to protect the social and cultural homogeneity of the nation by putting hurdles in the way of non-Western immigration. On the other hand, the dominant voices in the genetic modification discourse want to make it easier for the transfer of cross-species genes. What is common to both the discourses, however, is that the dominant voices in both cases do not want the country to be identified with the Third World. On the immigration front, there is an aversion to the country getting too many new residents from the Third World. And, on the genetic modification front, there is a fear that not keeping up with technology would push the country into the fold of the Third World. The clamping down on immigration of the Other, juxtaposed against the championing of genetic modification as an instrument of triumphalism of global capital, embodies the racialized and masculinized world of capitalics.

As Joan Acker (2004, 34) says, "capitalism can prosper from many different gender and race/ethnic patterns," and political elites implementing capitalist strategies have learned to fine-tune policies that are both raced and gendered in trying to negotiate business profitability and vote-gathering populism. Feminist researchers such as Saskia Sassen (1998), for example, have shown how capitalist structures have created labor markets in much of the Western world that thrive on low-wage workers from the Third World, a majority of whom are women, and yet institutionalize policies that obstruct such workers from gaining formal immigration and voting rights.

The masculinized logic of capitalics also becomes clear when we recognize the dominant economic and technical rationalities that underpin its functioning. Economic rationality, based on the principle of efficiency, involves the "maximum achievement of a plurality of goals" (Bartlett 1986, 227). Technical rationality is the "efficient achievement of a given end" (Diesing 1962, 9). By emphasizing "on instrumentalism, on hierarchical rankings and commodification of values, and in the objectification required by both, technical and economic rationalities represent a masculine perspective" (Kurian 2000, 28). Capitalics, driven by the objectification and commodification of both humans and nature, thus represents a largely monocultural and masculine world of the global market, where governments become complicit in the exploitation of migrant labor and natural resources as they connive to protect business interests.

IMMIGRATION

Its claims to a postcolonial status notwithstanding, New Zealand's history and geography as a nation "settled" by colonial Britain and the troubled existence of its citizens and residents of Third World origin lend themselves very easily to a study from TWCS perspectives. Although New Zealand is an immigrant nation, it remains wracked by a deep-rooted xenophobic antipathy to its Third World immigrants. Such antipathy is not only tied to the race-based interest in consolidating the British/New Zealand way of life, language, and sociocultural norms of its citizens but also to the masculinist ideal of protecting established (old white boys/girls) networks.

It is important to clarify here that we do not assume a homogeneous, undifferentiated dislike, intolerance, or hatred towards Third World immigrants in New Zealand. There are many who welcome the social and cultural diversity of the past two decades. Furthermore, despite the tightening of immigration provisions that work against potential Third World migrants, valuing "our diverse cultural heritage" has been identified as a focus under the "key government goal" of "strengthening national identity" by the then Labour-led government (Department of the Prime Minister and Cabinet 2002). What we are pointing to, rather, is the dominant discourse of valorizing what Ghassan Hage (1998, 58) calls the "everchanging, composite cultural historical construct" of whiteness that permeates all discussion of immigration and national identity. Hage's fascinating discussion of the yearning to become white in Australia resonates with New Zealand, and indeed, perhaps all European-dominated settler societies, and demonstrates how even liberal multiculturalism in Australia is caught up in the fantasy of a "white nation." We focus in this chapter on the ways in which old race/culture/ethnicity-based networks in New Zealand are entrenched by policies dictated by dominant worldviews.[5]

In radical new changes to immigration rules in 2003, policymakers in New Zealand replaced the erstwhile broad-based points system for skilled migrants by an invitational system with a much greater emphasis on a "job offer" and on a much tougher English language test as key criteria for permanent residency. The consequences of the changes were not unpredictable: "It is clear New Zealand is seeing a 'whitening' trend in migration. Last year, Britain was the greatest source of immigrants, making up a fifth of all approvals for permanent residency. Just over one-tenth came from China—a 4 per cent fall from earlier years" (Spratt 2005, 22). The policy changes reflected the significant anti-Asian public opinion in the country. A nationwide Massey University survey showed that New Zealanders generally, and Maori in particular, held negative views about Chinese, other Asians, and Pacific peoples (*The New Zealand Herald,* July 22, 2007). Another public opinion survey in March 2006 revealed that 72 percent of those polled agreed that Asians faced significant discrimination and prejudice (*The New Zealand Herald*, March 21, 2006).[6] These Third World migrants face the double burden of social and economic rejection and they find it much harder to meet the "job offer" criterion than those from the Euro-American world.

The combination of racist and masculinist ideologies in the discourses around immigration is evident in comments such as the following by one of our interviewees:

> No, they don't contribute enough to make it a viable prospect in New Zealand, you know, and if they're coming over and they're saying, you know we're giving you this amount of dollars well that's the only reason they're contributing this amount of dollars is because they're getting our land, our businesses, our housing, our you know, and to me that's not a contribution, you know, we're as a country being raped by Asians, well immigrants, and we do nothing about it. (J101)

The conflation of the term *Asians* with *immigrants* is especially noteworthy. Every time immigration is discussed in New Zealand as a policy or media issue, the discussion invariably is focused on Asian immigration (Munshi 1998; Spoonley and Trlin 2004). A recent English immigrant is not seen as an immigrant, but a second- or third-generation New Zealander of Chinese or Indian origin continues to be viewed as one. The institutional prejudice against people from the Third World based on the dichotomy of a First World "Us" versus a Third World "Them" is so entrenched that an academic study has shown how employers and recruitment agencies rejected applications from people with non-European names even if their qualifications and experience were stronger than those with European names (Ward and Masgoret 2004).

This cultural aversion to the Third World seeks justification by equating cultural difference with a lack of skills and even personal integrity, as these comments from interviews and media reports reveal:

> If you bring in unskilled, culturally incompatible people, it also becomes an economic issue because there's too much propping up, you know there's too much welfare involved. (F109)
>
> And there's all sorts of other things I mean, you know, I mean you hear of stuff and you hope that it's not true about people even getting into the door of some of our places and bribery and corruption. (F104)
>
> The huge movement of people from third-world countries, most of which are dominated by corrupt socialistic regimes and repressive religious cultures, to the free nations of the west is an unstoppable phenomenon. It is also one that exposes the critics of capitalism, who say the west is responsible for the oppression and poverty of these countries. (Editorial in the *National Business Review*, July 3, 2003)

These quotes exemplify what previous critical analyses of New Zealand immigration policy have insisted on, namely, an understanding of the way race permeates the discourse of immigration, facilitating the maintenance of racist social stratification (see, for example, Greif 1995; Munshi 1998). The frequent complaints of employers about the lack of appropriately skilled labor, the often strident anxieties about the importance of the "New Zealand way of life," the bemoaning of the despoilment of Queen Street in Auckland by the presence of Asians, and the fear of the "Third Worldization" of New Zealand, expressed most vocally by the leader of New Zealand First,[7] Winston Peters—all reflect, at one level, attempts to clutch at the parochial/local in a globalizing world:

> The Government is overseeing a wholesale replacement of New Zealand's population. For every New Zealander that leaves, three immigrants, mainly from the third world, replace them. (Winston Peters at a

> New Zealand First convention, reported in *The New Zealand Herald*, November 10, 2002)
>
> [There] is the need to keep a tight lid on immigration if we are to avoid New Zealand's identity, values, and heritage being swamped. New Zealand First believes our heritage is worth fighting for. I urge you to join us in the battle. (Peters 2002)

These comments also reflect a panic at what Nancy Tomes, in an analysis of "germ panics" in the United States, refers to as "societal incorporation"—a phenomenon "associated with expanding markets, transportation networks, and mass immigration" (2000, 191). Tomes points out that the germ panics "coincided with periods of heavy immigration to the United States of groups perceived as 'alien' and difficult to assimilate" (2000, 195). In recent years, these have included immigrants from Asia, Africa, and Latin America. It is precisely these kinds of social perceptions and anxieties that some politicians have tapped into in New Zealand in their ongoing efforts at winning parliamentary seats.

For instance, Peters sees the increase in the number of measles and meningitis cases in New Zealand as a manifestation of the "Third Worldization" of the country.

> Only this week we learned that we have a disgracefully low level of immunization for our children, and that we are heading for a measles epidemic. We have also had a meningitis epidemic for several years. These are Third World diseases—and while our children suffer from them, the Health Funding Authority bureaucrats are spending a thousand dollars each on new chairs for their new yuppie offices. (Winston Peters's speech to the Prostate Awareness and Support Society, June 13, 1999).

In many ways, the presence of the seeming "Third World" within New Zealand—in the form of immigrants—becomes a source of tension because, as Anna Tsing argued in the case of marginalized groups everywhere, those who cannot easily be classed as "primitives" in need of salvation or as romantic objects tend to "confuse boundaries of 'us' and 'them,' and they muddle universalizing standards of propriety, deference, and power" (Tsing 1993, 7). In a global context where marginality seems almost inevitable, given the perception of the South Pacific as geographically remote from the *real* centers of civilization in Europe, and compounded by New Zealand's lack of economic and military clout, Third Worldization becomes a "chromatized" issue (see Adesanmi 2004) where race appears to demarcate the status of being "developed" or not.

The stigmatizing and fear of the Third World reflects an enduring and deep-rooted Eurocentrism, a discourse that is "complex, contradictory and historically unstable" (Shohat and Stam 1994, 2). It is a discourse that claims for the West "an inherent progress toward democratic institutions;

. . . elides non-European democratic traditions; . . . minimizes the West's oppressive practices; and . . . appropriates the cultural and material production of non-Europeans while denying both their achievements and its own appropriation" (1994, 3). As Ella Shohat and Robert Stam argue, "Eurocentrism sanitizes Western history while patronizing and even demonizing the non-West; it thinks of itself in terms of its noblest achievements—science, progress, humanism—but of the non-West in terms of its deficiencies, real or imagined" (1994, 3). Maintaining this dichotomy between the imagined superiority of the West (the First World) and the imagined inferiority of the Rest (the Third World) is central to the logic of capitalics that drives the development project. For New Zealand, this logic poses a dilemma. On purely economic terms, it recognizes the need to open its doors to skilled immigrants regardless of their places of origin, and it is this recognition that prompted the liberalization of entry criteria in the 1990s. However, the logic of capitalics is derived not just from economics but a potent mix of business and politics. This logic seeks to give preeminence to the worldview that development is equivalent to the Western way of life, indeed the Western way of doing business and politics. This is a significant dilemma for New Zealand as the powerful discourses of civilization and progress that mark the development project are harder to lay claim to when the antithesis of these discourses—the Third World Other—appears in the belly of the beast as residents of New Zealand.

GENETIC MODIFICATION

As with the issue of immigration, genetic modification too is an issue that is enmeshed in economic, cultural, and political battles that play out against the backdrop of questions of New Zealand's national identity and its place in the world. Although genetic modification experiments have been under way in New Zealand since the 1970s, it was only in the 1990s that the issue shot into the limelight with massive public demonstrations against the use of genetic modification in food crops. So controversial did the issue become that the government set up a Royal Commission on Genetic Modification, which duly submitted its report in 2001, recommending that New Zealand "proceed with caution" (RCGM 2001). Opposition to genetic modification has come from environmentalists, Maori, animal rights activists, and those who saw "tampering with nature" as ethically and spiritually abhorrent (see Rogers-Hayden 2004; Wright 2006). In October 2003, however, the government decided to allow the moratorium on releasing genetic modification organisms into the environment to expire. What is even more striking is that the government, in a related development, allowed applications for experimenting with the introduction of human genes into cattle.

The government's implacable support for biotechnology, and bioengineering in particular, is evident from a series of policy documents and research reports produced by the Ministry of Research, Science and Technology (see, for example, MORST 2003, 2005, 2006). Much of the focus of these reports is on estimating the economic contributions of biotechnology to New Zealand, especially its primary agriculture sector—and the consequences of not investing in biotechnology, measured in dollar terms. There is only a brief reference to the "uncertainties of consumer acceptance of GM technologies" and the potential clash of "environmental values" (MORST 2006, 12–13).

The "logic and wisdom" of Western science that wants to push ahead with genetic experimentation is privileged over what is described as the "emotional outpourings" of a very large segment of the population, including significant numbers of women and minority groups, who want to keep New Zealand free of genetic modification. As Peter Glasner points out, "Public questioning of techno-scientific advances was predicated . . . upon equating understanding with support and appreciation, and resistance with misunderstanding or ignorance" (2002, 272). Indeed, in the New Zealand context, where public questioning of the scientific agenda has been vocal in recent years, we see a systematic attempt to portray the public as ignorant and antiscientific by the media, scientific experts, and policymakers (Fraser, Munshi, and Kurian 2006). Democratic processes and public forums created ostensibly to nurture dialogue and participation are instead openly subverted to suit the imperializing and masculinizing agenda of the scientific industry and political elite (see, for example, Wright 2006).

A key discourse that circulates in the support for genetic modification is a fear that not keeping up with technology would push the country into the fold of the Third World:

> If they don't adopt the technology then New Zealand's going to fall further economically behind, further behind in science and research, other advanced countries, and there's a definite fear that New Zealand's sort of gonna become one of those third world developing nations, and I think that that's a big issue. (F104)

Although there may be strong economic and moral reasons to use biotechnology—to eradicate some of the diseases faced by animals, plants, and humans, for example (MORST 2006)—it seemingly needs to be framed against the horror of becoming a Third World country for it to get public and political purchase.

This perceived horror is balanced by a superficially philanthropic urge to "save" the Third World from an impending disaster. For example, a Member of Parliament was quoted in a provincial daily newspaper, *The Timaru Herald*, as saying: "Starvation in Third World countries could be eliminated by New Zealand developments in genetically-modified foods" (*The Timaru Herald*, July 7, 1998). This view is echoed in a *National Business Review*[8] editorial which proclaims that "biotechnology offers a means of producing cheap and effective vaccines for many diseases in the Third World" (*National Business Review,* May 7, 1999). Such views mask the fact that within the logic of capitalics, "advanced biotechnology and the free flow of gene resources from South to North" actually make the Third World "economically more dependent on the North, and ecologically more vulnerable," while the First World becomes richer (Moser 1995, 13).

What makes the genetic modification debate particularly complex in New Zealand is that the process of "Othering" the Third World is not restricted to those who promote the advance of biotechnology unabashedly, either to prevent a Third Worldization of the country or to maintain a strategic economic supremacy over the Third World. At least some of those opposed to genetic modification too, wittingly or otherwise, strive to keep a racialized Other at bay by upholding a constructed identity of New Zealand based on issues of maintaining "purity." In response to questions about what was evoked in thinking about genetic modification and immigration as two overlapping issues, some interviewees touched on ideas of purity:

> We want New Zealand to be GE free so we don't, you know—we want this area of this part of the world on these islands to be free of impurities. (M209)
>
> The most important thing would be the purity of the food and its origins and that kind of thing. People do want to have pure, you know, pure food and you don't want things in the food chain or whatever it is, being tampered with. (J106)
>
> As a mixed heritage person, I'm quite passionate about the goodness of mixing people up, of racial impurity, I think it's right on! But I know that some people oppose GM on grounds of racial purity and I find that disturbing. (F108)
>
> For people with a very strong spiritual view of the world and this is where most Maori are coming from . . . and some of the fundamentalist Christians . . . to muck around with the genetic makeup is a violation [of nature]. (F110)

As Donna Haraway (1997) rightly pointed out, using a logic/rhetoric of purity and intrinsic properties—one that is implicated in the racist discourses of the histories of the colonizing First World—in challenging the many problems with genetic modification is deeply problematic. These are the very discourses that shape divisive immigration policies in the Western world, including in New Zealand. And with a few exceptions, most interviewees insisted on a focus on forces of globalization, capitalism, and economic control in articulating their views on genetic modification, steering away from the problematics of a discourse of racial purity.[9]

From a historical perspective, there are some profound ironies in the current debates over immigration and genetic modification, which reveal the fluid nature of social constructions of what we may consider to be "good" or "bad."[10] The first is the history of biotic transfer in New Zealand, which makes the introduction of genetic modification ironic. Immigration too, of course, is a continuing biotic transfer. Although ecologically the introduction of all exotic species (including humans) that subsequently flourished in New Zealand caused great harm to native species and tremendous changes in ecological relationships, this only belatedly led to policies to attempt to control it. Even then, there continues this distinction between good and bad introductions (humans, trees, farm crops—good; rabbits, weasels, stoats—bad) and efforts to manage introductions, such as for pest management or to exploit new markets. The second irony has to do with the historically evolving social construction of the concept of race. Before the mid-nineteenth century, race was often seen as synonymous with what we would now think of as ethnicity. For the English, for example, the Irish and Scots were different races, as were southern Europeans, Slavs, and Jews. Just as "whiteness" as a construct clearly has evolved and transformed over time, so also have understandings of who or what constitutes the Other. There is a racial past in the settlement of New Zealand between the English, the Scots, and the Irish that is glossed over today, but is still reflected in the high proportion of Catholics, the Scottish accents in Otago, and the very Anglican flavor of Christchurch, not to mention the racial discrimination toward the Dalmation gumdiggers on the North Island.[11]

For the most part now these intermingled ethnicities are not seen as Others but as Us (for example, the Irish immigrants to New Zealand were able to become "white" decades before they could have in Britain or even Ireland itself), which makes the anxiety over immigration of the new Others doubly ironic. Whiteness as a construct is thus as much a hybrid as the notion of the Third World Other is in New Zealand. Yet, if whiteness is aspirational, as Hage (1998) argues, then it is clear that for Third World immigrants and their descendants, it is an aspiration that is destined to remain unfulfilled given their physical visibility as Others. We would argue, therefore, that the racism and violence facing Third World immigrants in New Zealand, suffused as it is with the history and geopolitics of colonialism and neoimperialism, is materially distinct from the historical experience of marginalization that "other" Europeans faced.

In a discussion of whiteness and the move to "Western supremacism," Alastair Bonnett (2005) points out the troubled nature of "white racial solidarity" and the contradictions of class consciousness, which allowed the notion of "inferior" white classes. Even as the limits of white supremacism became evident, there has been a growing recognition of the idea of Western triumphalism and supremacy—something that allows such "geographical contortions" as claiming Australia (and New Zealand) as "Western" (Bonnett 2005, 14). Reflecting on the links between whiteness and "western civilization," Hage (1998, 58) argues that "White has become the ideal of being the bearer of 'Western' civilization." Framing the ironies of these contortions, and indeed driving them, in contemporary times, is the neoimperial imperative of the global capitalics system.

CONCLUSION

In an analysis of the "global cultural economy," Arjun Appadurai comments: "The central problem of today's global interactions is the tension between cultural homogenization and cultural heterogenization" (1990, 295). He argues that for smaller polities, there is "always a fear of cultural absorption by polities of larger scale" (1990, 157). Yet, what is striking in New Zealand is the reversal of this equation, whereby it is the larger, dominant polity that is marked by a fear of the Third World minority individual or community. The "imagined community" (Anderson 1991) of "mainstream" New Zealand can offer no meaningful place, nor a sense of actual belonging to the national space, for the cultural heterogeneities offered by Third World immigrants.

In the interplay between the discourses of immigration and genetic modification in New Zealand, we see how "discourses of race and nature provide the resources to express truths, forge identities, and justify inequalities" (Moore et al. 2003, 1). We can make most sense of the twin discourses of immigration and genetic modification when we situate ourselves in the context of (political, economic, and cultural) globalization where issues of politics, identity, and equality are never on a level plane. Globalization offers the promise of the borderless world, "of a unified humanity no longer divided by east and west, North and South, Europe and its Others, the rich and poor . . . these discourses set in motion the belief that the separate histories, geographies and cultures that have divided humanity are now being brought together by the warm embrace of globalization, understood as a progressive process of planetary integration" (Coronil 2000, 351–352). But as we have pointed out, "the globalized world is one that is not only hopelessly divided between the privileged and the underprivileged but is also one where dominant, often First World, elites have a lopsided share of the power to shape the world" (Kurian and Munshi 2003, 157). Third World Cultural Studies perspectives offer insights into this power equation, which become the basis for theory and praxis.

The power of the dominant elites in shaping policy is derived from the prevailing capitalics phenomenon, which not only provides a platform for the nexus between big business and politics but also creates an artificial division between discursively constructed notions of what is developed or underdeveloped (often euphemistically referred to as "developing"). This power is revealed quite explicitly in our study on the discourses of immigration and genetic modification in New Zealand. As far as immigration is concerned, dominant majority perspectives position non-European immigrants as a clearly defined Other. This is most evident in the conflation of

Asians with immigrants in general, paralleled by attributing social changes and "problems" associated with immigration to Asian immigrants specifically. On the genetic modification front, the dominant perspectives promote a support for technological advances in genetic engineering on the grounds that not keeping up with technology would consign the country into the imagined dustheap of the Third World.

Both of these discourses are situated within the mainstream development paradigm which, as Bill Cooke points out, draws on "an interweaving body of knowledge and practice that enable the management (in the most general sense) of the Third World" and "provides a false logic to and legitimation of processes such as, *inter alia*, the infliction of debt and of structural adjustment" (2004, 623). As Arturo Escobar says, development is not just "technocratic" with its focus on "universally applicable technical interventions" but also "ethnocentric" as it "proposes that the 'natives' will sooner or later be reformed" but at the same time "reproduces endlessly the separation between the reformers and those to be reformed by keeping alive the premise of the Third World as different and inferior" (1997, 91–93).

The mainstream development paradigm thrives under the logic of capitalics as it seeks parallel trajectories of homogenization of people and identities, one in a so-called "developed" space and another in what is deemed to be a "developing" space characterized by the Third World. In this paradigm, there is not much scope for articulations of difference, hybridity, or the opening up of national space for immigrants from the Third World except in limited, constrained roles as economic agents for the larger national good. This process of homogenization is also manifested in the monoculturalization of agriculture through genetic modification.

Development, therefore, is an ideological construct guided by the logic of capitalics. It is precisely for this reason that New Zealand, a self-proclaimed "developed" nation, is present in a book on development. The way New Zealand constructs its identity is reflected in the discourses around immigration and genetic modification, and much of this identity is shaped around its notions of what it aspires to be (a developed, First World, nation) as well as what it is determined not to be (its perceptions of an underdeveloped, Third World, nation). Its desire to be seen as a developed nation is based on the seductive, if flawed, logic that equates development with the dominant economic and technical rationalities of a political system energized by global capital.

ACKNOWLEDGMENTS

Research for this article was supported by grants from the Faculty of Arts and Social Sciences and the Waikato Management School, The University of Waikato. We thank Rebecca Fraser and Jeanette Wright for valuable research assistance; Robert Bartlett, Shiv Ganesh, Peter Gibbons, and a number of colleagues at the University of Waikato for insightful and helpful comments on earlier drafts of this paper; and participants of conferences where versions of this paper were presented, for critical engagement with some of the ideas put forward.

NOTES

1. New Zealand's GDP (gross domestic product) per capita was below the OECD average in 2003 and New Zealand is ranked 21 of 30 countries (Statistics New Zealand 2008).
2. Indeed, similar contradictions, often steeped in violence towards, and exploitation of, the marginalized sections of society, play themselves out in the development dramas in the Third World.
3. We used snowball sampling, interviewing a basic list of twenty-five people representing the various actors and agencies involved and then anyone else recommended by at least two of the original interviewees. Each interviewee has been assigned a numerical identifier to ensure anonymity. Our primary focus in these interviews was to gain insights into the points of view and perspectives of interviewees with regard to immigration and genetic modification and specifically on the notion of boundaries invoked by these issues. Thus, we do not specify identifying markers for interviewees in terms of their ethnicity, socioeconomic status, or occupation—the quotes used are in part a reflection of the nature of an ongoing process of constructing national identity, shaped by the dynamics of state-society relations.
4. The "Make Poverty History" campaign was a coalition of primarily British charities, trade unions, and religious organizations that came together in 2005 when Britain held the presidency of the European Union and the G8 (Group of Eight). In January 2006, a majority of the members of the campaign voted to disband the organization, a decision criticized by many activists.
5. Our discussion in this chapter does not touch on how Maori are situated in New Zealand, or the relationships between Maori and Third World immigrants (see Ip 2003; Liu et al. 2005).
6. In New Zealand, Asians from even affluent countries such as Hong Kong and Taiwan are identified with the Third World.
7. New Zealand First, a political party formed in 1993, is led by Winston Peters, and was a member of the 2005–2008 Labour-led government in New Zealand. With the introduction of Mixed Member Proportional (MMP) election system in 1996, New Zealand First won 17 seats in the 120-seat Parliament after a campaign run primarily on an anti-Asian immigration platform.
8. A prominent weekly conservative newspaper with national circulation.
9. A significant exception to this is among Maori activists who oppose genetic modification on grounds of *whakapapa* or genealogy, a central aspect of Maori identity and belief. See also Mere Roberts et al. (2004) for a detailed discussion of *whakapapa* as a "Maori mental construct" that has complex implications for genetic modification.
10. We are grateful to Robert Bartlett for his contribution to the discussion that follows.
11. The Dalmatians were, from the end of the nineteenth century into the early decades of the twentieth century, primarily gumdiggers, reworking areas in

Northland (the upper north of the North Island of New Zealand) for residues of kauri (a native tree) gum left by those who had previously skimmed off the more readily accessed gum. The antagonism towards the early Dalmatians has some parallels with attitudes towards the Chinese: both sets of people lived in primitive conditions, apart from the rest of the colonial community, making an income by "fossicking" after initial periods of extraction, maintained their own language, and so on (Gibbons, personal communication 2006; see also Trlin 1979, for a history of this community in New Zealand). But whereas people of European descent are today well-integrated into the "Pakeha" identity, no such prospect yet appears likely with the Chinese and other Third Worlders.

8 Overseas Filipino Workers' Tales, or Globalization Discourses and Development

Ming-Yan Lai

Pursuant to the apparent advance of capitalist development, globalization seems everywhere with us today. Not only has it become a ubiquitous term of reference in academic discussion of contemporary conditions, from the rather obvious matters of economics to the more controversial topics of cultural production and practices, but it has also saturated media wavelengths and captured public imagination. While this remarkable infiltration into our linguistic universe may paradoxically herald the term's eventual descent into the dustbin of discursive fashion, its currency has important implications that we cannot afford to ignore. This is particularly the case for scholars interested in the question of development because globalization appears to have taken over precisely the discursive space that was once claimed by development studies. This displacement of development discourse is, in part, what I want to suggest by globalization as fiction of development, which I will interrogate in this chapter with reference to narratives by and about overseas Filipino workers (OFWs).

Constituting a large contingent of temporary contract workers who oil the wheels of "globalization" with their hidden labor and services, OFWs are as much a part of so-called globalization as high-profile, powerful supra-state organizations like the World Bank, International Monetary Fund, or the World Trade Organization(WTO). Yet they are also worlds apart from these well-recognized global players, even though their life circumstances are inescapably structured by the latter's policies and practices. Just as their services and labor remain hidden in private homes, submerged in shipping vessels, or unrecognized in foreign factories and construction sites, their experiences and views are systematically excluded from received globalization discourses, suggestions of globalization from below notwithstanding. At the same time, as a major source of foreign exchange and national revenue for an underdeveloped, Third World state steeped in foreign debts, OFWs figure prominently in state policies and everyday struggles for "development," to the extent of being officially serenaded as "economic heroes." The recent global attempt to harness migration to development in the Global Forum on Migration and Development testifies precisely to the intensification of such state "management" of labor migration in lieu of sustainable development. OFWs thus stand discursively at the crossroads of globalization and development. Bringing their perspectives into the current discursive preoccupation with globalization, then, may help to illuminate globalization's unarticulated displacement of development from cultural examination and interrogation, and return development to the critical edge of debate and deliberation.

GLOBALIZATION AS FICTION OF DEVELOPMENT

To characterize globalization as fiction of development is not to dismiss whatever reality there is to the political, economic, and social changes in the past few decades that constitute the backdrop to all versions of globalization discourse, particularly the rapid increase in volume and speed of exchange and transactions across the world driven by trade and technology, culminating in what has been variously called "time-space compression" (Harvey 1989) or "time-space distanciation" (Giddens 1994). Rather, it is to highlight a contribution that the humanistic disciplines, particularly literary studies, can make to the discussion of globalization and development, namely, the awareness that whatever the reality, it acquires meaning and significance only through discursive construction and forms of representation that are never merely a transparent or neutral medium (for examples of discussion of globalization as discourse, see Gibson-Graham 1996b; Dirlik 2000; O'Brien and Szeman 2001). So, the current dominance of globalization discourse demands critical reflection and interrogation in terms of its politics of representation. Specifically, we need to examine the particular lens through which it sees and represents the social, political, and economic changes; what subject positions thus acquire legitimacy, normativity, and visibility; what development trajectories it plots; and what time-space configuration underlies such trajectories. In other words, by "fiction," I do not mean to suggest "fictive" as "unreal." Rather, I seek to highlight the politics of representation and draw attention to globalization as a particular way of representing the world, engaging imagination and narrative projection of development that carries with it what Michel Foucault (1972) calls "enunciative modality," or subject positions from and to which the narrative and imaginative projection makes sense. In this light, globalization is not only an interpretation of reality or social, political, and economic changes under the advancement of flexible capitalism, but it also inscribes visions, aspirations, and social projections that correspond to the normative subject positions from which the trajectory of events and changes are mapped out and represented.

In these terms, globalization discourse invariably projects and normativizes a vision and imagery of a world "compressed" and integrated into a "global whole," which serves as a focus for or a premise in shaping human activities (Albrow 1996), regardless of differences in the exact mechanisms or driving forces identified by its various versions. This applies not only to the dominant versions of what Richard Falk (1995) calls "globalization from above," or globalization driven by and identified with the operations of such entities as multinational corporations and the WTO, but also the counterversions of "globalization from below," featuring the activities of nongovernmental organizations to address issues like human rights abuses and market inequality through transnational alliances and coalition. A key dimension of this vision is what Arjun Appadurai (1996) called deterritorialization in his influential study of the cultural flows of globalization. Deterritorialization here pertains not only to the obvious transnational corporations and money markets but, more significantly, to ethnic groups, sectarian movements, political formations, images, and ideas, which, according to Appadurai, increasingly operate in ways that transcend territorial boundaries and identities. Though Appadurai is careful to point out that "not all deterritorialization is global in its scope, and not all imagined lives span vast international panoramas" (1996, 61), the very notion of deterritorialization as characteristic of globalization projects a vision of the world moving beyond boundaries and a future when the global whole is within reach of all imagined lives. Underlying Appadurai's representation of globalization is thus the universal projection of a culture-straddling, potentially globe-spanning world citizen whose imagined, if not real, life makes short shrift of territories and boundaries.

Though predicated on the ease and frequency of travel and mobility, this representation privileges and normativizes not so much the actual practices of boundary crossing as the disposition and orientation towards a world unlimited and unfettered by boundaries, especially national boundaries, and a fundamental disavowal of attachment to particular places as the physical embodiment of communal histories and identities. In other words, whether all corners and cultures of the world are actually within reach or not, the belief in the desirability and possibility of such global traversal of boundaries to yield a "shopping mall of cultures" (Trouillot 2002) that is potentially open and accessible to all defines the spirit and ethos here. This corresponds to a normativization of cosmopolitanism that, in Ulf Hannerz's (1990, 239) stark characterization, maintains "a stance toward the coexistence of cultures in the individual experience . . . an intellectual and aesthetic stance of openness toward divergent cultural experiences, a search for contrasts rather than uniformity." The cosmopolitan unencumbered by the affective, moral, and intellectual claims of national origins and indigenous cultural identities, in short, constitutes the "enunciative modality" or normative subject of globalization discourse.

The affinity between cosmopolitanism and globalization has indeed been noted before. As Timothy Brennan (2001) points out, the proponents of cosmopolitanism tout it as "the new ethos" responding to the new material reality of globalization. In identifying cosmopolitanism as the enunciative modality of globalization, I am turning the argument around to question globalization as not so much an objective "fact" of new material reality but as a "fiction," a discursive construction and representation that makes sense of the world and projects its future from a cosmopolitan subject position. Furthermore, despite various contemporary attempts to divest cosmopolitanism of its past grounding in universalism to meet current spirits of multiculturalism (see, for example, Cheah and Robbins 1998), globalization discourse obscures the inescapably local circumstances on which particular cosmopolitanisms are grounded. It naturalizes a particular representation of contemporary conditions, normativizing the experiences and perspectives of privileged social groups with the resources for unfettered border crossing. Thus, though "actually existing cosmopolitanisms" may very well work together with nationalism in some instances (Robbins 1998), the cosmopolitanism ensconced in globalization discourse rather serves the ideological function of undermining the critical role of existing nation-states to administer and oversee the organization of economic activities, the provision of social welfare and security, and the redress of inequality and injustice.

Inasmuch as a relatively free movement across boundaries, especially national boundaries, necessarily underlies the cosmopolitan's open access to global imaginative and cultural resources, the cultural vision inscribed in globalization as fiction of development prescribes the diminishing role of "hollowing out" of the nation-state. In other words, whatever the material reality, the persistently observed (eventual) demise of the nation-state in our globalized world of weblike interconnections is scripted in the cultural vision of cosmopolitanism underlying globalization discourse. This presumed trajectory of the nation-state substantially shapes the particularities of globalization as fiction of development.

For better or worse, a key role the nation-state has always assumed, despite the (neo)liberal touting of laissez-faire beliefs, is the regulation of economic activities and, for Third World countries, the planning and overseeing of economic development as well. Indeed, the nation-state's strategic planning and policy directives are widely credited for bringing about the "miraculous" economic development of Asia, especially the East Asian "little tigers," which played a significant part in the transnationalization of capitalist financing and the institution of offshore production that precipitated so-called globalization (see, for example, Berger 1988). Yet, with a rhetorical shift of dynamics to the global-local nexus, globalization discourse plots a "hollowing out" of the nation-state. In particular, the processes of globalization are said to have compromised "four critical aspects of the nation-state," specifically its competence, its forms, its autonomy, and ultimately its authority and legitimacy (McGrew 1992). The typical plotline runs as follows: current conditions marked by the instant mobility of global finances and intricate links of global market forces make it increasingly difficult for nation-states to regulate their internal economies, diminishing both their capabilities and effectiveness in delivering the goods of economic, social, or environmental security to their citizens, thus also undermining their legitimacy and authority.

This narrative projection of the nation-state's trajectory under globalization is remarkably revealing in its global claim. Presuming a singular class of nation-states and national subjects, it offers a universal representation of the fate of nation-states that glosses over the differential power of nation-states like the United States and the Philippines vis-à-vis global market forces, as well as the differential impacts and meaning of the nation-state's putative inabilities to regulate economic matters on different peoples' lives. For the transnational class of elites in the service of mobile capital and technology, which constitutes the cosmopolitan normative subject of globalization discourse, the ease with which capital moves around the world and plays havoc with (some) national economies may indeed translate into an overall weakening of the nation-states' ability and effectiveness in regulating their own physical, financial, cultural, and other forms of traveling worldwide. The ensuing ease and scope of sampling, collecting, and appropriating different cultures and ways of life for this class of transnational elites are indeed the precondition and linchpin of cosmopolitanism. For migrant workers and peoples variously displaced by the havocs wrought by capital on the run for maximum profits, however, it is an entirely different story or, I should say, different stories in the plural. Travel is incontrovertibly a fact of life for them, too. But it is a kind of travel that is fraught with pain and contradictions, entailing as much coercion as freedom, if not more. The power and possibilities of nation-states' intervention, both positive and detrimental, in their lives of compelled movement make for trajectories other than, or at least besides, cosmopolitan freedom. Yet their experiences and stories are elided in globalization as fiction of development. Overseas Filipino/a workers are a good case in point.

For the millions of Filipino/as working overseas, the power of nation-states in their lives is redoubled in some ways rather than reduced. On the "home" front, the Philippines government actively regulates, transports, and taxes them, regardless of its inabilities to offer much in terms of effective economic, social, and/or personal security and protection. Indeed, overseas contract work was initiated and promoted by the Marcos regime in the 1970s as a state developmental strategy to supposedly enhance the country's economic competitiveness. Quickly becoming a major source of national revenue through substantial remittances, it has, since then, continued to be a major instrument for the state to finance its huge foreign debt, manage the national economy, and formulate economic development policies (Battistella and Paganoni 1992; Rosca 1995; Constantino 1998). Even the state's limited efforts at protection through predeparture training of OFWs in particularly vulnerable jobs such as entertainment or domestic work arguably serves to further subject migrant workers under the regulatory and disciplinary power of patriarchal nationalism to support national development (see Guevarra 2006). In sum, the very emergence of a large contingent of OFWs and their life conditions dramatize the paradoxical disempowerment of the nation-state in its inability to maintain its border and sovereignty against the transnational forces and institutions of global capitalism, on the one hand, and the concentration and intensification of state power to enforce sacrifice from labor in the name of the embattled nation, on the other hand. With such an internationally weak and nationally still relatively powerful state, the possibility of cosmopolitan transcendence of national attachments for OFWs is significantly circumscribed.

On top of the Philippines government, receiving states also exercise remarkable power to regulate the lives of OFWs. Government authorities in Singapore and Hong Kong, for instance, have established strict and rigid employment rules for foreign domestic workers, in which capacity many OFWs earn their livings (Huang and Yeoh 1996; Constable 1997; Yeoh and Huang 1998; Cheng 2006; Lan 2006). Categorically excluded from citizenship programs catered to migrants with professional qualifications or capital for investment, no matter how long they have worked there, foreign domestic workers in Singapore, Taiwan, and Hong Kong toll under severe immigration and labor conditions that restrict their rights to change employers, types of employment, or even terminate their jobs. Singapore goes so far as to require a mandatory six-month pregnancy test to check the "employability" of foreign domestic workers. Following the lead of Singapore, the Hong Kong government recently also instituted a tax on foreign domestic service levied through local employers, in effect taxing the foreign domestic workers without extending any social services to them. Under these discriminatory regulations, the deliberately scripted position of temporary contract workers from overseas bars the foreign domestic workers from most institutional mechanisms of appeal and redress in either the sending or the receiving state. Thus, as conveniently exploitable labor reserves of globalization, OFWs often find themselves caught between the control and regulation of two nation-states, yet falling through the cracks of welfare and security protection in the nation-state system.

The experiences and life conditions of OFWs, then, expose the trajectory of demise for the nation-state plotted in globalization discourse as a partisan representation whereby the alibi of globalization not only partially excuses the nation-state from providing security and protection to its people, but also absolves it from the responsibility of formulating and implementing economic and/or development policies that are accountable to its people and take accounts of their rights and welfare. While particularly acute and consequential for Third World countries in the south, this absolution of state responsibilities under the guise of globalization's restraint on the nation-state's power of economic and, by extension, political jurisdiction and intervention is also discernible in "developed" countries, as Paul du Gay (2000) argues with reference to Britain. Simply put, globalization as fiction of development serves to legitimize the increasingly unfettered course of neoliberal economic transformation of the world and let the governing elites of nation-states, especially "developing" countries, off the hook in maintaining policies that give mobile capital free reins over their resources, labor, and market, and in failing to provide their citizens with minimum security or to protect and represent the interests and rights of their workers in the globalized market place. Globalization discourse in this sense is an ideological representation that disavows its role in displacing development as a critical issue for debates and absolves its normative subject from acknowledging privileges thus conferred. Against this displacement of development as a subject of debate involving incompatible priorities and competing visions and values, I turn to the narratives and representational efforts of OFWs in the rest of this chapter to explore other envisionings of development in the world of migrant workers and dislocated subjects. To the extent that the social locations and subject positions of migrant workers like OFWs are excluded from the enunciative modality of globalization discourse, OFW tales afford critical reflections on and interventions in globalization's displacement of development.

OVERSEAS FILIPINO/A WORKERS AND NARRATIVES OF DEVELOPMENT

Though they also travel across national boundaries, migrant workers like OFWs fall outside Hannerz's (1990) definition of cosmopolitans because they ostensibly maintain an indigenous cultural identity even while living and working overseas. This exclusion is noteworthy for revealing the class assumption behind the classic construct of cosmopolitanism, which makes the cultural connoisseurship and deterritorialization of elite travel a defining feature of the cosmopolitan ethos. Interestingly, James Clifford's (1997, 34–36) much lauded effort to extend cosmopolitanism beyond the privileged mobility of capitalist elites by coining "discrepant cosmopolitanisms" to include "cultures of displacement and transplantation" under violent histories such as those where "mobility is coerced, organized within regimes of dependent, highly disciplined labor" only accentuates this defining characteristic of cultural distanciation from particular places or roots underlying the (normative) cosmopolitanism of the traveling elites. Despite their different inclusiveness, both characterizations of migrant workers' relation to cosmopolitanism tend to obfuscate the structural forces circumscribing migrant workers' possibilities of cultural border crossing and denationalizing identity.

Whether they so desire or not, migrant workers like Filipina domestic workers in Hong Kong find it difficult to forget their national origins or cultural identity because their status as temporary contract workers is precisely designed to maintain such distinctions, and their reception in the receiving countries reinforce and enforce their national cultural identity. Caught between the needs of both sending and receiving states, they are not allowed to forget their place of origins even if they want to. In Hong Kong, Filipinas find themselves marketed for cheap nurturing and educating help in childcare yet also stigmatized for sexual promiscuity (Constable 1997a; Chang and Groves 2000). On the Philippines front, public discourses reinforce their national identification and attachment by making them mobile national symbols, alternatively hailed as "new heroes" essential to national economic development or mourned as martyrs sacrificed by the state-sponsored developmentalism (see Rafael 1997; Tadiar 2004a). Their narratives of personal experiences and hopes and visions of opportunities overseas thus remain deeply entwined with development back "home," including the nation's ideological needs and goals in the course of development. Consciously or not, the narratives illuminate questions of (national) development.

This is evident in many OFW narratives collected in *Tinig Filipino*, literally Voice of the Filipino, an internationally distributed monthly magazine published in Hong Kong from the late 1980s to the 1990s, which pledged in its contents page to be a "dedicated outlet for the views and expressions of the millions of Filipinos working overseas" with "no political, commercial, or religious allegiances" ("Our Promise" 1995). To channel OFW voices, the magazine solicited and published articles and creative writings from its readers besides representing OFW concerns in its feature articles and regular columns. The impossibility of forgetting one's national origins and cultural identities while being overseas finds palpable expressions in both feature articles and reader contributions. One reader's short essay makes clear a key aspect of this impossibility:

> It's tough to talk about the expectations of the Hong Kong people about the Filipinos . . . the image they've created for the Filipinos doesn't coincide with who the real Filipinos are . . . Are we Filipinos lazy, idiots, stupid, dishonest, evil necessity, environmental nuisance, and many more to tell? . . . They are treating us so unfairly! Nevertheless, we'll try to be very tactful about this, to show we are not as they've created in their minds. Let's prove that *we are not here to disgrace our country* but to work and earn money . . . Let's have self-value, self-respect and self-discipline. (Padua 1991, 65, emphasis added)

Clearly expressed here is the double-sided reinforcement of national identities by the receiving state's practice of casting OFWs into negative stereotypes of national characteristics and the OFWs' own impulse to counter negative stereotypes with self-discipline to project positive national images. Under this double reinforcement, OFWs cannot escape representing the Filipino nation or being a living embodiment of national culture. As such, they are a far cry from the denationalized and deterritorialized cosmopolitan subjects of globalization discourse, even if they similarly engage in frequent border crossing.

The magazine's drive for a "Let's Clean Up Our Image" campaign in the early 1990s further shows how such reinforcement of national identities easily recuperates problematic patriarchal values which are destabilized by Filipinas assuming the role of economic providers in working overseas. The campaign's concerted effort to discourage Filipinas from going to discos and pubs, where they are supposedly often taken to be prostitutes or cheap one-night stands, on the one hand, and to remind them of their worthwhile sacrifices as "economic heroes" of the country and loving responsibilities as mothers, wives, and daughters, on the other hand, puts women squarely back into an ethics of feminine sacrifice and sexual repression (Madamba 1991). This reflects a reactive emphasis on national identity from the marginalized position of migrant workers that has led some critics to discern a retrenchment into a romanticized conservatism of family and nation among some OFWs, particularly Filipina domestic workers in Hong Kong (Chang and Ling 2000). Yet, despite the general conservative orientation of the magazine's editorial line, other possibilities are expressed in the pages of *Tinig Filipino*, including possibilities that foreground the need to question the goals of (national) development and their underlying values.

Such possibilities are particularly inscribed in narratives on personal relationships, which are the focus of many feature articles and most of the reader contributions. Many of these narratives question the value of working overseas and ask specifically whether the material gains are worth the toll of lengthy separation on family relationships, especially that between couples and with one's children. Not a few consciously propose a "happy ending" with the mother leaving her overseas job to return "home" to the children. A short story serialized in four issues of the magazine poignantly expresses such questioning and deliberate resolution in a happy homecoming through the emotional travails of a fictional character Lorna:

> Circumstances compelled her to work abroad . . . But sometimes, her conscience would nag her, most especially when she would help her "alaga" with her homeworks [sic] or take care of her when she'd get sick. But how about her own children, her very own flesh and blood? Who is helping them now with their homeworks? . . . What is the use of a woman getting married and bear children, then leave them in order to work in a far country? These and many other sentimental thoughts would come rushing into her mind, making her heart ache with so much pain and longings for home.
>
> [In a phone conversation one day] "No, Ging. I'm not going home yet. I will still work here so that I will have plenty of money to buy you toys, chocolates, shoes."
>
> "No, no, no, I don't want them!" cried Mark, interrupting Lorna's sentence. "I want you, Mom."
>
> Lorna was unprepared for Mark's unusual outburst. It greatly shook her. . . . Lorna took a deep breath and cleared her throat. . . ." If that

> will make you happy, then, I'll be going home soon. I'll bring home with me . . . your Daddy."

This is the happy ending story (San Juan 1991–1992; see Maniwang 1989 for another example).

Without directly mentioning the nation or national development, this emotional account of pain and suffering for the OFW and her family implicitly questions labor export as a strategy of national development that the Philippines pioneered. The expressed concern with the intellectual and emotional development of children left parentless back home accentuates the story's interrogation of the meaning and goals of development. While the inscription of homecoming to the children as a "happy" ending risks reconfining women within the family and motherhood, in highlighting the priority of family togetherness and affective richness over economic advancement and material gratification as personal and collective goals, it nonetheless opens up the goals and values of development for critical reflection. Insofar as overseas contract work is a linchpin of the Philippine government's economic policies and strategy of financing foreign debts for national development, such narratives constitute an indirect interrogation of the government's development policies, calling attention to the need to see development as irreducibly a matter of debate and deliberation, not only at the state level but especially among the people as an everyday issue of personal and familial choices about the desirable way of life and appropriate course of action. Thus, OFW tales of personal experiences and relations can be read as narratives about (national) development.

This is underscored in a recent collection of OFW personal stories published by the Philippine Migrants Rights Watch (Arboleda and Nuqui 2007). The twelve testimonies of OFW experiences explicitly raise the question of the relative gain and social cost of labor migration as a way of family and national survival, foregrounding the toll on personal and family relationships even in cases of impressive economic gains, professional advancement, and contribution to community development. In a personal account consciously titled "Was working abroad for a quarter of a century worth it?" an OFW, who managed to rise to the top of a Saudi-owned but Western-managed company and experience the world-trotting life of a corporate executive that constitutes the normative cosmopolitan subject of globalization discourse, tells of irredeemable loss of family intimacy and attachment despite significant "personal development" and philanthropic contribution to the social welfare and development of his home community in the Philippines. He concludes:

> To me, working abroad doesn't seem really worth it. If you were to ask me, I think it is still best to work here, close to one's family. This is the best situation because money is not everything, especially for women. It is tough enough for a family when the father is not there. It is even

> tougher when it is the mother who is not around to hold the family together.
>
> In terms of our country, ideally, we should find jobs here. There should be no need to go abroad. . . . It appears to me that the risk is high and the probability is great that the children may not grow up like those with both parents around them most of the time. In which case, is the social cost worth it? Most OFWs would say they had no choice. (Bolos 2007, 67–68).

Ending a regretful account of financially successful labor migration with a resigned note of the lack of choice at personal and familial levels, this OFW narrative unambiguously links individual overseas employment to the sorry state of national development. Particularly noteworthy is its pointed reference to women's absence from the family. Though problematic in its patriarchal assumption of the gender division of labor, this comment calls attention to the plight of women who are increasingly caught in the dilemmas and contradictions of "national development" under "globalization," like Lorna in the story discussed earlier. Indeed, reflecting the escalating trend of so-called feminization of migration, it is in accounts of Filipina experiences of migrant work overseas, mostly as caretakers and domestic workers, that the impacts of "national development" under global capitalism on personal experiences and visions of life possibilities are most telling.

Even if the language of global restructuring of capitalism or structural adjustment programs hardly surfaces in these OFW narratives, the effects of such macrostructural changes on the course of development and the life chances of Filipinas are reflected in the personal experiences and visions they relate. Confronting the dire consequences of stringent government spending cuts pursuant on conditionalities of foreign debts and the skewed and stunted development of national industries in a globally connected economy of privatization, export orientation, and import liberalization, Filipinas are doubly pinched by an intensification of demands on their traditional feminine role as care providers and a contraction of their employment options in the labor market. Overseas employment in the low-end service sectors of what Saskia Sassen (2003) calls "global cities," where the centralization of top-level management, control centers, and advanced specialized professions of the global economy has created a great demand for maids, nannies, and servants of all kinds, ironically, becomes a plausible path of relief from this double burden or an imaginable course of immediate forbearance and sacrifice towards a more secure future "back home" under such conditions. Operative here is not only the deterritorialization of imaginable lives that Appadurai highlights in his account of globalization, but also the increasingly insurmountable barriers to a national construction of equitable and just ends and means of development. For the women concerned, moreover, exporting their caretaking services in what Rhacel Parrenas (2001) calls an international division of reproductive labor entails a displacement in some forms of their established identities as family caretakers within the nation-state, creating an ambivalent space of individual freedom, new possibilities, longing, homesickness, dislocation, alienation, and guilt in different degrees of combination that puts forth acutely the question of the values and ends of development. Shaping their life possibilities and trajectories are the promises, dilemmas, and contradictions of development at the intersection of the national, the familial, and the personal in an entangled nexus of travel, transactions, exploitation, and domination normativized in the name of globalization.

In this light, OFW tales in *Tinig Filipino* that do not recuperate relationships along traditional patterns or find resolution in a return to home in the Philippines are particularly illuminating. A series on personal experiences of "mixed relationships" that the magazine started early in its publication, for instance, explicitly raises and affirms the possibility of pursuing personal happiness and fulfillment across national boundaries, even if somewhat cautiously. While these tales of "long-term relationships" between Filipinas and men of other nationalities do not all end "happily," they invariably affirm the viability of establishing enriching relationships and promising futures across and beyond national and ethnic boundaries (Layosa and Neil 1990). In a tale of marriage between a Filipina domestic worker and a Chinese chef, who have to overcome even language barriers to come together, the woman, Rhoda, explicitly expresses satisfaction with her marriage over those she has observed in the Philippines:

> The thoughtfulness and good-naturedness of my husband pamper me . . . Unlike typical Filipino husbands, my Chinese husband does not drink. Thus, I do not experience headaches and heartaches waiting for him to return home at midnight . . . Yes, with him, I don't experience the bickers and brawls of couples I have witnessed in our neighborhood back in the Philippines. Although we are living quite simply, I feel secured with him since he's workaholic and has a strong determination to prepare our kids' future. (Layosa 1991, 29)

This affirmation of a mixed marriage is noteworthy in two aspects. First, in its uncritical reiteration of dominant racial stereotypes of the "workaholic" and responsible Chinese family man and the profligate, hard-drinking Filipino husband, the Filipina migrant domestic worker's self-understanding of her cross-national marriage reveals the tenacity of popular cultural understanding and beliefs even among border crossers with opportunities of direct contacts with other nationalities that belies the normative cosmopolitanism of travelers assumed in globalization discourse. The magazine article's verbatim report of Rhoda's account further implies an unreflective endorsement of such understanding. Ideological subject constitutions along gender, race/ethnic, and national lines are apparently not so easily erased or realigned as the fiction of globalization suggests. Second, Rhoda's story and its narration in *Tinig Filipino* highlight hope for the future, emotional fulfillment, and security besides and above material gains as goals that some Filipinas reach for in working overseas. In a different context, these may seem like unexceptional individual aspirations in life. Against the highly gendered national and nationalist backdrop to overseas employment for Filipinas, however, the narrative's celebration of such a cross-cultural union indirectly asserts the right of women to pursue personal happiness that has been systematically repressed and short-shrifted in the ethos and rhetoric of selfless sacrifice for the family and nation. Rather than the dutiful daughter, caring sister, sacrificing mother, and patriotic "economic hero" celebrated in hegemonic discourses, the migrant Filipina in this narrative is foremost an individual striving hard to ensure her own security and fulfillment with a family of her own making. Notwithstanding problematic ideological assumptions in terms of gender, race/ethnicity, and nation, the narrative establishes the legitimacy of a Filipina making personal choices and building her life and future outside the dominant frame of national development and homecoming. It thus opens up the meaning and ends of (national) development for interrogation, even though neither challenges nor alternatives are explicitly advanced to the state's "development" strategy of labor export.

This individual Filipina's assertion to find her own way and desirable ends of life against the failure of national development is echoed in the personal narrative of a Filipina migrant domestic worker who defends her repeated decision to leave her country and try "my luck in Taiwan":

> Because when one is earning more, one gets to dream more . . . and one must be prepared to shed tears, to experience pain and do some sacrifices.
>
> I brought with me enough ammunition to survive the battle between dreams and tears in which Taiwan has become the battleground. I ask myself the following questions: "Why do I have to go through this again? Is it the hopelessness of the situation in the Philippines that made me run away, or is it because I became ambitious? Is it wrong if I wanted more than what my country can offer?"
>
> After all, I am the one who's fighting, if I win my country gains, if I lose, I alone am the loser. (Buenavista 2007, 15–16)

If the arduous self-questioning in this OFW's personal narrative reveals a deep ambivalence towards pursuing individual development outside of and even away from her native country, which makes clear the power and tenacity of the claims of national development on the Filipina migrant worker, the affirmative statement following the self-questioning forcefully quells any qualms. In emphatically pointing out the individual "I" as the ultimate stakeholder and bearer of responsibility in the win or lose gamble of overseas work, it evinces a critical awareness of the power asymmetry underlying an individual migrant worker's struggle for development that justifies her caring about her own life and "ambitions" apart from the demands and circumstances of the development of her country. After all, her country never loses vis-à-vis the OFWs.

CONCLUSION

Because of OFWs' inseverable links to the Philippines as home and nation-state, OFW narratives of personal relationships in the light of development under the global restructuring of capitalism reveal the normative exclusion of globalization as fiction of development. The nationally circumscribed border crossing of the OFWs who are the subject of these narratives falls outside the elite cosmopolitanism that is the enunciative modality of globalization discourse. Though not averse to the border-crossing, culture-straddling ethos privileged in the cosmopolitan subject position of globalization discourse, the OFW narratives expose its incongeniality to the circumstances of migrant labor by foregrounding key issues of development for Third World peoples who still face recalcitrant boundaries of national sovereignty and state jurisdiction in our age of interconnectedness. In so doing, they return development to the political arena of national and popular debates and afford critical reflection on the possible meaning and course of development under the global penetration and dominance of capitalism. Neither circumscribing OFWs within nor overlooking boundaries and constraints confronting contract workers overseas, the narratives openly embrace all available possibilities for fulfilling and enriching relationships that a world of multifarious links and moving boundaries has to offer. Rather than deterritorialized imaginations or conservative retrenchment into family and nation, what emerges clearly from the narratives is a longing for and affirmation of the importance of emotional fulfillment, affective connectedness, and personal choices in formulating a common goal and future together with one's loved ones. Taken together, they articulate a vision of development that goes beyond economic advancement to encompass and embrace values that have been relegated to the feminine realm of family and reproduction. Though such a vision often takes traditional forms, it is not incompatible with or antithetical to border crossings and cultural rearticulations. More important, it reprioritizes a whole realm of values and needs that are marginalized in the dominant, neoliberal imagination of development naturalized in globalization discourse. Thus, it powerfully exposes the constitutive silence of globalization as fiction of development and recenters development as a subject of debate and contestation.

ACKNOWLEDGMENTS

Research on OFWs, the majority of whom are women migrant domestic workers, was supported by a grant from the Research Grants Council of the Hong Kong Special Administrative Region, China (project no. CUHK4700/05H).

9 Erratic Hopes and Inconsistent Expectations for Mexican Rural Women

A Critique of Economic Thinking on Alternatives to Poverty

Magdalena Villarreal

A favorite depiction of Mexican rural women is Diego Rivera's painting of a dark-skinned, braided "*torteadora*" (tortilla maker) kneeling over a stone *metate*, grinding maize for tortillas. Her plump yet strong arms press forcefully to produce the smooth dough, part of which she has already made into perfectly round tortillas and has placed on a makeshift griddle. The bright-colored artwork clearly bears notions of local knowledge and traditional ways as well as indigenous beauty. The artist might not have intended to convey the now common interpretation of these women as thriving in solidarity, rich folklore, and true experience, uncontaminated by capitalist ways of life and harmoniously linked to nature, but this is certainly what comes across to many viewers, who, in good will, might desire to help women such as these stand against the incursion of the "outside" world. Their traditions must be rescued and their social organization preserved. Their future lies in the retrieval of their past.

In contrast, one frequently comes across photographic representations of the very same scenario, mostly in dark colors, showing a similar brown-skinned, braided woman kneeling over a stone *metate*. Although her position is analogous to that of the woman in Diego Rivera's painting, her body, her back, and the angle at which she is bent communicates penury and hardship. The hand that holds the tortilla is sturdy rather than plump, showing prominent veins and uneven fingernails. The floor upon which she is kneeling is plain dirt. Behind her, the twig walls are smoke-tainted, and a table is swarming with flies. Sweat is streaking down her forehead, and a dour face of resignation replaces the complacent smile. The message delivered is that of poverty and adversity. These women have no future. It follows that they require financial resources, empowerment, discernment, education, and technology in order to develop and liberate themselves. Modernity is the basis upon which the development apparatus should operate in order to "build them a future."

These apparently contradictory images represent partial "truths" that coalesce in commonly held representations of Mexican rural women and their life prospects. While acknowledging them as valuable and worthy, there is a tendency to slip into stereotypical—and often naive—notions of their circumstances and their selves. On the one hand, their past must be retrieved to save their future, and on the other, a modern future must be concocted for them. All too often, in development planning and practice, images such as these taint expectations regarding rural women's options leading to the formulation of weak and misplaced alternatives.

In this chapter, I show that the ways in which these women's futures are conceived influence their present conditions. In so doing, I discuss some of the assumptions—economic and financial as well as social and cultural—that underlie much development practice oriented to women in Mexico.[1] I argue that these are framed within flawed portrayals of the economy, leading to the omission of a host of variables.

I build upon the premise that women are not excluded from the economy, in which they in fact play a critical role, nor are they, strictly speaking, excluded from development. However, the nature and scope of their participation tends to be overlooked by a large number of analysts, planners, and development practitioners who disregard the value of noncommoditized forms of production and exchange and fail to take into account the contradictions, ambiguities, and vulnerabilities of market-oriented economies. I believe that, in envisaging better living conditions for them, women's actions and their personae should be acknowledged as situated within a more encompassing economic scenario and that failure to do so leads to inaccurate foresight and expectations, thus obscuring avenues for change.

WOMEN AND POVERTY ALLEVIATION PROGRAMS IN MEXICO

Quantifying poverty has acquired great importance in Mexico, not so much because it helps us understand the phenomenon in order to deal with it, but because it has become a crucial element in assessing government's performance. According to recent calculations, 70 percent of all Mexican rural inhabitants are poor and 42.4 percent are extremely poor (Reporte del Comité Técnico para la Medición de la Pobreza en México 2000). Most rural incomes are below what is considered the poverty line. Access to medical services is reported as insufficient, as are educational options and adequate living conditions. Lively debates take place between academics and politicians, wherein the criteria to measure poverty are closely examined, reviewed, and reestablished. Changes in the final figures often seem to result from variations in these measurement criteria rather than as outcomes of the multiple poverty-alleviation programs set in place.

Such programs, implemented by governmental, nongovernmental, and civil organizations, have not been solely driven by economic agendas. Health, nutrition, and education are generally considered critical aspects of poverty alleviation, and issues of participation, democratization, and empowerment have—albeit from different angles and with different purposes in mind—constituted important concerns. Yet, as I discuss , the ways in which social, cultural, and economic issues are articulated and framed in the formulation of alternatives is problematic, not only within programs following capitalist or neoliberal guidelines, but also within some of those seeking to tackle root causes of poverty and trigger processes of structural change.

General trends in poverty-alleviation endeavors in the country include a number of governmental programs that have succeeded each other. In the 1970s and 1980s, COPLAMAR (*Coordinación General del Plan Nacional de Zonas Deprimidas y Grupos Marginados* [General Coordination of the National Plan for Deprived Regions and Marginalized Groups]) was implemented to encourage production and bolster social welfare, both in the construction of infrastructure and by subsidizing basic goods for consumption, PIDER (Programa de Inversiones Públicas para el Desarrollo Rural [Program for Public Investment in Rural Development]) was oriented to the promotion of cooperatives but also reinforced better health and education services, and SAM (Sistema Alimentario Mexicano) provided credit and subsidies to increase agricultural production of basic grains. All three were later dissolved by President Salinas, who instead created the National Solidarity Program (PRONASOL) as the spearhead of his social policy, which included social welfare programs oriented to health, education, housing, food supplies, and urban services; regional development programs involving the construction of roads and other infrastructure; as well as funds to be managed by the different municipalities and production programs, including agropecuarian and agroindustrial projects. Because he started his presidential period in the midst of social discontent and accusations of election fraud, poverty alleviation—in terms of social compensation for those most affected by the harsh structural adjustment measures—became central to his policies as a means to legitimate his government and ward against political unrest. Despite the fact that the president had decreed severe cuts in expenditures for social programs, PRONASOL itself held an extremely high budget. In 1992 PRONASOL disbursements represented 4 percent of the national public expenditures and 7.7 percent of the social expenditures. While in 1989 PRONASOL represented 6.6 percent of the total public investment, in 1992 it had reached 17.3 percent (Valencia Lomelí and Aguirre Reveles 1998, 69). However, during this period, poverty continued to increase.

Rural women have not been altogether absent from the agenda. The percentage of women in poverty is reported to be 10 percent higher than that of men. Hence, current trends in government development endeavors target women, enticing them to join health and education campaigns, learn new trades, and participate in micro-entrepreneurial schemes and community finance projects. Parallel to the International Women's Conference held in Mexico City in the 1970s, agroindustrial units for peasant women (UAIMs) were installed all over the country, with the expectation that women would "incorporate themselves into the economy" and the world of production. PROMUJER (Program for Action and Participation of Peasant Women in the Attainment of Rural Development) and PINMUDE (Community Development and Women's Participation Program) were later put in place as well. Because Mexican politics requires minimizing any association to factions previously in power in order to secure political control, programs are renamed. Thus, some of these groups were later enrolled into MUSOL (Women in Solidarity, which formed part of PRONASOL) and renamed as "solidarity" groups. In the next presidential period, mothers and wives living in extreme poverty were the focal point of PROGRESA, a welfare program focused on education, health, and nutrition, established by President Zedillo under the explicit premise that investing on the reproduction of human capital would provide returns to the economy (Escobar Latapí 2000; Riquer Fernández 2000). This program was in turn replaced by *Oportunidades*, set up by President Fox. The terms are quite similar: those in poverty first need to improve their health and nutrition in order to take advantage of opportunities and undertake risks.

It is not surprising that for more than three decades, health has been a major component of social policies oriented to women in Mexico. The association of deficit with overpopulation is a common one—hence the need to reach the rural population with family planning measures. This requires the involvement of women, as do nutrition plans for children, vaccine campaigns, and anticancer agendas. And women registered to receive benefits from the *Oportunidades* program—which include a small monthly allowance conditional on children's enrollment and regular school attendance, as well as medical checkups for the women—must show up every month to the talks imparted by a nurse, accept to undergo pap tests, and in many cases, carry out community tasks such as cleaning the medical dispensary, sweeping streets, and other such tasks. They are made responsible for their family's health, education, and nutrition, often including that of their husband, which, in rural Mexico, is no small issue. He who is represented as head of the household must be persuaded, compelled, or cajoled into undergoing medical checkups if the woman is to receive the bimonthly stipend. Also, that women and not men receive the allowance has occasioned more than a few household conflicts, which in some cases has led to violence from men who endeavor to embezzle the money from their wives.

In addition, a host of programs targeting rural women identified as poor are carried out by different government ministries and state departments, both at national and regional levels. These include DIF (Integral Development for the Family), the Ministry of Rural Development, the Ministry of Agriculture and the Environment, and the Ministry of Work. All need to show that they are gender conscious and politically correct. Thus, women are encouraged to promote family health, nutrition, and education; learn new trades; and participate in micro-entrepreneurial schemes and community finance projects. Conflict avoidance is high on the agenda, although it is seldom explicitly stated. And the ways in which poverty alleviation measures are established for electoral purposes, to garner political support, or to ward off social unrest have been discussed at length in multiple studies (see, for example, Dresser 1994; Fox 1994; Bruhn 1996).

It is clear that social and cultural matters are considered in such plans and programs and that women's contribution to development is regarded as indispensible. However, social, cultural, and gender issues are cast into a category that is deemed external to mainstream economics and "real progress." Women's activities as caretakers or even breadwinners might be acknowledged as important, but these are classified within the spheres of the social and the cultural, which tend to be perceived as separate from the economic sphere. Indeed, most of these programs pertain to what are labeled "social policies," clearly differentiated from economic ones. The generalized assumption is that dealing with rural women is dealing with those not participating in the economy. In this setting, as Luis Román (2000) points out for the case of PROGRESA, there is a tendency to categorize wealth as related to the sphere of "the economic" and poverty to that of "the social."

This is less often the case with nongovernment organizations (NGOs; particularly those seeking longer-term social change through economic but also political activities), who have invested large efforts in poverty alleviation. Yet, expectations vary between them. While they all hope producers will take off towards some sort of economic growth, for some, economic organization is a means to attain a degree of political autonomy. These also emphasize and promote actions of solidarity and resistance.

Micro-lending has also become an important focus for some of these organizations, mostly in response to the immediate demands of grassroots groups, whose options for finance have diminished considerably. Thus, organizations that provide credit and financial support for production and commercialization of agricultural products have mushroomed, many of them becoming alternative financial institutions. Due to their experience in working at the grassroots, a number of NGOs are now being hired as implementers of government programs and consultants. NGOs have accepted these new challenges, mostly because of the reduction of international funding,[2] but complain that the government is adopting a neoliberal stance to development intervention. Some of these organizations are now doing piecework under a "flexible organization" pattern (Angulo and Villarreal 2003), according to which they must incorporate economic markers to address growth, efficiency, and cost-benefit analyses of investments in human, intellectual, and organizational resources.

Civil organizations that seek processes of change have come to play important political as well as economic and social roles. These social organizations take up diverse voices from civil society. There is consensus in seeking greater justice, equality, and democracy, and they join in a common purpose for better development and the eradication of poverty. However, there are differences when it comes to the point of defining the immediate course to be followed, the most adequate procedures to struggle against or adapt to change, the means to be resorted to, organizational configurations, and the types of alliance that can be forged along the way.

The range of expectations with regard to women and poverty alleviation is thus quite wide, both within NGOs and governmental programs, and between them. Some NGOs rightly focus on issues of entitlements, autonomy, and democratization as important elements in poverty alleviation. They openly contest the separation between social and economic processes. The issue is not always solved, however, when it comes to formulating short- or medium-term alternatives. Vague notions of social capital are resorted to, but the ways in which social assets are articulated in economic processes within market economies is seldom clearly elucidated. The "market" tends to be thrust into the enemies' camp and women's options framed within a narrow view of the economy.

ECONOMIC AND FINANCIAL ASSUMPTIONS

In simplified terms, poverty-alleviation programs can thus be classified in three very general categories: (1) those aimed at increasing production, under the assumption that production leads to wealth; (2) those that seek social change, arguing that the economy does not work well for the poor; (3) and those oriented to welfare, envisioned as social compensation for those who, for different reasons, cannot provide for themselves. Here expectations are scant in terms of upward mobility as compared to programs oriented to production and industrialization, which squarely address the economy. Of course, agendas overlap and intertwine within and between programs. As mentioned before, government programs oriented to production can embrace some sort of welfare, and a number of those seeking social change also engage in production in the procurement of income. In general terms, however, the economy is considered the critical setting for the creation of wealth, and poor women are excluded from it.

The more commonly held view among development agents is that the path to emancipation for rural women—towards which the latter are expected to yearn—lies in their "incorporation" into the world of production, assuming that they are tied to the household, external to the world of economy and to agricultural and commercial activities. They need to enhance their entrepreneurial skills and operate in the real world: that is, learn to work for the market and pay for money at "market value." They should become "real" entrepreneurs. Modernity is the answer to the chains of tradition. Expectations tend to be established in terms of acquiring "financial culture" to enter the "modern" economy.

A host of inaccurate assumptions sustain such hopes and expectations. Three assumptions critical to the formulation of alternatives for rural women are listed next. These three are misconceptions of the nature of the economy, where the antidote to poverty is expected to reside.

1. The economy is equal to the market.
2. The household economy is not part of the "real" economy.
3. The economy is efficient.

If the market is the place where wealth is created, it must also constitute a critical site for poverty alleviation. Entrepreneurship and financial literacy become priorities for development endeavors. Quickly the rules of the game prevalent in commodity exchange take over. Premises of efficiency forwarded in this context become benchmarks, to the exclusion of what are considered nonmarket sites (such as the household), as well as noncommoditized resources and relationships. The economy, as Polanyi (1944) warned more than half a century ago, has been reduced to a simplified notion of the market.

The unrealistic notion that the economy (that is, market) is efficient does not require a great deal of argumentation. Most will not hesitate to acknowledge rampant irrationality in patterns of consumption, speculation, and corruption that commonly sustain economic practices. Yet what is surprising is the way a number of development planners, practitioners, and analysts choose to disregard common sense, resorting to market codes of belief in judging such practices as mere deviations. From this, it follows that plans and projections should be set to fine-tuning adequate techniques so as to "play by the book."

This brings us to what Michel Callon (1998) identifies as "framing." The market is performed, he says, by calculating agents—including financial experts, brokers, buyers and sellers, and economists themselves—who are involved in drawing boundaries between the relations that will be taken into account and which will serve in their calculations and those which will be thrown out of the calculation as such. Economists use the term *externalities* for those relations that remain outside the frame. Certain ties must be cut in order to disentangle an object or a relation, to "purify" products that are marketed and adjust the relation to a measurable, mathematical equation that can be subject to prediction.

The entanglement of household production and consumption with nonmeasurable and nonpredictable sets of relations, including gift giving, solidarity, altruism, and conflict, as well as noncommodified production and distribution, contributes to its classification as an externality.

But a great deal of production and distribution of resources take place in the context of household relations. By simply taking into account the number of people involved and the value of output, one comes to the realization that—as J. K. Gibson-Graham (1996a, 261), following the analyses of Nancy Folbre (1993) and H. Fraad, S. Resnick, and R. Wolff (1994), points out—the household sector can hardly be called marginal. These authors explain that more people are involved in household production than in capitalist production and that the discursive marginalization of the household does not reflect the status of the household economy itself.

In the development scenario, Irene Tinker (1995) argues that contemporary paradigms overlook the fact that women work within the frame of a human economy that addresses social, cultural, and familial angles of people's livelihoods. Her point is well taken, but it would be misleading to categorize women's work a priori as pertaining to a different economy, which can take us to separating off analytically the world of the "poor and/or marginalized" from the world of the "wealthy and/or dominant" with its consequent mystification.

We have to consider the ways in which a capitalist economy inhabits and survives on human and social resources and categories as well as financial ones. Social, cultural, domestic, ethnic, and power relations are part of the economy's constituent elements. These relations, although they might not, strictly speaking, be defined as capitalist, may act to mediate and structure monetary elements (see Long 1984, 13–14; 2001, 106–107; see also Wilson 1999 and Chapter 3, this volume). While social and cultural relations are frequently mentioned in the explanation of poverty and exclusion, the expectation is that these will be ironed out in the process of insertion within the capitalist economy. The hope is that rural women will leap out of poverty with entrepreneurial zeal and that this will lead to empowerment.

More critical change agents tend to view empowerment and the economy under different light. Empowerment has more to do with changing power relations and acquiring control over one's economy. Culture and social relations thus have everything to do with economic processes. Yet, in some cases, there remains a problem when referring to capital. The capitalist economy is reified to the degree that it is deemed efficient: efficient to accumulate, exploit, and dominate. Underpinning such views are notions of capital that need revising.

DEMYTHOLOGIZING CAPITAL

Three economic and financial assumptions that have to do with the nature of capital are the following:

1. Capital is measured in monetary terms.
2. Production leads to capitalization.
3. Saving and accumulation leads to wealth.

As I have reiterated elsewhere (Villarreal 2004), a specific resource—be it monetary or nonmonetary—can only become "capital" when it is brought into circulation within particular circuits of signification where its value is assessed and negotiated according to particular standards, rules, and expectations. But such processes of value definition are frequently disregarded in development efforts oriented to increasing production and accumulation in the hands of the poor. Capital is presumed material wealth measured in bona fide monetary terms.

For example, following the concern to transcend social compensation strategies, charity, and welfare, a number of development programs in Mexico set part of their goals on the establishment of small enterprises in the hands of the poor. The UAIM (Agricultural and Industrial Units for Women) program and MUSOL (Women in Solidarity), for instance, promoted micro-enterprises as mechanisms for poverty alleviation. These allowed low-income producers, manufacturers, and retailers to involve themselves actively in seeking ways out of their precarious situations. The belief was that, with the provision of "seed" capital, the poor could be "introduced" into the market. Well nurtured, the enterprise would expand, capital would grow, and the poor would be able to pull themselves out of poverty. Capital was expected to multiply itself and produce profit.

A number of interesting processes were triggered by such programs, but the fact is that many small enterprises did not survive more than a couple of years and most failed to expand. The "seed" resources that were injected were often diverted, disappearing into everyday consumption, or were turned into what Hernando de Soto (2000) labels "dead capital," which he claims is unable to do "economic things" for the impoverished.

De Soto has recently been influential in Mexican development planning (particularly during the period of President Fox, who hired him as a consultant). He claims that the poor already possess the resources they need to make a success of capitalism, but their resources are dead capital because they lack proper legal documents to prove legitimate property. He has a point. Those identified as poor hold or have access to a host of resources that are not activated within capitalist circuits of profit making. More than a few of the women engaged in micro-enterprises within the UAIM and MUSOL programs did own their small houses and urban plots, their husbands often possessed agricultural land, and some had access to water resources and forests. They definitively had skills, knowledge, networks, and rich cultural heritages that could become valuable assets in economic transactions. However, the fact that most of these were not gainfully articulated with commodity or financial markets had less to do with a lack of proper titles than with social constraints built into processes of capitalization. These included the ways in which markers of class, race, gender and other forms of social differentiation were entangled in the measurement of capital itself.

Women's work, skills, and knowledge were awarded little value within their circuits of interaction. Even the buildings they managed to construct with government aid were often considered community property—not so much because they lacked proper titles, which, they, like all other villagers, often did, but because they belonged to a group of women. They were thus easily taken over by other local (mostly male) groups, after which they were quickly revalued. The women also faced multiple obstacles in their efforts to access relevant markets, and when they did so, class and gender considerations hampered their possibilities to negotiate fair prices. After long and painful struggles, many chicken farms, sewing machines, ovens, and other equipment lost their status as capital and were abandoned or sold for next to nothing.

This is not surprising, since capital, as Steve Keen (2002, 141–145) explains, is in fact only a guesstimate of profit, calculated according to the price of expected revenues in the market. But markets are constituted in social interaction. The power to negotiate, for example, becomes a critical and quite unmeasurable factor in determining the value of goods and assets. The ways in which social and symbolic resources are deployed and made significant are thus essential.

In this scenario, the key is not to accumulate resources, but to capitalize and gain a degree of economic control, profiting from the value attributed to a particular resource. Processes of capitalization involve the ways in which assets (and identities as discussed next) are weighed, measured, and mobilized, and how their perceived virtues and attributes are included or not in economic calculations.

I am here speaking of different frameworks of calculation that coexist and interrelate in the definition of value equivalences, where, although money is *represented* as the standard measure of value, it does not necessarily function as such. What money does do is "delimit the circle of actions between which equivalences can be formulated" (Callon 1998, 21). By providing the façade of a universal yardstick, monetary calculations can brush off a number of social and economic relations (generally considered erratic, volatile, or subjective) as externalities. To be sure, some of these dimensions are taken into account in the now trendy notion of "social capital," which is used to address social resources that yield benefits such as improved material conditions, increased income, and social status. This is not difficult to conceptualize in today's world, where the range of what can be identified as assets yielding monetary benefits seems to have increased. Intangibles such as information, security, and knowledge are quite explicitly priced and allocated in ways that were previously not thought of. Notions of social, environmental, and cultural capital have eagerly been taken up in the development scenario, where projects and enterprises depend on the goodwill of donors and other stakeholders who are keen to measure the cost-benefit ratio of their investments. To think of social, environmental, kin, friendship and other resources as capital is to recognize their potential to produce profit in terms that can in some way be made equivalent to financial gain. Social and cultural resources become assets that are deemed measurable, presuming that they can be accumulated and even distributed to the poor.

But social resources are not external to the actions that invoke, generate, and constitute them (Long and Villarreal 2004). They do not exist as a supply of goods that can be stockpiled and exchanged. It is only in their mobilization that we can visualize them as resources. Activating capital, in this scenario, involves the manipulation of symbols, the imposition of interpretations, and anticipation of the future.

De Soto overlooks the fact that market currencies are based on particular information, predictions, speculation, promises, social links, trust, myths, and fallacies. Financial transactions include games of interpretation, inferences, and contests over the value to be attributed to a resource, over meanings and identities. Value is established through speculations that include the interpretation of the possible interpretation others will make concerning the value of a particular resource.

Viviane Forrester sees this as part of the economic horror we are facing today. She argues that these are transactions of what does not exist, that what is exchanged are not real assets, not even symbols of such assets, but, for example, the risks presumed in long- or medium-term contracts that have not yet been signed or only exist in someone's imagination (2000, 95). Quoting Robert Reich (1997), Forrester explains that decision makers of our times are the "manipulators of symbols," whom we can hardly identify with the old world of patrons.

The material base in terms of direct cash is no longer the main currency in international markets, which, with the turn towards a more virtual existence, recognize preexisting and new currencies framed in terms of information and trust (Weatherford 1997; Forrester 2000; Hart 2001). And information—crucial in today's world—is not constituted by the sum of objective data, but by flows of references interpreted within complex webs of networks, where hoaxes, tricks, and mystifications are frequently resorted to in order to gain edge. What is being circulated are not cold, scientifically proven data, but—as George Soros (1999) points out—the generalized acceptance of a "truth" until it is recognized as false. Thus, a great deal of capital exists until it is defined differently. Whether wealth is virtual or real remains ambiguous until a drastic event (however predictable) precipitates the need to define its nature.

Who are, then, the "owners of capital"? What kind of capital do they own? And, in the face of such ill-defined and erratic capital—which nonetheless appears to sustain a firm foot over people's livelihood prospects—what kind of hopes and expectations dare those of us interested in social change nourish?

POVERTY AND THE ISSUE OF VALUE AND RESOURCES

An important consideration to start with is that the apparently straightforward dichotomy between "having" and "not having" is placed on shaky grounds when delving into the workings of capital. One cannot assume that the problem of poverty is essentially an issue of faulty distribution of resources.

In Mexico, for example, the concentration of income has reached drastic dimensions. Millions of people are not able to access basic resources such as food and shelter in an adequate way. The country has been classified by the World Bank as a middle-class country, and this implies that Mexicans have enough wealth so as not to have a problem of extreme poverty. It would appear that, more than wealth creation, Mexico's problem is that of distribution.

However, many impoverished areas possess high-quality soils, mineral reserves, forests, and water reservoirs that are not exploited. Land reform schemes have, in the past, redistributed agricultural properties without seeming to redress poverty in a drastic way, and some poverty-stricken zones have been flooded with governmental and nongovernmental aid, including credit schemes, projects, subsidies for production, and social compensation programs with meager success. The notion of distribution fails to capture the dynamics of resource allocation and valuation. It provides too static a scenario, wherein it is commonly inferred that such resources cannot be put to good use because the poor lack intangible resources, such as knowledge, education, and information.

Fortunately academic discussion on this issue has moved beyond this rather simplistic view. Issues of entitlements, freedoms, capabilities, exclusion, and access have been addressed in development literature. While some perspectives highlight cultural differences, others stress class distinctions and power relations between elites and the underprivileged, and/or the role of the State in maintaining such inequalities. Amartya Sen (1981, 45)—whose insightful work on entitlements has inspired much work on poverty—discusses legal ownership rights, but also includes moral and other factors that enter into the allocation systems. He explains that it is not only the existence of resources (in this case, food) that is important, but people's *command* over them, taking into account social processes that enter into the allocation of legitimacy to access and ownership, how people's rights are formulated, and their possibilities of controlling mechanisms of exchange.

As has been discussed previously, it is not only the number of assets or resources (be they tangible or intangible) that makes for wealth or poverty, but the ways in which these are assessed in specific economic transactions, the contexts in which such valuation takes place, and the social relations entailed in these processes. Today most enterprises operate on the basis of credit, loans, and debt. Errors in the classification of debts can lead to failure, whereas opportune labeling can allow the use of debt as a resource. For entrepreneurs, it is not so much the amount outstanding that changes the definition of debt as a resource to that of a burden and default. Debts in the name of a company considered successful can function as a warranty of trustworthiness (as proof that financial institutions rely on them) and entrepreneurship. A number of considerations enter into this process of categorization, many of which are based on guesstimates and speculations.

An important point to bear in mind is that resources are also being created in the process. They are not always preexisting and predistributed. Clean air, security, authenticity, and historic relevance can be re-created as assets in particular transactions, as also can the non-use of chemicals in production and the utilization of artisan techniques. Resources, then, are not static. They do not exist in a given supply. Our conceptualization of their economic qualities (or the conceptualization we are able to impose on others) is crucial, because such resources need to be mobilized and leveraged. However, this can only be done within fields where their value is acknowledged and can be negotiated in accordance with certain conventions and expectations. And here, of course, patterns of exclusion and discrimination are reproduced and reinforced. Calculations and predictions vis-à-vis the future structure of opportunities—where processes of image construction and identification are crucial—enter into the equation.

In business contexts, successful entrepreneurs capitalize on their identities and prestige (or the prestige of their product). They build an image and profit from it. The future of a person can be seen, it is measured beforehand in the image projected. Unlike the poor, a prestigious entrepreneur has a future, an implicit promise of success in the socially attributed image of prestige. An "aspiring entrepreneur" must send signals that a banker or client must recognize as firm promises. These need to predict the success and credibility of the partner in whom they deposit their trust. Soros, known in the corporate world for his capacity to mobilize markets, makes this clear when he recognizes that much of his success was based on how he resorted to what he calls "value leverages": "When an enterprise or sector are overvalued, they can issue shares and use the benefits to justify to a degree exaggerated expectations. Inversely, when an enterprise that is going through rapid growth is undervalued, it may face difficulties in taking advantage of the opportunities it faces, which justifies its undervaluation" (Soros 1999, 71).

Undervalued as they are, it is no wonder that De Soto finds that the poor countries cannot seem to be able to produce capital. But their problem is only increased by reducing their assets to monetary value, since in the process of being defined as a resource linked to capital, these have been resignified and assessed in a language that, as mentioned before, delimits the circle of actions between which equivalences can be formulated. We thus lose sight of the key issue, namely, the power-laden contexts in which equivalences are defined, weighed, attributed value, and mobilized as capital.

Overvaluation eases the conduit for those considered wealthy to take advantage of their prestige to create and use opportunities, while undervaluation restricts such a possibility. The assessment of social standing, class, rank, and prestige attached to identity becomes critical. To a degree, the identity attributed to a person, a social group, or a country forecasts her future.

SOCIAL AND CULTURAL ASSUMPTIONS

In this context, social and cultural assumptions concerning rural women's future acquire great relevance. In most poverty-alleviation programs, women's identities are based on the idea of what they are *not* and do *not* have.

Using an unrealistic model of "progressive" and "free" women as a point of comparison, their actions and personae are quickly associated with poverty, ignorance, illiteracy, low productivity, malnutrition, and underdevelopment. That is, they are lacking. They lack income, education, and access to resources. They also lack power and control over their lives. And, not only are they are deemed illiterate, but it is frequently deduced that they lack the necessary skills to help themselves. Most importantly, they lack a future. Lacking is the quintessence of their identity, the definition of their being.

Obviously these women do lack: they live in the midst of poverty, a number of their children are malnourished, and they have limited access to proper educational and health facilities. And it is important to stress such images in development practice, since they pump the passion of practitioners as well as donors. But the problem is that dearth is woven discursively into particular relations of power, subordination, and status.

The notion of "poor" condemns the bearer to a lesser status, a half person who needs to be "developed:" to be educated, trained to acquire basic skills. What is needed is the intervention of "providers," who automatically bear a higher status—where power and control are accessible—and "experts." Experts are legitimately recognized as such by a salary; a title; physical distance (living, as they generally do, outside the site of intervention); symbolic distance, in terms of status, authority, and hierarchies; and social distance, which separates the "beneficiaries" from access to procedures, techniques, and the operation of markets.

The script concerning gender and poverty marks boundaries and excludes women, who are either idealistically depicted as living in the past (untainted by capitalism and thus needing to be "preserved" as part of Mexico's national heritage) or as lacking a future, a future that will be adequately constructed through development. Thus the invisibility of women—so reiteratively denounced in academic texts—appears to be giving way to what could be an even more pernicious practice: the discursive production of a "woman subject to development" which has contributed to create new forms of subjection of women in the Third World (Mohanty 1991; Kabeer 1994; Escobar 1995; Parpart 1995; Viola 1999). Escobar (1995, 8–9) insists that it is important to "make visible the power of the development apparatus to name women in ways that lead us to take for granted certain descriptions and solutions," for in the very process of naming "habitates the possibility of a colonialist effect."

What is disturbing is that the victim role that is ascribed to women within the script does not change drastically within the "counter-script," where women "subject to development" must first recognize themselves as poor and powerless in order to subvert the system. They are vulnerable, invaded, penetrated by the development apparatus and capital. Global capital dictates the script within which women are already constituted as subjects.[2]

The problem is accurately identified by Gibson-Graham who, in analogy with rape scripts, explain how the "globalization script normalizes an act of nonreciprocal penetration." In the rape script, men are portrayed as "naturally stronger than women, . . . biologically endowed with the strength to commit rape." "Women are the subjects of fear. Their bodies are soft, empty, vulnerable, open" (1996a, 124–125). The victim role prescribed by the script remains unchallenged, thus discouraging certain forms of activism that could enable a different script altogether. In the globalization script, capitalism is "large, powerful, active, expansive, penetrating, systematic, self-reproducing, dynamic, victorious, and capable of conferring identity and meaning." In this way, the future does not seem to offer hope for escape. Everything in its vicinity is likely to be drawn into capitalism, overpowered, and subsumed by it (1996a, 9). Moreover, this "generates a representation of the social world and endows it with a performative force that can influence the potential for successful political interventions." Thus, "the project of understanding the beast has itself produced a beast." It gives it a platform from which to speak its dominance (1996a, 23).

But, cloaked in what has come to be identified as dominant discourse is a simplification of whole sets of processes and negotiations, which, when observed closely, reveal the vulnerabilities of power. Disclosing such vulnerabilities is part of the process of un-naturalizing power and undermining the practices that uphold it.

SCRIPTS AND POWER

It is evident that processes of naming, classifying, and framing enclose, as Bourdieu (1994, 122) points out, those who are characterized within the limits that are assigned and that must be recognized. And, as Geof Wood (1985) and Erving Goffman (1972) assert, labeling and naming imply processes of control and regulation, wherein positions of status are created, granted, and occupied. Poverty is all too frequently associated with ignorance, filth, dishonesty, and violence, and such associations—often implicit in discourses, which makes them difficult to contest—close up possibilities of access to information and decision-making circles.

Paths are restricted by establishing boundaries, attributing values, and providing categories and hierarchies to order and structure social life. However, although scripts used to characterize rural women in development scenarios mark boundaries and delimit roles, serving as devices for exclusion, it would be a mistake to attribute power to the script itself. Scripts are compelling tools for power. But they are not in themselves powerful. Behind representations are agents, people who wield political and economic agency by operating cultural, social, and emotional triggers. Boundaries are thus reworked, positions negotiated and disowned, and meanings reinterpreted. Scripts always contain ambiguities and gaps, and they coexist with other scripts that oppose and contradict them. While labels are used to define status, social standards, and behavior, their meaning is situated and reinterpreted according to the different contexts in which they are applied. Claims to truth are negotiated, calling upon different connotations of the concepts. And different, opposing scripts concur in the same contexts, even expressed by the same people. Discourses can be far from consistent.

To come to terms with the complexity of power relations, we must acknowledge the webs of routines that are triggered or channeled in specific directions, not only by the power wielder but by the social constituency that attributes identities and roles including ethnic, class, and social differentiations (Villarreal 1994, 2000). Hence, power is seldom an individual accomplishment.

Discourses are constituted through social interaction, through processes involving the interlocking and segregation of voices, and in this way are shaped by the actors themselves. In everyday life, the interests and projects of individuals and social groups—including beneficiaries of poverty alleviation programs as well as implementers, planners, academics, and others—become ensnared within the scripts, thus constituting "voices" through which to express, defend, and challenge practices and discourses. Challenging, discrediting, dislocating, and reinterpreting meanings and values are common strategies in the struggles for access to resources. But most often, it is more a matter of exploiting ambiguities in institutionalized practices.

More than a few Mexican rural women have learned to exploit such ambiguities and contradictions. They might use their husband's authority as an excuse to avoid commitment to an enterprise they do not want to take on, and they may willingly adopt an identity as poor and destitute in order to obtain funds from development organizations and the State, even though they might disown such labels in other arenas. Some do not hesitate to disregard local officers who do not meet their terms. They quickly learn the "language of development" and use it to advantage. Their control over crucial contacts allows them to take hold of several projects at once or at least influence their allocation within their local networks. They soon detect cleavages and animosities among officers and project staff and play one party against the other. In the process, they manage to use their image as vulnerable women to a degree of advantage. In fact, these programs have kindled lively disputes and open conflicts in rural villages concerning who is legitimately entitled to such resources, who "is poorest," who is really needy and thus merits aid.

But in terms of subverting a "dominant discourse," these strategies can be seen as short- term and short-sighted. They do not touch the basis upon which an unequal relation is sustained. Subverting the script is difficult because it is already incarnated within many others in different domains of interaction, where multiple interests are at stake. It has become a consecrated and accepted truth. Turning a deaf ear to the voices that undermine the script makes it more difficult.

To subvert the script, we must first identify its nonalienating voices, sweep them out from under the rug. We must see how the women's world is not limited to typically capitalist circuits, and we must demythologize our own concepts of capital. Subversions of capitalism might in fact be found within what we identify as the capitalist system itself. Studying capitalists' actions, one is able to identify how even the most hard-core capitalist activities are not circumscribed to what one might describe as capitalist circuits. It is an aspiration rather than an achievement.

OMITTED VARIABLES

The corporate world, commonly credited with the power to control the economy, requires constant efforts of bridging gaps and covering up inconsistencies. Fear and uncertainty guide market behavior at least as much as "rational" cost-benefit analysis does. Capitalization takes place under fragile conditions. However, these are all too often missed in the design of possible alternatives to poverty, which are guided by illusory models of success. Failure to identify the weaknesses of market-oriented economies thwarts the potential to identify possible niches for social change.

It is important to acknowledge that this limited view of economic processes also entraps many participatory rural development endeavors, including some of those explicitly pursuing economic organization as a means for social change. Efficiency and cost-benefit markers are often drawn upon to assess achievement, which is all the more difficult, since economic success is expected to be collective and the outcomes must benefit the community as a whole. The effort is worthy. Yet, it tends to fall through, not least because key variables concerning both the sites and the nature of interaction between social and economic spheres are not adequately dealt with in the formulation of alternative expectations.

Recent trends in development thinking that orient social movements and initiatives are, to be sure, providing new avenues for hope and ideas as to alternative expectations. In Mexico, social organizations and even some government-supported programs have been focusing on fair trade, for example. Fair trade initiatives build upon recognition of the double standards, incongruence, and contradictions that prevail in market interaction. This is an important step. Yet, there is still a long stretch ahead in terms of acknowledging contradictions in the very terms in which the economy is formulated and framed.

The central role of household production, the relevance of noncommoditized transactions, and the differential value attributed to goods, property, money, and intangible qualities require more encompassing notions of the economy itself. As I have discussed, a series of generally omitted variables must be taken into account in conceiving options for rural women's struggle against poverty. These include the following:

1. The vulnerabilities, contradictions, and gaps in market economies
2. The differential value of goods and money
3. How resources can be created in interaction and how they are weighed and mobilized
4. The relevance of noncommoditized relations
5. The scope and scale of household economies
6. The impact of a victimized identity in thwarting trust and reproducing exclusion
7. The ways in which those identified as destitute deploy resources and act in pursuing their livelihoods

The aforementioned micro-financial programs could have become more meaningful change endeavors had they taken women's strengths as the point of departure, contextualizing such strengths in the face of capitalist markets' weaknesses. Such weaknesses include the capitalist need to frame out the value of household economy itself, as well as the ways in which power relies on subordination, omission, and compliance. These matters should be considered in tackling the issue of assessment and mobilization of resources. Needless to say, such efforts would be uphill. On the one hand, immediate electoral or political gain from these programs—particularly in the case of government endeavors—would likely be meager. On the other, women themselves tend to undervalue their strengths and resources, and, in the face of their pressing need for money, are willing to forego longer-term change for immediate benefits. Such a scenario is enhanced by the fact that a significant number of scientific studies feeding theoretical insights into development praxis still revolve around misplaced notions of the economy.

Those of us pursuing change live in very complex forms of give and take with capitalist ideas, practices, events, and relationships and simply cannot abandon market-oriented options altogether. But we should be able to detect cleavages and nonalienating voices. We can recognize our role in defining the value of noncommoditized transactions, crucial to both large- and small-scale economic enterprises, and we can begin to question the nature of capital in order to highlight the vulnerabilities of the structures we are not only abiding by, but also contributing to reproduce.

Here power relations will surely make their glaring appearance, not least because the context-specific social processes within which value equivalences are defined will be revealed. Power relations are generally incorporated in the formal design of antipoverty programs and projects. The notion of power is often present, whether in conceiving the poor as excluded from the market, in mentioning the problem of distribution of resources, or in reiterating the need for empowerment, particularly in the case of women. But the tendency is to visualize all scenarios involving "the poor" in terms of power and resistance, the latter being identified with the poor and the former with the affluent, capitalism, and the state. This is not enough. We need to pin down the processes of reproduction of power, including the gaps, inconsistencies, and ambiguities wherein space for maneuver and possibilities of subversion can be identified. By overlooking the ways in which power relies on subordination, omission, and compliance, we tend to obscure its weaknesses, and with them, the potential for alternative paths in the actions that run counter to typical market behavior. We fail to perceive the scope for change found within the complex flux of contradictory and muddled processes.

In this view, capital is the foundation of progress, capitalism is large, powerful, and victorious, but our hopes for rural women are erratic, our expectations inconsistent.

ACKNOWLEDGMENTS

Research for this article has been carried out under the auspices of an ECOS ANUIES project: *La pobreza: ciudadanización, discursos y políticas, una investigación comparativa.*

NOTES

1. Although I must say that the critique targets generalized trends that are quite prevalent around the world, both in government and nongovernment endeavors.

10 From Old to New Political Cultures of Opposition

Radical Social Change in an Era of Globalization

John Foran

If it is true that revolutions are the product of both structural conditions and human agency, and that they are born out of both political economic and cultural causes, then we may ask: in the current structural, political economic conjuncture of globalization, what are the human and cultural dimensions of revolutionary social change in the modern world? Certainly, in the post–Cold War, post–September 11 world, the space for revolutionary projects seems constrained by the collapse of older ideals and models. The socialist vision of the twentieth century has been tarnished by the authoritarian shape it took in the Soviet Union and in Eastern Europe, the return of savage forms of capitalism to China's new economy, the reversal of the Sandinista revolution in Nicaragua in the 1990s, and the uncertain future that lies ahead in a post-Castro Cuba. Zimbabwe, Mozambique, Angola, Vietnam, and Algeria all experienced anticolonial social revolutions in the latter half of the twentieth century and now find their prospects circumscribed by global capitalism and leaderships whose socialist credentials have given way to a hunger for power and money. The end of dictatorships in Haiti, the Philippines, and Zaire through political revolutions has not been accompanied by economic growth or betterment of life for their populations. Even the momentous toppling of apartheid in South Africa in 1994 has not been matched by any measurable gains for much of the black social base whose sacrifices brought it about.

Yet to conclude from this survey of broken dreams and promises that the path of revolution has failed for good, or that the future offers little prospect for positive social change, seems premature. For since the early 1990s a variety of new projects of radical social change have emerged, particularly in Latin America, where the left has been elected in Venezuela (1998), Brazil (2002), Uruguay (2004), and Bolivia (2005); joined in 2006 by Ecuador and Nicaragua and a second term for the left in Brazil and Venezuela; and came close to victory in Mexico in 2006, while the Zapatistas continue to build autonomous communities in Chiapas. And on a global scale, a vast "movement of movements" has emerged in the past ten years to counter neoliberal capitalism in the form of the global justice movement, transnational feminist networks, the gatherings of the World Social Forum, and the spirited protests at meetings of the World Trade Organization and the G8 (Group of Eight) nations, in Seattle, Genoa, Cancún, and elsewhere.

The confluence of the demise of twentieth-century social revolutions and the emergence of radical new struggles in the twenty-first suggests that the present moment is one of transition in the revolutionary tradition, in which armed struggle led by a vanguard in the name of socialism is yielding to more inclusive, democratic struggles in the name of something else. Students and proponents of revolution alike would do well to attend to the forms of this transition in seeking to understand and further the prospects for deep social change in an age of globalization and crisis. This chapter offers one way of thinking about the changes that are under way, by focusing on the ways in which revolutionary cultures are shifting from older forms to newer ones.

POLITICAL CULTURES OF OPPOSITION: A LENS ON HOW PEOPLE BECOME AGENTS OF RADICAL SOCIAL CHANGE

My own work on the history of twentieth-century revolutions led me to explore the link between the structural conditions that figure in their origins and the coming together of a coalition of social forces broad enough to take power. I attempt to work out a synthesis that balances attention to such perennial (and all too often reified) dichotomies as structure and agency, political economy and culture, state and social structure, internal and external factors. I have argued that five interrelated causal factors must combine in a given conjuncture to produce a social revolution (see Diagram 10.1):

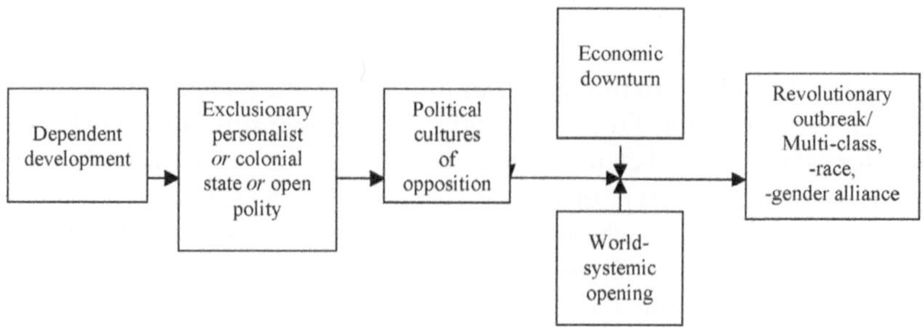

Diagram 10.1 A model of Third World social revolutions.

The coming together in a single place of five factors has led to the formation of the broad revolutionary coalitions which succeeded in gaining power in Mexico 1911, Russia 1917, China 1949, Cuba 1959, Iran 1979, and Nicaragua 1979. These include the following:

- *Dependent development* (Cardoso and Faletto 1979; Evans 1979), essentially a process of growth within limits set by a country's insertion into the capitalist world-economy, which creates social and economic grievances among diverse sectors of the population;
- *A repressive, exclusionary, personalist state*, led by a dictator or colonial power who provides a solid target for social movements from below, often alienating even the middle and upper classes;
- A revolutionary crisis produced by the combination of *an economic downturn*, either the result of processes in the world and national economies or the creation of revolutionaries in the course of their struggle, and
- *A world-systemic opening* or let-up of external controls, originating in the distraction in the core economies by world war or depression, rivalries between one or more core powers, mixed messages sent to Third World dictators, or a divided foreign policy when faced with an insurrection.

At the center of this combination of forces lies the elaboration of *effective and powerful political cultures of resistance*[1] among a broad array of actors, drawing upon formal ideologies such as socialism; folk traditions such as memories of past struggles; and popular idioms such as nationalism, social justice, or an end to dictatorship. In a look first at the Iranian revolution of 1979 (Foran 1993), and then at a wider set of cases (Foran 2005), I came to see this in terms of the articulation of political cultures of opposition and resistance (see Reed and Foran 2002). This refers to the process by which both ordinary citizens and revolutionary leaderships came to perceive the economic and political realities of their societies, and to fashion a set of understandings that simultaneously made sense of those conditions, gave voice to their grievances, and found a discourse capable of enjoining others to act with them in the attempt to remake their societies. The complexities of this process, and the several elements that work together to create a viable political culture of opposition, are suggested in Diagram 10.2.

The origins of revolutionary political cultures lie in the experiences of people and in the subjective emotions and dynamics that animate their politics. At the same time, revolutionary discourses in the form of consciously articulated ideologies travel from revolutionary groups into local settings, as well as circulate between revolutions. Meanwhile, more popular "idioms" also circulate in communities, putting people's concerns in everyday terms such as *fairness*, *justice*, or *freedom*. Political cultures are forged

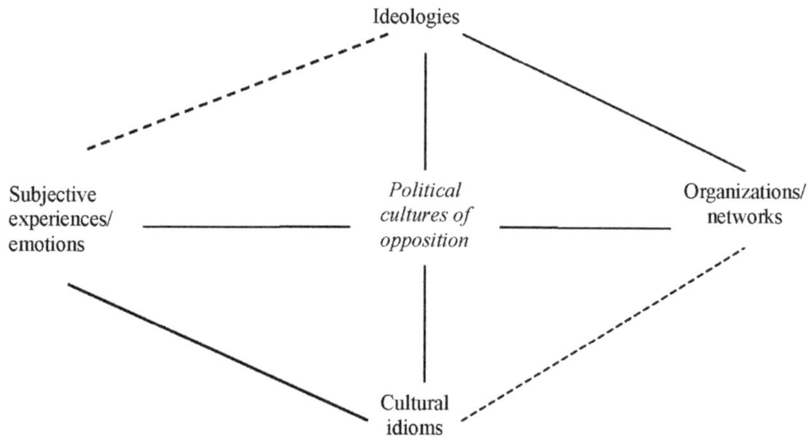

Diagram 10.2 The making of political cultures of opposition.

out of the encounter of these different elements and can become generalized when groups of people organize themselves into networks and organizations seeking to change the established order. It should be pointed out that in any given society, there may exist more than one political culture of opposition, for people do not necessarily share the same experiences, speak the same idioms, or respond to the same formal ideologies. The most effective revolutionary movements find ways of tapping into whatever political cultures emerge in their society, often through the creation of a common goal—"the regime must step down," "the foreign companies should leave"—or through an ability to speak to people's experiences and cultural understandings in a way that acknowledges and builds upon their diversity. When this happens, a revolutionary movement can gain enough committed followers to contest power with the state. The forging of a strong and vibrant political culture of opposition is thus an accomplishment, carried through by the actions of many people, and, like revolutions themselves, is relatively rare in human history.

"OLD" POLITICAL CULTURES OF OPPOSITION AND THE RECORD OF THE TWENTIETH-CENTURY REVOLUTIONS

To test our thesis that political cultures of opposition may be undergoing important changes in the current conjuncture, we should begin with an attempt to characterize the political cultures that animated the great social revolutions of the twentieth century, in Mexico, Russia, China, Cuba, Iran, and Nicaragua. What follows is necessarily a great simplification of the complexity and historical uniqueness of these events, and is done for the purpose not of suppressing that uniqueness, but for exploring possible patterns of similarity across them.

In each of these cases, the economic process of dependent development and the internal political structure of dictatorship produced experiences of exploitation and political exclusion, in turn eliciting emotions of anger and rage. The subjective side of these revolutions drew on an enormous reservoir of human aspiration and courage, difficult to document and impossible to present in this (or any) space. As the Cuban revolutionary Enrique Olutski put it, "No book can ever convey the greatness of a people in revolt" (2002, n.p.). One of the emotions at work in each case was surely a combination of anger and indignation at the conditions imposed. Teodor Shanin's work on the Russian revolution gives it expression: "At the very centre of revolution lies an emotional upheaval of moral indignation, revulsion and fury with the powers-that-be, such that one cannot demur or remain silent, whatever the cost" (1986, 31). Positive feelings of solidarity and love can also animate revolutions; as Che Guevara famously put it, "At the risk of seeming ridiculous, let me say that the true revolutionary is guided by great feelings of love" (1965).

The formal discourses that revolutionaries put forward varied from case to case, from the radical agrarian programs of Zapata in Mexico to the militant Islam of Khomeini in Iran. One core discourse was that of nationalism, the notion that foreign influence over the economy and national politics must come to an end. A second, in the cases of Russia, China, Cuba, and Nicaragua, was a more or less formal appeal to socialism (present also in an inchoate form in Mexico and as a minor current in Iran, and more subterranean in Cuba until after the movement came to power). A third strand, in Nicaragua and Iran especially, was a radical interpretation of religion, in the form of liberation theology in the first case, and an activist Islam in the second.

Identifying the less formal, popular idioms that animated revolutionary action is more difficult. The distrust of foreign power can be discerned across these cases, a visceral hatred for the alliance of the government with rapacious outsiders: "Death to America" was a prominent slogan at the mass demonstrations against the Shah, as was "Mexico for the Mexicans" in the 1910s. This extended to dislike of the dictator's monopoly of power, a factor which brought middle-class groups into opposition in Mexico, Russia, Cuba, Nicaragua, and Iran. Behind these lay a sense that social justice should be served: "Land, liberty, and freedom" in Mexico was one slogan that embodied this; the peasantry's desire for land reform in China another measure of it.

The organizations that emerged in five of the six cases—all but Iran (and less than the others in Russia)—consisted of armed insurgents who directly engaged the state, though these were aided in all cases by non-armed groups and organizations who engaged in support activities of many kinds (on Cuba, see Klouzal 2005). In Russia and China, and more loosely in Nicaragua, political parties existed alongside the armies and gave direction to them (in Cuba, the July 26 Movement acted as an organizational anchor for the insurgency, a quasi-political party). In Iran, the network of mosques and clerics, most of them loyal to the Ayatollah Khomeini, provided the organizational base for the mass demonstrations and general strike that undermined the shah's government without taking up arms. A common thread across cases is the hierarchical structure of the movements, with well-identified individuals at their head—Emiliano Zapata and Pancho Villa, Vladimir I. Lenin and Leon Trotsky, Mao Tse-Tung, Fidel Castro and Che Guevara, Khomeini, and the Sandinista leadership under the Ortega brothers and other commanders. This hierarchical nature of guerrilla militaries, socialist parties, and of religious leadership meant that influential figures—always male, and usually privileged in background—would lead in the name of the people.

Despite the variations from case to case, we may discern a rough but common pattern among the "old" political cultures of opposition that made the great revolutions of the twentieth century, as suggested in Diagram 10.3.

These political cultures produced broad and powerful revolutionary movements, all of which took state power (in Mexico, power fell to less radical forces, but the dictatorship of Porfirio Díaz was definitively toppled). Once in power, all the movements encountered internal and external pressures, and each produced new states whose leaderships held power close: Mexico's Party of the Institutionalized Revolution for eight decades, the

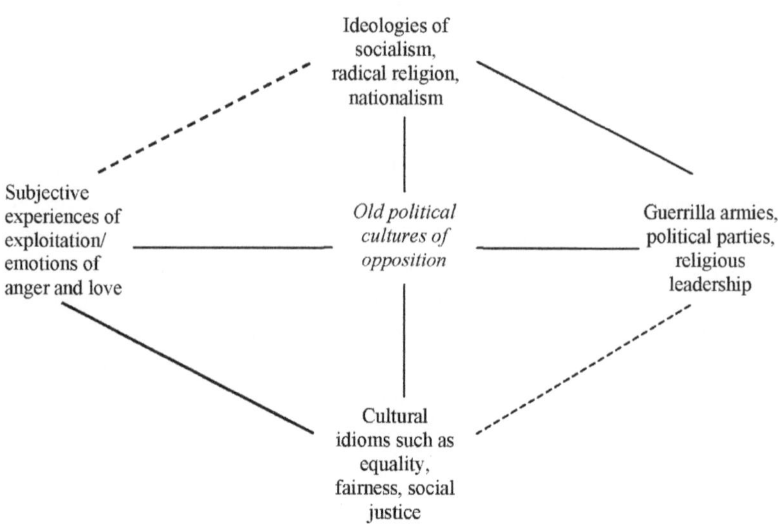

Diagram 10.3 The making of "old" political cultures of opposition in the Mexican, Russian, Chinese, Cuban, Iranian, and Nicaraguan revolutions.

Communist Party of the Soviet Union for almost as long, Castro's reign of almost fifty years, the Chinese Communist Party's monopoly of power since 1949, the strong hold of the Islamist leadership in Iran down to the present. Only in Nicaragua was a polity created which ran the risk of ceding power, and there the Sandinistas did indeed yield power in the 1990 elections; their subsequent presidential campaigns, all under Daniel Ortega, indicate that the party did not democratize internally, however, and this shared characteristic with the other cases has been an obstacle to their return to power. Ortega would win the November 2006 elections, aided by a change in the electoral rules enabling a candidate with 40 percent of the vote to win in the first round. This signals perhaps the hybrid or transitional character of Sandinismo, ahead of the older tradition in its espousal of an open, democratic polity, yet behind the new political cultures of opposition to come in its freezing of the leadership under Ortega.

I am not suggesting that the limits of these revolutions can be laid entirely at the feet of the political cultures which made them. For one thing, all of the revolutions produced gains for the population of some depth and duration (most notably in Russia and Cuba, for a short time in Nicaragua, and for a long time in China). For another, the fashioning of powerful political cultures was a remarkable accomplishment, and each possessed admirable features, particularly in the phase of the insurrection. These were not always preserved by the winners afterward, who faced the daunting task of holding together broad and heterogeneous social forces, typically with divergent interests. Of substantial weight in the outcomes of each were other factors that acted independently of political culture and human agency: external intervention and disadvantageous positions in the world-economy chief among them (see Foran and Goodwin 1993). We see here, as attested at the outset of this chapter, the profound intersection of political economy and culture, of impersonal structures and human agency.

But the possibility remains that the strength and solidity of these revolutionary political cultures, so crucial in overthrowing the states they opposed, yet possessed features—especially the combination of the leaderships' emphases on ideology over popular idiom, and the hierarchical nature of the organizations that came to power—which must be counted among the Achilles heels of the outcomes that followed. If we compare them with the emergent shape of their counterparts in the twenty-first century, we may find further clues to the nature and power of political culture in processes of radical social change.

THE EMERGENCE OF "NEW" POLITICAL CULTURES OF OPPOSITION IN THE TWENTY-FIRST CENTURY

The Zapatista uprising of 1994, the election of left governments in a number of Latin American countries, and the emergence of a movement for global justice have also been animated by resilient political cultures of opposition. The old and new political cultures of opposition are *not* dichotomous, of course: the same elements are present in every political culture of opposition. But even while retaining the same elements as older political cultures, the new political cultures of opposition accord different weights to them, with different contents and novel forms in some of them. They have also experienced a variety of outcomes to date, coming to power in a so-called pink tide in Venezuela, Brazil, Uruguay, Bolivia, Ecuador, Paraguay, and elsewhere, establishing autonomous communities but not taking national power in Chiapas, and organizing across borders without a clear or singular goal in the case of the global justice movement. We should explore not only these variations, but also the ways in which, as a group of movements, they differ from their twentieth-century revolutionary counterparts.

A New Left Comes to Power in Latin America

In Venezuela, Brazil, Uruguay, Bolivia, Ecuador, Nicaragua, and most recently, in Paraguay, left parties have succeeded in gaining political power through elections. (The following analysis is based in part on a reading of news media including *The New York Times*, *Latinamerica Press*, *The Guardian Weekly*, and *NACLA Report on the Americas*.) The impact of globalization on the populations of each country has exacerbated social inequalities of class and ethnicity (the latter especially in Bolivia and Ecuador), such that people's experiences of exploitation were sharply felt. Anger against established political elites animated the bases of the left parties—the Workers Party in Brazil, the aptly named Frente Amplio (Broad Front) coalition in Uruguay, the Movement Toward Socialism in Bolivia, the born-again Sandinistas in Nicaragua, and the emergence of the Patriotic Alliance for Change in Paraguay. The Argentine slogan—"que se vayan todos" (get all the politicians out)—resonated across working-class, indigenous, and middle-class communities and voters tired of the older governing parties in all of these countries (cf. the *New York Times* reference to "a strong throw-the-bums-out sentiment" in Nicaragua: November 7, 2006). There was also far less emphasis on an ideological appeal to socialism by the leaderships: Brazil's Luis Inacio da Silva (universally known as "Lula"), Uruguay's Tabaré Vázquez, Bolivia's Evo Morales, or Paraguayan Fernando Lugo. When asked what he and the Movement Toward Socialism understood by "socialism," Morales replied:

> To live in community and equality. . . . It is an economic model based on solidarity, reciprocity, community, and consensus. Because, for us, democracy is a consensus. In the community there is consensus, in the trade union there are majorities and minorities. . . . And beyond that, [it means] respecting Mother Earth, the Pacha Mama. (Dieterich 2006)

The notion of democracy as a consensus comes out of the popular idiom of the indigenous communities of Bolivia and has its deepest expression in the rebellion in Chiapas, as we shall see. In Uruguay, the Frente Amplio has governed with an emphasis on documenting the human rights abuses of the 1970s dictatorship and on strengthening worker participation in wage negotiations (Long 2005); they have moved on to a "mini-agrarian reform" and an ambitious reform of the health care system, and are being sustained and pushed further by a deep culture of protest (Fernando Lopez-Alves, personal communication, July 25, 2007). Lula's campaigns for the presidency of Brazil stressed social programs and relief for the landless. In all three cases, socialism was translated into concerns close to those of the populations who brought the left to power. Daniel Ortega's 2006 campaign in Nicaragua did not refer to socialism, instead emphasizing peace and reconciliation, choosing pink as the symbolic color of his candidacy, and adapting John Lennon's "Give Peace a Chance" as his anthem (*New York Times*, November 7, 2006). Known as "the bishop of the poor" and advocating land reform and other measures to combat endemic poverty in Paraguay, ex-clergyman Lugo described himself as neither left- nor right-wing but "in the middle" and vowed on election night, "We'll make democracy together!" (*The Guardian Weekly*, April 25, 2008).

Nationalism has persisted as a revolutionary current as well, again inflected away from any formal, ideological focus and rooted more in popular idioms. In the era of globalization, its content has shifted somewhat from confrontation with outside powers such as the United States (except for Venezuela and Cuba, the latter resolutely part of the older political cultures of opposition) to the newer targets of the transnational corporations and global financial institutions. Lula proclaimed, "The victory is Brazil's," when he was elected to a second term in October 2006; during the campaign he told the International Monetary Fund to "keep its nose out of Brazil's affairs" (paraphrased in the *New York Times*, October 30, 2006).

This has been evidenced most spectacularly in Bolivia, where it has been conjoined with the rise and acceptance of indigenous demands expressed in a new political idiom that has not had a national-level voice in the past. The Bechtel Corporation was notably forced to withdraw its bid to privatize water in Cochabamba in 2000. Starting in 2003, a movement to reclaim Bolivia's extensive natural gas holdings began to press for control against the Spanish, British, Argentine, and Brazilian corporations that operated the gas fields. On May 1, 2006, Morales declared "The looting by the foreign companies has ended" (Zuazo 2006), passing a decree requiring them to deliver their production to the Bolivian state and to renegotiate their contracts to pay 82 percent of their profits to Bolivia (*Latinamerica Press*, May 17, 2006). Felipe Quispe, an Aymara indigenous leader who is critical of all politicians, including Morales, puts it this way: "The foreigners can stay as long as we get 90 percent of the power. If not, there will be war. . . . We will rewrite history with our own blood. There will be a new sun, and even the rocks and the trees will be happy" (Parenti 2005, 18). In this there are echoes of previous indigenous movements which argued: "*Ya es otro tiempo el presente* (The present is a new time)" (Hylton and Thomson 2004, 19). Carlos Laime, a 33-year-old tailor, makes this connection: "I feel more Bolivian since an Aymara is in power. Now we can talk about majorities, and in [public] offices the people who are served are not only those wearing ties" (Manrique 2006, 8).

Bolivia's Evo Morales consciously acknowledges the influence of the continent's old and new political cultures: when speaking of new forms of democracy, he notes that Fidel Castro told him, "Don't do what I've done. Do what Chávez is doing: transformations through a constituent assembly" (Morales 2007). When asked about the legacy of Che Guevara to the people of Latin America, Morales replied:

> First of all, in the '40s, in the '50s, in the '60s—of course, when I hadn't been born yet—my first perception was that people rose up in arms to struggle against the empire. Now, I see quite the opposite, that it's the empire that's raising up arms against the peoples. What I think is that back then, that the peoples, they got organized and struggled, looking for justice, for equality. And now I think that these transformations, these structural transformations, are being forged through democracies. (Morales 2007)

But "democracy" now means something more than elections and political representation by a leadership: "This is something I've learned from Subcomandante Marcos, from his messages—that is, to govern by obeying the people" (Morales 2007). Speaking of the drawbacks of pursuing corn-grown ethanol as a biofuel, he avers:

> And we want to debate this, but we don't want to debate it just as governments or presidents. We want to debate with our peoples, with the social forces in our countries, and I would even dare to say, at the South American regional level, submit this to a referendum of the peoples of South America and let the people say yes or no . . . about what the future [of] biofuels is going to be. That would be the most democratic thing. (Morales 2007)

For Morales, "if globalization does not admit difference and pluralism, it's a selective globalization, therefore it will be almost impossible to resolve environmental issues and save humanity. . . . So we're talking about a profound change in the economic models and systems" (Morales 2007). Such a change will clearly draw on and require the embrace of new political cultures of opposition by a wide coalition of people, differently located but imbued with some common desires and dreams of deeply radical social change.

The November 2006 election of left-leaning Rafael Correa in Ecuador with support from leading indigenous organizations further illustrates the current trend in Latin America. Correa campaigned against global capital ("It is necessary to overcome all the fallacies of neoliberalism"), the US military airbase on the coast at Manta ("If they want, we won't close the base in 2009, but the United States would have to allow us to have an Ecuadoran base in Miami in return"), and prioritizing spending on social programs over debt repayment (Kozloff 2006). Correa also enjoyed the close support of Hugo Chávez and took much of the indigenous vote (40 percent of the population of 13 million) with the backing of CONAIE (the Confederation of Indigenous Nationalities of Ecuador). Charting a fairly moderate course economically and in foreign relations, Correa also moved to gain control of the military and intelligence services, which had been tightly tied to the United States, calling the latter "totally infiltrated and subjugated to the C.I.A. [Central Intelligence Agency]." In April 2008, he appointed his personal secretary Javier Ponce as defense minister; Ponce is a poet and former journalist who has been highly critical of the armed forces and the United States: "We must get past our legacy of relying too much on military relations with the United States, with President Bush showing little regard for national borders or sovereignty. . . . The risk of remaining too close to such a partner is one of ideological contagion" (*New York Times*, April 21, 2008).

One of the best pieces of evidence for the arrival of new political cultures of opposition to the furthest corners of Latin America is the election of former Roman Catholic bishop Fernando Lugo to the presidency of Paraguay in April 2008. In a society dominated by strongman rulers ever since independence—notably the rule of caudillo José Gaspar Rodríguez de Francia from 1814 to 1840, and then, after a period of 31 presidents in 22 years in the 1930s to the 1950s, the 35-year reign of corrupt patronage and highly repressive terror by Nazi admirer General Alfredo Stroessner from 1954 to 1989. This was followed by continued rule by Stroessner's Colorado Party until 2008, making it the longest governing political party still left in the world (Instituto del Tercer Mundo 2001, 432). Lugo's approach to social problems comes out of a liberation theology that taught him "how the poor live in this country. That inspires me to work on behalf of this class that is so demeaned, so abandoned, so forgotten" (*New York Times*, April 20, 2008). Three years after leaving the priesthood, believing he was powerless to help the poor, Lugo was put forward by the aptly named Patriotic Alliance for Change, a coalition of opposition parties and social movements from across the political spectrum representing "unions, Indians, and poor farmers" (*The Guardian Weekly*, April 25, 2008), and took 41 percent of the vote in a three-way race to wrest control of the country from the Colorado Party, which had run the political system and much of the economy uninterruptedly for over six decades. Time will tell if he has the means to translate this into his vision of authentic popular participation and greater national sovereignty, which means trying to alleviate endemic poverty with basic land reform while governing with Colorado Party members entrenched in most of the institutions of the state. He will also seek a better economic deal with Brazil for Paraguay's massive hydroelectricity output, and, in keeping with the new regional perspective, he has said, "The United States . . . has sustained the great dictatorships, but afterward lifted the banner of democracy," but that now Latin American governments "won't accept any type of intervention from any country, no matter how big it is" (Fox 2008; see also *New York Times*, April 21 and 22, 2008).

The Chávez phenomenon is more complex, both as a more self-identified left government than any of the other progressive elected Latin American governments to date and as more vested than the others in a single figure as leader, the paradoxical Hugo Chávez, who was first elected in 1998. Coming out of a military tradition and after having engaged in a failed coup in 1992, Chávez remade himself into a political candidate who challenged the popular legitimacy of the existing parties. In the course of the decade, Chávez came to articulate an original political discourse based on what he termed *Bolivarianism*—an appeal to the vision of Simón Bolívar for liberation from foreign powers and the development of a unity of purpose among Latin American nations, especially in the Andean region. This has also translated into calls for improving the lives of rural residents and the urban poor, integration of the indigenous and black populations into the national project, and using Venezuela's oil wealth for development and investment in human capital (Gott 2005). Venezuela presents the puzzle of a nation solidly enmeshed in global financial and economic circles which also represents a regional solidarity and counter-development that is not transnational capitalist in spirit.

Even in power, Chávez's relationship with the population was more loosely organized than the formal political parties of Brazil, Uruguay, Nicaragua, and Bolivia. His original organization, the Bolivarian Revolutionary Movement, became a political party, the Fifth Republic Movement, that participated in an alliance of left parties to bring him to power in 1998 (Gott 2005, 134–139); a new alliance of some twenty-four parties would help reelect him in 2006, after which a number of parties moved to establish the United Socialist Party of Venezuela in 2008 (Ingham 2008). In his first term, he moved away from both the established left parties and his own organization to establish a more personal link to his social base and a quest for larger executive powers and a longer term as president. The new constitution that enshrined the principles of Bolivarianism into law was passed by a nonpartisan referendum. Chávez addresses the nation in a weekly radio program in which he speaks with humor and candor in a popular idiom, with a language reminiscent of "an evangelical preacher, invoking pain and love and redemption" (Gott 2005, 137). Institutionally, the government has also reached deeply into communities in the form of social campaigns known as "missions" charged with addressing critical needs in health, education, housing, food, and jobs (Boudin, Gonzalez, and Rumbos 2006, 65–77). The depth of this new political culture was proven in the events of the April 2002 coup attempt, which, against almost all precedent in Latin American history, saw the restoration of a deposed president through popular mobilization and the loyalty of a part of the military. It was reaffirmed with the president's reelection in the 2006 election. Chávez's plans for his second term include a movement toward "Bolivarian socialism," based on "[a] new geometry of power" to be carried through by popular education to "deepen the new values and demolish the old values of individualism, capitalism, of egotism" (Wilpert 2007; see Wilpert 2006 for in-depth analysis). Despite the narrow defeat of wide-ranging constitutional reforms at the end of 2007, Chávez's project continues apace.

Despite their differences, the left governments of Brazil, Uruguay, Bolivia, Ecuador, Nicaragua, Paraguay, and Venezuela tap into a political culture that differs in some key respects from the older revolutionary tradition. Chief among these are the democratic route to power and the effort to build a more participatory political system on the parts of significant sectors of their populations. In this, the relative weight of formal ideology and popular idiom can be seen as shifting in the direction of popular demands for social justice and national sovereignty, more loosely expressed in terms of the socialist tradition. Perhaps better put, the current of socialism is being reworked in subterranean directions in the post–Cold War era, and the depth of the democratic ideal is arguably proving a more solid barrier to external and internal intervention than in the more polarized era of the Allende experiment with this form of revolution in the 1970s.

The Future May Be Now: The Zapatistas and the Global Justice Movement

The most radical developments in political cultures of opposition have occurred further from the limelight of elections on a national stage, at levels both above and below it. They differ from the Latin American left parties in not aiming to take national political power at all (cf. Holloway 2002). The Zapatista movement in Mexico offers one instance of this, and its genesis and subsequent trajectory are instructive. When student intellectuals sought to organize resistance in the indigenous south of Mexico after the government's massacre of their movement in 1968, they came to the local communities with Marxist ideas of socialism, tinged with a new left respect for nonauthoritarian organizing. After many stumbles and little success in the 1980s, the group that included future Zapatista spokesperson Subcomandante Marcos began to learn from the indigenous Mayan communities of Chiapas, rather than try to lead them from above or outside (Kampwirth 2002, 107–109; Womack 1999).

This encounter was shaped by practices and visions that had never been incorporated in the visible or official histories of revolutionary struggle in

Mexico. Drawing on their own political idioms, indigenous communities provided such core Zapatista principles as *mandar obedeciendo* ("to rule, obeying"): the view that leaders serve the community and the struggle for its issues, rather than the community existing to further the vision of the leadership. This would be embodied after 2002 in the institution of the *Juntas de Buen Gobierno* (Councils of Good Government), chosen on a rotating basis within each community to work with residents to determine their goals and projects. The assumption behind these councils was that every community member possessed the ability to lead the group, and that the community is strengthened when all are given this opportunity. The charismatic nonindigenous Subcomandante Marcos is the best-known figure among the Zapatistas by virtue of his gift for powerfully evocative political writing and speech, but he acknowledges the higher rank of the indigenous leadership of the guerrilla army: he is a *sub*comandante.

Another innovative Zapatista practice is suggested by the phrase *dar su palabra* (literally, "to have one's say"). One way this has been expressed is "allowing your true word to speak to my true word" (Martínez and García 2004, 215). This speaks to the effort to include all members of a group in the discussions that concern the group's plans. Behind this lies the respect that is accorded to each and the value attached to the views of differently situated members of a community. The goal is to make decisions that benefit from the unique insights of all present, to find solutions which have eluded them in the past. Such discussions can take much longer than formal debates followed by votes, but they endow the group's choices with a broader legitimacy. When a consensus does not emerge, the process has the merit of identifying where the points of disagreement lie.

The degree to which women have been truly empowered in the autonomous communities remains an open question, but it is worth considering whether their role in the Zapatista struggle may also portend a new face of revolution. Women have been prominent since before the movement publicly declared its existence, advocating and obtaining passage of the ten-point Women's Revolutionary Laws, which gave women the right to work and own land, to choose their partners and the number of their children, to be educated and to receive health care, and to take positions of revolutionary leadership. Women serve at the highest level of the Zapatista army and indigenous leadership; as Comandanta Ramona put it in 1994, "We [women] demand respect, true respect as Indians. We also have rights . . . and my message to all women who feel exploited, ignored, is take up arms as a Zapatista" (Collier 1994, 60, quoting *Tiempo*, February 6, 1994). Blanca Flor, a member of the group Kinal Antzetik (Women's Territory), points to the emotions driving women's participation: "Every day the women get madder. And the madder they get, the stronger they get" (quoted in Flinchum 1998, 31). This is not to obscure the fact that some scholars have treated the participation of women in the Zapatista movement more skeptically[2] (Belausteguigoitia

2000; Eber and Kovic 2003; Kalinic 2005; Speed, Castillo, and Stephen 2006; Speed 2007).

For Javier Eloriaga, a member of the National Coordinating Commission of the FZLN (the unarmed, civil society political wing of the Zapatista movement until it became inactive in the fall of 2005), "We have to do politics in a new way. You can't accept only what is possible because it will bring you into the hands of the system. This is a very difficult struggle. It is very, very difficult" (quoted in Zugman 2001, 113). Part of this involves "walking at a slower pace," acknowledging that change is a long and slow process, not secured with the mere seizure of power or electoral victories. Indeed, Zapatistas have said that they do not aspire to *take* state power in the traditional sense, but rather, to create "a free and democratic space for political struggle" (EZLN 2002, 226). To this end, they have engaged in campaigns of international solidarity against neoliberalism and in gathering together the many groups in Mexico who feel excluded from the political system. Above all, they have worked to implement their own visions of autonomy in those parts of the Lacandón forest of Chiapas where they have enough support to keep the Mexican government and military at bay, even in the face of continued violence and low-intensity warfare.

The movement, though formally armed at the level of the Zapatista Army of National Liberation, has concerned itself not with fighting but with building positive alternatives to the capitalist exploitation of Chiapas and its inhabitants. While some of the rebels initially said that their goal is "for socialism, like the Cubans have, but better" (*New York Times* January 4, 1994), their demands have been for such things as land, health care, education, autonomy for indigenous peoples, and deeper forms of democracy than elections. The rebellion thus marks very clearly the movement away from ideologies and toward idioms of resistance and opposition, tinged with visionary alternatives. The terms that have been introduced, along with others, are evidence of the depth of this shift: *dignidad y esperanza* ("dignity and hope"), *caminamos preguntando* ("we walk asking"), *nunca jamás un mundo sin nosotros* ("never again a world without us"); and *todo para todos y nada para nostros* ("everything for everyone and nothing for ourselves"). Manuel Callahan (2004, 218) believes, rightly I think, that we should see these as personal and communal conceptions rather than political slogans. As Marcos has put it: "Zapatismo is not an ideology. It is not a bought and paid for doctrine. It is an intuition" (*Zapatista* 1998).

The Zapatistas emerged in tandem with and as part of an international movement of resistance to capitalist globalization that has many parts and its own history. While its first prominent manifestation was arguably the spectacular shutting down of the meetings of the World Trade Organization (WTO) in Seattle in late 1999 (Cockburn, St. Clair, and Sekula 2001), its roots go deeper and further, ranging from actions that started in the late 1980s in South Korea, Venezuela, India, Germany, and many other countries on campaigns against Third World debt and structural adjustment programs, environmental struggles against states and corporations, new labor movements, women's actions, indigenous organizing, and antiwar demonstrations. After Seattle, they range forward to the militant protests at subsequent meetings of the WTO and the G8 nations from Genoa in 2001 to Gleneagles, Scotland, in 2006 and include the millions of people throughout the world who went to the streets on February 15, 2003, to protest the imminent US attack on Iraq (key works include Fisher and Ponniah 2003; Notes from Nowhere 2003; Mertes 2004; Solnit 2004a; Starr 2005; Yuen, Burton-Rose, and Katsiaficas 2004). And they include the considerable grassroots organizing that takes place without attention from either the media or academics, much of this being done by women and people of color.

As Kevin Danaher and Roger Burbach suggest:

> If we look closely we can see the pieces of the first global revolution being put together. Every revolution up until now has been a national revolution, aimed at seizing control of a national government. But the blatant corporate bias of global rule-making institutions such as the IMF [International Monetary Fund], World Bank and WTO have forced the grassroots democracy movement to start planning a global revolution. It is a revolution in values as well as institutions. It seeks to replace the money values of the current system with the life values of a truly democratic system. (2000, 9)

If we focus on the political cultures that animate the global justice movement, we can see some novel features, many of them parallel with the Zapatista rebellion, but coming from movements with many distinct locations around the world and occasionally gathering in places such as the World Social Forum for action or reflection.

On the subjective side of experience and emotion, it is useful to point out that love—of life, of people, of justice—often provides the vital force that impels ordinary people into extraordinary acts. Expressing hope and optimism, love provides a constructive counterpoint to those other powerful animating emotions, hatred and anger. I am not arguing here that a change has been wrought in the emotional tenor of revolutions per se, but I am suggesting that this thread may be gaining in prominence as movements come together in new ways. L. A. Kauffman, who has participated in anti-WTO protests, describes it this way:

> The central idea behind the carnival is that protests gain in power if they reflect the world we want to create. And I, for one, want to create a world that is full of color and life and creativity and art and music and dance. It's a celebration of life against the forces of greed and death. (Shepard and Kauffman 2004, 380–381)

Compassion, caring, and creativity have roles to play. To this, we may add the subjective experience of hope (is it an emotion?). In the words of David Solnit, one of the key organizers of the spectacular Seattle action of 1999 against the WTO: "Hope is key. If our organizations, analysis, visions and strategies are lanterns, then hope is the fuel that makes them burn bright and attracts people to them" (Neumann and Solnit 2004). Interestingly, the Zapatistas are sometimes referred to as "professionals of hope."

As with the Zapatistas, we can also discern a turn toward popular idioms over ideology. John Walton puts it thus: "The broader lesson is the emergence of a new global political consciousness . . . which attempts to define a coherent code of global justice embracing indigenous people, peasants, the urban poor, labor, democrats and dolphins" (Walton 2003, 225). We have seen that a concern with social justice has not been absent in the great revolutions of the twentieth century; one can readily see it in the demands for "Bread, Land, and Peace" in 1917 Russia, "Socialism with a Human Face" in 1968 Czechoslovakia, and "a preferential option for the poor" in the 1970s language of liberation theology in Central America. It has now taken the form of demands for "Hope and Dignity" in Chiapas, and "Fair Trade" and "This Is What Democracy Looks Like" in Seattle. For Patrick Reinsborough,

> When we say we want a better world, we mean it. We want a world that reflects basic life-centered values. We've got the vision and the other side doesn't. We've got biocentrism, organic food production, direct democracy, renewable energy, diversity, people's globalization, and justice. What have they got? Styrofoam? Neoliberalism? Eating disorders? Designer jeans, manic depression, and global warming? (Reinsborough 2004, 178–180)

This vision includes radically different modes of struggle for an age of globalization where the location of the enemy is the increasingly interlocked institutions of global capitalism in the form of the WTO, World Bank, transnational corporations, and First and Third World states. These modes of struggle include sit-ins, boycotts, strikes, civil disobedience, occupation of land or factories, all forms of direct action aimed at uprooting the system rather than reproducing it. In a no doubt conscious echo of the Zapatistas, direct action activist David Solnit writes, "The world cannot be changed for the better by taking power. . . . Capturing positions of state power, either through elections or insurrection, misses the point that the aim of uprooting the system is to fundamentally change the relations of power at the root of our problems" (2004b, xix).

Organizationally, new forms are being developed that depart from the past practice of revolutions. The global justice movement "has no international headquarters, no political party, no traditional leaders or politicians running for office, and no uniform ideology or ten-point platform" (Solnit

2004b, xii), or as imprisoned activist Mumia Abu-Jamal puts it, it is "a fight that has no nationality" (*This Is What Democracy Looks Like* 2000).

> This is a movement about reinventing democracy. It is not opposed to organization. It is about creating new forms of organization. It is not lacking in ideology [better put, "its political culture"]. These new forms of organization are its ideology. It is about creating and enacting horizontal networks . . . based on principles of decentralized, non-hierarchical consensus democracy. (Graeber 2004, 212, bracketed comment mine)

Mexican artist and scholar Manuel De Landa (1997) suggests we use the term *meshworks* for such self-organizing, nonhierarchical, and heterogeneous networks. It is for this reason also that one name for the whole is "the movement of movements."

Diagram 10.4 attempts to sum up this argument about the emergence of new political cultures of opposition, particularly those of the Zapatistas and the global justice movement (the elected left governments also share some of these features, except for their organizational forms, as noted on the diagram).

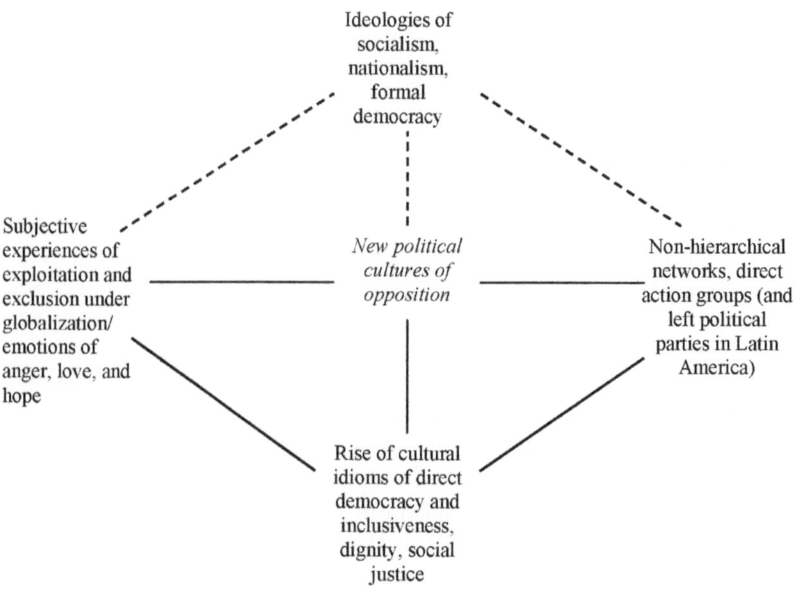

Diagram 10.4 The emergence of "new" political cultures of opposition in the twenty-first century: The Zapatistas, the Global Justice Movement, and the elected left governments of Latin America.

PROBLEMS AND PROSPECTS

Can these new political cultures produce some sort of revolution? The left has achieved state power or is on the verge of it in an important set of Latin American countries: does it have the will, internal support, and global room for maneuver to redirect resources to the poorest sectors of society? The Zapatistas have registered concrete gains on a local level: will they be able to generalize these accomplishments beyond Chiapas? The global justice movement has registered significant opposition to elite globalization projects and has mustered its forces at the successive World Social Forums. It has also made gains in many local settings around the world. Can this movement reverse the tide of neoliberal capitalism? No one can say. If millions of ordinary citizens around the world can be attracted to these movements, then maybe so (a big *if* and a modest *maybe* are to be read here).

Whether this can be done depends, in some measure, on how their new political cultures of opposition build on the past and how they read the lessons of each other's bold experiments. These cases have shown their ability to move beyond ideology in favor of the strengths of popular idioms demanding social justice; they have shown us some of the advantages of horizontal networks over vertical hierarchies. But how to fashion large-scale popular spaces for democracy and how to articulate the discourses that will bring together the broadest coalition ever seen on a global stage constitute great challenges, which are thus far unresolved.

As the Zapatistas argue, and the disappointing experience of Lula and the Workers Party in Brazil (watering down their radical program once in power) has shown, elections are not a magic solution to undoing fundamental structures of exploitation. But neither is direct democracy. Both can be subverted by new forms of domination even as they seek to avoid old ones. There are no guarantees that either can spread in conditions of crisis and scarcity. Fighting a system is not as easy as overthrowing a state (and the latter was rarely achieved in the past century in any case). Behind the institutions of global capital lie other forms of internal oppression and power: patriarchy, militarism, racism, fundamentalism, nationalism, environmental destruction, consumerism, media control, and the privileging of cultures that oppress others. None of this is going to be undone swiftly or without cost.

Meanwhile, the US response to the September 11 attacks has effected a large setback for a future of deep social change. It has militarized the course of globalization from above by a transnational elite and opened up a new and uncertain period in the global political economy (for a brilliant analysis of the options and divisions faced by proponents of globalization from above, see Engler 2008). It has also broken the growing momentum of the global justice movement by its "war on terrorism" discourse. It has created facts on the ground in a shattered Iraq that defy restitution, and it has conjured paralyzing new fears and amorphous threats in the United

States where none had previously existed. The Bush administration finally overplayed its hand, at home and abroad, as the Democratic sweep of the 2008 elections signaled. Bush's project certainly stumbled in terms of its prosecution of the war, its response to Hurricane Katrina, its wire-tapping of its own citizens, its budget priorities and massive indebtedness, and its inaction on global warming and peak oil. But can those who oppose it regain the initiative? The Democratic Party is not to be relied upon to do this work, yet the rules of the political game in the United States leave little space for other parties. The possibility for radical social change of a positive kind depends on a recovery from this enormous setback, and the election of Barack Obama may open up new avenues of social change; as Greg Grandin has put it in a piece otherwise very critical of the Obama effect: "Barack Obama is obviously the candidate best positioned to walk the United States back from the edge of irrelevance. Though no one hoping for a job in the White House would put it in such defeatist terms, the historic task of the next president will not be to win this president's Global War on Terror, but to negotiate America's reentry into a community of nations" (Grandin 2008).

What, then, lies between direct action and elections? Do we have the imagination to know? The tensions between the new left projects of taking state power through elections, and the Zapatista goal of not taking power but seeking to subvert it at the local level, are palpable. This was brought clearly into focus in the July 2006 election in Mexico, where Andrés Manuel López Obrador, the candidate of the Party of the Democratic Revolution (PRD), was narrowly defeated in the official vote count but claimed that the government had engaged in massive fraud to retain power. If the Zapatistas had not put forward sharp critiques of his revolutionary credentials, could he have won outright? And if he had, could he have shifted the bases of Mexican development to any meaningful degree in favor of the poor? What common ground might be found between these two approaches to revolutionizing Mexico? In the immediate aftermath of the elections, López Obrador took his protest into the streets, pushing beyond the bounds imposed by legal frameworks of opposition. The Zapatistas, for their part, had been calling for an alliance of all progressive forces to challenge the country's economic and political arrangements at their core. What are the prospects for these currents to converge, and what might such a convergence look like and accomplish? A strong grassroots movement of teachers, workers, students, and ordinary citizens rose up in Oaxaca in the fall of 2006, shutting down the state capital and provoking a violent response from the government. Mexico remains a very important site in the struggle to cultivate effective new political cultures of opposition, and what happens there will tell much about their potential for deep social transformation.

Other hints are provided by the actions of the world's Green parties and the movement for radical reforms in Kerala, India. The various Green parties certainly embody the elements of the new political cultures of opposition, and to some extent, operate in ways that bridge the divide between those who seek to take state power and those who seek to transform the very nature of power. Though far from power in many places (notably in the United States), and having made compromises with less radical forces where they have obtained a role in government (as in Germany), they represent fledgling embodiments of the powerful combination of social movement dynamism and party organization that are one possible future for a new political culture. They are also organically transnational in vision and organization in a way that other parties, including those on the left, are not. Meanwhile, in the Indian state of Kerala, a five decade–long synergetic relationship between a noncharismatic (in a positive sense) left coalition and strong, independent social movements in civil society has succeeded in forging relatively equitable, participatory conditions of life for more than 27 million people (Franke and Chasin 1994).

Is this combination a solution? It's hard to know (and, as Zhou Enlai is meant to have said of the outcome of the French revolution, "It is too soon to say"). The future of radical social change may well lie at the many possible intersections of deeply democratic social movements and political coalitions: the World Social Forum, the global justice movement, the Zapatistas' meshworks and sympathizers worldwide, the Kerala model, Chávez's experiment, the overthrow of the monarchy in Nepal in 2007, and their radical precursors in Czechoslovakia and France in 1968, or the Allende years, and elsewhere—are each valuable guides with multiple tools ("weapons"?) if we know how to read their lessons and make them concrete, human, and real in today's world and that of tomorrow. Honesty and love seem as indispensable as ever. When we are in search of what seems a utopian outcome, we need to cast a web wide enough to intertwine diverse possibilities: all such experiments offer much to global activists in search of workable models, and the growing ability for movements everywhere to learn from each other is also a part of the process of arriving at a better future.

In a 2003 essay, I observed that the revolutionaries of the present and future are faced with a new set of paradoxes and challenges:

- To find a language capable of uniting diverse forces and allowing their not necessarily mutually compatible desires full expression
- To find organizational forms capable of nurturing this expression and debate as well as enabling decisive action when needed, both locally and across borders
- To articulate an economic alternative to neoliberalism and capitalism that can sustain itself against the systemic weight of the past and the pervasive and hostile reach of the present global economic system
- To make all this happen, in many places and at different levels (local, national, "global") over time, working with both the deep strengths and frailties of the experiences and emotions of human liberation (Foran 2003, 282)

These tasks remain as pressing as ever. The new revolutionary movements and the political cultures they repose upon have opened them up for consideration. The categories we have used to think about revolutions may be the same—economic, political, cultural—but the content is shifting in all these domains. We need a fresh look at the current conjuncture to take us from it toward the future—unknown, yes; unknowable, granted; but in need of our careful attention.

ACKNOWLEDGMENTS

I thank my research assistant Molly Talcott for much of the material reported on the global justice movement, and Jordan Camp for tracking down the details of key references. I have learned much from the constructive comments of Jordan Camp, Fernando Lopez-Alves, and Eric Selbin on earlier versions of this chapter.

NOTES

1. I first coined the term *effective and powerful political cultures of resistance* in my 1981 master's thesis: John Foran, "Dependency and Social Change in Iran, 1501–1925." It is fully employed in Fragile Resistance (1993), further theorized in my essay, "Discourses and Social Forces: The Role of Culture and Cultural Studies in Understanding Revolutions" (1997), and most extensively discussed and illustrated in Jean-Pierre Reed and John Foran, "Political Cultures of Opposition: Exploring Idioms, Ideologies, and Revolutionary Agency in the Case of Nicaragua" (2002). In formulating it, I have drawn greatly on the work of A. Sivanandan ([1979] 1980), James Scott (1990), Farideh Farhi (1990), Stuart Hall (1978a, 1978b, 1986), Ann Swidler (1986), Raymond Williams (1960), Clifford Geertz (1973), E. P. Thompson ([1963] 1966), and Antonio Gramsci (1971), among many others.
2. Consider the assessment of Paloma, an activist in a women's group in Chiapas interviewed by Karen Kampwirth: "What I think is that the EZLN is not a feminist movement but rather a movement that is military, hierarchical, and authoritarian. Not all of them have gender consciousness but some of them do. The EZLN is not against working with women but I think that it has been a little careless about work with women. The topic of women is always treated as less important than other topics. But it does try to break with a patriarchal system" (interview in Kampwirth 2004, 114).

Part III

Fictions of Development

11 *Mama Benz and the Taste of Money*
A Critical View of a "Homespun" Rags-to-Riches Story of Post-Independence Africa

Lena Khor

The "Mama Benzes" of West Africa are often regarded by the West as striking examples of African rags-to-riches stories, of African women triumphing against the odds, and thus of Africa's capacity to self-develop. Robert Press and Betty Press, for example, consider the Mama Benzes of Lome, Togo, success stories of "personal freedom" in post-independence Africa (1999, 296). They and other Western reporters spotlight Madame Sanvee, the "queen of the Mama Benz," who started as "a spindly-legged 8-year-old hawking cigarettes and perfume on the streets of" Lome (Brooke 1987, 8; see also Mahoney 1990).

In many ways, the Presses' classification of the Mama Benzes like Madame Sanvee as "personal freedom" success stories makes sense. These women, for the most part, lack formal education; some are even illiterate, but through a remarkable combination of diligence, determination, street smarts, and business savvy, they have made a fortune and raised their standard of living from the status of "developing" to "developed." In this chapter, however, I suggest that the Mama Benzes may be neither an ideal model of development nor an authentically "African" mode of development for Africa, much less African women, as Press and Press (1999) might have us believe. Indeed, as my analysis of Karin Junger's documentary, *Mama Benz and the Taste of Money* (2002), reveals, the symbol of the Mama Benz as an icon of how post-independence Africa can become "developed" needs to be questioned.

THE "MAMA BENZES"

Wealthy businesswomen like Madame Sanvee are called Mama Benzes because of their signature mode of transportation, the Mercedes Benz car. They are identified by their penchant for these German-made luxury cars, which they drive or are driven in around Lome. As millionaires, the Mama Benzes of Lome live in "palatial mansions," send their children to expensive private schools and foreign universities, make frequent trips overseas for business and pleasure, and have apartments in Paris and Geneva to accommodate their international travels (Brooke 1987, 8; see also Godwin 2002). The power of their wealth extends their influence to the arena of national politics as well, where they command "spontaneous salutes from the police at state functions" and where they once loaned their fleet of luxury cars to Togo's long-time leader President Gnassingbe Eyadema to accommodate state visitors (Brooke 1987, 8; Godwin 2002). Due to their influence in the economic, political, social, and cultural arenas of Togolese society specifically, and West Africa generally, the Mama Benzes are often heralded as icons of female African ingenuity and indomitable spirit.

The Mama Benzes built their fortunes in the batik cloth trade in West Africa, selling wax-print fabrics that today characterize the cultural identity of traditional West African fashion. Although only a dozen Togolese women in Lome who control the batik trade in West Africa truly qualify for the title, the reputation of the Mama Benzes of Lome is such that many market women in West Africa, wealthy and not so wealthy, have come to be loosely called *Mama Benzes* (Mahoney 1990). The term thus has expanded from its initial Togolese batik cloth trader confines and come to symbolize the image of a formidable, successful West African businesswoman. In the fashion industry, however, the title still carries the power of its roots in the fabric business. The reputation of the Mama Benz title and the influence of its image in the fashion world are such that there is even a Montreal-based multicultural magazine on art, fashion, and culture that carries the name *Mama Benz*. The editor of *Mama Benz* magazine, 24-year-old Benin native and five-year resident in Montreal Edwige Dazobgo, identified the tantalizing mix of money, power, and status in the world of fabric and fashion that the term *Mama Benz* represents as the reason for her choice of the magazine's name (Friede 2002).

My interest in the Mama Benz as a symbol of economic success and "personal freedom" lies with the place of these businesswomen in the African batik fabric industry at the local and global levels. Hence, I use the term *Mama Benz* here to refer to an exceptionally wealthy, Mercedes-driving woman engaged in the batik cloth trade in West Africa. In this chapter, I employ Karin Junger's film, *Mama Benz and the Taste of Money*, to reexamine the figure of the Mama Benz in post-independence Africa. By tracing the surprising foreign and colonial past of the Mama Benzes, the present monopoly of the Mama Benzes in a hierarchically structured local batik cloth market, and the current struggles for control among three players in the West African batik fabric industry—the foreign supplier, the Mama Benz wholesaler, and the market woman cloth seller—I seek to highlight the complex relationships among women, culture, and development in the West African batik cloth market that complicate any declaration of the Mama Benz as an icon of "personal freedom" and economic development.

MAMA BENZ AND THE TASTE OF MONEY

Dutch filmmaker Karin Junger's documentary, *Mama Benz and the Taste of Money*, was produced for Netherlands-based RNTV and first screened in the United States at the 2002 Margaret Mead Film Festival. Set in Burkina Faso and Holland, the 52-minute film documents how the opening of a new wholesale store by Dutch textile company, Vlisco, affects the women cloth vendors in the central market of the capital of Burkina Faso, Ouagadougou. In the film, Junger reveals the darker sides of the Mama Benz model of development by capturing the complex relationship (historical and ongoing) among three parties in Ouagadougou's main batik fabric market: (1) West African women cloth vendors; (2) Mama Benzes; and (3) Vlisco, the Dutch textile company that monopolizes the high-end batik industry of Africa.

The Vlisco representatives in the film include Henk Bremer, a young, white, managing director; Kamidigha, a young, black, general manager of the new Burkina Faso store; and Fabrice, a young, white, Vlisco representative responsible for researching the cloth market in Burkina Faso and establishing contact with the cloth vendors. In keeping with the method of Junger's film, I address all individuals by their first names. Henk, stationed in Vlisco headquarters in the southern Dutch town of Helmond, is Kami's immediate supervisor. He flies in to Ouagadougou for the first meeting between Vlisco and the cloth vendors, for the official opening of the store, and for interim on-site progress reports from Kami.

The women cloth vendors are represented primarily by Alice Gouba, a young, black African woman who sells cloth in a booth in the central market of Ouagadougou, and Pauline Ilboudo, an older, black African woman who runs a large cloth shop in the same market. Junger introduces Pauline as a "Mama Benz" and Alice as a "Young Mama Benz." Pauline's position in the marketplace is such that she has the status of a Mama Benz whereas Alice, who envisions a future when she will run her own cloth store instead of her current stall and commute in a luxury car instead of on her present motorcycle, is an aspiring Mama Benz.

Mama Benz and the Taste of Money represents, in thoughtful and nuanced ways, the challenges these different groups of women (women cloth vendors like Alice and Mama Benzes like Pauline) and men (Vlisco representatives like Kami, Henk, and Fabrice) face in the batik market of Burkina Faso. They all wrestle with the possibilities and problems presented to them by a globalizing economic market that overtly boasts no limits of personal and economic development opportunities, yet covertly reinforces economic, social, and cultural power structures that restrict them from easily realizing these opportunities. Most significantly, the film uncovers the power dynamics between the women cloth vendors in the market and the Mama Benzes, thereby revealing the complexities of development even at a local level.

At the same time, however, the film does not reduce these enterprising women into mere victims, or these corporate men into simple vultures, of global capitalism. Rather, it underscores how the women, despite their often disadvantaged position in a global and even local economic market, leverage whatever power they have as buyers and sellers (economic power); mothers, wives, sisters, and friends (social influence); and West African women (cultural authority) to negotiate the challenges posed by such local and global power systems as they strive to fulfill their own personal and economic goals. The film also highlights how the Vlisco men, in spite of their, typically, advantageous position in a global economic market, find themselves relying on the local women (less affluent cloth vendors and more established Mama Benzes alike) as a source of indigenous knowledge, cultural influence, and social networks to develop their private and corporate ambitions.

Mama Benz and the Taste of Money, thus, presents a near perfect specimen of why any discussion of "development," especially top-down development plans for the global south, must take into account the three-pronged paradigm of women, culture, and development (WCD) first articulated by Kum-Kum Bhavnani, John Foran, and Priya A. Kurian (2003a). Drawing from feminist studies, cultural studies, and Third World/development studies, these scholars assert the importance of locating the agency of women, and of attending to the context of culture, when proposing projects for development in the Third World. I have chosen to analyze Junger's film not only because it serves as a timely reminder of Bhavnani, Foran, and Kurian's WCD premise but also because it forces us to question each aspect of this paradigm. By analyzing the historical and ongoing moments of vulnerability and power experienced by these different groups (the West African women cloth vendors, the Mama Benzes, and the Vlisco men) throughout the film, I show that the Mama Benz model of development is not the homegrown rags-to-riches success story that many Westerners would like to believe. In so doing, I seek to suggest that before we become too enamored with an idealized notion that some combination of women, culture, and development is the best practice for "globalization-from-below," we should reexamine, not just the constructed concept of "development," as Bhavnani, Foran, and Kurian argue, but also the construed notions of "women" and "culture." Doing so may reveal that there may be as many "fictions" about "women" and "culture," as there are for "development."

REVISIONING "DEVELOPMENT:" VLISCO'S COLONIAL PAST

Mama Benz and the Taste of Money's central premise—that Vlisco shapes West Africa and its women in its development of culture and its culture of development, historically and contemporarily—is represented in the way Junger interweaves the historical narrative of Vlisco in West Africa with the contemporary event of Vlisco's new store in Burkina Faso. Although ostensibly about the opening of Vlisco's new store, the film includes historical footage that depicts the history of Vlisco's presence in West Africa as being deeply rooted in the enterprise of Dutch colonialism. By doing so, as I explain in a moment, Junger reveals the double-edged sword of colonialism in the past and neocolonialism in the present; a sword that even as it carves development opportunities for West African women to improve their economic, social, and cultural position also exposes them to an increased vulnerability of economic dependence, social alienation, and cultural indoctrination.

Vlisco was founded in 1846 when a son of the famous Dutch merchant family, the van Vlissingens, appropriated the Indonesian wax printing technique, industrialized it, and sold the Dutch wax batik cloth in the then Dutch colony of Indonesia (Steinglass 2000). By the late 1800s, Dutch manufacturers dominated the majority of the Indonesian batik market. Since Dutch freighters stopped at various African ports between Holland and Indonesia, Vlisco began to sell their cloth in Africa as well. Vlisco started to concentrate on West Africa as a market in the beginning of the twentieth century when their previous market, the former Dutch colony of Indonesia, sought to protect its own batik industry. By the 1960s, Vlisco had acquired most of its competitors and become "the exclusive supplier" for West Africa (Steinglass 2000). Thus, the appropriation and privatization of Indonesian culture (the Indonesian wax printing technique) came to be a kind of indoctrination of, and an injection of foreign influence into, African culture. As Vlisco insinuated itself into West Africa, it made its batik the most desired, even the signature, fabric of the region.

Interestingly, this cultural indoctrination not only targeted but also used the women of the region. Besides clearly depicting Vlisco as a colonizing cultural force in West Africa, the historical segments in Junger's film also elucidate Vlisco's calculated decision to engage the local women in their commercial enterprise. As members of the local community, the West African women were poised to create a loyal market for Vlisco cloth. Following the tradition of female traders in West Africa, these women were better positioned to sell Vlisco cloth in the local marketplaces than were the Vlisco men (Coquery-Vidrovitch 1997, 30). Therefore, by initially giving the women Vlisco cloth to trade, the company eventually won a local demand and a local sales team. Vlisco's marketing strategy paved the way for the rise of the Mama Benzes, who later made their fortunes selling the Dutch company's batik cloth. In this way, then, Vlisco slowly but surely penetrated the female-dominated West African market of batik buyers and sellers, securing for itself a loyal customer base and an efficient network of distributors and advertisers. At best, this situation brought improved economic, social, and cultural conditions for the market women, especially those who eventually became Mama Benzes. At worst, this development meant that the gendered cultural indoctrination continued, not just from without but also from within. The West African women were now the very agents of Vlisco's cultural indoctrination.

Although Vlisco's business pursuits may have alleviated the conditions of the market women economically, as evidenced by the Mama Benzes, the presence of the Vlisco men did not always improve the circumstances of all West African women's lives in general. Junger depicts how the relationships between Vlisco men and West African women often went beyond business transactions into intimate relationships. However, these personal attachments usually lasted only for the time the men were stationed in West Africa. When their posting was over, the Vlisco men typically returned to Holland, leaving their West African wives and/or lovers behind in extremely vulnerable social positions. These women and their mixed-race offspring commonly experienced social alienation, and their situations altered local society and affected local culture in new ways. The presence of Vlisco, then, not only influenced West African culture in terms of fabric and fashion, but also West African society in terms of genetics and genealogy. Here too, as with the cultural indoctrination previously discussed , it was the local women who were most affected by these foreign influences.

Thus, by invoking the history of Vlisco in West Africa as a strand of Dutch colonialism, Junger highlights how the company's influence on the region has primarily consisted of manipulating West African women and reconstructing West African culture, in the name of economic development. She shows that although the presence of Vlisco may have improved the economic, social, and cultural position of some West African women because the company opened more business opportunities for the women, it also exposed them to new positions of vulnerability in these very economic, social, and cultural arenas. For some women, their income became dependent on the supply of fabric by Vlisco. For others, their social standing and that of their children, fathered by Vlisco men, relied on the continued presence and favor of these company men. In general, these women's senses of their local and regional cultural identity, not to mention their personal socioeconomic standing, became tied to a foreign fabric they neither produced nor designed.

By revealing the troubled history of Vlisco in West Africa, and by implication the roots of the Mama Benzes in the region, Junger not only exposes the less than "African" underpinnings of the Mama Benzes successes but also forces us to question the value of purely economic progress fostered by a foreign company like Vlisco, and to consider instead a fuller picture of "development." For instance, even though Vlisco brought economic growth and personal advancement for the Mama Benzes, was the opportunity cost for this "development"—cultural indoctrination, foreign dependence, social alienation—worthwhile? For Junger, the answer appears to be "no." Although Vlisco raised the socioeconomic status of the Mama Benzes from "developing" to "developed," the company's presence also changed, not always for the better, the women and culture in West Africa.

REVISITING "CULTURE:" VLISCO'S NEOCOLONIAL PRESENT

Besides the historical colonization of women and culture, *Mama Benz and the Taste of Money* also highlights Vlisco's ongoing colonization—a contemporary neocolonization—of West African women and culture in terms of fashion and lifestyle. The film precisely captures how this female-focused form of cultural colonization works. In her opening scenes of Vlisco in its Holland office, Junger depicts a team of Vlisco men evaluating the advertising campaign for the opening of their Burkina Faso store. The advertising slides show young, beautiful, wealthy African women models, including one emerging from a stretch limousine with a cell phone in one hand in "real Vlisco dress" (Junger 2002). As the images flash across the office projection screen, Vlisco Managing Director Henk Bremer notes, "the pattern of the fabric underlines the air of wealth and success and the American Dream come true" (Junger 2002). The advertisements, Henk explains, are meant to imply that "people who wear Vlisco get more respect from their social peers. They are more beautiful, feel stronger, are more self-possessed and convincing" (Junger 2002). Clearly, Vlisco's advertisement strategy is intended to foster a connection between Vlisco—the fabric and the name—and all that is fashionable, and more significantly, all that is desirable and desired. If one wears the Vlisco label, one lives "the good life" and vice versa.

In this advertising process of creating a brand name and market for Vlisco, however, the company constructs and propagates a particular image of women, especially African women, and of a certain type of lifestyle. According to Vlisco's advertisements, the successful African woman is wealthy (symbolized by the stretch limousine), modern or technologically savvy (represented by the cell phone), thin (all the models are waiflike), and basking in leisure and luxury (demonstrated by the models' relaxed poses and their dresses and heels that would make any work, much less movement, difficult). This image of a successful African woman and a leisurely lifestyle, of course, contradicts the often poverty-ridden, work-infused, and technologically limited realities of the vast majority of West African women's lived experiences. Moreover, thinness has never been considered a desirable quality for an African woman, not in the eyes of African men or women. Nevertheless, this image of womanhood and of lifestyle is what Vlisco circulates as that which African women should desire. This figure of wealth and modernity is what African women should aspire to. This vision of leisure and luxury is what Vlisco dictates African women should aim for. Most importantly, realizing these images of womanhood and lifestyle are what Vlisco determines is the goal of "development." This is "the American Dream come true" (Junger 2002). Vlisco's advertising plan, hence, constructs, for West Africa, the meaning of "woman" (in terms of the desirable qualities in a woman), "culture" (in terms of the desired lifestyle), and "development" (in terms of the definitive aims of development). The company's advertisement strategy is, consequently, also an ideology, a form of cultural indoctrination tantamount to mental colonization, albeit one practiced by all advertising campaigns.

Despite these apparent contradictions between Vlisco's image and the reality of West African women and lifestyle, Vlisco's marketing methods are highly successful in dictating fashion and in determining what is desirable and desired, not just in the region, but across the African continent. In terms of fashion, *New African* writer Tom Mbakwe states that the Vlisco name holds "hundreds of millions of Africans (all the way from Senegal right down to Angola) in thrall" (2002, 8). He adds that Vlisco is known as "the Yves Saint Laurent of Ghana" and their "Guaranteed Dutch Wax" label is "to West and Central Africans (particularly the women) what the Bible is to Christians" (Mbakwe 2002, 8). The demand for "Guaranteed Dutch Wax" batik cloth is such that the market abounds with cheaper local imitations, mostly made in enterprising Nigeria. The speed with which these imitations flood the market, often within eight days of a new design entering the market, speaks to the popularity of Vlisco's batik fabric (Steinglass 2000).

The efficiency, if not the quality, of these imitations also testifies to the entrepreneurial acumen of West Africans in leveraging Vlisco's prestige and popularity for their own profit. This move might perhaps be read as a kind of counter-colonization: if Vlisco colonized the women and culture of West Africa for its profit margins, these West African entrepreneurs now capitalize on Vlisco's brand name and image for their own gain. They trade their cheap imitations on the very prestige and popularity that Vlisco's advertising strategies have built for batik fabrics in West African women and culture. Hence, these imitators, or "pirates," as our increasingly privatized and propertized culture insists on calling (and thus criminalizing them), turn the tables on Vlisco's colonization of and monopoly over West Africa's culture and textile market (Hardt and Negri 2004; Lessig 2004). They leech, in fact, upon the cultural cachet Vlisco has developed for batik cloth and hijack the possible consumer pool for Vlisco's products.

Although these "pirates" may be in the wrong when they cheat customers by selling them fake Vlisco cloth at real Vlisco prices, they are entirely right (business wise, if not in morals or law) in capitalizing on Vlisco's brand name and image. The prestige and popularity of the Vlisco brand is such that over the years it has come to represent the "traditional" fabric and "cultural" costume for West Africa. Mbakwe (2002), for example, points out that Vlisco's dominance in the textile industry all but pushed aside traditionally woven textiles like Kente cloth to the sidelines. And Yvette Turlings (2002) observes that Vlisco prints have become the "Ghanaian national costume." In fact, Vlisco's influence on West African fashion is such that when one thinks of traditional West African attire, one pictures colorful batik print dresses, gowns, and headscarves with bold "African" designs (Wentholt 2000). Such is the degree to which Vlisco's textiles (and all the ideas and images associated with it) have permeated, if not reconstructed, West African culture.

Yet as Wyger Wentholt (2000) reminds us, "the textiles with the vivid colors and African designs are neither traditional nor African" but Dutch. What is presented and considered as traditional to West African culture turns out to be a product of Dutch design. Vlisco's designs cannot be considered exactly "African" since all their designers are Dutch men. Instead, they are what Vlisco's Head of Design, Frans van Rood, calls "a European imagination of African tastes" (Wentholt 2000). Although Vlisco is happy to employ Africans to work in its many production plants in the African continent, the company keeps the design work an exclusively male European affair. This entirely Dutch and male control over the creation of a product for African and female consumption could be seen as a classic example of neocolonialism (a twentieth-century form of colonialism): we can easily discern the dominance of a masculine European and corporate power over a feminized African and community culture. Yet, to arrive at this preliminary conclusion and go no further would be to miss the subtle and complex workings of this form of neocolonialism.

If, in the traditional colonialism of the nineteenth century, powerful European states extracted the people and materials of Asian, African, and Latin American countries to supply the growing consumption of their home countries, then in neocolonialism, dominant global north corporations exploit the resources of global south countries to develop their businesses. What is particularly pernicious about neocolonialism, especially the form of cultural neocolonization practiced by Vlisco, is that it is often supported, especially by the elite, from within the global south itself. Years of indoctrination that foreign colonizers were somehow superior to the local people seems to have engendered, if not an inferiority complex, then at least a "foreign-equals-superior" framework in the postcolonial imagination. It turns out that this notion that "foreign," more precisely "Western," is somehow better than "indigenous" or "African," is what drives Vlisco's design policies. Indeed, Van Rood identifies Africa's desire for the "foreign" as Vlisco's rationale for its Dutch-designers-only hiring practices. He explains, "Most Africans appreciate innovations that come from abroad, not those that come from within. As long as those foreign influences are somehow recognizable, and as long as they fit within the realm of social ideas and traditions, the influences are accepted" (Wentholt 2000). According to Vlisco, then, it simply maintains its Dutch-designers-only policy to satisfy Africa's demand for foreign, and by implication superior, products.

Although Van Rood's comments may seem culturally offensive, if not absurd, *Mama Benz and the Taste of Money* demonstrates that privileging the foreign is prevalent among the West African female ruling elite. Even as the film highlights how Vlisco's reputation is in large part self-fashioned, it alludes to the complicity of the ruling elite in forging Vlisco's reputation. At the opening of the Vlisco store in the film, for example, the First Lady of

Burkina Faso expresses her preference for Dutch cloth. She states, "I go for Dutch Wax prints" (Junger 2002). The film also names wives of political ministers and businessmen as Vlisco's most frequent customers. As such, Junger marks how the elite women serve to propagate Vlisco's control over West African fashion and, thereby, to perpetuate the company's influence on West African women and culture. It turns out that the very representatives associated with leadership in West Africa are privileging the foreign, the European, and the colonial as superior to the local, the African, and the indigenous. In its advertising, marketing, and designing strategies, then, Vlisco continues a contemporary neocolonization of West African women and culture, not without a little help from the elite women of West Africa.

Still, things may not be as bleak as they seem under what sounds like a most sinister, because most ingrained, form of cultural neocolonization. Although West Africa desires this "foreign" influence, it demands that the "foreign" remains in keeping with its "traditional" social and cultural norms. To ensure that the designers understand the "social ideas and traditions," Vlisco sends its designers to Africa for market research and cultural immersion every two or three years (Wentholt 2000). The company also depends on its important buyers in the markets, wealthy African women cloth traders, to let them know which patterns are popular and which are culturally inappropriate (Steinglass 2000). Most significantly, although the designs may not be entirely "African," the names for the cloths are. Each design is given a number by Vlisco, but it is the African market women who come up with nicknames for the designs (Turlings 2002). Oftentimes it is the symbolic name that creates the market for the material (Turlings 2002). One particular design, called "*Mon mari est capable*" (My husband is capable), was so popular that many of the market women made enough money to divorce their less-than-capable husbands (Turlings 2002). This inclusion of West African women in the creation, if not the design, process reveals that Vlisco's success, in fact, depends on the input of these women. The company relies on them for their indigenous knowledge of "social ideas and traditions," their social networks of friends and family members as potential customers and advertisers, and their imagination of culturally resonant names for the different prints. Might this then suggest that Vlisco's neocolonization of women and culture in West Africa may not be as totalizing (all Dutch-determined) as it first appears?

While I hesitate to say that the West African women have a lot of control over Vlisco's form of neocolonization, it is clear that Vlisco cannot assert its power over the women and culture of West Africa on its own. What Junger's film does quite well, as I describe in the next section, is highlight the interdependence between Vlisco and these women in constructing "culture." Each counts on the other's strengths and weaknesses to create the lived experiences of women in West Africa. This interdependent relationship does not make Vlisco any less of a neocolonizer of West African women or culture, nor does it make the West African market women any more in control of their culture. But it does call attention to the different historical and contemporary factors, and local and global actors, which generate and regenerate what we often lump under the rubric of "culture."

Mama Benz and the Taste of Money, thus, deconstructs the idea of "culture," especially the conventions of equating "culture" with an essentialized notion of the indigenous and the traditional. As the colonial history behind the Mama Benzes shows, these purportedly "indigenous" icons of "African" success stories actually carry a mixed past of foreign domination and native entrepreneurship. And as the background of Vlisco's Dutch designers to West Africa's "traditional" dress or costume reveals, "tradition" may really be a combination of foreign influence and native flavor. Hence, by including the archival footage of Vlisco in West Africa as part of Dutch colonialism, and highlighting how Vlisco, with the help of the West African women, continue to dominate the region's culture, Junger challenges us to discard any reductive idea of "culture." She reminds us that "culture" is neither a natural (always already present) nor a static (never changing) category. "Culture" (and all the other practices that we group under this heading) are produced and reproduced by a multiplicity of actors (indigenous and foreign, local and global) and through a multitude of factors (economic and political, social and cultural, historical and contemporary).

REFIGURING "WOMEN:" WEST AFRICAN MARKET WOMEN AS A "COMMUNITY"

Despite the way I emphasize the heavy hand of Vlisco on the shape of West African women, culture, and development in Junger's film and beyond, it is not my intention to create the impression that West African women were, and are, mere pawns in the hands of Vlisco's men. Nor is it my intention to fashion West African "culture" as infinitely pliable and wholly dominated, then and now, by Vlisco's design. Indeed, Junger is careful in her film not to diminish the complexities of the market women as individuals or as a community and of the culture in its plurality of forms. The women in Junger's film are never portrayed without intelligence or without some recognition, if not some action, of their agency. They are shown as enterprising, diligent, determined, and savvy businesswomen. They are also depicted working in cooperation and, if one is feeling particularly idealistic, in solidarity and in harmony.

To dismiss the women as happily compliant to or unsuspectingly ignorant of Vlisco's manipulations, or to construe them as innocent of desire for personal gain is to be overly simplistic, and Junger does none of this in her film. Instead, she illuminates, in intelligent and nuanced ways, the various methods that the different market women use to interpret, react to, and manage Vlisco's presence in their marketplace. In so doing, Junger invites us to recognize the agency of "women" in the face of the dominant forces of global capitalism like Vlisco. Indeed, she also forces us to grapple with the heterogeneity of this category of "women" and the power dynamics within this category in the batik market of Burkina Faso's capital city.

The two market women that Junger focuses on are Madam Pauline Ilboudo, a Mama Benz, and Alice Gouba, an aspiring Mama Benz. In order to illustrate how Junger reveals the different subsets and various power structures within this "community" of market women, I analyze Pauline's and Alice's interactions with Kami and Henk, the Vlisco representatives who have been charged with setting up the new wholesale store. At the same time, I analyze their dealings with the other women cloth sellers in the market. How these women each deal with Vlisco's male representatives and the other female cloth sellers, and how they are each dealt with by these other actors will undoubtedly dismiss any further simplistic use of "women" as a homogenous category, or any romanticized notion of "women" as being somehow less ruthless, more fair-minded, and thus the championed alternative to a male-dominated global capitalist system. In her critiques of treating women as a uniform class, Junger echoes not just the standard charge of essentialism or biological determinism raised by social-constructivist theories of feminism since Simone de Beauvoir observed, "One is not born, but rather becomes, a woman" (Beauvoir 1949, 267). Rather, Junger also responds to the classic critique of homogenization, a concern that nonwhite feminists like Audre Lorde have raised, for instance with Mary Daly's controversial book *Gyn/Ecology* (1978) whereby Lorde finds Daly to be overlooking the experiences of Black women (African and African-American; Lorde 1984). Junger further contests the tendency most graphically identified by Shulamith Firestone in *The Dialectic of Sex* (1970), a tendency still prevalent in most patriarchal societies, of heralding "women" as a gentler and kinder alternative to a male-dominated global system of capitalism.

Let us begin with Pauline and her interactions with other market women. Junger's introduction of Madam Pauline Ilboudo, the Mama Benz, into the film speaks to her sensitive appraisal of the complexities and the culture within the community of market women. The presence of Pauline underscores the unspoken but understood hierarchy in the cloth market. As a Mama Benz, she is at the top of the hierarchy that less wealthy market women, like Alice Gouba, the young Mama Benz, are trying to climb (Junger 2002). As the owner of a large and prosperous establishment, Pauline has economic, political, and social presence. Pauline knows this, as do the other market women. We can see this in the way Pauline dismisses the other market women lower down the hierarchy like Alice, as nonentities, as irrelevant as fruit-sellers, in the cloth business. By highlighting Pauline's position as top-dog in a competitive female-dominated marketplace, Junger calls attention to the power dynamics and differentials among this so-called community of women. As Pauline's interactions with other market women show, Pauline and Alice may both be business owners and members of the town society, but they each hold and exercise very different types of authority and degrees of agency. Moreover, Pauline is as intent upon maintaining her dominance, as Alice is upon improving her economic and social position. And both of them are willing to do so at the expense of other women. Thus, Junger cautions us that we overlook the heterogeneity of the market women (Pauline and Alice are almost polar opposites) when we refer to "women" as a homogenous category. And we stereotype "women," effeminate them even, when we herald them as the kinder alternative to a male-dominated global system of capitalism.

Pauline's dealings with the Vlisco men are equally revealing. In the film, Pauline's dominant presence is undermined when Vlisco neglects to invite her to their first meeting with the market's cloth sellers. The company does, however, invite other market women, including Alice. Understandably, Pauline complains to Junger that the Vlisco men have shown disrespect by not inviting her to their first sales meeting. From Pauline's complaints, one comes to understand that she is disgruntled not only by the loss of social respect (the Vlisco men have snubbed her on her very own home turf) but also by the potential loss of economic power. With the Vlisco store right in town and the company apparently willing to deal directly with even smaller business ventures like Alice's, market women with less capital and smaller cash flows would no longer have to depend on establishments like Pauline's to trade them a few pieces of Vlisco cloth to sell. Ordinarily, market women like Alice were Pauline's clients because they lacked the resources to buy the cloth in larger quantities or from across the border. Pauline therefore perceives Vlisco as a threat to both her social position and her economic position in the marketplace.

Although Pauline's initial reaction is indignation, she eventually copes with Vlisco's intrusion on her turf by sending her niece as mediator. Aware of her vulnerable position, Pauline swallows her pride and makes the first move towards a relationship with Vlisco. The moment in which her niece negotiates with Vlisco on Pauline's behalf is arguably Pauline's greatest moment of vulnerability. She has humbled herself, if not literally, at least figuratively, and the ball is in Vlisco's court. However, the manner in which Pauline's niece persuades Kami and Hank to telephone Pauline and invite her to their store is worth considering. The niece emphasizes the size of Pauline's purse and the strength of Pauline's clout in the marketplace to the two Vlisco men who finally mockingly comply. What, in effect, does Pauline's act of self-imposed vulnerability achieve? This act of mediation that shifts the balance of power to Vlisco, a condition that I am calling a moment of vulnerability, is an attempt to establish a relationship with Vlisco as, if not exactly a contending force, at least an influential client. As such, even at her most vulnerable (Pauline, Kami, and Henk are each aware that it is in Pauline's best business interest to be able to buy Vlisco's cloth from the new store), Pauline asserts herself as a powerful client, one with wealth and influence.

But what about Alice and her interactions with Vlisco and the other market women? In the figure of Alice Gouba, the aspiring Mama Benz who sells cloth from a booth in the central market of Burkina Faso, Junger offers us a quite different response to Vlisco's entry into the cloth market of Burkina Faso. While Pauline's initial reaction is to perceive Vlisco as a threat and to respond by leveraging her economic and social power as best she can, Alice's initial response is to see Vlisco as an opportunity. But she does so in a way that almost jeopardizes her economic and social position, as well as that of other market women like herself.

Ambitious Alice decides to break away from the collective silence of the market women and answer all of Vlisco's inquiries about the workings of the batik business in Burkina Faso. She agrees to divulge the market women's closely kept trade secrets to Vlisco in exchange for buying on credit and getting first picks on new designs. Alice tells Junger that she did not see the harm in furnishing Vlisco with such information. Whether Alice was actually acting out of calculated self-interest or simply being young and naive when she divulged these trade secrets is open to debate. What is certain, however, is that she acted, individually, against the grain of the "community," in order to seize what she saw as an opportunity to improve her economic position and achieve her dream of becoming a Mama Benz. While I would not go so far as to insist that Alice behaves ruthlessly, she is at least shrewdly taking advantage of opportunities that arise for the sake of her individual development. She is not as concerned with the other market women as she is about herself. Alice's self-serving actions, like Pauline's self-interested ones, should again lay to rest stereotyped and romanticized ideas of women as always privileging their community at the expense of their individual selves.

Indeed, Alice's decision to cooperate with Vlisco really puts the whole "community" of market women at risk. The danger of Alice's self-serving disclosure soon comes to light in the market women's second business meeting with Vlisco where Kami, the general manager of the Vlisco store, dictates the "draconian" terms of sale that Vlisco has to offer. The terms include a nonnegotiable price set by Vlisco, a minimum purchase of at least 150 pieces of cloth (three bales), and cash-only transactions. One of the women sitting close to Alice remarks, "It's obvious they've been getting information. They know our prices. They know how we work and what our margins are. They know everything about us. Somebody has told them everything" (Junger 2002). Armed with the information (provided by Alice) of strengths and limitations of the market women, Vlisco is able to design business conditions that pin the market women into a corner. Alice's indiscretion, thus, exposes the market women to Vlisco's manipulations, leaving them (and Alice) in a position of vulnerability. The strength this group of women had as a community of traders, with agreements about prices and margins to secure their business as a whole in the marketplace, falls apart because of Alice. In effect, then, Alice's attempt to develop herself comes at the expense of the development of the group of market women as a whole. What might have been a way to pit strength in numbers and insider knowledge (the very factors the market women have in their favor) against the corporate clout of Vlisco is now lost.

Ironically, Alice's disclosure does not even prove very helpful for Alice. Indeed, it appears to hurt her present economic and social position. Her indiscretion endangers herself since she is vulnerable to estrangement from the market women community should they discover her role as informant. The importance of that community to Alice's development—economic and otherwise—is highlighted when Alice informs Junger that she cannot independently afford to purchase Vlisco cloth according to Vlisco terms. As such, although Vlisco allows Alice to buy on credit, she eventually joins with the market women who pool their cash together in subgroups of three or four to meet Vlisco's terms of sale. So, when Alice tells Junger that she is afraid of the "anger" of the market women if they discover her role as Vlisco's informant, one understands that the consequences of community "anger" go beyond mere emotion. Indeed, they are economic since the repercussions critically affect Alice's ability to make a living.

Here, Junger's film shows how market women like Alice may achieve "development" more easily and, probably more fully, collectively, rather than individually. Although their resources are limited individually, when they pool these resources together, they can achieve much more. For start-ups like Alice, the path to development may not be an individual one that one walks alone, but a communal one along which one travels with others. Junger seems to suggest, that although one may have individual ambitions, they are sometimes best achieved with the help of (or at least not at the expense, of) one's social networks. Fulfilling ambitions individually may seem to be the way to economic prosperity but it may also be the road to social alienation. Ultimately, is that the kind of "development" that we truly desire?

It is clear from the film that the kind of development Junger favors is not just economic but also social and cultural. And she believes the means to such holistic development involves community and culture. The Vlisco representative, Kami, however, ascribes to the individual and economic mode of development. He understands neither the importance of the market women's community nor their ways of working and living. He insists that Alice only encumbers her business by teaming up with other market women because in sharing the advantage of the popular prints with other sellers, she blunts her competitive edge. Kami explains his development plan to Junger in these terms, "You must develop on your own." For Kami, despite his earlier rhetoric of "family"—he calls the market women "mothers," "aunts," and "sisters" who are part of the Vlisco family in their first business meeting—the business world functions according to "natural selection," and it is the individual with the most competitive advantages who will succeed (Junger 2002).

This scene clearly highlights problems of applying generic theories and practices of development to all cultures and all people. Western-dominant notions of development often privilege the individual as a lone agent, rather than seeing individuals as members of families and communities. Typically, such concepts of development also focus on economic growth as the ends, or even the means, to improved overall personal development. In such typically individualistic societies, the notion of family and community ties taking precedent over economic wealth remains perhaps less comprehensible. In the different ways that Pauline and Alice manage their interactions with the Vlisco men and the market women, then, Junger not only asks us to question the monolithic term *women*, but also to recognize the place that other often used (and abused) constructs like "community" and "culture" hold in defining and achieving "development."

RECONSTRUCTING "AGENCY:" THE POWER OF VULNERABILITY, THE VULNERABILITY OF POWER

Although the market women, as individuals or as a community, are almost certainly at a disadvantage when dealing with a corporate giant like Vlisco, this power imbalance does not prevent them from asserting whatever agency they have at hand. Junger calls attention to these acts of self-assertion that interestingly coincide with the characters' moments of deepest vulnerability. As always, however, Junger cautions that "agency" too should not be idealized as a form of entirely positive empowerment and action. Indeed, even "agency" can have negative outcomes.

The penultimate scene in the film is a particularly illustrative example of Junger's nuanced and complicated depiction of "agency." Here, Kami rebukes Alice at her stall ostensibly for doing "bad" business. In front of other Vlisco general managers who have come in from various parts of West Africa to celebrate the opening of the new store, Kami criticizes Alice for selling the Vlisco cloth below the agreed-upon price and making a paltry profit. Pushed in this way, Alice tries to explain the challenges of selling expensive Vlisco cloth—in 2002, eleven meters of Vlisco cloth cost nearly 100 Euros (US$124)—in a market where the gross national income per capita in 2002 is $270, according to the World Bank, and selling it at a fixed price in a market schooled in the art of bargaining (Turlings 2002). In essence, Alice is critiquing structural conditions—Vlisco's culturally inappropriate terms of sale—that create the very circumstances that prevent market women like her from increasing their profit and developing their business. Alice's response is in fact an attempt at self-assertion—she criticizes Vlisco with insight and strength, explaining her position and that of other market women. Alice's greatest moment of vulnerability is, thus, also, paradoxically, shown to be where Alice's most powerful exercise of agency arises.

Junger dwells on this moment, arguably the film's most pronounced moment of vulnerability and agency, between Alice and the Vlisco men. The film pauses. The camera lingers on Alice's profile as Junger allows Alice to recover from the emotionally charged moment. Publicly rebuked and humiliated by the very representatives of a company she had so recently helped, Alice struggles with the realization that she has been taken for a fool and treated as such by Kami and the Vlisco representatives. To Junger's eventual question of how she feels, Alice responds, "I was unhappy. I was thinking: The men you were so busy trying to help are reproaching you now . . . You're helping someone and now they're coming to laugh at you. It's not the first time they laugh at me . . . If I had known in advance I'd never have done it" (Junger 2002). To her credit, even as Junger registers Alice's regret for helping the Vlisco men, she neither heaps judgment on nor denies sympathy to Alice's plight. Because Alice's betrayal of the market women community was voluntary and yet at the same time partially instigated by Vlisco, Junger's film does not explicitly blame Vlisco nor completely acquit Alice of responsibility. Indeed, Junger seems to suggest that vulnerability and power are perhaps two sides of the same coin, on the edge of which we are all—men and women, global corporations and local businesses—perched precariously, armed only with our agency, our capacity to act, for better or worse, in the face of such weakness and strength.

Throughout the film, Junger repeatedly calls attention to other such moments of paradoxical vulnerability and power. So far I have discussed primarily the vulnerability of the market women to Vlisco and their acts of agency in the way they attempt to manage Vlisco's arrival. But the film also gestures towards other kinds of vulnerable positions and respective assertions of power. One of these places of potential weakness (and strength) in the film is that of the market women within their own community as seen in the potential estrangement of Alice from the other market women and in the market hierarchy where the Mama Benzes like Pauline hold a monopoly over the market and the resources—capital, credit, and superior cloth—for doing business. Although each of these women competes with each other for market share and profits in their businesses, they also rely on each other as a financial network for credit and capital, and social network for friendship and contacts.

Another juncture of vulnerability and power in the film is seen in the figure of Kami as he is held accountable to Vlisco, specifically to his superior, Hank, for the success of the new store in Burkina Faso. As we see in the scene where he criticizes Alice for her "bad" business skills, Kami is too concerned with his personal loss of face (not to mention his job with Vlisco) to heed Alice's explanations. He is intent on locating the problem in the person of Alice, blaming her dearth of business acumen for her lack of success with the Vlisco cloth. Again, although Kami seems to hold all the cards over Alice, he needs her to follow through on her promise to buy and sell Vlisco cloth at prices Vlisco has set. It is in Vlisco's interest to keep its fabric pricey so as to maintain its image of luxury and exclusivity. Moreover, although Junger does not specifically address this in her film, the presence of Kami, as an African man working for a Dutch company like Vlisco, raises inevitable questions about identity politics. Kami, selected probably for his "African" identity, presumably has to negotiate various kinds of identity issues that a Dutch employee may not. He may have more to prove and more to deliver, and his assertion of power in the Burkina Faso marketplace may have much to do with this position of vulnerability in the Vlisco Corporation.

Last, but not least, there is the vulnerability of Vlisco to (and exertion of power over) its new market in Burkina Faso. The company has put time, money, and energy into opening a new store and, yet, its success finally depends on the cooperation of the market women to sell Vlisco cloth and the wealthy African women to buy Vlisco cloth. Why might Junger call attention to these various paradoxical moments of weakness and strength throughout her film? What is at stake in such a portrayal of vulnerability and power?

I propose that Junger focuses on the interconnection between vulnerability and power in such scenes to underscore that the "powerful," however strong, still rely on the "weak," and, consequently, the less powerful, however vulnerable, still have some power. In her attention to the vulnerability of the West African market women in their relationships with Vlisco, Junger recognizes also the presence of strength. Pauline, the contemporary market women, and Alice are revealed in their very moments of vulnerability to be asserting their power. Here is agency in action from the perspective of the typically less powerful group. The women are fighting, with whatever means they have available, for the power to decide, to define for their society and themselves, the meaning and construction of culture, and the means and ends of development.

In their dominance of the textile industry and the fashion identity of West Africa, Vlisco may impose on West Africa and on West African society their view of what constitutes culture and development. In their manipulation of the market women, historically and contemporarily, Vlisco may determine what can and should be done in the name of culture and development. They may dictate who does what, when, and how in that batik cloth market of Burkina Faso, for example, but their dominance is not absolute and not met without resistance. Junger's film, thus, recognizes how Vlisco's power to define culture and development in the West African cloth market is not inherently stable and does not go unchallenged by the people most affected by this foreign influence—the market women. In their negotiations—voluntary or necessary—with Vlisco, it is certainly the West African market women who have more to gain and more to lose. The higher stakes of culture and development on their side of the struggle increase their vulnerability to the erosions of control that colonizing forces like Vlisco represents, but they may also magnify their determination and resolve.

And yet, Junger reminds us that this agency, this capacity to act from a position of vulnerability in the face of power, can have negative, as well as positive, means and outcomes. For some people like Pauline, agency can manifest itself as cannibalizing on other, less established market women to protect her position. For other folks like Alice, agency can take the form of selling out the market secrets of the community women and hurting not only the bargaining position of the market women with Vlisco but also her own place in that social network. As for other people like Kami, agency can mean capitalizing on his "African" identity to further the cultural colonization of West African women and culture. And for some corporations like Vlisco, agency can appear as colonizing a new West African market when it loses control over an old Indonesian one. By showing us both the productive and destructive acts and effects of agency, Junger's film problematizes any simple understanding of agency and its relationship to positions of vulnerability and power.

CONCLUSION

In this chapter, I have tried to demonstrate how Junger's film *Mama Benz and the Taste of Money* invites us to reexamine what have become increasingly monolithic terms—*development*, *culture*, *women*, and *agency*. In terms of *development*, perhaps one of the film's greatest strengths is that it manages, subtly yet pointedly, to question the value of purely economic development, that is, when development is synonymous with financial advancement or monetary gain. It problematizes such a limited view of development by showing us the ultimate opportunity cost of such relentless economic progress—the loss of a sense of social security, that is, the certainty of knowing that you are accepted by a community and will be protected by its members when you need it. As such, it suggests that "development" may need to be measured against other noneconomic markers like social well-being, rather than mere economic production. And "development" may need to be conceived more holistically instead of simply by the accumulation of wealth.

As for *culture*, Junger's film completely dismantles any stock understanding of this term. It questions the convention of linking "culture" with the "traditional" by showing us how the "traditional" batik fabric of West Africa comes courtesy of Vlisco, a Dutch company with deeply colonial roots, and via Indonesia, a former Dutch colony. It also quickly refutes the misguided tendency to presume that African "culture," the "natural" African way of living (read non-Western, noncapitalist, and nonindividualist) will necessarily present a more socially just and communally centered social life. After all, Pauline, Alice, and the other market women appear quite ready to pursue their individual advancement, even at the expense of the other members of their market community. Therefore, it suggests that even as any development projects must consider the particular way of life of the communities involved as a major factor, they should neither presume any essentialized, pure, or static notion of "culture" nor glorify any romanticized idea of it.

The film makes a similar observation with the term *women*. It challenges the practice of reducing Third World women, especially African women, to symbols of the victimized or the oppressed by portraying a wealthy and shrewd Pauline and an ambitious and independent Alice. It also problematizes the opposing practice of heralding Third World women as the true source of productive labor and moral strength and, hence, the real beacon of hope for their respective nations. It shows, instead, how even the Mama Benzes, repeatedly proclaimed as icons of miraculous female and African successes, actually have their roots in a colonial past and willingly collaborate in a neocolonial present. Women like Pauline and Alice may be the real backbone of Burkina Faso's economy, but they are neither self-sacrificing saints nor altruistic angels. They are women, with dreams and desires, schemes and sins. Thus, Junger's film suggests that although feminists and activists may advocate a larger role for women in development and community projects, they too should not presume that including women necessarily means things will change for the better.

As for *agency*, possibly one of the most fascinating aspects of Junger's film is that it even deconstructs arguably one of the most precious terms in the vocabulary and ideology of Third World development and antiglobalization activists as well as feminist and cultural studies scholars. It problematizes the tendency to associate "agency" with the weak, the oppressed, and the victimized, and to proclaim this capacity to act as the cure-all against social injustices and global inequality. It does so by uncovering the paradoxical relationship between vulnerability and power. Instead of showing only the dominance of Vlisco men over the West African market women, it reveals the interdependence among Pauline, Alice, Kami, and Vlisco. Each needs the other to succeed (each is vulnerable in this way). And each has something the other wants (each is powerful in this way). Most importantly, each at once preys upon the vulnerability of the others and grafts herself or himself upon the power of the others in order to develop. In so doing, the film demonstrates how agency, one's capacity to act, resides in both the weak and the strong, the oppressed and the oppressor, the victimized and the victimizer. Moreover, these actions, when undertaken by both the more powerful and the less powerful can include both disempowerment (feeding upon the others' weaknesses) and empowerment (feeding into the others' strengths). In this way, Junger's film suggests that even as scholars and activists may seek to champion "agency" as signs of resistance by the weak against the strong and as means of revolution by the local against the global, they should remember not only the paradoxical relationship between vulnerability and power, but also how agency in the less powerful may not necessarily translate into greater social justice or global equality.

In asking us to reexamine our understanding and use of these terms, *Mama Benz and the Taste of Money* also elaborates on the paradigm of women, culture, and development as conceived by Bhavnani, Foran, and Kurian, which I described at the beginning of this chapter. It does so by raising provocative questions about the agency of women like Pauline and Alice in their local community and a global world—both the means and effects of their individual and collective agency. It also poses difficult queries about the role of culture (historical background, social norms, community practices, lifestyle aspirations, and even fashion) in the "development" of the Third World. Although the film does not offer any easy answers, it does open up the conversation to a more nuanced understanding of the role of women especially—the market women, the Mama Benzes, and the elite women—in deciding what constitutes culture and development. Ultimately, Junger's success with *Mama Benz and the Taste of Money* is in capturing the complexities of the relationship between Vlisco and the market women; how, even as they collaborate with each other to conduct business, the two factions are wrestling for the power to decide what will comprise culture and development. Pauline, the contemporary market women, and Alice are revealed by Junger, in their very moments of vulnerability and power to be, if not already contesting for, at least reflecting on their capacity to design their own "fictions" of culture and development.

12 History, Development, and Transformation in Paule Marshall's *The Chosen Place, The Timeless People*

A Conversation among Students of Development

Erin Kennedy, Edwin López, Moira O'Neil, and Molly Talcott

As social science graduate students at the University of California in Santa Barbara, we have had the opportunity to interrogate the meanings, histories, and outcomes of Third World development practices in innovative ways. An unorthodox method of studying development we have encountered—through our participation in graduate courses in *Development and Its Alternatives* and *Women, Culture, and Development*—is the study of fictional accounts of peoples' experiences of development. One such critically important narrative is Paule Marshall's 1969 description of development in the fictional community of Bournehills on the West Indian Bourne Island in her novel, *The Chosen Place, The Timeless People*. What follows is a conversation among the four of us about the lessons Marshall's novel offers about the powerful interrelations of history, development, and social transformation in Third World contexts such as Bournehills.

Moira O'Neil: My experiences in the seminar *Development and Its Alternatives* changed my thinking about teaching and learning about development in the Third World while sitting in a classroom in the United States. I have come to see how novels can serve as a crucial complement to the academic study of nearly any social phenomenon, but I think especially to theories of development. Like ethnographic work that allows us to think about how development as an idea and a social practice works in people's lives, the novel may offer an even more complex vision of how development is experienced. Marshall's book allows for this complexity and points to the ways theoretical writings about development are lacking.

Molly Talcott: I agree with you, Moira, that we need to challenge the social scientific canons that are routinely taught so that a work like Marshall's novel can take its place alongside Mead, Geertz, Marx, and the rest. I think that this novel is a must-read for any scholar of development, especially those of us who conduct fieldwork. It's as if Marshall, through her microcosmic story, is holding up a mirror to the development establishment. Perhaps it is up to those of us who are involved in it—either as academics, practitioners, social activists, or some of each—to study the image she has created and learn from it. Marshall's *The Chosen Place, The Timeless People* is so illuminating, in part, because it exposes not only the colonial gaze of traditional anthropological and elite-led development studies and projects, but also because it actually reveals the rather provincial and shallow understandings that guide such top-down approaches to development. This rendering is so valuable; it reminds me that, as a social scientist who critiques top-down, (neo)colonial, and capitalist approaches to "development," I run the risk of exaggerating their power. *The Chosen Place, The Timeless People* demonstrates that although hegemonic development produces social effects that are often devastating, it is not omnipotent; it can be, and often is, contested by those subaltern communities who are surviving in spite of it.

Erin Kennedy: I think it is necessary at this point in time to recognize the importance of integrating voices not typically heard in academic discourse in order to challenge the very foundations upon which knowledge is produced. Just as Marshall offers an unorthodox vision of development ahead of its time in her text, taking into account the many faults that have characterized notions of progress and development, she also challenges us to think about the ways we as individuals are integrated into a larger community of people worldwide and, in doing so, she problematizes such dichotomous distinctions as self and other, insider and outsider, and the global and the local. Furthermore, she requires us to acknowledge our own complicity in reproducing these false dualisms.

MT: Indeed, *The Chosen Place, The Timeless People* (henceforth, *TCP*) reads nearly as a documentation of the premise you've hinted at, Erin, that development—as it has been overwhelmingly conceived, funded, and carried out—has failed the peoples of the Third World. Marshall's protagonist, Merle Kinbono, is acutely aware of this. She sees development, as it has been practiced on her island, as a new form of colonization, albeit one with a nicer appearance.

EK: Marshall does imply that grand schemes of development devised by corporations will not truly develop communities such as Bournehills. In *TCP*, it is clear that factories and resorts that cater to the First World will not provide the much-needed transformations required to create an environmentally and socially sustainable form of development.

MO: And what is striking is that the novel was first published in 1969, around the same period that Andre Gunder Frank began formulating his critique of modernization theory and ten years prior to the publication of Cardoso and Faletto's classic work, *Dependency and Development in Latin America*. Modernization theory was beginning to come under fire in large part because of the ahistorical nature of the paradigm and a specific unwillingness to consider colonialism as very much a living part of development projects in the Third World.

Edwin López: Yes, Marshall demonstrates that this form of "development from above" is about the exercise of power and the extraction of resources. And that development has historically been a racialized process. The setting of *TCP* is Bourne Island, a remote isle in the West Indies that recently gained its independence from England. Its economy, based on a sugar cane monoculture, is largely unstable; a reality that compels many men to seek temporary labor contracts in the United States. Bournehills is a small community on the island that serves as the primary labor pool for the local sugar refinery. The island's residents are descendants of African slaves, and they endure hardships that go beyond the economic. Marshall shows that after generations of exploitation and discrimination, they are overshadowed by a sense of hopelessness, a misery that seeps into every corner of their lives.

MO: *TCP* is so powerful in the way that Marshall captures the historical relationship between the legacy of colonialism and development that often eludes social scientific studies of development. To me, her narrative calls forth Walter Benjamin's redemptive philosophy of history. In his "Theses on the Philosophy of History" (1968), he discusses history's direct grip on the present of human lived experience, and the ability of the past to move among the living. The dead and things past are not secure—they can be forgotten, purposefully erased, or annihilated. At the same time, Benjamin's concept of history implies that there is a chance to redeem the past; direct acknowledgment, reenactment, and confrontation with the past as a living force are potential strategies for social change for the characters in *TCP*. This acknowledgment is a way of transgressing the collective despair of which you just spoke, Edwin. Specifically, I am thinking of the ritual reenactment of Cuffee Ned's rebellion against the colonial powers on the island. Each year during carnival, the people of Bournehills reconstruct Pyre Hill, the mythic place where Cuffee Ned slit the throat of colonist Percy Bryam. This annual ritual becomes a way of experiencing the violence, pain, and humiliation of the colonial encounter, which—as you mentioned, Edwin—is still very much a part of life in Bournehills. Marshall writes:

> They were . . . simply telling their story as they did each year. Yet as those fused voices continued to mount the air, shaking the old town at its mooring on the bay, it didn't seem like they were singing only of themselves and Bournehills, but of people like them everywhere. The struggle on the hill which had seen Cuffee triumphant and Bryam brought low was, their insistent voices seemed to be saying, but the experience through which any people who find themselves ill-used, dispossessed, at the mercy of the powerful, must pass." (1969, 286–287)

And yet, Marshall is not overly romantic about the political efficacy of this ritual. It is simply a necessary part of the process by which people deal with colonial and neocolonial forms of domination, and therefore *begin* to effect social transformation.

MT: *TCP* emphasizes the weight of history on contemporary cultures of development. Moira, you mentioned Benjamin's philosophy of history and the ritual performance of Cuffee Ned's rebellion. And there are so many instances where this novel concretely demonstrates the operation of theoretical concepts like Benjamin's. I am reminded of the work of poet and historian Aurora Levins Morales, who calls for the resurrection and creation of what she calls "medicinal histories"—those which counter the claims of imperial history and instead "seek to re-establish connections between peoples and their histories, to reveal the mechanisms of power, the steps by which their current condition of oppression was achieved through a series of decisions made by real people to dispossess them; but also to reveal the multiplicity, creativity, and persistence of resistance among the oppressed" (1998, 24). Morales argues that this practice of medicinal history is guided by a *politics of integrity*, which she describes as "a political practice that sacrifices neither the global nor the local, ignores neither institutional power structures, nor their most personal impact on the lives of people. . . . That restores connections, not only in the future we dream of, but right here, in the gory, tumultuous, hopeful, messy, and inconsistent present" (1998, 5). To me, Marshall's novel embodies this politics of integrity of which Morales speaks. And the residents of Bournehills themselves act as medicinal historians in their persistent and proud retelling of the uprising of Cuffee Ned. They do so with conviction each year, despite the ridicule of other Bourne Island residents and the superficial response of visiting tourists. And of course it is Merle who is the key medicinal historian in Bournehills; she loses her teaching job after insisting on teaching the children about Cuffee Ned's uprising.

EL: Moira and Molly, you have noted some conceptual links between Marshall's novel and the writings of Benjamin and Morales, on the subject of history. After reading *TCP,* I could not help but draw some connections between the Bournehills context and my own work (Lopez 2004) on indigenous cultural resistance during the Guatemalan revolution of 1944–1954, with respect to the historically racialized nature of development.

MO: Yes, development has been linked to Eurocentric notions of progress, evolution.

EK: And because Marshall centers on racially marginalized voices, she is able to capture the depths of racialized historical constructs of inferiority, as well as the persistence of ideas about civilization and savagery, which are closely linked to racialization processes.

EL: Race relationships are of particular interest to me, and I have written about what I call "racialized political cultures," that is, how racialized groups use culture to meet their needs. In the case of Guatemala, Ladinos used culture to subordinate the indigenous majority and maintain the racial order. These Ladinos in question were political leftists—it was they who led the move for greater democracy and freedom in Guatemala. For instance, President Arbenz (1952–1954) took great risks and was left-leaning. He signed the most controversial reform law in Guatemalan history, the Agrarian Reform Law Decree 900. His plan was to provide a direct benefit to Guatemala's rural poor. Yet, the redistribution of land was very discriminatory, with Ladinos consistently favored over the indigenous. In the end, the Ladinos' revolutionary efforts were thwarted by their belief that "Indian" culture was primitive, and their experiment with modernization aimed to Westernize and "Ladinoize" the indigenous. So while the plight of Guatemala's indigenous majority was of concern in revolutionary discourse, the development plan was to make them efficient manual laborers, while the mestizo elite remained their managers. And this pattern is evident in *TCP* as well. As was the case with indigenous communities of Guatemala, the residents of Bournehills had more than sufficient reason to distrust the government and their employers. Attempts to modernize the area had failed many times over, with blame for the collapse always placed on the supposedly "stubborn" and "backward" comportment of the Bournehills community. And, the intraracial conflicts among blacks in *TCP* are profound. While well-to-do blacks feel superior to black plantation workers, their sense of inferiority to whites is firm. The varying shades of blackness that make up the island's population affect how people are judged and how they view themselves. It is not uncommon in Bournehills for women to apply white powder to their black skin as they ride the bus into town.

MT: Yes, and this expression of racialized shame illustrates Morales's point that institutional power structures also have very personal effects on people. The intraracial conflicts you speak of, Edwin, are indeed evident in *TCP*. Marshall brilliantly narrates the complexities of such conflicts, including how intraracial tensions are linked with processes of class formation, colonization, and development. I want to come back to Merle Kinbona because she is a very powerful character in the novel. Marshall does not romanticize Merle; her life is messy, her history painful, and she grapples with personal contradictions. But it is she who recognizes the racialized and classed cleavages that continually shape what might be called the development of "underdevelopment" in Bournehills. I am thinking specifically of the way Merle confronts Lyle Hutson about the development plan that is adopted by the Bournehills legislature. Lyle is a London-educated, upwardly mobile politician, lawyer, and black native of Bournehills. When he describes a plan to boost foreign investment and tourism on the island by means of offering many perks and tax breaks to the companies involved, Merle takes him to task on this "development" plan, saying to him:

> Signed, sealed, and delivered. The whole bloody place. And to the lowest bidder. Who says the auction block isn't still with us? . . . Is that

> what we threw out the white pack who ruled us for years and put you chaps in office for? For you to give away the island? For you to literally pay people to come and make money off us? . . . Is that all that's possible for us in these small islands? . . . Well, if so, it's no different now than when they were around here selling us for thirty pounds sterling. Not really. Not when you look deep. . . . The chains are still on. Oh, Lyle, can't you see that? . . . Haven't you fellows in Legco learned anything from all that's gone on in this island over the past four hundred years? Read your history, man! (1969, 209–210)

And here Merle brings the reader, once again, back to history.

EK: While race is integral throughout the text and the history of colonization, we see that Marshall is concerned with the erasure of boundaries, going beyond class and race to include gender and sexuality in her quest to propose alternative modes of understanding and dealing with notions of development. Indeed, through Merle, Marshall invokes the very idea of liminality. Merle belongs neither here nor there; she traverses boundaries of race, class, gender, and sexuality. As Marshall exhibits through Merle's shifting boundaries of self and identity, community development is what is ultimately necessary for true development—social, political, economic and otherwise—requiring the breakdown of divisive societal structures and acceptance of individuals regardless of their background. In this spirit, Marshall asserts the need for a larger definition of community, one that includes not simply people in the local area, but also allies across the globe.

EL: And yet, development projects are usually directed toward racially disenfranchised groups, and what I have found in my research is that political strategy (i.e., development strategy) relies heavily on lived experience and cultural values, so that when both dominant and subordinate groups accept the idea of development and change, these visions differ. How they define "progress" and what equals "justice" can result in new fields of contention. The lesson here is that race, class, and culture shape the way people experience the world, and they thus influence the blueprints for change and the way these projects are received.

MT: Erin, you mentioned the issue of gender in the novel. And in the beginning of our conversation, Moira, you spoke of the pedagogical value of *TCP*. What I have been reminded of is the importance of historicizing any ethnography or story told about Third World development as a reflexive and feminist practice. The four of us have been influenced by the teaching and writing of Kum-Kum Bhavnani, who has taught me that historically mediated power structures *always* affect the micropolitics of any research project (Bhavnani 1993). This is evident in *TCP*, particularly with respect to Saul and his research in Bournehills. Saul does not effectively engage with the power dynamics related to his social position. His research (and thus the report and recommendations that followed) is heavily masculinist. For instance, he instructs his wife Harriet that, along with typing up his fieldnotes, her "job" is to talk to the women. He conducts most of his own participant observation in predominantly male contexts, whether drinking rum with the local men, at the exclusively male pig slaughter, or in the sugarcane processing factory. As a result, Saul comes to see the men of Bournehills as the key agents of development, and he implements an all-male village council and leadership training program. And despite the problem of male violence against women on the island, Saul never integrates the issue of women's physical security into his development plan. Toward the end of the novel, he begins to think more historically with respect to the project and his own life, yet his reflexive attention to the micropolitics of his study remains quite limited. So for me, the pedagogical value of *TCP* is that it teaches me—in vivid narrative detail—the importance of attending to the micropolitics of my own research projects, in order to try to see for myself what Saul, like so many development researchers who travel from west to east and from north to south, could not.

MO: There are, indeed, myriad lessons within the pages of *TCP* for both the study and practice of development projects. One that we seem to agree on is that attention must be paid to the historical context in which development projects are implemented. And finally, Marshall's novel demonstrates that conceptions of history and processes of development and social transformation sometimes transcend the rigid boundaries of social scientific models.

MT: Yes, the continuing relevance of Marshall's *TCP* is indisputable, as is the persistence of the crisis of development, and thus, of development studies, which has at present failed to center social justice and human rights over global capitalist market expansion. Perhaps a proliferation of "medicinal" histories, ethnographies, and stories like Marshall's, including those that the four of us will generate, may facilitate the turning of this troubling tide, alongside and in cooperation with the growing waves of worldwide movements for social justice and sustainable, equitable, and grassroots development.

ON THE EDGE OF A CONCLUSION, A QUESTION

Reading Marshall's *TCP* in the *Development and Its Alternatives* and *Women, Culture, and Development* courses presented us with a valuable learning experience. For us, *TCP* has demonstrated the power of fiction to illuminate complex social realities and convey myriad subjectivities, and thus it has enabled us to rethink development "from the edge"—that is, at the intersections of social science and cultural production. In *TCP* and with the grace and nuance afforded by her "fictional" approach, Marshall explores key theoretical concepts within contemporary development studies—the impact of colonial histories on Third World development, the ways gender, race, and class work as complex and interlocking systems of oppression within the Third World and globally, and the centrality of culture as well as political-economic systems. Furthermore, for students of development living in the First World, these concepts are not abstract as with some social scientific accounts of them, but come alive through Marshall's characters.

Marshall's *TCP* also encourages readers to see the fictions of development that social science itself has historically produced, and continues to manufacture. Thus we can imagine the possibility of new forms of development that might take root when social scientific models become displaced from center to margin—for at least some of the time. *TCP*'s deep critique of the role of "experts" in Third World development projects calls into question the ways that such outsiders engage with people who are its subjects. And yet, Marshall simultaneously refuses easy romanticisms that portray victims, heroes, and the gender and racial essentialisms therein (Sturgeon 1997), in tales of development.

On a final note, *TCP* encourages us to reexamine our roles and positions as researchers vis-à-vis the communities and people that we study. While issues of power and method have been theorized within and across scholarly disciplines, this novel prompts us to think even more deeply, and perhaps with more vivid imaginations, about what possible paths forward might resemble. *The Chosen Place, The Timeless People* is a powerful teaching tool, for it continues to edge us toward new explorations of the ever-relevant question, "Development for, and by, whom?"

13 Urduja through the Looking Glass

A Response to Colonial Trauma

Tera Maxwell

> *The story is older than my body, my mother's, my grandmother's. For years we have been passing it on so that it may live, shift, and circulate. So that it may become larger than its proper measure, always larger than its own in-significance.*
>
> Trinh (1989, 137)

> *Following the ghosts . . . is about putting life back in where only a vague memory or a bare trace was visible to those who bothered to look. It is sometimes about writing ghost stories, stories that not only repair representational mistakes, but also strive to understand the conditions under which a memory was produced in the first place, toward a countermemory, for the future.*
>
> Gordon (1997, 22)

INTRODUCTION

The story of Princess Urduja and her presence in Filipino popular culture points to the gendered, traumatic nature of empire, specifically American empire (McClintock 1995, 74). For Filipinos, this memory of a warrior princess who once ruled the South China Sea marks a truth countering colonial mentality, yet recent scholars insist this tale is the stuff of legends, not history. Urduja is a ghostly figure because, although dismissed by historians, she continues to haunt Filipino imagination.

The story of an Amazonian warrior princess suggests an enlightened kingdom where women rank equal status with men in thirteenth-century Southeast Asia, before the advent of European colonization. The first written record of Princess Urduja appears in the Arab historian Ibn Batuta's account of his world travels from 1325 to 1354. Batuta encounters the lovely princess on the island of Tawalisi, on his way to China. Impressed by her courtly grace and intelligence, Batuta notes that she speaks Arabic and Turkish, reads from the Qur'an, and leads an army of men and women soldiers. Adept in archery and hand-to-hand combat, Urduja proves her bravery in battle when she breaks through enemy lines, kills the enemy king, and brings back his head on a spear (Ibn and Mackintosh-Smith 2002, 259). As a reward, her father King Dalisay appoints her governor of the port of Kailukari. Surrounded by an entourage of women soldiers, Urduja revels in her independent life, and like many other legendary heroines, vows only to marry the man who could beat her in single combat. No suitors dare to challenge her. Furthermore, Batuta describes Tawalisi's inhabitants as "brave and intrepid . . . their women ride horses, understand archery, and fight just like the men" (Ibn and Mackintosh-Smith 2002, 258). While Urduja as a national heroine was initially introduced through the public school curriculum as part of the American colonial machine, Filipina feminists and activists recuperate the medieval legend not only to articulate Filipino longing for a lost past but also to invoke alternate ways of being in response to current economic conditions (Magno 1992, 47).[1]

How is Princess Urduja an empowering fiction, what Gordon calls a "fiction of the real" (Gordon 1997, 147)? This chapter examines how a local memory of Urduja shapes agency for women—whether it be women's participation in the Tayug uprising; how a local nongovernmental organization in Pangasinan trains prospective overseas contract workers how to protect themselves abroad; women's rights organization GABRIELA's use of Urduja to reinforce activism; or artist Alma Quinto's interpretation of the Urduja/ancient priestess tradition to not only help abused children heal but also tap into this precolonial knowledge to empower Filipinas.

By carving out a fertile space for imagining change, the reinvention of Urduja counters the terms of development. How is she used to negotiate the trauma of a colonial past, as well as the ever-present traumas of decolonization? How does her presence mark loss and resistance to loss? By examining Urduja's palimpsest-like quality, Urduja's continued appearances or ghostly haunting speak to how Filipinos have resisted history's erasure of their precolonial past and how specifically *Filipina* groups continue to sustain her so that Urduja's life continues (Brewer 2004, 5).

This chapter adduces memories of Urduja, by marking where she crops up in the Filipino imaginary and decoding what her figure reveals about desire and loss. Thus, Princess Urduja is a figure seen "through the looking glass" of Filipino desire.[2] As one stage of recovering an archive of memory, my reading implicitly incorporates a kind of politics that David Eng and David Kazanjian call "a politics of mourning" (2003, 2). They note, "if loss is known only by what remains of it, then the politics and ethics of mourning lie in the interpretation of what remains—how remains are produced and animated, how they are read and sustained" (Eng and Kazanjian 2003, ix). This chapter is thus as much about the living as it is about the dead, as much about Filipinos across the diaspora as about the ghostly Urduja. My interest is not to establish Urduja's authenticity because it little matters whether Urduja existed or not. Instead, I seek to understand, as Gordon puts it, the conditions under which memories of Urduja cropped up in the first place (Gordon 1997, 22). Gordon remarks that ghosts are "a symptom of what is missing" and points to what they represent: "a loss, sometimes of life, sometimes of a path not taken," but also "a future possibility, a hope" (Gordon 1997, 63–64). In other words, ghost stories might occur in the violent gap between hope and reality. This chapter thus aims to not only excavate an archive of memories of Urduja but also speak to a collective loss and its reparation. Thus, the recovery of Urduja re-presents a narratological map, tracing a trajectory from nationalist dreams to concrete articulations of feminist activism. Her recuperation ushers a response to centuries of oppression—from colonial regimes to its contemporary face, globalization—in particular, the present-day trafficking of Filipina bodies to developed countries.

URDUJA AND THE BIRTH OF FILIPINO IDENTITY

The narrative of Urduja—from medieval legend to Filipino pop icon—tells a sweeping history spanning the centuries—the emergence of print capitalism, the subsequent colonial expansion and the West's hunger for tales of the exotic, and twentieth-century decolonization followed by the rise of transnational capital and globalization—dictating the range of possible movement for human bodies through time and space. Ironically, Urduja's figure is marshaled to refuse the very forces that nourished her popularity. Henry Yule's 1866 English translation of Ibn Batuta's travels in *Cathay and the Way Thither* transports Urduja from a figure in an arcane medieval text into circulation in the modern, industrial West. It is José Rizal, however, who launches Urduja from a local legend to a cultural icon of Filipino identity when he tries to establish the location of Tawalisi as Northern Luzon. Rizal is considered one of the founding fathers of the Philippines and is dubbed "the First Filipino" because he was the first "to define Filipinos as a politico-ethnic people" (Delmendo 2004, 22). In reaction to Spanish imperialism, Rizal aimed to foster a cultural nationalism. Sharon Delmendo describes how Rizal, while visiting Buffalo Bill's show in Paris, was fascinated with the romantic portrayal of Indians as *Los Indios Bravos*. Previously, the term *Filipinos* referred exclusively to those of Spanish blood born in the Philippines (Delmendo 2004, 26). Members of this privileged class were also known as *insulares* or *creoles*. In the Philippines the term *indios*, meaning the indigenous inhabitants of the Philippines, was a derogatory term. In contradistinction to the racist meaning of *indio*, Rizal decided to form an association called Los Indios Bravos in what Delmendo calls a "critical moment in the early stages of nationalism" (Delmendo 2004, 26). Although he was a Spanish-speaking *ilustrado*, Rizal called himself an *indio* to appropriate the term *Filipino* and use it to designate all indigenous peoples of the Philippine islands.

Rizal's interest in Tawalisi performs similar cultural work: the recovery of a precolonial past, a history to make Filipinos proud of their indigenous heritage. Just as he recuperates *indio* from racist meanings by insisting on calling himself *indio* and the indigenous *Filipino,* he also recuperates the Philippines' ancient history by insisting on the historicity of the kingdom of Tawalisi. Disagreeing with Yule's dismissal of Batuta's travelogue as fiction, in 1888 Rizal writes in a private letter to Adolf B. Meyer of the Dresden Museum: "While I have doubts regarding the accuracy of Ibn Batuta's details, still I believe in the voyage to Tawalisi. . . . Besides, what possible interest could Ibn Batuta have had in falsifying?" (Rizal 1888).

Rizal establishes the location of Tawalisi as a region in Northern Luzon, Philippines, by taking into account Batuta's geographical description of his voyage and ancient trade routes and calculating the coordinates of Batuta's journey according to the days or distance sailed. Proving the existence of the kingdom of Tawalisi and Urduja furthers Rizal's nationalist project, which links Rizal's Urduja with the birth of Filipino identity. His interest in Urduja's kingdom and in establishing its legitimacy bespeaks his own desire for recovery, to allay the trauma of a colonial past and loss of cultural heritage.

Rizal's endorsement launches Urduja into the public realm when Rizal's private letter enters public circulation. Austin Craig's publication of José Rizal's letter in his 1916 pamphlet "Particulars of the Philippines Pre-Spanish Past" first brings the public's attention to Rizal's letter (Zafra 1977). Later, Craig publishes *Gems of Philippine Oratory,* a collection of short excerpts of the speeches of famous personages throughout Philippine history, in which one section, titled "Ancient Filipino Culture and Prominence of Women," features Ibn Batuta's account of Princess Urduja (Craig 1924, 11). This book was written as a textbook for readers of English. According to Nicolas Zafra, Craig's suggestion that the kingdom of Tawalisi was in the northern Philippines went "unchallenged" for decades (Zafra 1977, 152). Zafra explains that Urduja's historicity received "general acceptance and approbation" due to "the fact that Prof. Craig's assumption had for its basis the opinion of a man of the standing, integrity and reputation of Dr. Rizal" (Zafra 1977). José Rizal's status as national hero[3] lends to Urduja legitimacy as a cultural icon.

Thus, Urduja's status in public consciousness is solidified when she is absorbed into the public school curriculum in the two decades preceding the Pacific War of 1937 to 1945. According to Rosa Maria Magno, Francisco and Conrado Benitez's *Stories of Great Filipinos*, published in 1923, served as the impetus for disseminating Urduja in Filipino popular culture (Magno 1992). Benitez's textbook states as its purpose to offer "examples of worthy lives among the pupils' own countrymen who rendered valuable service to the community in some line of national activity" (Magno 1992). After Benitez's textbook, a flurry of other books—Zoilo M. Galang's entry on Urduja in the *Encyclopedia of the Philippines* (1935); Gregorio Zaide's entry on Urduja in *The Philippines Since Pre-Spanish*; and Pedrito Reyes and Jose Karasig's *Brief Biographies* (1940)—further solidify Urduja's standing in public consciousness (Magno 1992). Rosa Maria Magno argues that Urduja becomes popularized in the Filipino consciousness through public school education, an education that spread the belief in Urduja even as more contemporary historians refute her existence (Magno 1992, 48).

While it may seem ironic that American colonial rule through public school education fostered this interest in Urduja as a national heroine, I suggest that Urduja served American interests because she represents a casualty of Spanish imperialism. Marking a lost history, the figure of Urduja performs the ideological work of casting American occupation as benign, democratic, and magnanimous, a far cry from the tyranny of the Spaniards. Through the public school curriculum and Rizal's endorsement, Princess Urduja achieves the status of national heroine.

The eagerness with which Rizal and later scholars embrace her as one of their own suggests their own anxiety about their history, a past occluded by Spanish imperialism. Until the 1970s, scholars classified the period before the Spanish conquest as "prehistory," and books abound with that classification in their title. Such a rubric suggests that history started with the Spanish contact, and elides a long history of civilization in the Philippines. Rather than reading Rizal's appropriation of Urduja's kingdom as wistful or fabricated scholarship, one might interpret Rizal's "rememory" as a conscious choice negotiating the trauma of colonization.

URDUJA AND LOCAL RESISTANCE

In contrast to the West's courting of Urduja as history and subsequent dismissal as mere fable, local lore in Pangasinan, a province in Northern Luzon, Philippines, faithfully maintains Urduja existed (see this area in Figure 13.1).

Predating Spanish colonization of the Philippine archipelago in the sixteenth century, Pangasinan's rich oral history claims lineage with Urduja. The memories of a 1931 revolt in Pangasinan reveal the strength of the Urduja legend in popular memory and suggest that past collective memory shapes future memories and narratives.

Fe A. Andico, professor of Pangasinan State University invokes Urduja in the retelling of the Tayug uprising. On the Philippine Culture and Arts website, she writes, "The legendary Princess Urduja was renowned for her intelligence and her enlightened rule. *Significantly*, the women of the province figured prominently in the agrarian Colorum movement of the 1930s and in the women's suffrage movement" (Andico 2004). Juxtaposing a sentence on Urduja next to a statement on Pangasinan women's participation in revolt suggests a connection between Pangasinans' claimed lineage with Urduja and their women's participation in both the suffrage movement and the 1931 Colorum uprising. Although Andico admits that Urduja may be just a legend that nevertheless persists in the imagination, Andico's own invocation of Urduja summons ethnic pride and suggests a long history of resistance, a memory that reaches back to before the Spanish conquest. Alluding to a mythic origin suggests that women's participation in revolt transcends time and can be traced back to the beginning of time.

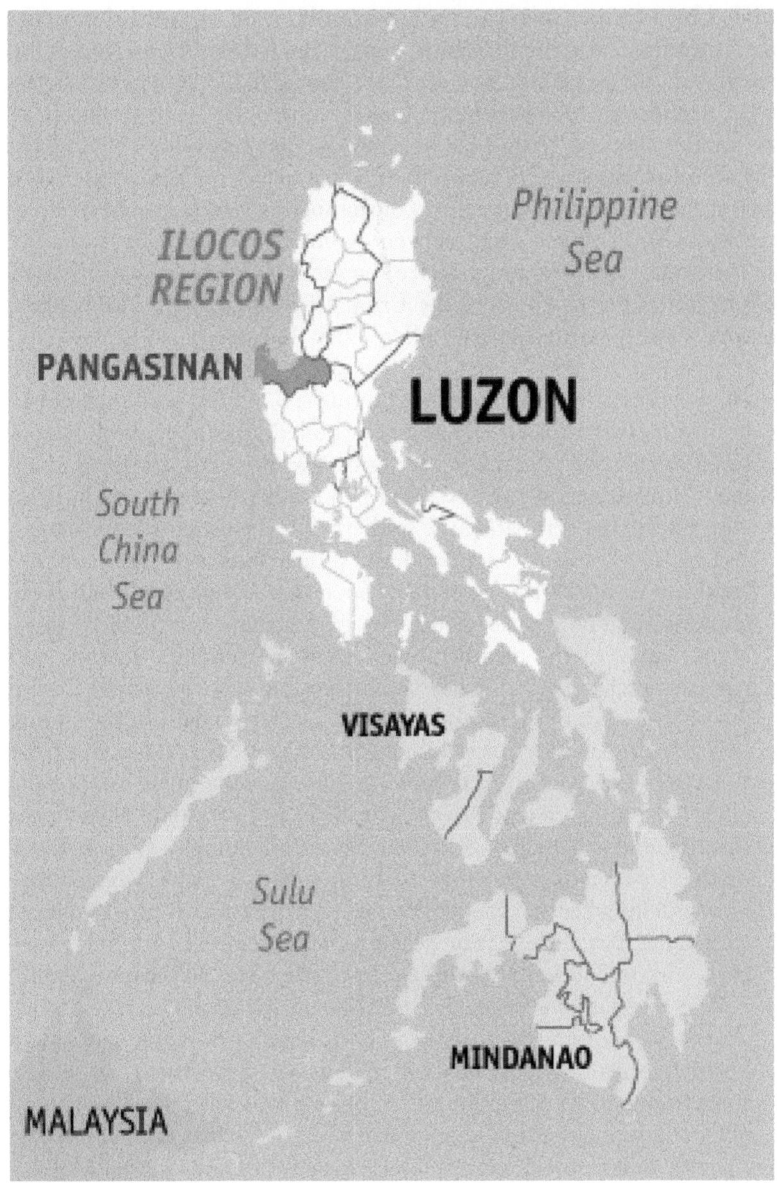

Figure 13.1 Pangasinan province in the Philippines.

In her paper on the Tayug uprising, Andico interviews several informants who participated in, or were witnesses to, the 1931 uprising to reconstruct what transpired during this revolt (Andico 1998). The narratives of several informants coalesce around a girl named Laura Cruz who participated in and was a key actor in the revolt. The Colorum Society, a secret society founded by a former migrant worker from Hawaii, opposed the American government and sought to reform unfair land distribution and rampant poverty among peasants. The society "stormed the soldier's quarters in Brgy. Carreido, burned the municipio, [and] then fled to the church which they forcibly opened," recalls informant Jose Cruz (Andico 1998, 162). Initially stunned, the soldiers received reinforcement from Lingayen and retaliated on the rebels. Many members of the society were arrested while a few were shot. Andico's research recovers women's involvement in the revolt. The historical accounts romanticize the memory of Laura Cruz's involvement in a manner that echoes the Urduja legend. Excerpts from Andico's interviews are presented here (Andico 1998, 162–166):

> She was the society's "Princesa Laura." . . . Laura was shot dead, her body was tied to a vehicle and was pulled, "paranggoyod iti kotse ti soldado" all over the town. Her body was not claimed by relatives for they were all afraid to do so. No one knows where she was buried and who buried her. Probably, the soldiers did. (Informant Jose Cruz)
>
> Laura was said to be a good and industrious girl who learned judo from her father. Her suitors had much reservation regarding their intentions because she seemed to be better than any of them in many ways. Three of the members were women from San Manuel, two of who were teachers. . . . They convinced Laura to surrender that night during the siege in the church, but she decided to fight to the end, more so when she saw her father killed. (Informant Mrs. Visitacion Briz)
>
> Laura Cruz was a pretty girl. . . . She was one of the beautiful girls in this place. There was a day when she went to the field where we were planting and she invited us to their place for a compleano. She asked my mother's permission to allow us to attend that night. I remember my mother telling her that we, her daughters, did not know how to dance and so told her that there was no sense going therefore. Laura just answered back with a request to permit us. (Informant Ms. Filomeno Avelino)
>
> The night of the siege, the members of the group retreated into the church . . . one of the women members [Laura Cruz] inside came out with a white flag in her hand. Her coming out was to probably encourage her companions to come out and fight, but she was felled by a shot. . . . The body of Laura Cruz was just left in front of the church although there was a rumor that it was eaten by pigs. (Informant Fauston Fernandez)
>
> Laura did not surrender even if her companions that night persuaded her to do so, especially upon knowing that her father had been killed during the siege. So when the officer came to arrest her (as the others did after the surrender), she hacked him with a bolo instead (and thus, she was shot to death). (Informant Mrs. Angelina Abad)

To describe Laura, the informants invoke the archetypal woman-warrior to explain and make sense of what turns out to be a failure.

These narratives witness the trappings of trauma: a violent battle scene, an unsettling death which resists the closure of a dignified burial, the shame of defeat and returning to the same circumstances as before. As one daughter of an officer in the attack writes, "When it was over, many things were gone. Not just relatives dead, and houses burned and important papers missing from the municipio, but something else again: a certain innocence, a graciousness, gone from the town" (Cortes 1974). This testimony touches upon irrevocable loss, how innocence is stolen from the community, yet the informants' description of Laura as an Urduja-like figure suggests an underlying hope, or at least hints at how loss might be reenvisioned.

The story foregrounds colonial trauma, how the locals never accepted American occupation. Andico writes, "The ideal for political independence . . . never waned in the revolutionaries' consciousness" (Andico 1998, 162). The memory of this event reveals how American colonialism failed to correct what Andico describes as "the seemingly unending cycle of poverty and toil brought about by the prevalent and pernicious tenancy system and practices" (Andico 1998, 162). The traumatic retelling evokes an earlier trauma of Spanish imperialism in the story of Laura's father Amado, who changes his name and moves his family to escape the Spanish authorities in the period before the American occupation. This forced displacement due to Spanish tyranny was a common occurrence among Filipinos. Furthermore, the 1931 Colorum uprising reenacts an earlier trauma, the brutal annihilation of the villagers on Mactan Island, Philippines, who upon encountering Magellan's visit in 1521, refused to accept Christianity or submit to the Spanish king. These layers of painful collective memory, buried and revisited at such moments as precipitated by the slaughter of the Tayug rebels, stultifies speech. The informants resort to the Urduja archetype to process mentally the inexplicable violence and to communicate through speech what is always removed from actual experience.

In addition, the Urduja figure points to the trauma of erasure, of having the memory of Urduja blotted out from history, as well as resistance to that erasure. The archetype rises to the surface because the legend of Urduja frames how the informants remember the 1931 revolt. The memory of Urduja informs the informants' memories of Laura Cruz and provides the scaffolding for constructing narrative about her participation in the revolt, in part, because the Urduja figure provides a vocabulary and framework to make sense of women's participation in the revolt. As the beautiful "Princesa," Laura performs the role of flag keeper in the group. Just as Princess Urduja is skilled in martial arts, Princesa Laura learns judo from her father. Just as Urduja intimidates suitors from courting her because they fear defeat by her in combat, Laura intimidates potential suitors who "[have] much reservation . . . because she [seems] to be better than any of them in many ways" (Andico 1998, 166). Just as Urduja, with her woman warriors, assists her father King Dalisay in governing his kingdom, Laura stands out as a leader among the women in the Colorum society and helps her father Amado in the revolt. She persuades the women in her community to join the Colorum group. Furthermore, the women rebels are given *bolos*, which suggest that the men "deemed their women-members capable of engaging in physical battle" (Andico 1998, 166). This constructed image of Laura's women rebels evokes the women warriors who surround Urduja. Laura leads her group of women in the fight and even sacrifices her safety to leave their retreat in order to encourage the others to follow her. In the two versions of how Laura was shot, one account is that she was shot when she left the church in an effort to lead the others, while the other account is that she was shot after she "hacked" a soldier with a bolo (Andico 1998, 166). Both accounts evoke a brave warrior princess who leads her woman warriors in battle.

In describing the Colorum uprising, Andico's reference to Urduja is a rhetorical move that resists the dominant narrative of a unified people and resists Rizal's Urduja as a nationalist icon. In the section on Urduja and the Birth of Filipino Identity, I examined how Rizal and later scholars used Urduja to create a unified ethnic identity, an employment of Urduja that elides regional and ethnic differences. In contrast, Andico refers to Urduja to highlight a peasant revolt. Lisa Lowe writes,

> Radical historians of India and the Philippines have argued that official colonialist histories, as well as the elite nationalist histories they have informed and engendered, have favored the narrative structure of progressive, stage-bound development of a unified subject and people, a structure that has subjugated the fragmented, decentralized activities of mass uprisings, peasant revolts, and laborer rebellions. (1996, 104)

Unlike a call for a unified nationalism, Andico's invocation of Urduja privileges a localized, peasant revolt, one that strategically forgets Urduja's royalty and place in the noble class and realigns her as a feminist and a fighter. Unlike the mainstream historiography of Urduja that plots her rise and fall as a historical figure, this idiosyncratic and fractured account of the Tayug uprising and its resonance with the Urduja memory presents an alternate truth that defies the categorization of Western epistemology. However, in suggesting an alternate history, these Urduja threads undermine the unspoken seamlessness of the dominant narrative and carve out a space to "imagine otherwise" (Chuh 2003, x).

This collective memory not only inculcates a language of militant opposition but also provides a cultural device to counter marginalization. For example, the Women in Development Foundation, a local nongovernmental organization in Pangasinan, Philippines, taps into the archive of Urduja to educate and empower Pangasinan women about to embark as overseas contract workers (OCWs) or start their own businesses. Virginia Pasalo, executive director of Women in Development, explains that Urduja is used as a training tool because women from Pangasinan recognize the legend of Urduja passed on through songs from "the old ones" (interview, February 2005). The Overseas Workers Program is a one-day workshop intent on teaching protection and safety to OCWs before they work outside of the country. By addressing the rampant abuse of Filipina migrant domestic workers who are only granted "partial citizenship" in a global economy, this program makes a localized, micro-intervention in the dysfunctional nexus called globalization (Parrenas 2001, 49).[4]

While circumventing the limitations of language, Urduja triggers alternate knowledge through recalling collective memory. During the Overseas Worker Program the moderators invite the participants to draw on the strength of their ancestors and leaders. In focus groups the participants are invited to contribute to the discussion and to envision what kind of women they want to be and what is useful or not useful to them. Pasalos notes, "We try to give the background of Urduja as a leader. And then we ask what they want as women. What is their notion of power and spirituality? They decide among themselves" (interview, February 2005). For instance, one group dismissed the "princess" title before Urduja's name because this tradition did not resonate with their experiences. Similarly, in the Micro Enterprise Development Program the moderators ask the participants which qualities of Urduja women should possess. The participants are invited to connect with images of Urduja to develop "confidence" and autonomy (interview, February 2005). The Urduja figure touches upon a subconscious, archetypal truth, a possibility of being and acting that challenges prescribed norms. In fact, Pasalos insists that Pangasinan women are "the living Urduja," so that Urduja names what already exists within these women" (interview, February 2005). By suggesting these women embody Urduja, Urduja's memory is thrust from legend to physical reality. Drawing upon the notion of "strategic essentialism"—glossing over differences and simplifying a group's identity in order to serves a larger good—Urduja helps the women develop feminist awareness as they share a common bond in an ancestral memory. Urduja simply represents what feminist scholar and nun Mary Mananzan calls the Filipina's "valuable heritage, . . . the memory of her egalitarian status in pre-colonial Philippines" (Mananzan 1998, 1). Regardless of whether Urduja's existence can be proven (it cannot), she serves as a metonym for this precolonial past as a memory of women's power. During this precolonial time, Mananzan suggests, girl babies were as welcome as boy babies. Women owned property and practiced sexual autonomy. Divorce was easy, and virginity was not valued. In fact, upon marriage men often took on the women's name. Women in Development Foundation, as well as other women's organizations in the Philippines, consciously invoke this memory of Urduja to reinscribe women's power and effect change.

Perhaps only a starting point, Urduja's memory presents an alternate way of knowing that refuses the First World's commodification of Filipina women as docile, nurturing bodies.[5] To meet the developed world's demand for caretaking, Filipina migrant workers must rely upon extended family and domestic help to care for their own children and elderly back home in what Parrenas argues is a "growing crisis of care" (Parrenas 2005, 12). The sheer enormity of this crisis necessitates storytelling, tapping into the collective unconscious to negotiate an alternate way of being.

URDUJA, A MAP FOR HUMAN RIGHTS ADVOCACY

Indeed, the very invocation of Urduja's memory signals a conflict between competing discourses: the celebration of a free market, a global economy clashing with the forced migration of predominantly college-educated, middle-class Filipinas, displaced from home and family to improve the family's standard of living back home (Parrenas 2005, 13). GABRIELA, a network of Philippines-based and United States–based women's organizations advocating women's rights, features an article about Princess Urduja in its spring 2003 edition of *kaWOMENan*. Urduja is juxtaposed next to articles about the exploitation of Filipinas, such as the plight of mail-order brides or the outrage of domestic workers auctioned online. Urduja's archetypal figure is used to negotiate the failure of language to represent "insidious"[6] everyday trauma (Brown 1995, 107). Using Urduja as a kind of mascot, the article strives to correct the stereotype of the docile, subservient Filipina. Dorotea Mendoza, president of GABRIELA and author of the Urduja article, writes: "In times when the Filipina is stereotyped as submissive, shy, and always service-oriented, women of Philippine ancestry cling to figures like Urduja to help them break out of that mold. . . . Urduja, fact or fiction, gives women of Philippine ancestry a much needed sense of hope and self-worth" (2003, 10). The newsletter employs Urduja to invoke a "warrior woman's legacy" that renders Filipina feminism timeless. Here, Urduja champions human rights in the newsletter's implicit critique of globalization.

Mendoza's article invokes Urduja's militancy in a way that serves to sanction Filipina activism. In the process, however, Urduja's penchant for war and piracy, her act of bringing the enemy king's head home on a spear, is conveniently elided in this newsletter that is adamant in its critique of the war in Iraq. In fact, when Ibn Batuta tells Urduja that he has visited India, she says, "Tell me about the Pepper Country. . . . I should like to conquer it someday" (Ibn and Mackintosh-Smith 2002, 259). It's plain that the use of Urduja by feminists is a strategy that foregrounds some characteristics of Urduja, like her independent spirit, while eliding others, like her desire for territorial domination and conquest. Urduja's thirstiness for battle is elided in the newsletter that actively endeavors to protest US occupation of Iraq. Trinh argues that storytelling can be a politically conscious act:

> Storytelling, the oldest form of building historical consciousness in community, constitutes a rich oral legacy. . . . by re-establishing the contact with her foremothers, so that living tradition can never be congealed into fixed forms, so that life keeps on nurturing life, so that

> what is understood as the Past continues to provide the link for the Present and the Future. (Trinh 1989, 148–149)

Storytelling engages selective memory. In this newsletter Mendoza retells the Urduja legend to sanction activism that resists US imperialism and the exploitation of Filipinos as a result of globalization.

Furthermore, the newsletter's illustration of the warrior princess reinforces this message of an activist, feminist ethos rooted in Filipino identity. Artist Monica A. Bauer portrays Urduja as an embodiment of the homeland (Figure 13.2).

Figure 13.2 Princess Urduja (Bauer).

In a sleeveless dress a woman warrior wields a *bolo* or sword. Behind her, a parallel image suggests her shadow or perhaps, an abstract rendering of Urduja. Clearly, the "inkblot" behind the foregrounded Urduja is a map of the Philippine islands.[6] Thus, Urduja is not only inextricably tied to the homeland through her shadow, but also the map of the islands is a silhouette of the warrior princess. Palawan is Urduja's sword. Luzon is her head crowned with a headdress. Urduja is literally mapped as the Philippines Islands so that Urduja embodies the homeland. In other words, it is not enough, the painting and GABRIELA newsletter suggest, to simply claim Filipina identity, unless this identity is grounded in Filipina activism.

URDUJA AND THE ART OF HEALING

Employing an ethos of Filpina feminist activism, Alma "Urduja" Quinto's work highlights Urduja's potential as a healer, particularly for recovery from trauma. Quinto is an artist, art educator, and social activist who intentionally adopted the name of "Urduja" to remind people of the legendary warrior princess. As Quinto puts it, she appropriated Urduja's name legally "to disseminate information about Urduja" or "to educate others" (interview, February 2005). Urduja serves not only as a muse for Quinto's art but also as an inspiration for her work in the community. As art educator and president of the Philippine Art Educators Association, Quinto uses art to help sexually abused girls build self-esteem and reinvent their lives in recovery. The program is called New Beginnings, a home for girls who have been victims of rape and incest. The girls use art as a way to acknowledge their pain, reclaim their bodies, and heal within a community of survivors through a process that Quinto calls "creative visual autobiography" (Datuin 2003). Quinto believes in art's transformative power. In a large installation in which Quinto works collaboratively with six girls from New Beginnings, she creates "Soft Dreams and Bed Stories" featuring the bed in the shape of a *babaylan* priestess (Figure 13.3).

The babaylan tradition recalls indigenous spiritual practice before the Spanish colonized the Philippines in which women, as priestesses, were healers and officiators of public rituals. Although this tradition was suppressed by the Spanish, it remains a part of Filipino culture. Filipina feminists return to the *babaylan* tradition for its subversive potential. In this art installation, the bed represents domestic space. Although formerly not a safe place for these girls at New Beginnings, the bed is transformed into a safe haven to play and rest. The bed is surrounded by soft sculpture toys, inspired by Philippine indigenous icons. Urduja and the *babaylan* tradition help the girls to create new memories for themselves, not only as a form of catharsis but also as a way to address the pain and, as Flaudette Datuin puts it, to "rejoin the public sphere of community and communion" (Datuin 2004, 4). Quinto points out that she uses the Urduja archetype

Figure 13.3 Babaylan soft sculptures.

or *babaylan* archetype, not in its original form but as a new memory that serves the present. Urduja and the *babaylan* become conflated, perhaps a calculated slippage for many Filipinas. According to art critic Fe Managhas, "You cannot talk about Urduja without discussing the *babaylan* tradition because Urduja was part of the *babaylan* tradition" (interview, February 2005). Since there is no mention in the legend of Urduja as a *babaylan* priestess, I suggest that in this conflation, the babaylan's power for healing is recuperated and highlighted in Urduja. As Quinto points out, it is not important to recover the pristine form of the *babaylan* (or Urduja for that matter; Quinto 2003). Rather, Filipinas create a "rememory," to use Toni Morrison's words (1987), of this priestess tradition, as well as the warrior princess tradition, by strategically conflating these two traditions.

Quinto's work, titled "Dait tan Buknol" (Sew and Tie), epitomizes the conflation of the priestess and Urduja tradition (Figure 13.4).

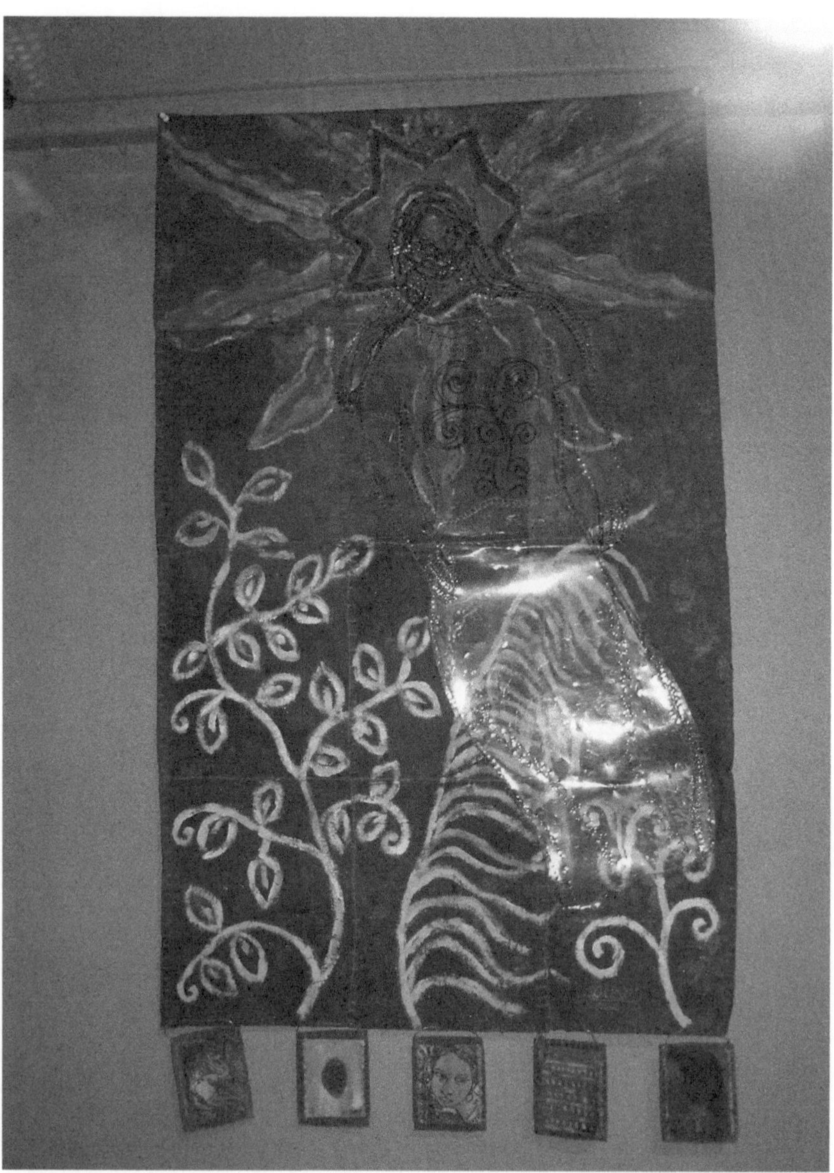

Figure 13.4 Princess Urduja (Quinto).

Quinto (2005) describes her works as "small estampita-like paintings—mostly attributed to the legend of Urduja—attached to the bigger painting of a babaylan (priestess) and a powerful woman or Urduja." The background is comprised of pieces of fabric stitched together to create an organic whole. Quinto says that she uses this technique of stitching to blend the distinction between low and high art. She writes against the tradition that esteems high art (historically created by men) over "women's work" such as quilting. Urduja's body is cut-out plastic draped over the stitched canvas. Urduja's transparency highlights her spectral quality, suggesting that her spirit rather than her "authentic" person is the source of inspiration. Stitches of yarn adumbrate her body, while attaching her to the "canvas." Underneath Urduja's body, there are five pieces of plastic *estampitas* that dangle beneath the larger Urduja. The see-through-ness of the larger Urduja ornamented with the smaller versions of Urduja emphasizes Urduja's multiplicity: her identity proliferates as many things to many people, ever elusive to a monolithic definition. These smaller pieces were used in the 1999 group exhibition Mga Ni Anak (Urduja's Children) by eight women artists from Pangasinan. To use pieces from an earlier exhibition, and to incorporate them into this individual artwork, not only gestures to the custom of women's quilting that borrows from available materials but also underscores the memory-making required to conjure up Urduja. She is pieced together through generations of stories, a patchwork of memories that constitute the legendary princess. In Quinto's work Urduja suggests a trajectory from imperial trauma, the loss of an earlier history, to the trauma of decolonization and to the private trauma of incest and rape, but more importantly, to recovery or a reworking of memory in a way that empowers women.

URDUJA IN CYBERSPACE

While cyberspace increases knowledge-sharing and communication about an otherwise esoteric legend, the Internet also provides a market for the commodification of Urduja, whereas the emphasis is on consumption rather than recovery. Ranked first in any Google search on Urduja, Mary Ubaldo's website Urduja Designs—www.urduja.com—dominates as a site of knowledge about Urduja.[8] This website hawks Filipina jewelry inscribed with the ancient Tagalog script *Baybayin* (Figure 13.5).

Naming her company after Princess Urduja, artist Mary Ubaldo invites her audience, presumably Filipinos, to hearken back to their roots through purchasing her jewelry. Princess Urduja, she claims, is the "first Filipina feminist and a symbol of Filipina strength and wisdom." (Ubaldo 2002).

Owning a piece of Urduja Designs, Ubaldo implies, taps into this mythic power, which is interestingly enough, more accessible *outside the homeland*. Ubaldo, who lives in New York, believes this "rediscovery of her ethnic roots . . . would have been unheard of had she stayed in Manila" (2002 1). Ubaldo's location outside of the Philippines allows her to gaze back to the homeland. Ubaldo's use of Urduja presumes a privileged class: mobile with computer and Internet access, an audience of Filipinos across the diaspora, longing for a lost homeland. This search for origins is the result of colonial trauma. E. San Juan, Jr. writes:

Figure 13.5 Kalikasan, meaning nature (Ubaldo).

> Of all the Asian American groups, the Filipino community is perhaps the only one obsessed with the impossible desire of returning to the homeland, whether in reality or fantasy. It is impossible because, given the break in our history . . . the authentic homeland doesn't exist except as a simulacrum of Hollywood. (1992, 123–124)

Thus, the commercialization of Urduja as a commodity to be purchased and worn gestures to this loss of an irrecoverable past and a desire for rootedness, masquerading as ethnic pride. While on the one hand, the Internet's circumvention of time-space barriers and relative accessibility fosters knowledge-sharing and community-building, on the other hand, the Internet simply adds another front to a media industry creating "good," compliant consumers.

Indeed, Urduja's very figure reflects the complicated and contradictory forces of the Internet. Google Princess Urduja to find the articles and websites discussed here, as well as Filipina "pen pals" who use the pseudonym Urduja or Filipina mail-order bride names of Urduja. Such pimping of Urduja's name dampens celebratory praise of the web as a kind of "cyberdemocracy." While it is true that Internet users could publish information about Princess Urduja as well as access this information, Vernadette V. Gonzalez and Robyn Magalit Rodriquez question this utopian vision of cyberspace as a place that crosses gender, racial, and national boundaries in their article that points to how Filipina bodies continue to be exoticized on the Internet. They write:

> The bodies of Filipinas haunt this dawning Asian "cyberdemocracy" in a historically specific way. . . . Trafficking in women has intensified globally with the advent of telecommunications technology, and

> while Filipinas are not the sole commodity in this traffic, they represent unique sites where histories of U.S. and Asian imperialisms, militarisms, and capitalisms coalesce." (2003, 216–217)

By association, Urduja posits an alternative history, spanning time and space to connect this medieval legend with a digitized global world and to reveal colonial trauma reincarnate.

Yet both the Urduja Designs website and GABRIELA's website, featuring a newsletter article on Urduja, engage with the legend to allay the trauma of a colonial past. Each manifestation of Urduja reflects a specific loss. Princess Urduja continues to haunt the present with a story that has been dismissed by history, and this ghostly presence points to present-day traumas. Gordon writes that "perceiving the lost subjects of history—the missing and lost ones and the blind fields they inhabit—makes all the difference to any project trying to find the address of the present" (Gordon 1997, 195). Urduja persists as a vibrant presence ironically marked by absence. We know very little of the historical figure whom Urduja represents. In fact, one might say she is wiped away, yet she continues to haunt the margins of Filipino collective imagination and refuses to be erased. In the many faces of Urduja there is the repetition of a signifier, each time with a difference, so that the meaning of what constitutes Urduja proliferates. We see so many images and stories of Urduja that it no longer matters if the original referent does not exist, that the thing which Urduja is supposed to represent, the *authentic* person, did not historically exist.

When I began to study the medieval Philippines and first encountered Princess Urduja, I was surprised by the paucity of scholarly material on this time period. Urduja is linked to the medieval Philippines on the World Wide Web because in part she stands for an absence of Filipino history, not because the history did not exist but because it was erased upon Spanish contact. Before the Spanish conquest, the ancestors of the Filipinos used a written script recorded on bamboo or leaves rather than permanent material. Their records and religious relics were destroyed in the name of Christianity. Colonialism in this context enacts a particular kind of trauma that occludes a whole body of earlier history that the body of Urduja—gendered and regendered anew—animates. Princess Urduja gives Filipinos something to embrace, a way of perceiving identity that rebukes the colonialist mentality of inferiority.

Despite history's negation of Urduja, she still persists. Militant Urduja, aristocratic Urduja, and Muslim Urduja (even the pronunciation of her name reveals the influence of the Spanish (urdu-ha rather than urdu-ja): these identities are all elided in order to focus on her independence, strength, leadership, bravery, and solidarity with other women. Urduja's continued appearances speak not only to how Filipinas have resisted history's erasure of their precolonial past but also to how Filipina women, in response to colonial trauma and the ever-present challenges of globalization, continue to sustain Urduja so that she has a life of her own.

NOTES

1. For instance, 50 percent of the Philippines population lives below the poverty line. Overseas contract workers (OCWs) are listed as the second largest export (1,062,057 OCWs in 2006, which translates to over 12 billion dollars in remittances received by the families of OCWs; Philippines Overseas Employment Administration 2006, 6). The Philippines' labor export is caused by unemployment (8 percent in January 2007) and underemployment (over 20 percent in January 2007; Philippines National Statistics). Over 35 percent of the unemployed are college graduates (Philippines National Statistics). Although there is a large, educated middle class, the dearth of job opportunities at home compel many to go abroad to seek out a better life.
2. I am indebted to Geraldine Heng's reading of an earlier version of this chapter, as well as her team-taught seminar, Global Interconnections in the Medieval World, for prompting my interest in Urduja.
3. Delmendo points out that Rizal's status as national hero is in debate, particularly because he did not advocate independence from Spain. Also, the United States' endorsement of José Rizal problematizes Rizal as a national hero because he embodied a nationalism that furthered their colonial project (Delmendo 2004, 24–25).
4. Massive national debt, high unemployment, and underemployment prompt the Philippines' overreliance on exporting Filipino labor (Parrenas 2001, 51).
5. Neferti Tadiar's *Fantasy-Production: Sexual Economies and Other Philippine Consequences for the New World Order* and Rhacel Parrenas's *Servants of Globalization* provide a starting point for thinking about the commodification of Filipina women in the global marketplace.
6. Laura Brown borrows from Maria Root's 1992 definition of "insidious trauma."
7. I am grateful to Lena Khor and Allison Perry for their suggestions on this paper.
8. Internet users interested in Urduja may read Guiterrez's (2004) article on Urduja and view Ubaldo's jewelry designs. Wandering through Ubaldo's website, the Internet user encounters an online Filipino community. The website offers links to the Filipino American National Historical Society, information on Tagalog, as well as links to Filipino American photographer Norman Montifar, whose work documents the Filipino American experience. Urduja marks this online community since she is the link by which a user might have access. Conversely, a Filipino interested in *Baybayin* or Ubaldo's designs might encounter the legend of Urduja for the first time.

14 Fictions of (Under)Development

Hunger Artists in the Global Economy

Françoise Lionnet

> *It is not sufficient to know the personal but to know—to speak it in a different way. Knowing the personal might mean naming spaces of ignorance, gaps in knowledge, ones that render us unable to link the personal with the political.*
>
> bell hooks (1989, 107)

> *Different narrative strategies may be authorized at specific moments in history by complex negotiations of community, identity, and accountability. Fiction, as we know, is political.*
>
> Kamala Visweswaran (1994, 15)

Walk into any supermarket in Mauritius, one of the Indian Ocean Rim countries known among economists as an "African tiger cub," and you get a picture of abundance: neat rows of packaged foods, aisles crowded with customers, entire families shopping for bargains (*The Economist*, February 28, 1988, 51). The lines at the cash registers are long, even at the French-owned mega-stores Continent and Prisunic, which charge inflated prices, or at the South African–owned Winners and Spar, which import merchandise from not quite as far away as Europe. In a country where the 2007 average annual income per capita is approximately $11,900, the disposable income of the middle and working classes is limited, and people will spend their paychecks in the first few days of the month on the basic necessities of life (*Jeune Afrique*, March 31, 1998, 55). But what counts as "basic necessities of life" in the midst of this consumer revolution? How has the concept of individual need been inflected by the availability of imported merchandise, the lure of easy credit, and the promise of a more satisfying lifestyle? How have these issues affected women's lives? And what do we know about the impact of these economic changes on the quotidian practices of a new generation of Mauritian women today? This essay attempts to answer some of these questions by analyzing a fictional text, *There Is a Tide,* by Lindsey Collen (1990), and situating it within the context of those changing socioeconomic conditions. Collen, a South African–born Mauritian citizen for more than thirty years, is an award-winning Anglophone and Creolophone novelist and a political activist who has fought for human rights and worked closely with grassroots organizations. Her fictional treatments of critical social issues offer unique insights into the personal experiences of ordinary citizens, whose social and cultural histories have yet to be fully included in the narratives of "world history."

The transformation of the world's markets and the resulting changes in patterns of consumption have affected the daily habits of the population and the balance of payments of remote, developing nations such as Mauritius. Once adequately fed by multiple small-scale local resources such as fish and vegetables and imported staples such as rice and lentils, the population is now persuaded by advertising and the proliferation of malls and supermarkets to value imports and fast food: the best of the food grown locally or fished from the sea is reserved for the luxury hotels and their hard-currency-paying guests. At the supermarkets, you can stare at prepackaged imported apples and oranges (and at fellow shoppers) while dealing with well-groomed, uniformed, and politely distant cashiers. The depersonalization of shopping and the promotion of items that have questionable use-value in the general context of the culture, and the nation reached exceptional levels in the 1990s. By contrast, the open-air market or Creole bazaar continues to be the preferred choice for cheaper local produce and other staples. Market day in the towns of Mauritius is the shopper's opportunity to discuss freshness and prices with jocular growers who will boast, "pas fin met di sel dans sa legim la" ("my vegetables are organically grown"). These open-air markets also serve as outlets for garment-industry "seconds" and defective items that are sold at cut-rate prices. The unlabeled designer clothes that you find there run the gamut, from Ralph Lauren Polo shirts to Gap sweatshirts or jeans and Pierre Cardin ties and sweaters—all made in Mauritius in the export processing zone (EPZ) factories by a largely female workforce.

Food and clothing are two of the most basic necessities of life, and they form part of the range of material practices central to the identity of a people. It is a truism that what we eat and how we eat tend to define us as social beings (Weismantel 1989), and that there is a dynamic relationship between the body, clothing, and the changing self-representations of citizens (Hendrickson 1996). The worldwide expansion of capitalism and the phenomenon vaguely known as "globalization" bring about new forms of social interaction which are superimposed on more traditional ones, resulting in stresses on gender roles and familial arrangements and in conflicted responses to new job opportunities. People's bodies exhibit the mark of their changing relationship to the symbolic realm of culture. Thus, in Mauritius, the new consumerism spells a less complex diet, even causing nutritional disorders of all kinds, like those prevalent in the West: obesity, anemia, anorexia, or bulimia, as I was able to observe among adolescent girls of my acquaintance in the mid-1990s. Women who are employed in the service sector are given tailored uniforms that minimize their clothing expenses but also affect their self-image and their demeanor. Add to this the omnipresent billboards promoting the products of the offshore garment industry and the tourist sector's objectification of the exotic Mauritian feminine body in its advertising of this "island paradise," and you have the ingredients for making women appearance-conscious in a more Western way, suspended between their roles as producers and consumers, on the one hand, and as lures for both tourists and foreign capital investments, on the other.

Women's relationship to food and shopping, work, language, and sexuality is shifting rapidly and creating new pathologies of identification. The social and economic forces which normalize slenderness and gender identity (Bordo 1993) and conflate the exotic Creole or Asian body with stereotypical forms of "mysterious" femininity are reinforced by public health warnings against the dangers of malnutrition and obesity. Faced with these modern stereotypes (which many well-intentioned government campaigns only serve to reinforce) *and* having to cope with aspects of their traditional culture that put a definite premium on "plumpness," Mauritian women have to sort out conflicting signals about body shape, health, and food. From breast milk and baby formula to the preparation of quotidian family meals, everyday choices now carry a heavy symbolic load and generate stressful reactions. More women than ever are developing symptomatic reactions of alienation and disembodiment, which continue a pattern of psychosomatic ailments dating from slavery and indentured labor and amount to internalized forms of social and gender oppression, as anthropologists such as Aihwa Ong have argued. To my knowledge, there is no medical or social science literature pertaining to this topic in relation to the distinct historical and cultural circumstances of Mauritius; but literary texts, such as Collen's, that stage specifically female modes of alienation, are the tip of the iceberg. Writers like Ananda Devi (1989, 2000, 2001, 2006) or Natacha Appanah (2004), both award-winning Francophone novelists, have also treated such issues with insight and elegance. Devi, in particular, who is trained as an anthropologist (and whose scholarly work is published under the last name Nirsimloo-Anenden), delves relentlessly into the darker narratives of gender oppression in Hindu and Creole communities in Mauritius (Lionnet 1995, 48–68).

In the industrial sector—especially the garment factories—stress-related fainting spells, screaming fits, seizures, and spirit possession are common occurrences. They create disturbances and cause production shutdowns, and can thus be interpreted as tactics of resistance, nonverbal ruses against authority, or surreptitious forms of protest (de Certeau 1984). They are also physical reactions to, and ways of dealing with, the traumas of colonial and neocolonial exploitation (Ong 1986). This behavior is increasingly recognized and disciplined by the medicocultural discourses that regulate health and normalcy on an international scale. Mental illness has become a big business. It is treated by growing numbers of health professionals who practice at the old Brown Sequard Hospital, aptly named after the nineteenth-century Franco-Mauritian neurologist who became famous in Paris for his research on glandular secretions and hormonal therapy for mental disorders, including hysteria and anorexia (Brumberg 1988, 206–208). Today, among the affluent classes, even Prozac has become a drug of choice for depression. But since psychosomatic reactions are still largely read as narcissistic or hysterical, women have been the primary targets for experimental treatments, drugs, and psychotherapy that together aim at "normalizing" their behavior.

Eating disorders are commonly associated with a warped self-image, and a distorted sense of one's body shape and appearance. Feminist research has shown, however, that these disorders are closely related to larger social issues, including work and wage-labor, rather than being the result of a narcissistic or neurotic focus on personal appearance. Women's self-image cannot be divorced or decontextualized from the use- or exchange-value of the body within the political economy of a given culture. Extrapolating from the work of cultural critics (such as Przybylowicz 1990), I argue that it is possible to view the increasing fixation on personal appearance as a result of the relationship we are obliged to have to our productive capabilities and to the concurrent need to discipline our laboring bodies. Anorexia and bulimia can thus be seen as the consequences of a social need generated not just by unrealistic standards of beauty but also by the conditions governing rules in the workplace and by the history of the culture and the nation. Mauritius is now a postcolonial and developing nation with a history of trauma related to its past and to the demands which were put on its workforce (from slavery to neocolonial exploitation). Somatic disorders linked to the globalization of the economy are thus a multilayered syndrome, symptomatic of the survival of the past in the present.

SOCIAL REALITY AND PERSONAL STORIES

Few cultural historians and anthropologists have done work on Mauritius (Arno and Orian 1986; Eriksen 1988; Nirsimloo-Anenden 1990). Only Nirsimloo-Anenden has asked gender-related questions, but her research is limited to the Telegu ethnic group. No one else has used gender as a systematic category of analysis or conducted extensive interviews with women. Information about popular culture is found mostly in the work of folklorists such as Lee Haring, who bemoans the fact that oral tales are not taken seriously by the educated elites who have internalized Western values and standards of literacy and rationality (Haring 1992). Sociologists, on the other hand, have recently begun to document some of the changes in labor reorganization, while economists have always shown a great deal of interest in the resilience of the local markets and the productive capacity of women workers.

In the 1980s, free-trade zones and EPZs were set up in Mauritius, as in a number of developing countries, as an instrument of economic stabilization and structural adjustment. The international banking community devised EPZs to help indebted governments redress their balance-of-payments deficits by producing goods for the international market. As Cynthia Enloe (1989, 159) describes it: "Governments lure overseas companies to move their plants to these EPZs by offering them sewers, electricity, ports, runways, tax holidays and police protection. Most attractive of all is the government's offer of cheap labor. Women's labor has been the easiest to cheapen, so it shouldn't be surprising that in most Export Processing Zones at least 70 per cent of the workers are women." In Mauritius, women's share of manufacturing employment was 6.6 percent in 1962, climbed to 57.4 percent in 1982 (Pearson in Nababsing and Kothari 1996, 25), and hovered at around 66 percent in the mid-1990s (personal communication with Vidula Nababsing, November 7, 1996). These new forms of industrialization have helped create a precariously affluent middle class. If the new shopping malls exemplify this affluence in the urban areas, the garment factories that have sprouted in the middle of sugarcane fields have transformed the rural areas, providing employment where the poorest people live. Sociologists Vidula Nababsing and Uma Kothari, who have studied these patterns in Mauritius, Bangladesh, and Sri Lanka, note that the socioeconomic benefits to women have been considerable, even where employment conditions, wages, labor laws, and low unionization levels have created less than optimal working environments. Their findings indicate that in Mauritius, "new employment opportunities were taken up either by those who would otherwise have gone into an already declining agricultural sector or domestic service" (Nababsing and Kothari 1996, 134) or would not have been job seekers in the first place.

For these sociologists, the single criterion of "new employment opportunities" is a value, since it is helping women to acquire a measure of independence. Such independence can then allow them to escape some of their more rigid religious and patriarchal traditions and to support themselves and their families in ways that improve upon the arduous labor in the sugarcane fields. The benefits of modernization should not be discounted, their argument goes, even when the mobility of international capital renders industrialization ephemeral: consciousness-raising has been an important impact of industrialization. "In fact, the empowerment of women in terms of their increased participation in social, economic and political arenas [became] a primary objective for many development agencies and projects" (Nababsing and Kothari 1996, 152), as women pushed for reforms in the areas of social and welfare services. The "moral panic" (Nababsing and Kothari 1996, 148) expressed by some religious leaders at the prospects of liberalization, and their fear that it would impact negatively on "family values," has been largely unfounded as women have organized to support one another and strengthen community bonds.

The psychosocial aspects of this industrialization process, however, have been largely neglected by development "experts." The intimate feelings of the women and their working conditions have recently been articulated in fictional texts. These feelings must give us pause as we listen to the worker's own voice against the sociologists' account of empowerment and participatory democracy. As Collen's (1990) fictional autobiographical character, Shynee, reports in *There Is a Tide*:

> I'll be twenty-three soon and I've got already ten years' experience behind me. Ten years making woollen threads out of bundles of wool or sewing collars, collars and more collars. Don't know who I'm making it all for, not even what'll become of it. I feel old and tired. Don't we all. Some of us climbing up and down. It is like an animal, that I feel? Like an ox, to be more precise, working bowed and cowed. Over a sitting machine. Others like me, in my first job, watch the thread on the machine, and when it breaks, which it does every few minutes, they climb up on the stool and tie it up again fast, and do this day in and day out, on an eight hour shift, ever rotating. Seven to three, three to eleven, eleven to seven. And then again.
>
> And I've never moaned. Please don't misunderstand me. Even now I am not moaning. In any case I prefer working on the twister running backwards and forwards after the "mule" like my mates have to. Other workers work harder than I do. Especially now that I am a machinist, bottom to my chair, back aching, sewing away at collars. . . . Sometimes I feel all angry inside about it. I don't know what it is. I am humiliated by my turning this eight hours into my bread. I had to eat a lot. We all do in the factory. I was quite proud that I got a bit round. . . . And being a machinist, I jumped about less. Much less than on the twister. . . . So a general plumpness rounded me off. (Collen 1990, 44–45)

As is made clear by this monologue, the physical impositions and the manipulation of the body of the worker create feelings of anger and humiliation that convey the concrete material and psychic consequences of exploitation. Food becomes a substitute for free expression and freedom of movement. It compensates for the physical discomforts of wage-labor: food is what one works for, but also that which can soothe the humiliation of "turning this eight hours into bread." It is the sign of one's alienation. While a new global culture makes women more conscious of the "shape" they are in, they, on the other hand, tend to use food to take comfort in the soothing quality of its sensual aspects. Their individual anguish is made visible and is shared in these nonverbal ways of coping.

A polyvocal text that looks back on twenty-five years of post-independence Mauritius, *There Is a Tide* is a testimonial narrative which stages and authorizes different perspectives on this contested reality. There are three parallel testimonies: 22-year-old Shynee Pillay, an anorexic Hindu worker in a shirt factory in the free-trade zone, writes an "auto-analysis" (Collen 1990, 7) for her psychiatrist at the Brown Sequard Hospital; Fatma, a midwife, recounts the life of Shynee's grandmother and father and the latter's public role as union and strike organizer during the revolutionary struggles for independence; finally, the unnamed psychiatrist's stream-of-consciousness diary reveals a disconnected and disaffected postmodern subjectivity. These three voices are themselves embedded within a futuristic frame that projects the reader into the twenty-first century and a utopian postglobalization world. The narratives provide a multifaceted critique of social victimization and agency during what the framing story calls the prerevolutionary "dark ages." Two autobiographical modes are contrasted with a historical and biographical one, and their relative status as sources of information is foregrounded by the utopian quest for useful and enabling knowledge. Each narrator's act of witnessing articulates for the reader the interconnectedness of the local and the global, of gender, ethnic, and class subject positions. Taken together, the stories add up to counter-history and visionary feminine ethnography, since they inscribe these muted realities into discourse, thus giving them symbolic purchase. These stories perform identity and citizenship on three levels across time and space, rewriting the history of independence movements, exposing the complacent attitudes of local elites, denouncing the politics of female labor in the EPZs, and questioning neocolonial consumerism as well as religious fundamentalism.

The women writers who bear witness to these efforts simultaneously document the vulnerabilities and strengths of this new exploited class of global capital. As women workers struggle to become the subjects of their own stories, the narrators of their own history, they also engage with the public scripts that attempt to define them as chattel and cheap labor (for example, "ox," "animal," "mule") useful to the neoliberal (or neocolonial) economy. Collen's *There Is a Tide* fictionalizes the material and symbolic changes of the 1980s by reinterpreting current somatic symptoms in terms of a history of social and political events. As the contemporary "labor politics of postmodernity" (Ong 1986) infiltrates communities that had remained largely rural and self-sufficient, ethnicity, gender, and class are redefined and intertwined with shifting economic relations of domination and insubordination. Fictional and personal narratives become the sites where contradictions are worked out and solutions begin to be imagined.

In her study of the testimonial genre, Doris Sommer (1988, 129–130) has shown how Latin American testimonies are related "to a general text of struggle . . . written from interpersonal class and ethnic positions" that engage the reader in a relationship of "respectful distance" where difference is acknowledged and the goal is "to raise the reader's consciousness by linking her to the writer's testimony." In *There Is a Tide*, the plurality of subject positions (which cannot in any way be collapsed into one another) challenges the reader to consider more inclusive definitions of citizenship and to question the clichés of democracy. Each story foregrounds coping mechanisms and ways of witnessing directly linked to the social practices that are implicitly being critiqued. Sommer (1988, 120) makes the point that "one of the most fascinating features of [testimonies] is their unpredictable pattern, the sense that the discourse of analysis and struggle is being created in an open-ended and syncretic process of trial, error, and surprise."

The three alternating narratives of *There Is a Tide* provide this sense of "surprise" as they function as interpretative frameworks for one another. Fatma tells of the father's experiences of political solidarity: the historic dockers' strike of 1971 and the general strike of 1979, which culminated in a hunger strike by the jailed activists. Listening to her, Shynee is able to recast her own choices and motivations—to "name the spaces of ignorance," as bell hooks puts it (1989, 107)—and to appropriate the realm of the political. History's hidden scripts gradually emerge, along with an alternative reading of her anorexia not just as individualized protest against social constraints, but also as an echo of the heroism of a previous generation of political agents. The public theater of nationalist politics and the private realm of women's lives are brought together by the same spectacular gestures of refusal and rejection and by analogous ways of dealing with inequities and refusing consumption. The narrative thus mediates the performance of self-starvation and its gendered contexts by weaving together the symptoms and the cure, the seeming solitariness of anorexia and the public statement of hunger strikers.

The different styles of each section of the novel force a constant readjustment on the part of the reader, enacting a deconstruction of the seamless narratives of neocolonialism that promote unambiguous and linear progress; the stylistic shifts simultaneously expose the postmodern fragmentation of the new nation, its divided allegiances, mosaic of cultures, and uneven development. Fatma's and Shynee's voices interrupt the ironic and self-deprecating flow of the medical expert. The psychiatrist's breathless style of enunciation, intensified by the lack of punctuation, mirrors the penetrating flow of capital as it infiltrates every aspect of the local economy. While the cumulative effect of his words on the page aestheticizes and "privatizes" his experiences, his soliloquy is a form of excess that interrupts the narrative or testimonial economy of the women's dialogues, and his tone reveals the disciplining power of money and privilege. The testimonies of the women, on the other hand, their stories of embodied struggle within the regulative discourses of culture, labor, and capital, assert the dissolution of the very concept of "privacy," making visible the concrete material conditions of their existence and the "collective assemblage" of their enunciation (Deleuze and Guattari 1986). Their conversation thus puts the reader (rather than the psychiatrist) in the position of witness to the cultural and historical trauma of the nation and its working class.

When small oppositional practices of everyday life (de Certeau 1984) proliferate outside hegemonic relations, in the interstices of systems of domination hidden from public scrutiny, testimonial narratives help to articulate personal experiences as forms of collective struggle, as "structures of feeling" (Williams 1977, 128) and emergent sensibilities. The public scenarios of globalization, their norms and disciplining power, are sundered by the multiplication of unscripted behaviors revealed by the dissenting voices of the women. The storytelling in which they engage shifts the focus from "expert" and professional testimony (medicine, anthropology, sociology, economy) on to their own concrete experiences. The act of telling and remembering is thus part of a process of symbolization, a sharing of values, the logic of which produces more self-aware and politicized subjectivities. As a literary text, *There Is a Tide* draws attention to the casualties of the new labor markets while remaining an open-ended and utopian engagement with the desire for long-term political change. As literature, then, it is the space where issues that are not immediately resolvable politically can be articulated and symbolized, leading its readers towards both a personal and a national confrontation with the issues and traumas that have occluded discussions about the past, the histories of colonialism and independence struggles, their gendered subtexts, and the way these issues continue to have an effect in the present.

BLOOD, MILK, AND MONEY

At the hospital where she begins her narrative, Shynee is required to give all elements of her identity using a questionnaire meant to establish the "facts" of her life: name, age, occupation, education, and so on. When she gets to the last line, "food preferences," she writes: "I refuse to answer this. This question is, in my case, not in the realm of fact, at all" (Collen 1990, 20). She adds: "What I am about to write is the reason why I do not eat" (Collen 1990, 27). Her first explanation is the obvious one: wanting to conform to new models of beauty, to be "thin. Slim, lithe. Svelte. Light as a feather" (Collen 1990, 43), she thinks of it as a necessary "diet" after becoming a bit too "plump" on the factory job. Dieting now becomes an issue of self-control, and the focus broadens from body size to contours and appearance in general. Factory workers who have fits are tagged "wild women." Shynee's head of "unruly hair" becomes a symbol of unbridled sexuality that connotes a femininity out of control. It needs to be tied "up into a neat plait" (Collen 1990, 43), just as her clothing needs to conform to certain rules. Hair and skin imperfections become signs of the "madness escaped from inside of me" (Collen 1990, 163), as she puts it. The fear of revealing her inner reality translates into a need to restrain and stabilize the inner self within impermeable borders: "I had two linked worries. Not wanting to take anything in. And not wanting to let anything break out" (Collen 1990,

47). Susie Orbach (1986) has shown how anorexia is precipitated by the tensions and paradoxes women experience about their place in the world: "Anorexia symbolizes the restraint on women's desire. In the most tortuous denial of need and dependency and the most persistent and insistent expression of independence, women with anorexia live out the contrariness of contemporary cultural dictates. . . . Anorexia is at once an embodiment of stereotyped femininity and its very opposite" (Orbach 1986, 29–30). As Shynee moves out of the sphere of the home, where the matriarchs of the village praise a well-rounded body, and goes to work in the factory, her values are jolted by advertising dictates and factory rules which encourage uniformity, but succeed only in generating schizophrenic reactions.

The power to refuse food becomes performative on other levels as well. It leads to dissent and defiance with regard to the technologies of identity used by the hospital. Each line on the questionnaire now raises more questions than it enables Shynee to answer: "Name. I have already given my name. It is a fact. A known fact. But facts are difficult. The fact of Shynee Pillay is fraught with problems" (Collen 1990, 17). As Kamala Visweswaran (1994, 61) has pointed out in *Fictions of Feminist Ethnography*, "facts" have a way of being misperceived, of constructing the subject "as" something other than she wants to be seen (Visweswaran 1994, 61). Referring to a woman who "refused . . . to be [her] subject," and whom she calls simply "M" in her research, Visweswaran (1994, 61) asks: "What if I were to call this resisting subject Françoise or Ghislaine? Surely my audience, anticipating the story of an Indian woman, would object knowing that the anthropological pseudonym connotes placename if not ethnic identity." Shynee's "paper name" too connotes a specific caste and ethnic identity—and refusing to use it is a proclamation of distrust for printed information, for government or religious "archives" (Collen 1990, 19) that immediately demarcate her as representative of a distinct political class, with a civil status that she has not chosen. Her musings echo those of her father, who had pondered the wisdom of "changing" names handed down in slave cultures: "To change it seems to be to sell out. To abandon the last memory. . . . To somehow bury something that should not be buried. To forget what should be remembered. And yet, to leave it the same seems to mean you accept the slave-owners' definition of you" (Collen 1990, 75). Names are linked to "blood-lines," but as Fatma's commentary stresses, the seemingly ambivalent identity (both Indian and African Creole) of Shynee's father, his double name—Lallmohar/Larmwar and Laval—was a force in the struggles for independence, a symbol against the "race war" (Collen 1990, 29), and a means of avoiding essentialist notions of self and other: "Nothing is in your blood, girl. It's all out there, around you, moulding you, making you. That is the only moral my story will have" (Collen 1990, 75). The physical and the social body are conflated in this reminder that religious beliefs encourage arbitrary notions of racialized and gendered purity and posit definitions of selfhood that can lead to ethnic cleansing. When workers at the factory break up into race and religious groups to eat their meals, Shynee reacts with "morbid horror" (Collen 1990, 148–149), realizing that efforts to unionize them are bound to be difficult if even the sharing of food becomes an index of the fragmentations and divisions that the bosses can now easily exploit. Her refusal to be named and circumscribed by the rules of patriarchal logic extends to food choices and cultural notions of purity and transgression.

In her study of pollution and taboo, *Purity and Danger*, Mary Douglas (1966, 27) stresses that, "food is not likely to be polluting at all unless external boundaries of the social system are under pressure." The fear of social destabilization is brought about by the proliferation of new social practices—from prepackaged and precooked foodstuffs and objects whose use-value is at issue, to new work opportunities. This fear serves to reinforce archaic models of purity at all levels of society. As Douglas (1966, 126) puts it: "If we treat ritual protection of bodily orifices as a symbol of social preoccupations about exits and entrances, the purity of cooked food becomes important." Quoting from commentators who have studied Indian pollution symbolism, Douglas (1966, 126) explains that "cooking may be taken to imply a complete appropriation of the food by the household. It is almost as if, before being 'internally absorbed' by the individual, food was, by cooking, collectively predigested. One cannot share the food prepared by people without sharing in their nature." Thus the preparation and consumption of food are symbolically marked, and changes in eating habits can lead to symptomatic disorders at the individual and collective levels.

Refusing to consume what is external to the household, the culture, and the nation, the anorexic appears to be making visible the paradoxical yet logical parallel between self-starvation and the utopian need to feel autonomous in the face of global capitalism. When Shynee states, "Milk was my first food, and I don't want to drink milk" (Collen 1990, 27), she emphasizes its ambiguous meaning. The most basic food of life, it carries a set of unsettling connotations. "Milk," Roland Barthes (1972, 60) has said, "is cosmetic, it joins, covers, restores . . . its purity, associated with the innocence of the child, is a token of strength, of a strength which is not revulsive, not congestive, but calm, white, lucid, the equal of reality." But the production and circulation of milk in rural Mauritius are fraught with taboos that are anything but "calm" and comforting. In those rural areas, the cows are cared for by women who collect and sell the fresh milk to a middleman. Shynee's stepfather is such a milkman who circulates in the countryside, puts diluted milk in an "aluminium tank soldered to his bicycle" (Collen 1990, 164), and resells the watered-down product to other families for a fat profit.

Although milk is generally linked to the notion of purity and motherhood, in this context it becomes, like bloodlines, the sign of an oppressive system of exchange, and of an imposed identity. It marks the numerous ways in which women lack control over their own labor and bodies, which can be exploited by those who are freer to circulate at will in society. The nature and use-value of milk thus foregrounds the links between production and reproduction, especially unwanted pregnancies: "My mother did not want me. I was foisted upon her. . . . Nor did she want my father. He was also foist upon her" (Collen 1990, 29). Shynee exposes the notion of "family" as artificial, and the traditional role of mothers as bearers of culture as damaging to their relationship to the child. "She breastfed reluctance into me," says Shynee, denouncing the corporeal struggle involved in reluctant motherhood, the hardships that biology visits upon the women who do not have the luxury of sentimentalizing the maternal instinct.

Resentment against sexuality and reproduction—as well as other "natural" functions of the body such as digestion, evacuation, and menstruation—becomes confused within a symbolic economy that attempts to conflate nature and culture. Shynee's refusal to conform becomes a leitmotiv against the perversion of natural needs. When her mother dies—"in a pool of blood on her bed" (Collen 1990, 59)—from a botched illegal abortion, Shynee is confirmed in her "reluctant" subjectivity, that of a woman who refuses to be defined by the feminine realm of the "fluid" (Irigaray 1985) and by the products of her body: blood and milk. The oppressive structures of religious taboos, in Hinduism as in other religions, associate traditional views of femininity with uncleanliness and filth. The significations attached to blood and milk, and the role women play in reproducing gender differences, is central to Shynee's developing feelings of repulsion. As Caroline Bynum (1987) has shown in her study of medieval women's fasts, fasting is impelled by the pious need to feel "clean," "pure," and "holy." The anorexic's wish for disembodied spirituality, for a state of being that will be divorced from the pollution associated with the flesh, stems from the religious conflation of the impure with the feminine (Bynum 1987). "I have stopped eating, doctor, in order to be cleaner. The more I stop, the cleaner. The cleaner, the holier. I want to be holy . . . I would prefer never to get my periods, if it's unclean. If I don't eat, maybe I won't," confesses Shynee (Collen 1990, 59). Since menstruation is what banishes women to the realm of immanence, that of the unchaste and the desecrated, it is not surprising that Shynee, "not wanting to let anything break out" of her, should also resist "tak[ing] anything in" (Collen 1990, 47). Caught in a double bind, she would "rather not risk living," since life might mean passing on to a daughter the mark of gender and its weight of shame, guilt, self-hatred, and despair. Refusal becomes empowering, since it is what allows her to go against the grain of femininity and motherhood, to step out of the shackles of patriarchal culture.

Self-awareness and negativity finally culminate in Shynee's realization that her behavior is not simply culturally driven (dieting, fasting) but economically and politically motivated as well:

> I have no objection to eating, to using food. I just happen to refuse to consume food. I am a producer. I work . . . I don't always know what

> I produce. Nor do I know who I produce it for. But I know for sure I am a producer. I make shirts. . . . I am not a consumer of things. . . . This refusing to consume is what turns out to be my not eating. (Collen 1990, 104–105)

The distinction between "using" and "consuming," between need and want, the necessary and the superfluous, is hard to establish, however, since money corrupts the use-value of things. When even milk becomes a commodity like any other, it can be exchanged for money. Its exchangeability corrupts its inaugural meaning and perverts its original usage.

For Marx, only "superfluous products become exchangeable products," only those "whose use-value falls outside the sphere of mere necessaries" (Marx 1904, 168). Milk, like bread and money, becomes what one works for rather than the source of life. The milkman who collects it from the rural women and sells it for a profit to his high-caste clients is in a position to legislate the standards of "purity" which must accompany the handling of milk by the womenfolk whose impure nature (according to Hindu beliefs) can cause the milk to curdle when they are menstruating. But Shynee suggests that the man's ability to turn this "product" into a consumer good, to water it down in order to make more money, contaminates its meaning with regard to the "basic necessities of life." Milk thus loses its purity, its "innocence" (Barthes 1972). It becomes the "abject" (Kristeva 1986)—something that is both self and other, but feared as foreign; something against which the self must be guarded. The throat contracts against the invasion by this substance, thus rejecting what does not enter into "the satisfaction of immediate need" (Marx 1904, 208) or what is already denied by its association with the notions of superfluity and excess. No longer the natural means of satisfying a natural need, milk becomes a medium of exchange which further oppresses those who are subjected to its symbolic economy. It becomes that which can be dispensed with, expelled, evacuated—in other words, it becomes, in Freudian terms, linked to feces and excrements within the archaic economy of the social subject (Goux 1990, 29–31).

Milk becomes a metaphor for what Shynee's body refuses to ingest and for what the nation's EPZs symbolize in this new world economy. The EPZs are sites which are both within the country, and yet external to it, regulated by laws which transcend those that govern the nation and the lives of the ordinary citizens who labor in this zone yet reap few of its benefits. EPZs are useful to the developing country, but for Shynee they are the means by which her exploitation reaches a point of paroxysm. When the concept of need is perverted, the refusal of food corresponds to a very different logic of starvation from the one prevalent in either Western interpretations of narcissistic "dieting" or religious notions of purification and "fasting." It now corresponds paradoxical logic of survival, expressed in the contradiction at the heart of the statement made by Shynee just before her return to a more "earthy" acceptance of embodiment: "It is as though I want to say: I don't need to eat to stay alive" (Collen 1990,168).

With this declaration, Shynee comes full circle and experiences a form of epiphany that grounds her in unmediated nature. In a crucial scene, she is suddenly attracted by a smell: "I felt my nostrils flare open. I put my head back and sniffed. Loudly. Like a wild deer . . . I snorted. I panted with excitement. . . . It was a rotting tang" (Collen 1990, 174). The *tang* is a rodent which burrows and scavenges for food, "the lowliest of creatures" (Collen 1990, 173). This dead animal, the symbol of what is abject in nature and a frequent source of food for maroon slaves during the colonial period, becomes the catalyst that sets Shynee on the road to recovery. In a horrific attempt at ingesting that symbol of impurity, she becomes like a scavenging animal herself, merging with all that is abject, and recovering in this process an identity that she had been taught to deny (the fact that she is *also* a descendant of slaves). She becomes a "huntress" (Collen 1990, 175) and her appetite returns. She embraces nature and its life-affirming "filth" and transforms her relationship to culture. She asserts her independence from culturally defined functions of the body, but this is not an illusion of transcendence. Rather, it is her acknowledgment of the *utopian possibility* of being in harmony with unmediated nature, of surviving at the level of raw need, of feeding on wild creatures and uncooked substances. The fact that she then starts to eat normally (that is, processed foods) is an indication of the transformative power of this realization. In other words, she is tempted by, but recognizes the futility of, an escape from the encroachment of global society, from the uneven exchanges metaphorized by the whole process of feeding. She learns from the *tang* that to scavenge and to survive is a perfectly acceptable form of resistance, whereas anorexia and isolationism lead to self-destructiveness. Her discovery about food can be extended to the economic realm as well. If the products of the EPZs are meant for foreign markets, and if the local economy has to make do with "seconds" or "rejects," then the local producer/consumer becomes a form of scavenger who undoes the distinction between the local and the global, the pure and the impure, the raw and the cooked. She can decide to survive on the crumbs or leftovers of that global economy rather than letting it destroy her. She can learn to manipulate the system and benefit from its contradictions.[1]

HUNGER ARTISTS AND HUNGER STRIKERS

In this story, "normal" or patriarchal narrative logic would have required closure either in the form of death (anorexics often starve to death, as do political prisoners whose sole means of protest is fasting) or in complete separation from the realm of the social. But the initial rejection of food is only a means to a creative end. It permits the narrator's voice to come into its own, voraciously to enumerate possible explanations of her reluctance to be a "model consumer." Deleuze and Guattari (1986, 19–20) explain that "there is a certain disjunction between eating and speaking, and even more, despite all appearances, between eating and writing . . . writing transform[s] words into things capable of competing with food. . . . To speak, and above all to write, is to fast." In writing her "auto-analysis," Shynee progresses through different stages of negativity that offer a systematic critique of social "norms." She reaches a point of political and critical awareness that allows her to embrace life and affirm her local cultural values. Her fast is a form of consciousness-raising. It clears the path towards higher self-knowledge, even if this knowledge is embedded within multiple contradictions.

Like other "hunger artists" before her, Shynee performs linguistically and thus renders visible the gap between cultural survival and mere physical subsistence.[2] By contrasting what Maud Ellman has termed the "wordless testimony of the famished flesh" (Ellman 1993, 17) with the abundance of descriptive language in the local vernacular, Shynee is able to distinguish her anorexia from other forms of self-denial. By articulating her refusal as a form of hunger strike, and then attributing a series of meanings to her refusal, she is able to make her "self-starvation *readable* as protest" (Ellman 1993, emphasis added). The artistry and eloquence of the testimony serve to "master [the] destructive logic" (Ellman 1993, 21) of the act of starving. Rather than denying and disavowing her eating disorder, as women patients are generally supposed to do, Shynee's narrative allows her to claim agency and responsibility for the act of negation; rather than being a denial, her act is one of conscious refusal. By withholding the basic and "natural" needs of the body, she is simultaneously conferring upon it the status of a cipher, a slate upon which the notion of negation is inscribed. Her body now mirrors her father's body and those of other manual laborers who had their work "engraved" into it (Collen 1990, 34), marked, and broken by the weight of the burdens they carried and the repeated gestures they performed as dockers loading sugar on to the cargo ships. The mechanization of sugar loading has rendered the docker's job obsolete, but it is now the female workers of the EPZ who are put in the same situation of repetitive physical labor. Their physical trauma mirrors those of the past, which begs the question about modes of psychological healing that can take this long history into consideration instead of excising the gendered subject from its representations.

In the chronicle of revolutionary events narrated by Fatma, the heroic strike of the dockers serves as counterpoint and introduces another notion of purposiveness. Fourteen of them starve together, publicly, in the main park of the capital city (Collen 1990, 212). The collective aspect of this protest contrasts starkly with the woman's isolating refusal of food. Since eating and conviviality are very much a part of the activity of building social bonds, to refuse food would be to become hopelessly isolated. But if the gift and the sharing of food constitute the basis for building cohesion, while the nature of the food to be shared clearly undermines the constitution of the group or the nation, then it becomes logical to propose that it is in the collective refusal of the *inappropriate* meal that a proper community can begin to be imagined. If an earlier generation of workers embarked together on a hunger strike to solidify the communal means by which they might succeed in resisting oppression, then Shynee's accomplishment is of a different nature. By ceasing to refuse food indiscriminatingly, she learns the difference between the blanket denial of need and the discriminating approach of an enlightened subject who does not exist and survive only "by the gaze of others" (Ellman 1993, 17). She no longer needs to exhibit her physical body as an instrument of protest, to mortify it. She can make choices that will not be damaging to her being, just as—it is implied—the community, too, can resist rampant consumerism, benefit from the consolidation of its most vital and local needs, and survive by using the resources of its newly prosperous economy.

The narrative attempts to resolve these contradictions by slipping into the realm of utopia. The tone changes to one of prelapsarian reliance on the goodness of nature's bounty, on the quasi-mythic time of Shynee's childhood, when cultural and economic self-sufficiency seemed the norm. The flora and fauna are lovingly described in a style that combines English and Creole with meticulous precision:

> *bred murum* from trees, *bred sonz* in the marshes, and *bred gondol*, and *bred butat*, and *bred martin*, and these were our vegetables, they grew by themselves, and were free for the taking. . . . We would . . . cook the *karang* fish, or the *kapitenn*, or the *madam tonbe*, of the *vyel*, or the *kordonye*. . . . Or we'd go down to Belli River and catch and eat the *tilapya* and carp fried crisp. (Collen 1990, 105)

In those days, the small general store of the village was a site of festive diversity which allowed one to cross cultural borders simply by choosing different kinds of French (*franse*), Indian (*indyen*), or Chinese (*lasir*) sweets according to one's desires, or the holiday being celebrated:

> oven baked cakes called *gato franse* and sweets called *gato indyen*. During the cane cutting season, there was *gato lakerls*. . . . At Chinese New Year, there was *gato lasir*, called "wax cake" because it looks just like wax, somehow made from rice. There was *gato papay*, which was not made from pawpaw, but from Chinese pumpkin. (Collen 1990, 108)

The linguistic density and the poetry of these lists convey a playful use of language, a freedom from external constraints that seems possible only because the materiality of food is transformed into the materiality and magic of language. The lists go on to include objects of all sorts that used to coexist in the neighborhood shop tended by Lung Yu. But there, these objects' use-value was indisputable, as though the Creole terms that describe them (*paydefer, karay, koton perle, patang, rwa dezer, katora, kalchul, lakord filin, medsinn pis*—in Collen 1990, 110–114) could allow for their integration within a nonalienating symbolic economy. Says Shynee: "I have nothing against paying for things. . . . So long as I use them. So long as they are part of our lives" (Collen 1990, 116). As Shynee articulates her understanding of her own resistance to consumption, the logic of the narrative suggests that it is the process of *writing* and *communicating* in the *local* language which produces the possibility of considering choices that might still be within reach of informed, enlightened citizens.

Like Lung Yu's store, an anarchic space of diversity, language becomes a space of creative folly, unlike the well-ordered and uniformed existence of the pragmatic consumer or practical user of words in the European language. The excess (represented by the numerous recipes, the descriptions of Creole foods, and the "private" realm of female solidarity) becomes a metonymy for the excessive or supplementary nature of the Creole language—a language that is nevertheless the central element for continuity and survival of the community. The narrative excess emblematized by those lists thematizes the theoretical debates over the status and usefulness of Creole among the local elites. It is often dismissed as mere dialect, superfluous, "vulgar and disgusting and abusive" (Collen 1990, 81)—in other words, "impure" or "abject." Yet this is the language that allows Shynee to name those things that are "part of [her] life." It is the foundation of both her subjective and her social existence, and it allows her to name those basic necessities that reinforce her sense of identity and community. These passages become meaningful and useful in a way that contrasts sharply with the professional excesses of the psychiatrist's or "expert's" voice, and permits the author to integrate the local culture within the Standard English text.

Collen's fictional text, the women's voices it brings to the public sphere of English-language literature, and the Creole culture to which it bears witness are a rich contribution to international discourses on development. It is both a provocative look at the complex practices that are transforming everyday life on a global scale and a call to respect diversity in all its forms, especially linguistic ones. *There Is a Tide* represents the diversity of contemporary Mauritius and manages to raise serious questions about history, gender, and society that social scientists and economists would do well to ponder.

NOTES

1. I thank Kathleen McHugh and Tiffany Ana Lopez for pointing this out.
2. See Ellman (1993) for a thorough study of the spectacular aspects of starvation: "Self-starvation is above all a performance . . . it is staged to trick the conscience of its viewers, forcing them to recognize that they are implicated in the spectacle that they behold" (17).

Afterword

Susanne Schech

A decade ago, when Arturo Escobar's (1995) notion of development as a discourse and a system of knowledge and power was new and exciting, Jane Haggis and I started to write what, to our knowledge, was one of the first books to explore in some detail the different terrains where culture and development have operated. The idea that development is always also cultural has only fairly recently become a focus of attention by theorists and practitioners, who have tended to see development mainly in terms of economic and social transformation. In our book we argued that culture, and its interconnectedness with economic, political, and social change, is central to understanding development processes and their impacts on societies. Reading *On the Edges of Development*, its wonderfully varied and richly detailed case studies inspired by Escobar's challenging ideas, invites some reflection on where development studies is in its engagement with "the cultural," where it has come from, and where it might go.

DEVELOPMENT AFTER POSTDEVELOPMENT?

Seeing development as a cultural construct has many implications. One might be to dismiss development as steeped in Western ideologies of modernization and progress, as stained by its association with colonialism and imperialism, or simply as outdated and replaced by globalization, and to argue that new terms of reference are needed (Schech and Haggis 2000, xii). But years later, we continue to use the same old terms—*Third World, development, progress, poverty, Westernization*, to name a few—and development as a field of study and as an industry is far from dead. On the contrary, development appears to enjoy a revival in Australia, for example, where universities establish new development studies programs and the federal government promised in 2005 to double its aid budget by 2010 (AusAID 2006). This move is encouraged by international institutions like the World Bank and the United Nations reaffirming the need and the possibility for countries to achieve development, and setting targets to meet a basic standard of living for their populations within the near future through global strategies such as Poverty Reduction Strategies and Millennium Development Goals (MDG). Despite the many critiques (for example, Kabeer 2003), the MDG initiative has placed development firmly back on the global agenda.

At the same time, international development institutions and scholars have begun to pay some attention to the relationship between culture and development. The World Bank, usually a paragon of economist development knowledge, even commissioned a book on culture and public action (Rao and Walton 2004) because, it argued, "culture is relevant to development in terms of ends, by affecting what is of value in a society, and means, by influencing how individuals, communities, informal and formal institutions respond to developmental changes and opportunities" (World Bank n.d.). This suggests that for the World Bank, culture is principally a lens through which development is perceived. A different perspective is taken by the "culture and development paradigm" (Pieterse 2001), which sees culture as being constantly reworked and reproduced around and through development, and development as "embedded in 'imaginaries of desirability,' material culture, and social relations" (Radcliffe 2006, 17; see also K. Hart 2001). If you like poetry, it is difficult to go past Pred's (1992, 109) evocative articulation of culture's interconnectedness with the uneven articulations of capitalist economic processes that are never just material—labor, capital, goods, technologies, and the like—but always take on cultural forms:

> Culture does not stand
> isolated
>   on its own, immutable and uncontested.
> It is neither fixed, nor confined to the traditional,
>   neither completely stable, nor a unified monolith of coherence.
> It is not an autonomous entity,
>   existing in a territory of its own,
>   beyond the realms of materiality and social reality.
> Culture is embodied and lived,
>   actively produced and expressed,
> through all social practices,
> through all that is concrete and everyday,
> through all that is enmeshed in power relations
>   and their associated discourses,
>   their associated representations and rhetorics.

From this perspective, the limits and fragilities of spatially uneven capitalist development cannot be read off universal abstract notions of capital, structure of social relations, or cultural imperialism, but require fine-grained analysis of how people make sense of everyday life and the world around them (G. Hart 2002).

Escobar's withering critique of development as a dream that has turned into a nightmare, as a regime of government over the Third World which ensures control over "subject peoples" and keeps them in their place (Escobar 1995, 10) appears to leave little option other than to reject development. His critics accuse him of portraying Third World people as "docile slaves or zombie victims of Western development discourses" who have no agency (Robins 2003, 282). Others point out that adopting an antidevelopment stance is "politically and/or morally inappropriate" because it fails to engage with poverty (Simon 2006, 208). The problem with being against development, then, is that it offers no redress to injustices done in the name of development and does not acknowledge the agency of Third World actors in resisting, challenging, adapting, and adopting development. Politically, it can feed into neoliberal discourses of development that see no need for intervention and leave everything in the "invisible hands of the market." Development scholars argue that people, particularly the millions of poor people, want change that will bring them a better life, however they may define it. Reflecting on the antiglobalization movement, Amartya Sen (2006, 131) points out that the question is not whether the poor should be part of the global economy or refuse it:

> People from very deprived countries clamor for the fruits of modern technology (such as the use of newly invented drugs that have transformed the lives of AIDS patients in America and Europe); they seek greater access to the markets in the richer countries for a wide variety of commodities, from sugar to textiles; and they want more voice and attention to the affairs of the world. If there is skepticism of the results of globalization, it is not because suffering humanity wants to withdraw into its shell.

The real question, according to Sen, is "whether they can feasibly get a better—and fairer—deal, with less disparities of economic, social, and political opportunities, and if so, through what international and domestic rearrangements this could be brought about" (Sen 2006, 136). The antiglobalization protesters are justified, in his view, in pointing the finger at the vast inequalities and injustices in today's world, but not in claiming that globalization has nothing to offer to those at the bottom of the hierarchy.

Making actors and institutions visible in accounts of development enables us to attribute responsibility for change. The agency of the subaltern, the displaced, the objects of development, who are so often portrayed as passive beneficiaries or helpless victims, gives us insight into the cultural politics of development and globalization. At the same time these detailed studies of the local or micro-level complicate any simple model of development as colonization or as Westernization, in the sense of a "direct transference of Western imaginaries of development to the local context" (Schech and Haggis 2000, 75). They show, instead, how women and men resist but also negotiate, reject but also desire, adopt and modify "development" in its myriad manifestations, good and bad. For the "largely unsung but key protagonists" of development (Introduction, this volume) cases, the problem is not so much development as the fact that the development they desire was never on the table.

Arjun Appadurai's (2004) work on the "capacity to aspire" reveals how culture shapes the means and ends of development. His case study of a pro-poor alliance of housing activists and organizations (the Alliance), based in Mumbai, India, and linked to a global network, the Slum/Shackdwellers International, shows how the poor take charge of their development by using culture to expand the spaces of agency and representation. Forty percent of Mumbai's population lives in slums in cramped and poorly serviced spaces, on pavements, between railway lines, and next to industrial estates and dumps, and their dwellings are always at risk of demolition, disenfranchisement, as well as fire and the vagaries of the monsoon. The Alliance's approach to these problems emphasizes negotiation, accommodation, and pressure rather than confrontation or political reprisal, as well as patience, long-term asset building, and cumulative victories. In pursuing the goal to improve the quality and security of housing as defined by the poor themselves, the Alliance works with whomever is useful, including federal, state, and municipal agencies; the Mumbai underworld; and international development institutions and donors. Staging housing exhibitions is one of its strategies, in which the poor bring their needs, interests, and knowledge in direct discussion with architects, designers, and building professionals, and share their experience with slum communities in other cities. This strategy involves hijacking an upper-class form and orienting them towards the poor, subverting the class cultures in India and providing spaces for the poor to be seen and heard (Appadurai 2004). The Alliance is an example of globalization from below which gives reason for hope that globalization can work for the poor and dispossessed.

WHAT EDGES?

Many chapters in this book take up the challenge to examine where, when, and how culture and development interact, who is involved in these interactions, and what this means. *On the Edges of Development* conjures up the precarious positioning of the authors and their subjects, for want of a better term—the overseas Filipino/a workers, rural Mexican women, Jamaican informal traders—in relation to mainstream development discourse and development interventions. Being on the edges of development can refer to marginal positions from which any development interventions or programs are experienced as a distant echo, or as acts of dispossession and oppression. From the edge, one step further can mean sliding down a precipice into oblivion—or violence. Appadurai (2006) claims that exclusion, inequality and violence can be traced back to social uncertainty about who we are and what we are entitled to in the contemporary era of globalization. In his call to reject "globalized development," Molefi Kete Asante (Chapter 5, this volume) posits development as a monotonous monologue rather than a discourse, a one-way imposition which causes local cultures to disappear and destroys local ways of life. His account evokes Manuel Castells's point that segments of society able to harness the "formidable productive forces of the informational revolution" exist side by side with "black holes of human misery in the global economy," often in the same country (Castells 1996, 2). Castells argued that in global informational society, uneven development could no longer be understood in terms of the First World/Third World dichotomy. One of the few avenues for the marginalized and disconnected people to respond and act is through culture—by constructing alternative meanings around religion, ethnicity, territory, or nation. Through the rising power of identity politics, "the process of disconnection becomes reciprocal" by the excluded refusing globalization's "one-sided logic of structural domination and social exclusion" (Castells 1996, 25) and connecting with a different source of identity and meaning.

But the edge is not necessarily a black hole. It can also describe a position from which development is viewed differently and freshly, similar to the liminal, or in-between, location that Homi Bhabha sees as central to the creation of new cultural meaning. In this sense, *On the Edges of Development* deals with temporal and spatial liminality, undermining the idea "that people living in different spaces are living at different stages of 'progress'" (Huddart 2006, 7). Overseas Filipino/a workers, for example, live modern lives in metropolitan cities but cannot forget their national origins or cultural identity. Portrayed as sacrificial heroes in their home country, and as eternally temporary, always racialized migrants in the receiving country, their narratives remain deeply entwined with development back home even though many find it difficult to return home (Lai, Chapter 8, this volume). Liminality in space and time is also at work in Hume Johnson's (Chapter 2, this volume) account of Jamaican "higglers," who make a precarious living on Kingston's pavements between the road traffic and the "proper" shops. By resisting the local government's regular efforts to "clean up" informal squatter businesses, they do not only defend their livelihood but also assert the integral role of their informal trading activities in global and local capitalism. They pull down the shutters of established main street shops not only in retaliation for being removed from the pavement but also in denial of the old established distinction between formal and informal, modern and traditional forms of trading. One might ask, what would development be without the edge?

Another angle from which to approach the "edge of development" is to conceive of the spaces of development as "borderlands." This concept is often evoked in critical cultural studies as a metaphor for the experience of blurring cultural boundaries, unsettled demarcations between self and other, and ruptured truths, "as a site of radical openness where the 'resistive' forces of dialogic excess triumph over the dominant forces of discursive closure" (Ang 2001, 164). As Ien Ang points out, these claims often ignore the specificity and particularity of people's positions in the borderlands, the power relations, and the policing and controlling that go on there. Rather than being a site where the voices of others can be heard loud and clear, she sees the borderlands as a "contested terrain where concrete, differentially positioned subjects have to forge particular strategies to speak and to be heard" (Ang 2001, 169). The strength of cultural studies lies in its attention to context, specificity, and particularity, but it requires the sorts of detailed and nuanced explanations "which might not resonate with the curiosity and the interests of our interlocutors on the crossroads" who are more interested in the stylish abstractions of cultural theory (Ang 2001, 168). The challenge for cultural studies, and perhaps even more so for Third World Cultural Studies, is "how . . . to speak about the 'particular,' the 'specific,' the 'local' in a way which doesn't subsume and absorb these into the abstractions of the 'universal,' the 'general,' and the 'global,' while at the same time not succumbing to the conservative and essentialist notion of complete untranslatability of cultures" (Ang 2001, 172).

ENTER COSMOPOLITANISM

This is a dilemma which some scholars argue to have resolved through the notion of cosmopolitanism, which has experienced a revival of late in social science writing. Among them are Ulrich Beck and Kwame Appiah, who devoted their recent monographs to cosmopolitanism and its ethics. Both authors, one a sociologist and the other a philosopher, argue that globalization is associated much more with the economic than the cultural, and is widely understood to refer to world markets, capitalism, and neoliberalism. For Appiah (2006), cosmopolitanism captures the notion of the "citizen of the world" who is aware of her obligations to others that go beyond the bounds of family, tribe, or nation, and at the same time values and respects the right to be different. Appiah calls these two ideals of cosmopolitanism "universal concern and respect for legitimate difference." His cosmopolitanism works from the ground up, whereby "the points of entry to cross-cultural conversations are things that are shared by those who are in the conversation" (Appiah 2006, 97). When two people meet, they find that they have much in common as a result of a long history of flows of ideas, people, and goods, not just in recent decades of globalization. They realize that they are not, and cannot be, culturally pure; they are already culturally contaminated.

Beck (2004) takes the same two ideals but elaborates each. According to him, cosmopolitanism describes the awareness, aided among other things by global media and information technologies, that we are part of a civilizational community of fate (zivilisatorische Schicksalsgemeinschaft) which shares the experience of risks and crises, combined with empathy which comes from the recognition that what happens to "them" could happen to "us." Added to this is the acknowledgment of the difference of the "Other," to which we respond with curiosity and at times with conflict, even hatred, because the difference of the Other is transparent and we can no longer protect our world through institutional hostility and ignorance. We still draw boundaries to make sense of ourselves in the global world, but at the same time we know that the local, national, ethnic, and cosmopolitan cultures are all mixing with each other—provincialism is blind without cosmopolitanism, and cosmopolitanism is empty without provincialism (Beck 2004, 16). For Beck, cosmopolitanism acknowledges otherness inside and outside, and refuses to order otherness hierarchically, or erase it through universalism. Accepting the other as different and equal removes the ground from underneath racism, but also reveals the ethnocentric universalism of the West as an anachronism that can be transcended (Beck 2004, 89).

The questions that Beck's theoretical discussion does not answer are, how can ethnocentric universalism be transcended, and who does the accepting? It seems to me that Beck calls for the West to transcend its own ethnocentric universalism and to accept the Other's difference, but what about the agency of the Other? Do they wait to be included as equals? Is there a limit to acceptable difference? While I do not claim to have an answer to these questions, I want to reflect on and contextualize them in the difficult terrain of indigenous/nonindigenous relations in Australia, which is also a site of struggle over culture and difference. The "sub-standard of living" of indigenous Australians (Wilson 2005) in rural and remote Australia has been a long-standing issue described as "intractable" by many commentators. While governments in the 1980s and early 1990s emphasized symbolic recognition of past injustice and restoration of rights—acceptance of difference, one might call it—the conservative Coalition government, which took power in 1996, preferred a "practical reconciliation" approach focused more on improving housing, health, education, and employment among indigenous communities. This approach does not appear to have been successful, with most social indicators showing a deterioration rather than improvement (Altman and Hunter 2003), but it did not deter the government from pursuing its agenda. Long-serving Australian Prime Minister, John Howard, who led the Australian government from 1996 to 2007, stated that he favored a review of Aboriginal land titles—most of them granted under previous administrations—to allow for private ownership, as "all Australians should be able to aspire to owning their own home and having their own business" (Parliament of Australia 2007).

The assumption underlying Howard's point is that traditional rights and laws hinder the government's efforts to improve indigenous peoples' living standards, and that they constrain the rights of individuals to aspire to the fruits of modernity, such as owning a home, receiving quality health care, and so on. This assumption was also at work in September 2007, when Australia (along with New Zealand, Canada, and the United States) voted against the United Nations Declaration on the Rights of Indigenous Peoples. Rather than agreeing to give more control to tribal peoples over the land and resources they traditionally possessed, and return confiscated territory or pay compensation, as the Declaration is asking countries to do, the then Australian Indigenous Affairs Minister, Mal Brough, made a point about tradition and modernity: "There should only be one law for all Australians and we should not enshrine in law practices that are not acceptable in the modern world" (BBC 2007). One might ask, what aspects of indigenous cultural difference are not acceptable to the Australian government? Why should it not be possible to reconcile indigenous Australians' cultural reasons to maintain their attachment to land with their aspiration for a good life, including a home of their own? Some Australian indigenous leaders agree with some aspects of the government's approach because they are desperate to pull their communities out of poverty. Noel Pearson (2006) argues that communities living on Aboriginal lands live on "dead capital" because their assets are inalienable and the laws governing Aboriginal property are so complex as to defeat most professionals' comprehension. Pearson (2007) also questions why most Aboriginal communities have not benefited from the resource boom on their lands, despite the existence of a Native Title Act since 1992, but have instead been suffering the detrimental impacts of mining activities on their culture and social cohesion. These problems cannot be reduced to traditional rights, as many "traditional" property arrangements, laws, and entitlements have been made by modern Australian governments. Should indigenous Australians only be allowed to aspire if they are prepared to give up rights they have struggled to gain? If we agree with Appiah (2006, 105–106) that people should neither be forced into sustaining authentic cultural practices nor be required to abandon them, how then is it possible to ensure that the choice is not either modernity or tradition, and that they can freely choose the way they want to live?

Appadurai's point with his example of the Mumbai-based alliance of housing activists is that culture is not just about the past. It is, he argues, "in culture that ideas of the future, as much as of those about the past, are embedded and nurtured" (Appadurai 2004, 59). Important as it is to unbury hidden pasts to expose the "human costs of domination and bureaucratic administration of power" (Bayoumi, Chapter 1, this volume), culture is also about aspirations for the future. Sen (2006, 89) points out that allowing one's priorities today to be dominated by the past history of humiliation and domination can "vastly deflect attention from other objectives . . . [one has] reason to value and pursue in the contemporary world;" in other words, it shuts down alternative pathways into the future. We can philosophize until the proverbial cows come home about the importance of culture and how to best deal with difference, but we won't get very far unless we take on board, as the contributions to this book do, that "culture is embodied and lived, actively produced and expressed, through all social practices, through all that is concrete and everyday, through all that is enmeshed in power relations" (Pred 1992, 109). The idea that culture is the stuff people, and particularly women, draw on to build a meaningful future for themselves underpinned this book and its predecessor (Bhavnani, Foran, and Kurian 2003a). There clearly is more work to be done if we want to find answers to the many questions and respond to the ideas raised by both books, both at the theoretical and "broad canvas" end and the particular, specific, local end of the spectrum of critical cultural studies.

Contributors

Molefi Kete Asante is Professor, Department of African American Studies, Temple University. Dr. Asante has written 66 books, the latest being *An Afrocentric Manifesto: Toward an African Renaissance* (2008), and *The History of Africa: The Quest for Eternal Harmony* (2007).

Moustafa Bayoumi is Associate Professor of English at Brooklyn College, City University of New York (CUNY). He is the coeditor of *The Edward Said Reader* and author of the forthcoming *How Does It Feel to Be a Problem? Being Young and Arab in America.*

Kum-Kum Bhavnani is a filmmaker and Professor of Sociology at the University of California, Santa Barbara. Her books include *Talking Politics* (1991), *Feminism and "Race"* (2001), and *Feminist Futures* (2003). *The Shape of Water* (2006), narrated by Susan Sarandon, is her first documentary (http://www.theshapeofwatermovie.com).

Krista Bywater is a doctoral candidate in sociology at the University of California, Santa Barbara. She is working on her dissertation, "Water for Life, Not for Profit: Development, Globalization, and Water Struggles in India."

John Foran is Professor of Sociology at the University of California, Santa Barbara. He is the author of *Fragile Resistance: Social Transformation in Iran from 1500 to the Revolution* (1993) and *Taking Power: On the Origins of Third World Revolutions* (2005).

Hume N. Johnson is a Lecturer in Journalism and Communications at James Cook University, Queensland, Australia. Her current research focuses on popular citizen participation, civil society, and governance in Jamaica. Other research interests include media studies, political communication, elections, and political parties.

Erin Kennedy has an M.A. in sociocultural anthropology from the University of California, Santa Barbara. Her current interests include the history and culture of wine and winemaking in California's Central Coast, and wine as global enterprise.

Lena Khor is a Ph.D. candidate in English at the University of Texas at Austin. Her research interests include contemporary World Anglophone Literature, transnational storytelling, and human rights and humanitarian discourses.

Priya A. Kurian is Associate Professor in the Department of Political Science and Public Policy at the University of Waikato, New Zealand. She is the author of *Engendering the Environment? Gender in the World Bank's Environmental Policies* (2000) and coeditor of *Feminist Futures: Re-imagining Women, Culture and Development* (2003).

Ming-Yan Lai is Assistant Professor and Program Director of M.A. in Intercultural Studies at the Chinese University of Hong Kong. She is the author of *Nativism and Modernity: Cultural Contestations in China and Taiwan under Global Capitalism* (2008).

Françoise Lionnet is Professor of French and Francophone Studies and Comparative Literature at the University of California, Los Angeles. She is the author of *Autobiographical Voices: Race, Gender, Self-Portraiture* (1989), *Postcolonial Representations: Women, Literature, Identity* (1995); and the coeditor with Shu-mei Shih of *Minor Transnationalism* (2005).

Edwin López is a Ph.D. Candidate of Sociology at the University of California, Santa Barbara (UCSB), with an M.A. in Latin American and Iberian Studies from UCSB. He is currently conducting a critical global ethnography on local justice organizing in New Orleans, Louisiana.

Tera Maxwell is a doctoral candidate in English at the University of Texas at Austin. Spanning over a century of Philippine-American relations, her dissertation examines how imperial trauma resonates in the Filipino imaginary.

Debashish Munshi is Chair of, and Associate Professor in, the Department of Management Communication at the University of Waikato, New Zealand. He is the coauthor of *Reconfiguring Public Relations: Ecology, Equity and Enterprise* (2007) and his research straddles culture, communication, politics, and management.

Moira O'Neil is a doctoral candidate in the sociology department at the University of California, Santa Barbara. Her dissertation analyzes the social determinants of diagnosis and treatment of war-related mental distress in the United States from the 1890s to 1920s.

María Josefina Saldaña-Portillo is Director of the Latino Studies Program in the Department of Social and Cultural Analysis at New York University. She is the author of *The Revolutionary Imagination in the Americas and the Age of Development* (2003).

Susanne Schech is Associate Professor of Development Geography at Flinders University in South Australia. She publishes on culture and development, gender, and race and coauthored *Culture and Development: A Critical Introduction* (2000).

Molly Talcott is Assistant Professor in Social and Behavioral Sciences at Arizona State University. Her research analyzes how women and youth are reshaping indigenous-led struggles for human rights and against neoliberalism across southern Mexico.

Magdalena Villarreal is Professor of Anthropology at CIESAS in Guadalajara, Mexico. Her publications include *Antropología de la Deuda: Crédito, Ahorro, Fiado y Prestado en las Finanzas Cotidianas* (2004) and *Wielding and Yielding: Power, Gender and Intervention in Mexico* (1994).

Ara Wilson is Director of the Program in the Study of Sexualities and Associate Professor of Women's Studies at Duke University. She is the author of *The Intimate Economies of Bangkok: Tomboys, Tycoons, and Avon Ladies in a Global City* (2004).

Bibliography

Acheson, Dean. 1944. *Hearings of the House Special Committee on Postwar Policy and Planning, 78th Congress, 2nd session.* Washington: US Congressional Records.

Acker, Joan. 2004. "Gender, Capitalism, and Globalization." *Critical Sociology* 30 (1): 17–41.

Adams, Alexander B. 1990. *Geronimo.* New York: Perseus Publishing.

Adesanmi, Pius. 2004. "'Nous les Colonisés': Reflections on the Territorial Integrity of Oppression." *Social Text* 22 (1): 35–58.

Adorno, Theodore W. 1986. "What Does Coming to Terms with the Past Mean?" pp. 114–129 in Geoffrey H. Hartman, editor, *Bitburg in Moral and Political Perspective.* Bloomington: Indiana University Press.

Agarwal, Bina. 1998. "Environmental Action, Equity and Ecofeminism: Debating India's Experience." *Journal of Peasant Studies* 25 (4): 55–95.

Albrow, Martin. 1996. *The Global Age: State and Society Beyond Modernity.* Cambridge: Polity Press.

Alfred, Helen. Editor. 1943. *First Steps Toward World Economic Peace.* New York: Citizens Conference on International Economic Union.

Alfred, Helen. 1944. *The Bretton Woods Accord: Why It's Necessary.* New York: Citizens Conference on International Economic Union.

Altman, Jon and Boyd Hunter. 2003. "Evaluating Indigenous Socioeconomic Outcomes in the Reconciliation Decade, 1991–2001." *Economic Papers* 20 (4): 1–15.

Alvarez, Maribel. 2003. "Made in Mexico: Souvenirs, Artisans, Shoppers and the Meanings of Other 'Border-Type-Things.'" Ph.D. Dissertation. University of Arizona.

Anderson, Benedict. 1991. *Imagined Communities: Reflections on the Origin and Spread of Nationalism.* New York: Verso.

Andico, Fe. 1998. "The Involvement of Women in the 1931 Colorum Uprising in Tayug, Pangasinan," pp. 161–167 in National Centennial Commission of the Phillipines, editors, *Herstories: A Global Movement. Proceedings of the International Congress on Women's Role in History and Nation Building.* Manila: Women Sector and Asia-Pacific, D. I. f. W. i. NCC-WS Secretariat: PWU-DIWA.

Andico, Fe. 2004. "World Cultures: Links to Cultures Around the World." http://www.ncca.gov.ph/culture&arts/cularts/ccta/kapatagan/kapatag-lowland.htm. Accessed August 26, 2004.

Ang, Ien. 2001. *On Not Speaking Chinese: Living between Asia and the West.* London: Routledge.

Angulo, Lourdes and Magdalena Villarreal. 2003. "Voices of the Civil Society in Mexico," pp. 120–139 in Kanyinga, Jeremiah Owiti, Theunis Keulder, Anil

Bhattarai, et al., editors, *Voices from Southern Civil Societies: The Interplay of National and Global Contexts in the Performance of Civil Society Organisations in the South.* Institute of Development Studies: University of Helsinki.
Ani, Marimba. 1994. *Yurugu.* Lawrenceville: Africa World Press.
Antonio Gonzalez, Jose and Desmond McCarthy. Editors. 1999. *Bolivia Public Expenditure Review.* World Bank. http://wbln0018.worldbank.org/LAC/LAC-InfoClient.nsf/5996dfbf9847f67d85256736005dc67c/9ed46854cf6e89f0852567fd00703451. Accessed November 25, 2007.
Appadurai, Arjun. 1990. "Disjuncture and Difference in the Global Cultural Economy," pp. 295–310 in Michael Featherstone, editor, *Global Culture: Nationalism, Globalization and Modernity.* London: Sage Publications.
Appadurai, Arjun. 1996. *Modernity at Large: Cultural Dimensions of Globalization.* Minneapolis: University of Minnesota Press.
Appadurai, Arjun. 2004. "The Capacity to Aspire: Culture and the Terms of Recognition," pp. 59–84 in Vijayendra Rao and Michael Walton, editors, *Culture and Public Action.* Stanford: Stanford University Press.
Appadurai, Arjun. 2006. *Fear of Small Numbers: An Essay on the Geography of Anger.* Durham: Duke University Press.
Appanah, Natacha. 2004. *Blue Bay Palace.* Paris: Gallimard.
Appiah, Kwame Anthony. 2006. *Cosmopolitanism: Ethics in a World of Strangers.* New York: W. W. Norton.
Arboleda, Corazon R. and Carmelita G. Nuqui. Editors. 2007. *Migrants' Stories, Migrants' Voices.* Quezon City: Philippine Migrants Rights Watch.
Arendt, Hannah. 1968. *The Origins of Totalitarianism.* New York: Harcourt.
Arno, Toni and Claude Orian. 1986. *Ile Maurice: Une société multiraciale.* Paris: L'Harmattan.
Asante, Molefi. 1998. *The Afrocentric Idea.* Philadelphia: Temple University Press.
Asante, Molefi and Ama Mazama. 2002. *Egypt vs. Greece and the American Academy.* Chicago: AA Images.
AusAID. 2006. *Australian Aid: Promoting Growth and Stability—White Paper on the Australian Government's Overseas Aid Program.* White Paper, April 2006. Canberra: AusAID.
Barlow, Maude and Tony Clark. 2002. *Blue Gold: The Fight to Stop the Corporate Theft of the World's Water.* New York: The New Press.
Barthes, Roland. 1972. *Mythologies.* New York: Noonday Press.
Bartlett, Robert V. 1986. "Ecological Rationality: Reason and Environmental Policy." *Environmental Ethics* 8: 221–239.
Battistella, Graziano and Anthony Paganoni. Editors. 1992. *Philippine Labor Migration: Impact and Policy.* Quezon City: Scalabrini Migration Center.
Bauer, Monica A. 2003. "Urduja." In KaWOMANan. http://www.gabnet.org/publicationsresources/kawomenan/2003/kawomenan%20spring%202003.pdf. Accessed May 20, 2008.
Baviskar, Amita. 2003. "Tribal Politics and Discourses of Indian Environmentalism," pp. 289–318 in Paul Greenough and Anna Lowenhaupt Tsing, editors, *Nature in the Global South: Environmental Projects in South and Southeast Asia.* Durham: Duke University Press.
Bayat, Asef. 1997. "Un-civil Society: The Politics of the 'Informal People'." *Third World Quarterly* 18 (1) (March): 53–72.
Bechtel Corporation. 2006. "Cochabamba Water Dispute Settled." http://www.bechtel.com/2006–01–19.html. Accessed November 25, 2007.
Beck, Ulrich. 2004. *Der kosmopolitische Blick oder: Krieg ist Frieden.* Frankfurt am Main: Suhrkamp.

Beckles, Hilary, and Verene Shepherd. Editors. 1996. *Caribbean Freedom: Economy and Society from Emancipation to the Present.* London: James Curry.

Belausteguigoitia, Marisa. 2000. "The Right to Rest: Women's Struggle to Be Heard in the Zapatistas' Movement." *Development* 43 (3) (September): 1–8.

Benjamin, Walter. 1968. "Theses on the Philosophy of History," pp. 253–264 in Hannah Arendt, editor, *Illuminations.* New York: Harcourt Brace Jovanovich.

Berger, Peter. 1988. "An East Asian Development Model?" pp. 1–25 in Peter Berger and Hsin-huang Michael Hsiao, editors, *In Search of an East Asian Development Model.* New Brunswick: Transaction Books.

Besson, Jean. 1993. "Reputation and Respectability Considered: A New Perspective on Afro-Caribbean Peasant Women," pp. 15–37 in Janet Henshall Momsen, editor, *Women and Change in the Caribbean.* London: James Curry.

Bhavnani, Kum-Kum. 1993. "Tracing the Contours: Feminist Research and Feminist Objectivity." *Women's Studies International Forum* 16 (2): 95–104.

Bhavnani, Kum-Kum, John Foran, and Priya Kurian. Editors. 2003a. *Feminist Futures: Re-imagining Women, Culture and Development.* London: Zed Books.

Bhavnani, Kum-Kum, John Foran, and Priya Kurian. 2003b. "Introduction to Women, Culture and Development," pp. 1–21 in Kum-Kum Bhavnani, John Foran, and Priya Kurian, editors, *Feminist Futures: Re-imagining Women, Culture and Development.* London: Zed Books.

Bhavnani, Kum-Kum, John Foran, and Molly Talcott. 2005. "The Red, the Green, the Black, and the Purple: Reclaiming Development, Resisting Globalization," pp. 323–332 in Richard Appelbaum and William I. Robinson, editors, *Critical Globalization Studies.* New York: Routledge.

Bhowmik, Shari and Renana Jhabvala. 1996. "Rural Women Manage Their Own Producer Co-Operatives: Self Employed Women's Association (SEWA)/Banaskantha Women's Indian Association in Western India," pp. 105–141 in Marilyn Carr, Martha Chen, and Renana Jhabvala, editors, *Speaking Out: Women's Economic Empowerment in South Asia.* London: Intermediate Technology Publications.

Bijoy, C.R. 2006. "Kerala's Plachimada Struggle." *Economic and Political Weekly* (October 14): 4332–4339.

Blaikie, Piers. 2000. "Development, Post-, Anti-, and Populist: A Critical Review." *Environment and Planning A* 32: 1033–1050.

Bolos, Mike, Jr. 2007. "Was Working Abroad for a Quarter of a Century Worth It?" pp. 61–68 in Corazon R. Arboleda and Carmelita G. Nuqui, editors, *Migrants' Stories, Migrants' Voices.* Quezon City: Philippine Migrants Rights Watch.

Bond, Patrick. 2001. "The World Bank in the Time of Cholera." *ZNet* (April 13). http://www.zmag.org/sustainers/content/2001-04/13bond.htm. Accessed January 15, 2007.

Bonnett, Alastair. 2005. "From the Crises of Whiteness to Western Supramacism." *Australian Critical Race and Whiteness Studies Association Journal* 1: 8–20.

Bordo, Susan. 1993. *Unbearable Weight: Feminism, Western Culture, and the Body.* Berkeley: University of California Press.

Boudin, Chesa, Gabriel Gonzalez, and Wilmer Rumbos. 2006. *The Venezuelan Revolution: 100 Questions—100 Answers.* New York: Thunder's Mouth Press.

Bourdieu, Pierre. 1984. *Distinction: A Social Critique of the Judgment of Taste.* Cambridge: Harvard University Press.

Bourdieu, Pierre. [1991] 1994. *Language and Symbolic Power.* Cambridge: Polity Press.

Brennan, Timothy. 2001. "Cosmo-Theory." *The South Atlantic Quarterly* 100 (3) (Summer): 659–691.

Brewer, Carolyn. 2004. *Shamanism, Catholicism, and Gender Relations in Colonial Philippines, 1521–1685*. Aldershot, Hants, England, and Burlington: Ashgate.

Brigg, Morgan. 2002. "Post-development, Foucault and the Colonisation Metaphor." *Third World Quarterly* 23 (3): 421–436.

British Broadcasting Corporation (BBC). 2007. "Indigenous Rights Outlined by UN." *BBC News*, 13 September 2007. http://news.bbc.co.uk/2/hi/in_depth/6993776.stm Accessed October 22, 2007.

Brooke, James. 1987. "West African Women: Political Inroads." *The New York Times* (August 10): 8. *LexisNexis Academic*. Accessed September 12, 2004.

Brown, Laura. 1995. "Not Outside the Range: One Feminist Perspective on Psychic Trauma," pp. 100–112 in Cathy Caruth, editor, *Trauma: Explorations in Memory*. Baltimore: John Hopkins University Press.

Bruhn, Kathleen. 1996. "Social Spending and Political Support: The 'Lessons' of the National Solidarity Program in Mexico." *Comparative Politics* 28 (2): 151–177.

Brumberg, Joan Jacobs. 1988. *Fasting Girls: The Emergence of Anorexia Nervosa as a Modem Disease*. Cambridge: Harvard University Press.

Buenavista, Elsa. 2007. "Trying My Luck in Taiwan," pp. 11–16 in Corazon R. Arboleda and Carmelita G. Nuqui, editors, *Migrants' Stories, Migrants' Voices*. Quezon City: Philippine Migrants Rights Watch.

Butler, Judith. 1997. *The Psychic Life of Power: Theories in Subjection*. Stanford: Stanford University Press.

Bynum, Caroline Walker. 1987. *Holy Fast and Holy Feast: The Religious Significance of Food to Medieval Women*. Berkeley: University of California Press.

Callahan, Manuel. 2004. "Zapatismo beyond Chiapas," pp. 217–228 in David Solnit, editor, *Globalize Liberation: How to Uproot the System and Build a Better World*. San Francisco: City Lights Books.

Callon, Michel. 1998. "The Embeddedness of Economic Markets in Economics," pp. 1–58 in Michel Callon, editor, *The Laws of the Markets*. Oxford: Blackwell Publishers.

Cameron, Angus and Ronen Palan. 2004. *The Imagined Communities of Globalization*. London: Sage Publications.

Campbell, Connie. 1995. "Out on the Front Lines but Still Struggling for Voice: Women in the Rubber Tappers' Defense of the Forest in Xapuri, Acre, Brazil," pp. 27–61 in Diane Rocheleau, Barbara Thomas-Slayter, and Esther Wangari, editors, *Feminist Political Ecology: Global Issues and Local Experiences*. London: Routledge.

Cardoso, Fernando Henrique and Enzo Faletto. 1979. *Dependency and Development in Latin America*. Berkeley: University of California Press.

Carruyo, Light. 2008. *Producing Knowledge, Protecting Forests: Rural Encounters with Gender, Ecotourism, and International Aid in the Dominican Republic*. Philadelphia: Pennsylvania State University Press.

Castells, Manuel. 1996. *The Information Age: Economy, Society and Culture, Vol. 1*. Oxford: Blackwell.

Central Intelligence Agency. 2007. Map of Southeast Asia. http://www.lib.utexas.edu/maps/middle_east_and_asia/southeast_asia_ref_2007.jpg. Accessed May 20, 2008.

Césaire, Aimé. [1955] 2000. *Discourse on Colonialism*, trans. Joan Pinkham. New York: Monthly Review Press.

Chakrabarty, Dipesh. 2000. *Provincializing Europe: Postcolonial Thought and Historical Difference*. Princeton: Princeton University Press.

Chang, Kimberley A. and Julian M. Groves. 2000. "Neither 'Saints' Nor 'Prostitutes': Sexual Discourse in the Filipina Domestic Worker Community in Hong Kong." *Women's Studies International Forum* 23 (1): 73–87.

Chang, Kimberley A. and L. H. M. Ling. 2000. "Globalization and Its Intimate Other: Filipina Domestic Workers in Hong Kong," pp. 27–43 in Marianne H. Marchand and Anne Sisson Runyan, editors, *Gender and Global Restructuring: Sightings, Sites and Resistances*. London and New York: Routledge.

Cheah, Pheng and Bruce Robbins. Editors. 1998. *Cosmopolitics: Thinking and Feeling Beyond the Nation*. Minneapolis: University of Minnesota Press.

Cheng, Shu-Ju Ada. 2006. *Serving the Household and the Nation: Filipina Domestics and the Politics of Identity in Taiwan*. Lanham: Lexington Books.

Chevannes, Barry. 1992. "The Formation of Garrison Communities." Paper presented at symposium in honour of Carl Stone. Kingston: University of the West Indies. November 16–17.

Chinweizu. 1975. *The West and the Rest of Us: White Predators, Black Slavers, and the African Exile*. New York: Vintage.

Chua, Peter, Kum-Kum Bhavnani, and John Foran. 2000. "Women, Culture, Development: A New Paradigm for Development Studies?" *Ethnic and Racial Studies* 23 (September): 820–841.

Chuh, Kandice. 2003. *Imagine Otherwise on Asian Americanist Critique*. Durham: Duke University Press.

Clifford, James. 1997. *Routes: Travel and Translation in the Late Twentieth Century*. Cambridge: Harvard University Press.

Cockburn, Bruce, Jeffery St. Clair, and Allan Sekula. 2001. *Five Days That Shook the World: The Battle for Seattle and Beyond*. London: Verso.

Cockburn, Cynthia. 1999. "Being Able To Say Neither/Nor." Notes from a talk at a meeting organized by Peace Brigades International and the National Peace Council. London. (April 14).

Coles, Anne and Tina Wallace. 2005. *Gender, Water and Development*. New York: Oxford International Publishers Ltd.

Collen, Lindsey. 1990. *There Is a Tide*. Port Louis: Ledikasyon pu Travayer.

Collier, George. A. 1994. *Basta! Land and the Zapatista Rebellion in Chiapas*. With E. L. Quaratiello. Oakland: Food First/Institute for Food and Development Policy.

Conca, Ken. 2006. *Governing Water: Contentious Transnational Politics and Global Institution Building*. Cambridge: MIT Press.

Conrad, Joseph. [1902] 1990. *Heart of Darkness*. New York: Dover Publications.

Constable, Nicole. 1997a. *Maid to Order in Hong Kong: Stories of Filipina Workers*. Ithaca: Cornell University Press.

Constable, Nicole. 1997b. "Sexuality and Discipline Among Filipina Domestic Workers in Hong Kong." *American Ethnologist* 24 (3): 530–558.

Constantino, Renato. 1998. "Globalization and the South: The Philippines Experience," pp. 57–64 in Kuan-Hsing Chen, editor, *Trajectories: Inter-Asia Cultural Studies*. New York: Routledge.

Cooke, Bill. 2004. "The Managing of the Third World." *Organization* 11 (5): 603–629.

Coquery-Vidrovitch, Catherine. 1997. *African Women: A Modern History*. Boulder: Westview Press.

Coronil, Fernando. 2000. "Towards a Critique of Globalcentrism: Speculations on Capitalism's Nature." *Public Culture* 12 (2): 351–374.

Cortes, Rosa Maria. 1974. *Pangasinan*. Quezon City: University of the Philippines Press.

Craig, Austin. 1924. *Gems of Philippine Oratory*. Manila: University of Manila.

Cummings, J. F. 2005. *How to Rule the World: Lessons in Conquest for the Modern Prince*. Tokyo: Blue Ocean.

Daileader, Claudia. 2001. "Female Genital Mutilation: A Woman's Choice?" HealthLink 107 (February 1). http://www.globalhealth.org/publications/article.php3?id=475. Accessed November 21, 2008.

Daly, Mary. 1978. *Gyn/Ecology: The Metaethics of Radical Feminism*. Boston: Beacon Press.

Danaher, Kevin and Roger Burbach. 2000. "Introduction: Making History," pp. 7–11 in Kevin Danaher and Roger Burbacj, editors, *Globalize This! The Battle Against the World Trade Organization and Corporate Rule*. Monroe: Common Courage.

Dankelman, Irene and Davidson, Joan. 1988. *Women and Environment in the Third World: Alliance for the Future*. London: Earthscan Publications/The International Union for Conservation of Nature and Natural Resources.

Datuin, Flaudette May V. 2002. *Home, Body, Memory: Filipina Artists in the Visual Arts, 19th Century to the Present*. Quezon City: University of the Philippines Press.

de Beauvoir, Simone. [1949] 1957. *The Second Sex*, trans. H. M. Parshley. New York: Alfred A. Knopf.

de Certeau, Michel. 1984. *The Practice of Everyday Life*. Berkeley: University of California Press.

De Landa, Manuel. 1997. *A Thousand Years of Nonlinear History*. New York: Zone Books.

De Soto, Hernando. 2000. *The Mystery of Capital: Why Capitalism Triumphs in the West and Fails Everywhere Else*. New York: Basic Books.

De Villiers, Marq. 2000. *Water: The Fate of Our Most Precious Resource*. New York: Jacobus Communications Corporation.

Deleuze, Gilles and Felix Guattari. 1986. *Kafka: Toward a Minor Literature*. Minneapolis: University of Minnesota Press.

Delmendo, Sharon. 2004. *The Star-entangled Banner: One Hundred Years of America in the Philippines*. New Brunswick: Rutgers University Press.

Department of the Prime Minister and Cabinet. (2002). *Key Government Goals to Guide the Public Sector in Achieving Sustainable Development*. Wellington. http://www.dpmc.govt.nz/dpmc/publications/key_goals.html. Accessed July 15, 2007.

Devi, Ananda. 1989. *Rue la poudrière*. Abidjan: Nouvelles Editions Africaines.

Devi, Ananda. 2000. *Moi, L'interdite*. Paris: Editions Dapper.

Devi, Ananda. 2001. *Pagli*. Paris: Gallimard.

Devi, Ananda. 2006. *Eve de ses décombres*. Paris: Gallimard.

Diesing, Paul. 1962. *Reason in Society*. Westport: Greenwood Press.

Dieterich, Heintz. 2006. "Evo Morales, Communitarian Socialism, and the Regional Power Block." MRZine. http://mrzine.monthlyreview.org/dieterich070106.html. Accessed January 8, 2006.

Dirlik, Arif. 2000. "Globalization as the End and the Beginning of History." *Rethinking Marxism* 12 (4) (Fall): 4–27.

Dissanayake, Wimal. Editor. 1996. *Narrtives of Agency: Self-Making in China, India and Japan*. Minneapolis and London: University of Minnesota Press.

Domínguez, Jorge, Robert A. Pastor, and R. DeLisle Worrell. Editors. 1993. *Democracy in the Caribbean: Political, Economic and Social Perspectives*. Baltimore: The John Hopkins University Press.

Douglas, Mary. 1966. *Purity and Danger: An Analysis of the Concepts of Pollution and Taboo*. London: Routledge and Kegan Paul.

Dresser, Denise. 1994. "Bringing the Poor Back In: National Solidarity as a Strategy of Regime Legitimation," pp. 143–166 in Wayne A. Cornelius, Ann L. Craig, and Jonathan Fox, editors, *Transforming State-Society Relations in Mexico: The National Solidarity Strategy*. San Diego: Center for US-Mexican Studies.

Du Gay, Paul. 2000. "Representing 'Globalization': Notes on The Discursive Orderings of Economic Life," pp. 113–125 in Paul Gilroy, Lawrence Grossberg, and Angela McRobbie, editors, *Without Guarantees: In Honour of Stuart Hall*. London: Verso.

Eber, Christine and Christine Kovic. Editors. 2003. *Women of Chiapas: Making History in Times of Struggle and Hope*. New York: Routledge.

The Economist. 1988. "Mauritius: Miracle in Trouble" (February 28).

Einaudi, Jean-Luc. 1991. *La Bataille de Paris*. Paris: Le Seuil.

Ela, Jean-Marc. 1998. "Western Development has Failed: Looking to a New Africa," *Le Monde Diplomatique* (October). http://mondediplo.com/1998/10/06africa. Accessed November 24, 2008.

Ellman, Maud. 1993. *The Hunger Artists: Starving, Writing, and Imprisonment*. Cambridge, MA: Harvard University Press.

Eng, David L. and David Kazanjian. 2003. *Loss: The Politics of Mourning*. Berkeley: University of California Press.

Engler, Mark. 2008. "Globalizers, Neocons, or ?? The World after Bush." May 18, 2008. http://www.tomdispatch.com/post/174933/mark_engler_how_to_rule_the_world_after_bush. Accessed July 4, 2008.

Enloe, Cynthia. 1989. *Bananas, Beaches, and Bases*. Berkeley: University of California Press.

Eriksen, Thomas. 1988. *Communicating Cultural Differences and Identity: Ethnicity and Nationalism in Mauritius*. Oslo: Oslo Occasional Papers in Social Anthropology.

Escobar, Arturo. 1992. "Reflections on 'Development': Grassroots Approaches and Alternative Politics in the Third World." *Futures* 24 (5): 411–436.

Escobar, Arturo. 1995. *Encountering Development: The Making and Unmaking of the Third World*. Princeton: Princeton University Press.

Escobar, Arturo. 1997. "The Making and Unmaking of the Third World through Development," pp. 85–93 in Majid Rahnema and Victoria Bawtree, editors, *The Post-Development Reader*. London: Zed Books.

Escobar Latapí, Agustín. 2000. "PROGRESA y Cambio Social en el Campo Mexicano," pp. 257–282 in Valencia, Gendreau, and Tepichín, editors, *Los Dilemas de la Política Social: ¿Cómo Combatir la Pobreza?* México: Universidad de Guadalajara, ITESO, Universidad Iberoamericana, planteles Golfo y Santa Fe.

Espiritu, Yen Le. 2003. *Home Bound: Filipino Lives Across Cultures, Communities, and Countries*. Berkeley: University of California Press.

Esteva, Gustavo. 1992. "Development," pp. 6–25 in Wolfgang Sachs, editor, *The Development Dictionary: A Guide to Knowledge as Power*. London: Zed Books.

Esteva, Gustavo. 2006. "An Interview with Gustavo Esteva." *In Motion Magazine*. http://www.inmotionmagazine.com/global/gest_int_1.html. Accessed April 8, 2008.

Etounga-Manguelle, Daniel. 2000. "Does Africa Need a Cultural Adjustment Programme?" pp. 65–77 in Lawrence E. Harrison and Samuel P. Huntington, editors, *Culture Matters: How Values Shape Human Progress*. New York: Basic Books.

Evans, Peter. 1979. *Dependent Development: The Alliance of Multinational, State, and Local Capital in Brazil*. Princeton: Princeton University Press.

EZLN. 2002. "Second Declaration from the Lacandón Jungle: 'Today We Say: We Will Not Surrender!'" pp. 221–231 in Tom Hayden, editor, *The Zapatista Reader*. New York: Thunder's Mouth Press and Nation Books.

Falk, Richard. 1995. *On Humane Governance: Toward a New Global Politics*. University Park: Pennsylvania State University Press.

Fanon, Frantz. 1965. *The Wretched of the Earth*, trans. Constance Farrington. London: MacGibbon and Kee.

Farhi, Farideh. 1990. *States and Urban-Based Revolutions: Iran and Nicaragua.* Urbana and Chicago: University of Illinois Press.

Federici, Sylvia. Editor. 2005. *Enduring Western Civilization.* Westport: Praeger.

Ferguson, James. 1994. *The Anti-Politics Machine: "Development," Depoliticization, and Bureaucratic Power in Lesotho.* Minneapolis: University of Minnesota Press.

Fernandes, Walter, and Geeta Menon. 1987. *Tribal Women and Forest Economy: Deforestation, Exploitation and Status Change.* New Delhi: Indian Social Institute.

Figueroa, Mark. 1995. "Garrison Communities in Jamaica, 1962–1993: Their Growth and Impact on Political Culture." Paper presented at symposium on Democracy and Democratization in Jamaica: Fifty Years of Adult Suffrage. Kingston: University of the West Indies. December 6–7.

Figueroa, Mark and Amanda Sives. 2003. "Garrison Politics and Criminality in Jamaica: Does the 1997 Election Represent a Turning Point?" Pp. 63–66 in Anthony Harriott, editor, *Understanding Crime in Jamaica: New Challenges for Public Policy.* Kingston: The University of the West Indies Press.

Finger, Matthias and Jeremy Allouche. 2002. *Water Privatisation: Trans-National Corporations and the Re-Regulation of the Water Industry.* London: Spon Press.

Finnegan, William. 2002. "Leasing the Rain." *The New Yorker.* (April 8).

Firestone, Shulamith. 1970. *The Dialectic of Sex: The Case for Feminist Revolution.* New York: Morrow.

Fisher, William F. and Thomas Ponniah. Editors. 2003. *Another World Is Possible: Popular Alternatives to Globalization at the World Social Forum.* London: Zed Books.

Flinchum, Robert. 1998. "The Women of Chiapas." *The Progressive* (March): 30–31.

Folbre, Nancy. 1993. *Who Pays for the Kids? Gender and the Structures of Constraint.* New York and London: Routledge.

Foran, John. 1981. "Dependency and Social Change in Iran, 1501–1925," Department of Sociology, University of California, Santa Barbara.

Foran, John. 1993. *Fragile Resistance: Social Change in Iran from 1500 to the Revolution.* Boulder: Westview Press.

Foran, John. 1997. "Discourses and Social Forces: The Role of Culture and Cultural Studies in Understanding Revolutions," pp. 203–226 in John Foran, editor, *Theorizing Revolutions.* London: Routledge.

Foran, John. 2000. "Discursive Subversions: Time Magazine, the CIA Overthrow of Mussadiq, and the Installation of the Shah," pp. 157–182 in Christian G. Appy, editor, *Cold War Constructions: The Political Culture of United States Imperialism, 1945–1966.* Amherst: The University of Massachusetts Press.

Foran, John. 2002. "In the Margins of Culture: Towards a Third World Cultural Studies." *Culture*, Newsletter of the Sociology of Culture Section of the American Sociological Association 16 (3) (Spring): 1, 3–6.

Foran, John. 2003. "Magical Realism: How Might the Revolutions of the Future Have Better End(ing)s?" pp. 271–283 in John Foran, editor, *The Future of Revolutions: Rethinking Radical Change in the Age of Globalization.* London: Zed Books.

Foran, John. 2005. *Taking Power: On the Origins of Third World Revolutions.* Cambridge: Cambridge University Press.

Foran, John and Jeff Goodwin. 1993. "Revolutionary Outcomes in Iran and Nicaragua: Coalition Fragmentation, War, and the Limits of Social Transformation." *Theory and Society* 22 (2) (April): 209–247.

Forrester, Viviane. 2000. *El Horror Económico*. México: Fondo de Cultura Económica.

Foucault, Michel. 1972. *The Archaeology of Knowledge and the Discourse on Language*. New York: Pantheon.

Fox, Jonathan. 1994. "The Difficult Transition from Clientelism to Citizenship: Lessons from Mexico." *World Politics* 46 (2) (January): 151–184.

Fox, Michael. 2008. "'Bishop of Poor' Fernando Lugo Wins Paraguayan Elections Ending 61 Years of Conservative Rule." *Democracy Now!* (April 22, 2008). http://upsidedownworld.org/main/content/view/1247/68/. Accessed July 25, 2008.

Fraad, H., S. Resnick, and R. Wolff. 1994. *Bringing It All Back Home: Class, Gender and Power in the Modern Household*. London: Pluto Press.

Frank, Andre Gunder. 1967. *Capitalism and Underdevelopment in Latin America*. New York: Monthly Review Press.

Franke, Richard W. and Barbara H. Chasin. 1994. *Kerala: Radical Reform as Development in an Indian State*. San Francisco: The Institute for Food and Development Policy.

Fraser, Rebecca, Debashish Munshi, and Priya Kurian. 2006. "Analysis of Media Discourses Around Immigration and Genetic Modification." Paper presented at the New Zealand Political Science Association Conference, Christchurch, August 28–30.

Freeman, Carla. 2001. "Is Local: Global as Feminine: Masculine? Rethinking the Gender of Globalization." *Signs* 26 (4) (Summer): 1007–1037.

Freeman, Carla. 2005. "Neo-Liberalism, Respectability, and the Romance of Flexibility in Barbados." *Working Paper No. 40* (April): 1–29. Atlanta: Emory Centre for Myth and Ritual in American Life.

French, Joan. 1995. "Women and Colonial Policy in Jamaica," pp. 121–146 in Saskia Wieringa, editor, *Subversive Women: Women's Movements in Africa, Asia, Latin America and the Caribbean*. London: Zed Books.

Friede, Eva. 2002. "Material Woman: Montreal Mag Publisher Inspired by Fabled African Fabric-Traders Known as Mama Benz." *The Gazette*. Montreal (October 8): D1. *LexisNexis Academic*. Accessed September 12, 2004.

Geertz, Clifford. 1973. *The Interpretation of Culture*. New York: Basic Books.

George, Susan and Fabrizio Sabelli. 1994. *Faith and Credit: The World Bank's Secular Empire*. Boulder: Westview Press.

Gibson-Graham, J. K. 1996a. *The End of Capitalism (As We Knew It)*. London: Blackwell Publishers.

Gibson-Graham, J. K. 1996b. "Querying globalization." *Rethinking Marxism* 9 (1): 1–27.

Giddens, Anthony. 1994. *Beyond Left and Right: The Future of Radical Politics*. Cambridge: Polity Press.

Glasner, Peter. 2002. "Beyond the genome: Reconstituting the new genetics." *New Genetics and Society* 21 (3): 267–277.

Godwin, Ebow. 2002. "Trade-Togo: Once-Powerful Women Traders See Dwindling Empire." *IPS-Inter Press Service* (February 12). *LexisNexis Academic*. Accessed September 12, 2004.

Goffman, Erving. 1972. *Interaction Ritual*. Harmondsworth: Penguin.

Gonzalez, Vernadette V. and Robyn Magalit Rodriguez. 2003. "Filipina.com: Wives, Workers, and Whores on the Cyberfrontier," pp. 215-234 in Rachel Lee and Sau-Ling Cynthia Wong, editors, *Asian America.Net: Ethnicity, Nationalism, and Cyberspace*. New York: Routledge.

Gordon, Avery. 1997. *Ghostly Matters: Haunting and the Sociological Imagination*. Minneapolis: University of Minnesota Press.

Gordon, Derek, Patricia Anderson, and Don Robotham. 1997. "Jamaica: Urbanization during the Years of Crisis," pp. 190–226 in Alejandro Portes, Carlos

Dobre-Cabal, and Patricia Landolt, editors, *The Urban Caribbean: Transition to the New Global Economy*. Baltimore: The Johns Hopkins University Press.

Gott, Richard. 2005. *Hugo Chávez and the Bolivarian Revolution*. London: Verso.

Goux, Jean-Joseph. 1990. *Symbolic Economies: After Marx and Freud*. Ithaca: Cornell University Press.

Graeber, David. 2004. "The New Anarchists," pp. 202–215 in David Solnit, editor, *Globalize Liberation: How to Uproot the System and Build a Better World*. San Francisco: City Lights Books.

Graham, Mekada. 2002. *Social Work and African-Centred Worldviews*. Birmingham: Venture Press.

Gramsci, Antonio. 1971. *Selections from the Prison Notebooks*. New York: International.

Grandin, Greg. 2008. "Losing Latin America: What Will the Obama Doctrine Be Like?" http://www.venezuelanalysis.com/analysis/3543. Accessed July 8, 2008.

Grant-Wisdom, Dorith. 1994. "Constraints on the Caribbean State: The Global and Policy Contexts." *21st Century Policy Review* 2 (1/2) (Spring): 151–179.

Gray, Obika. 2004. *Demeaned but Empowered: The Social Power of the Urban Poor in Jamaica*. Kingston: The University of the West Indies Press.

Greif, Stuart. Editor. 1995. *Immigration and National Identity in New Zealand: One People-Two Peoples-Many Peoples?* Palmerston North: Dunmore Press.

Guevara, Che. 1965. "Socialism and Man in Cuba." In *The Che Reader*. Melbourne: Ocean Press, 2005. First published as "From Algiers, for *Marcha*. The Cuban Revolution Today" (March 12, 1965). Found at http://marxists.org/archive/guevara/1965/03/man-socialism.htm. Accessed June 21, 2008.

Guevarra, Anna Romina. 2006. "Managing 'Vulnerabilities' and 'Empowering' Migrant Filipina Workers: The Philippines' Overseas Employment Program." *Social Identities* 12 (5): 523–541.

Gutierrez, Chit. 1999. "In Search of a Princess." *Filipinas Magazine* (June 1999). http://www.urduja.com/princess.html. Accessed November 24, 2008.

Gupta, Ahkil. 1988. *Postcolonial Developments*. Durham: Duke University Press.

Hadjor, Kofi Buenor. 1992. *Dictionary of Third World Terms*. London: Penguin.

Hage, Ghassan. 1998. *White Nation: Fantasies of White Supremacy in a Multicultural Society*. Annandale: Pluto Press.

Hall, Stuart. 1978a. "Marxism and Culture." *Radical History Review* 18: 5–14.

Hall, Stuart. 1978b. "Politics and Ideology: Gramsci," pp. 45–76 in Stuart Hall, Bob Lumley, and Gregor McLennan, editors, *On Ideology*. London: Hutchinson.

Hall, Stuart. 1986. "The Problem of Ideology: Marxism Without Guarantees." *Journal of Communication Inquiry* 10 (2): 28–44.

Hannerz, Ulf. 1990. "Cosmopolitanism and Locals in World Culture," pp. 230–247 in Mike Featherstone, editor, *Global Culture: Nationalism, Globalization, and Modernity*. London: Sage Publications.

Haraway, Donna. 1985. "Manifesto for Cyborgs: Science, Technology, and Socialist Feminism in the 1980s." *Socialist Review* 80: 65–108.

Haraway, Donna. 1997. *Modest_Witness@Second_Millennium. FemaleMan_Meets_OncoMouse: Feminism and Technoscience*. New York: Routledge.

Hardt, Michael and Antonio Negri. 2004. *Multitude: War and Democracy in the Age of Empire*. New York: Penguin Press.

Haring, Lee. 1992. "Buried Treasure." *Journal of Mauritian Studies* 4 (1): 22–35.

Hart, Gillian. 2001. "Development Critiques in the 1990s: *Cul de sac* and Promising Paths." *Progress in Human Geography* 25 (4): 649–658.

Hart, Gillian. 2002. "Geography and Development: Development/s Beyond Neoliberalism? Power, Culture, Political Economy." *Progress in Human Geography*. 26 (6): 812–822.

Hart, Keith. 2001. *Money in an Unequal World*. New York and London: Texere.
Harvey, David. 1989. *The Condition of Postmodernity*. Oxford: Blackwell.
Hayes, Samuel P., Jr. 1951. "An Official Interpretation," pp. 12–16 in Walter M. Daniels, editor, *The Point Four Program*. Special issue of *The Reference Shelf* 23 (5). New York: Wilson.
Hendrickson, Hildi. Editor. 1996. *Clothing and Difference: Embodied Identities in Colonial and Post-Colonial Africa*. Durham: Duke University Press.
Hilliard, Asa. 2002. "Lefkowitz and the Myth of the Immaculate Conception of Western Civilization," pp. 51–67 in Molefi Asante and Ama Mazama, editors, *Egypt vs. Greece in the American Academy*. Chicago: AA Images.
Hobson, John A. [1938] 1965. *Imperialism*. Ann Arbor: University of Michigan Press.
Holloway, John. 2002. *Change the World Without Taking Power: The Meaning of Revolution Today*, London: Pluto.
hooks, bell. 1989. *Talking Back: Thinking Feminist, Thinking Black*. Boston: South End Press.
Hope, Donna. 2004. "The British Link Up Crew: Consumption Masquerading as Masculinity in the Dancehall." *Interventions: International Journal of Postcolonial Studies. Special Issue on Jamaican Popular Culture* 6 (1) (April): 101–117.
Hope, Donna. 2005. *Inna Di Dancehall: Socio-Cultural Politics of Identity in Jamaica*. Kingston: The University of the West Indies Press.
Horne, Alistair. 1987. *A Savage War of Peace: Algeria 1954–1962*. London: Macmillan.
Huang, Shirlena and Brenda S. A. Yeoh. 1996. "Ties that Bind: State Policy and Migrant Female Domestic Helpers in Singapore." *Geoforum* 27: 479–493.
Huddart, David. 2006. *Homi K. Bhabha*. Abington: Routledge.
Huntington, Samuel. 1993. "The Clash of Civilizations?" *Foreign Affairs* 72 (3) (Summer): 22–49.
Huntington, Samuel. 1996. *The Clash of Civilizations and the Remaking of the World Order*. New York: Simon and Schuster.
Hyden, Goran. 1983. *No Shortcuts to Progress*. Berkeley: University of California Press.
Hyden, Goran. 1987. "Capital Accumulation, Resource Distribution, and Governance in Kenya: The Role of the Economy of Affection," pp. 117–136 in Michael G. Schatzberg, editor, *The Political Economy of Kenya*. New York: Praeger.
Hylton, Forrest, and Sinclair Thomson. 2004. "The Roots of Rebellion: I: Insurgent Bolivia." *NACLA Report on the Americas* 38 (3) (November/December): 15–19.
Ibn, Batuta and Tim Mackintosh-Smith. 2002. *The Travels of Ibn Battutah*. London: Picador.
Ingham, James. "Crucial Year for Chavez Revolution." *BBC News* (January 11, 2008). http://news.bbc.co.uk/2/hi/americas/7179055.stm. Accessed June 29, 2008.
Instituto del Tercer Mundo. 2001. *The World Guide: An Alternative Reference to the Countries of Our Planet*. Oxford: New Internationalist Publications Ltd.
Ip, Manying. 2003. "Maori-Chinese Encounters: Indigene-Immigrant Interaction in New Zealand." *Asian Studies Review* 27 (2): 227–252.
Irigaray, Luce.1985. *This Sex Which Is Not One*. Ithaca: Cornell University Press.
Irin. 2007. "Muslims talk about female genital mutilation." *Spero News* (April 1, 2007). http://www.speroforum.com/site/article.asp?idcategory=33&idSub=121&idArticle=8773. Accessed November 21, 2008.
Jackson, Celia. 1993. "Doing What Comes Naturally? Women and Environment in Development." *World Development* 21 (12) (December): 1947–1963.

Jamaica Gleaner. 1998. "Mob Rule Downtown: Area Don's Detention Sparks Violent Demonstration." September 24.

Jamaica Gleaner. 1999. "Street Vending Dilemma." December 22. http://www.jamaica-gleaner.com/gleaner/19991222/cleisure/cl.html. Accessed August 15, 2005.

Jamaica Gleaner. 2000. "Congested Streets of Downtown Kingston." September 1a. http://www.jamaica-gleaner.com/gleaner/20000901/news/news2.html. Accessed August 15, 2005.

Jamaica Gleaner. 2000. "Dons Extort millions—Businesses, Sidewalk Vendors Said Paying $400m a Year." September 1b. http://www.jamaica-gleaner.com/gleaner/20000901/news/news3.html. Accessed August 15, 2005.

Jamaica Gleaner. 2001. "Downtown Shut Down—Streets Vendors Forcibly Close Businesses in Protest." November 20a. http://www.jamaica-gleaner.com/gleaner/20011120/lead/lead1.html. Accessed May 24, 2005.

Jamaica Gleaner. 2001. "Shutdown to Cost Businesses." November 20b. http://www.jamaica-gleaner.com/gleaner/20011120/business/business1.html. Accessed May 24, 2005.

Jamaica Gleaner. 2001. "Cat and Mouse Game Downtown Kingston—Vendors Remain Determined to Cash in on Xmas Sales." December 6. http://www.jamaica-gleaner.com/gleaner/20011206/news/news2.html. Accessed May 24, 2005.

Jamaica Gleaner. 2002. "Downtown Vendors Defiant." November 5. http://www.jamaica-gleaner.com/gleaner/20021105/lead/lead3.html. Accessed August 15, 2006.

Jamaica Gleaner. 2002. "Merchants Stand Firm on Shutdown." September 6. http://www.jamaica-gleaner.com/gleaner/20020906/lead/lead6.html. Accessed May 24, 2005.

Jamaica Gleaner. 2003. "Vendors Must Obey the Rules." December 2. http://www.jamaica-gleaner.com/gleaner/20031202/cleisure/cleisure1.html. Accessed October 24, 2005.

Jeune Afrique. 1998. "Examples à suivre" (March 31).

Johnson, Hume Nicola. 2005. "Incivility—The Politics of 'people on the margins' in Jamaica." *Political Studies* 53 (3) (October): 579–597.

Junger, Karin. 2002. *Mama Benz and the Taste of Money* [videocassette]. USA: Filmmakers Library.

Kabeer, Naila 1994. *Reversed Realities: Gender Hierarchies in Development Thought*. London and New York: Verso Press.

Kabeer, Naila. 2003. *Gender Mainstreaming in Poverty Eradication and the Millennium Development Goals: A Handbook for Policy-Makers and Other Stakeholders*. London: Commonwealth Secretariat and International Development Research Institute.

Kainer, Karen and Mary Duryea. 1992. "Tapping Women's Knowledge: Plant Resource Use in Extractive Reserves, Acre, Brazil." *Economic Botany* 46 (4): 408–425.

Kalinic, Ariana. 2005. "Everything for Everyone, Nothing for Ourselves: Zapatista Women in the Age of Autonomy." B.A. Honors Thesis. University of California, Santa Barbara.

Kampwirth, Karen. 2002. *Women and Guerrilla Movements: Nicaragua, El Salvador, Chiapas, Cuba*. University Park: Pennsylvania State University Press.

Kampwirth, Karen. 2004. *Feminism and the Legacy of Revolution: Nicaragua, El Salvador, Chiapas*. Athens: Ohio University Press.

Karenga, Maulana. 2006. *Maat: The Moral Ideal in Ancient Egypt*. Los Angeles: University of Sankore Press.

Kassindja, Fauziya and Layli Miller Bashir. 1998. *Do They Hear You When You Cry?* New York: Delacorte Press.

Keefe-Feldman, Mike. 2006. "Winning Hearts and Minds in the Water Wars." http://www.onthecommons.org/content.php?id=899. Accessed December 20, 2006.

Keen, Steve. 2002. *Debunking Economics: The Naked Emperor of the Social Sciences*. London: Zed Books.

Kennedy, John F. 1962. "Text of President's Speech on Alliance for Progress Program." *New York Times* (14 March), A–18.

Klein, Naomi. 2002. *Fences and Windows: Dispatches from the Front Lines of the Globalization Debate*. New York: St. Martin's Press.

Klouzal, Linda. 2005. "Rebellious Affinities: Narratives of Community, Resistance, and Women's Participation in the Cuban Revolution (1952–1959)." Ph.D. dissertation. University of California, Santa Barbara.

Kothari, Uma. 2001. "Power, Knowledge and Social Control in Participatory Development," pp. 139–152 in Bill Cooke and Uma Kothari, editors, *Participation: The New Tyranny*. London: Zed Books.

Kozloff, Nikolas. 2006. "The Rise of Rafael Correa: Ecuador and the Contradictions of Chavismo." *Counterpunch* (November 27): 1–6.

Kristeva, Julia. 1986. "Psychoanalysis and the Polis," pp. 302–320 in Toril Moi, editor, *The Kristeva Reader*. New York: Columbia University Press.

Kurian, Priya. 2000. *Engendering the Environment?: Gender in the World Bank's Environmental Policies*. Aldershot: Ashgate.

Kurian, Priya and Debashish Munshi. 2003. "Negotiating Human-Nature Boundaries, Cultural Hierarchies and Masculinist Paradigms of Development Studies," pp. 146–159 in Kum-Kum Bhavnani, John Foran, and Priya Kurian, editors, *Feminist Futures: Re-imagining Women, Culture, and Development*. London: Zed Books.

Kurian, Priya and Debashish Munshi. 2006. "Tense Borders: Culture, Identity, and Anxiety in New Zealand's Interweaving Discourses of Immigration and Genetic Modification." *Cultural Politics* 2 (3): 359–379.

Lan, Pei-chia. 2006. *Global Cinderellas: Migrant Domestics and Newly Rich Employers in Taiwan*. Durham: Duke University Press.

Larrain, Jorge. 1989. *Theories of Development: Capitalism, Colonial and Dependency*. Cambridge: Blackwell Publishers.

Layosa, Linda. 1991. "The Story of Rhoda," *Tinig Filipino* (January).

Layosa, Linda and Brian Neil. 1990. "Mixed Relationships—Do They Work?" *Tinig Filipino* (July/August).

Le Cour Grandmaison, Olivier. Editor. 2001. *Le 17 Octobre 1961: Un crime d' État à Paris*. Paris: La Dispute.

Le Franc, Elsie. Editor. 1994. *Consequences of Structural Adjustment: A Review of the Jamaican Experience*. Kingston: Canoe Press.

Lessig, Lawrence. 2004. *Free Culture: The Nature and Future of Creativity*. New York: Penguin Press.

Lind, Amy and Jessica Share. 2003. "Queering Development: Institutionalized Heterosexuality in Development Theory, Practice and Politics in Latin America," pp. 55–73 in Kum-Kum Bhavnani, John Foran, and Priya Kurian, editors, *Feminist Futures: Re-Imagining Women, Culture and Development*. London: Zed Books.

Lionnet, Françoise. 1995. *Postcolonial Representations: Women, Literature, Identity*. Ithaca: Cornell University Press.

Liu, James, Tim McCreanor, Tracey McIntosh, and Teresia Teaiwa. Editors. 2005. *New Zealand Identities: Departures and Destinations*. Wellington: Victoria University Press.

Long, Norman. Editor. 1984. *Family and Work in Rural Societies: Perspectives on Non-wage Labour*. London: Tavistock.

Long, Norman. 2001. *Development Sociology: Actor Perspectives*. London: Routledge.

Long, Norman and Magdalena Villarreal. 2004. "Redes de deudas y Compromisos: La Trascendencia del Dinero y las Divisas Sociales en las Cadenas Mercantiles," pp. 27–56 in Magdalena Villarreal, editor, *Antropología de la Deuda: Crédito, Ahorro, Fiado y Prestado en las Finanzas Cotidianas*. México, D.F.: Ciesas, Porrúa y La Cámara de Diputados.

Long, Pablo. 2005. "Broad Front Strengthens." *Latinamerica Press* (May 18): 2–3.

López, Edwin. 2004. "Through the Prism of Racialized Political Cultures: An Analysis of Racialized Cultural Hegemony and Resistance in Revolutionary Guatemala, 1944–1954." M.A. thesis. University of California, Santa Barbara.

Lorde, Audre. 1984. "An Open Letter to Mary Daly." In *Sister Outsider*. Freedom, CA: The Crossing Press, pp. 66–71.

Lott, Davis Newton. 1994. *The Presidents Speak: The Inaugural Addresses of the American Presidents from Washington to Clinton*. New York: H. Holt and Co.

Mackie, Gerry. 1998. "A Way to End Female Genital Cutting." http://www.fgm-network.org/articles/mackie1998.html. Accessed February 20, 2008.

Madamba, V. 1991. "Discotheque and Pubhouses: Let Us Avoid Them." *Tinig Filipino* (December).

Magno, Rosa Maria. 1992. *Urduja Beleaguered and Other Essays on Pangasinan Language, Literature, and Culture*. Manila: Kalikasan Press.

Mahoney, Robert. 1990. "Don't Get In the Way of West Africa's Market Women." *Reuters News* (May 6). *Factiva*. Accessed September 12, 2004.

Make Poverty History. 2005. http://www.makepovertyhistory.org/. Accessed November 24, 2008.

Mananzan, Mary John. 1998. "The Precolonial Filipina," in Alexander R. Magno, Teresa Ma Custodio, and Jose Y. Dalisay, editors, *Kasaysayan: The Story of a Filipino People*. vol.2. Manila: Asia Publishing Company Limited.

Maniwang, Auring. 1989. "It's Never Too Late." *Tinig Filipino* (December).

Manrique, Juan. 2006. "Bolivia: Evo's Friends and Foes." *Latinamerica Press* (14) (July 26): 8–9.

Marchand, Marianne and Jane Parpart. 1995. *Feminism/postmodernism/development*. New York: Routledge.

Marshall, Paule. 1969. *The Chosen Place, The Timeless People*. New York: Vintage.

Martínez, Elizabeth (Betita) and Arnoldo García. 2004. "What Is Zapatismo? A Brief Definition for Activists," pp. 213–216 in David Solnit, editor, *Globalize Liberation: How to Uproot the System and Build a Better World*. San Francisco: City Lights Books.

Marx, Karl. 1904. *A Contribution to the Critique of Political Economy*. New York: International Library.

Marx, Karl. 1978. "The Future Result of British Rule in India," pp. 659–664 in Robert Tucker, editor, *The Marx-Engels Reader*. New York: W. W. Norton & Co.

Maspero, François. 1999. "Les mensonges grossiers de M. Papon." *Le Monde* (February 24).

Matthews, Sally. 2004. "Post-development Theory and the Question of Alternatives: A View from Africa." *Third World Quarterly* 25 (2): 373–384.

M. A. Singamma Sreenivasan Foundation. 1993. "Integrating Women in Development Planning: The Role of Traditional Wisdom," pp. 280–300 in Joycelin Massiah, editor, *Women in Developing Economies: Making Visible the Invisible*. Providence and Paris: Berg/UNESCO.

Mazama, Ama. 2003. Editor. *The Afrocentric Paradigm*. Trenton: Africa World Press.

Mbakwe, Tom. 2002. "African Majesty." *New African* 408: 8–9. *Academic Search Premier*. Accessed July 8, 2004.

McClintock, Anne. 1995. *Imperial Leather: Race, Gender, and Sexuality in the Colonial Contest.* New York: Routledge.

McDonald, Bernadette and Douglas Jehl. Editors. 2003. *Whose Water Is It? The Unquenchable Thirst of a Water-Hungry World.* Washington: National Geographic Society.

McFarlane, Colin. 2006. "Knowledge, Learning, and Development: A Post-rationalist Approach." *Progress in Development Studies* 6 (4): 287–305.

McGrew, Anthony. 1992. *Global Politics: Globalization and the Nation State.* Cambridge, UK: Polity Press.

McMichael, Philip. 2003. *Development and Social Change: A Global Perspective* Third edition. Thousand Oaks: Pine Forge Press.

Mendoza, Dorotea. 2003. *Kawomenan.* http://www.gabnet.org/publicationsresources/kawomenan/2003/kawomenan%20spring%202003.pdf. Accessed May 20, 2008.

Mertes, Tom. Editor. 2004. *A Movement of Movements: Is Another World Really Possible?* New York: Verso.

Mies, Maria and Vandana Shiva. 1993. *Ecofeminism.* London: Zed Books.

Miller, Daniel. 1998. *A Theory of Shopping.* Ithaca: Cornell University Press.

Mills, Mary Beth. 1999. *Thai Women in the Global Labor Force: Consuming Desires, Contested Selves.* New Brunswick: Rutgers University Press.

Ministry of Research, Science and Technology (MORST). 2003. *New Zealand's Biotechnology Strategy.* http://www.morst.govt.nz/uploadedfiles/Documents/Publications/Govt%20policy%20statements/BiotechFinal2.pdf. Accessed July 15, 2007.

Ministry of Research, Science and Technology (MORST). 2005. *Futurewatch: Biotechnologies to 2025.* http://www.morst.govt.nz/uploadedfiles/Biotechnology/FutureWatchBookFull.pdf. Accessed July 15, 2007.

Ministry of Research, Science and Technology (MORST). 2006. *Estimating the economic contribution of biotechnology to New Zealand's primary sector.* http://www.morst.govt.nz/uploadedfiles/Documents/Publications/research%20reports/MoRSTBioPart2.pdf. Accessed July 15, 2007.

Mintz, Sidney. 1996. "Black Women, Economic Roles and Cultural Traditions," pp. 515–534 in Filomina Chioma Steady, editor, *The Black Woman Cross-Culturally.* Cambridge: Schenkman.

Mohanty, Chandra Talpade. 1991. "Under Western Eyes: Feminist Scholarship and Colonial Discourses," pp. 51–80 in Chandra Talpade Mohanty, Ann Russo, and Lourdes Torres, editors, *Third World Women and the Politics of Feminism.* Bloomington: Indiana University Press.

Momsen, Janet Henshall. 1996. "Gender Roles in Caribbean Agricultural Labour," pp. 216–224 in Hilary Beckles and Verene Shepherd, editors, *Caribbean Freedom: Economy and Society from Emancipation to the Present.* London: James Curry.

Moore, Donald, Jake Kosek, and Anand Pandian. 2003. *Race, Nature, and the Politics of Difference.* Durham: Duke University Press.

Morales, Aurora Levins. 1998. *Medicine Stories: History, Culture, and the Politics of Integrity.* Boston: South End Press.

Morales, Evo. 2007. "Bolivian President Evo Morales on Indigenous Rights, Climate Change, Establishing Diplomatic Relations with Iran, Che Guevara's Legacy and More." Interview with Amy Goodman and Juan Gonzalez for *Democracy Now!* (September 26, 2007). http://www.democracynow.org/2007/9/26/bolivian_president_evo_morales_on_indigenous. Accessed June 29, 2008.

Morris, Meaghan. 1988. "Things to Do with Shopping Centres," pp. 193–225 in Susan Sheridan, editor, *Grafts: Feminist Cultural Criticism.* London: Verso.

Moser, Ingunn. 1995. "Introduction: Mobilizing Critical Communities and Discourses on Modern Biotechnology," pp. 1–24 in Vandana Shiva and Ingunn

Moser, editors, *Biopolitics: A Feminist and Ecological Reader on Biotechnology*. London: Zed Books.
Munshi, Debashish. 1998. "Media, Politics, and the Asianisation of a Polarized Immigration Debate in New Zealand." *Australian Journal of Communication* 25 (1): 97–110.
Munshi, Debashish and Priya Kurian. 2005. "Imperializing Spin Cycles: A Postcolonial Look at Public Relations, Greenwashing, and the Separation of Publics." *Public Relations Review* 31 (4): 513–520.
Munshi, Debashish and Priya Kurian. 2007. "The Case of the Subaltern Public: A Postcolonial Investigation of CSR's (O)missions," pp. 438–447 in Steve May, George Cheney, and Juliet Roper, editors, *The Debate Over Corporate Social Responsibility*. Oxford: Oxford University Press.
Nababsing, Vidula and Uma Kothari. Editors. 1996. *Gender and Industrialization: Mauritius, Bangladesh, Sri Lanka*. Stanley Rose Hill: Editions de 1'Ocean Indien.
Narayan, Uma. 1997. *Dis-Locating Cultures: Identities, Traditions, and Third-World Feminism*. New York: Routledge.
Negri, Antonio and Michael Hardt. 2004. *Multitude: War and Democracy in the Age of Empire*. New York: Penguin.
Neumann, R. and David. Solnit. 2004. "The New Radicalism." AlterNet. http://www.alternet.org/story/19308/. Accessed August 19, 2006.
Nirsimloo-Anenden, Ananda. 1990. *The Primordial Link: Telegu Ethnic Identity in Mauritius*. Moka: Mahatma Gandhi Institute Press.
Notes from Nowhere. 2003. *We Are Everywhere: The Irresistible Rise of Global Anticapitalism*. London: Verso.
O'Brien, Suzie and Imre Szeman. 2001. "Introduction: The Globalization of Fiction and the Fiction of Globalization." *The South Atlantic Quarterly* 100 (3) (Summer): 603–626.
Obenga, Theophile. 1989. "African Philosophy of the Pharaonic Period" pp. 286–320 in Ivan Van Sertima, *Egypt Revisited*. New Brunswick: Transaction.
Okine, Vicky. 1993. "The Survival Strategies of Poor Families in Ghana and the Role of Women Therein," in Joycelin Massiah, editor, *Women in Developing Economies: Making Visible the Invisible*. Providence and Paris: Berg/UNESCO.
Olivera, Oscar, and Tom Lewis. 2004. *Cochabamba! Water Rebellion in Bolivia*. Cambridge: South End Press.
Olutski, Enrique. 2002. *Vida Clandestina: My Life in the Cuban Revolution*, trans. Thomas Christensen and Carol Christensen. New York: Wiley.
Ong, Aihwa. 1988. "Colonialism and Modernity: Feminist Re-presentations of Women in Non-Western Societies." *Inscriptions* 3–4: 79–93.
Ong, Aihwa. 1991. "The Gender and Labor Politics of Postmodernity." *Annual Reviews of Anthropology* 20: 279–309.
Orbach, Susie. 1986. *Hunger Strike: The Anorexic's Struggle as a Metaphor for Our Age*. London: Faber and Faber.
"Our Promise." 1995. *Tinig Filipino* (October).
Padua, Jerome. 1991. "Filipinos: Hong Kong's Evil Necessities or Environmental Nuisances?" *Tinig Filipino* (December).
Panijel, Jacques. Director. 1961. *Octobre à Paris*. Documentary. Paris.
Parenti, Christian. 2005. "Bolivia's Battle of Wills." *The Nation* (July 4): 13–18.
Parliament of Australia. 2007. "Bills Digest No. 18 2007–08. Northern Territory National Emergency Response Bills 2007—Interim Bills Digest." http://www.aph.gov.au/Library/Pubs/BD/2007-08/08bd018.htm. Accessed October 19, 2007.
Parpart, Jane L. 1995. "Post-Modernism, Gender and Development," pp. 247–258 in Jonathan Crush, editor, *Power of Development*. London: Routledge.

Parrenas, Rhacel Salazar. 2001. *Servants of Globalization: Women, Migration and Domestic Work.* Palo Alto: Stanford University Press.

Parrenas, Rhacel. 2005. *Children of Global Migration: Transnational Families and Gendered Woes.* Stanford: Stanford University Press.

Pasuk, Phongpaichit and Chris Baker. 1998. *Thailand's Boom and Bust.* Chiang Mai: Silkwork Books.

Pearson, Noel. 2006. "Review of Hernando de Soto *The Mystery of Capital: Why Capitalism triumphs in the West and Fails Everywhere Else* (2001, London: Bantam)." *API Review of Books*, Issue 44, http://www.api-network.com/cgi-bin/reviews/jrb.cgi?issue=44. Accessed October 22, 2007.

Pearson, Noel. 2007. "Boom and Dust Lifestyle." *The Australian*, September 27, 2007.

Péju, Paulette. [1961] 2000. *Ratonnades à Paris.* Paris: La Découverte.

Peredo Beltrán, Elizabeth. 2004. *Water, Privatization and Conflict: Women of the Cochabamba Valley.* Heinrich Böll Foundation North America. http://c1.cancun.boell-net.de/ES/download/peredowaterwomenboliviaeng.pdf. Accessed January 5, 2008.

Peters, Winston. 2002. "NZ First—The Lightning Rod for Immigration Changes." Address to a public meeting at Erinlea Lounge, Fahy's Motor Inn Greerton, Tauranga, November 24, 2002. http://www.nzfirst.org.nz/content/display_item.php?t=1&i=808. Retrieved July 25, 2007.

Peterson, V. Spike and Anne Sisson Runyan. 1999. *Global Gender Issues.* Boulder: Westview Press.

Philippines Overseas Employment Administration. 2006. *OFW Global Presence: A Compendium of Overseas Employment Statistics.* http://www.poea.gov.ph/stats/2006Stats.pdf. Accessed November 24, 2008.

Pieterse, Jan Nederveen. 1998. "My Paradigm or Yours? Alternative Development, Post-development, Reflexive Development." *Development and Change* 29: 343–373.

Pieterse, Jan Nederveen. 2000. "After Post-development." *Third World Quarterly* 21 (2): 175–191.

Pieterse, Jan Nederveen. 2001. *Development Theory: Deconstructions/Reconstructions.* London and Thousand Oaks: Sage Publications.

Polanyi, Karl. [1944] 2001. *The Great Transformation: The Political and Economic Origins of Our Time.* Boston: Beacon Press.

Polanyi, Karl. 1957. "The Economy as Instituted Process," pp. 240–270 in Karl Polanyi, Conrad M. Arensberg, and Harry W. Pearson, editors, *Trade and Market in the Early Empires.* Glencoe: The Free Press and the Falcon's Wing Press.

Postel, Sandra. 1992. *Last Oasis: Facing Water Scarcity.* New York: W. W. Norton.

Prahalad, C. Krishna Rao. 2005. *The Fortune at the Bottom of the Pyramid.* Upper Saddle River, NJ: Pearson Education and Wharton School Publishing.

Prashad, Vijay. 2007. *The Darker Nations: A People's History of the Third World.* New York: The New Press.

Pred, Allan. 1992. "Capitalisms, Crises, and Cultures II: Notes on Local Transformation and Everyday Cultural Struggles," pp. 106–117 in Allan Pred and Michael J. Watts, editors, *Reworking Modernity: Capitalisms and Symbolic Discontent*, Brunswick: Rutgers University Press.

Press, Robert and Betty Press. 1999. *The New Africa: Dispatches from a Changing Continent.* Gainesville: University Press of Florida.

Przybylowicz, Donna. 1990. "Toward a Feminist Cultural Criticism: Hegemony and Modes of Social Division." *Cultural Critique* 14 (Winter): 259–301.

Quinto, Alma Urduja. 1999. "Princess Urduja." Dait tan Buknol ("Sew and Tie") Art Exhibit. Mga Anak Ni Urduja (Urduja's Children) Walang Filipina Art Exhibit. Liongoren Gallery. Dagupan City, Pangasinan.

Quinto, Alma Urduja. 2003. "Babaylan." Soft Dreams and Bedtime Stories Exhibit. Havana Bieniale. http://www.trauma-interrupted. M ,org/alma/. Accessed May 20, 2008.

Quinto, Alma. 2005. Personal communication. Email to Tera Maxwell (March 2005).

Radcliffe, Sarah A. 2006. "Culture in Development Thinking: Geographies, Actors, and Paradigms," pp. 1–29 in Sarah A. Radcliffe, editor, *Culture and Development in a Globalizing World: Geographies, Actors, and Paradigms*. London: Routledge.

Rafael, Vicente L. 1997. "'Your Grief Is Our Gossip:' Overseas Filipinos and Other Spectral Presences." *Public Culture* 9: 267–291.

Rahnema, Majid, with Victoria Bawtree. 1997. *The Post-Development Reader*. London: Zed Books.

RAINBO. 2008. "Workshop on Innovative Tools for the Abandonment of the Practice of Female Genital Mutilation/Cutting (FGM/C) Nov 2006--Feb 2007 Kenya, Tanzania & Sudan." http://www.rainbo.org/trainingfgm.html. Accessed November 21, 2008.

Rao, Vijayendra and Michael Walton. 2004. Editors. *Culture and Public Action*. Stanford: Stanford University Press.

Reddock, Rhoda. 1995. "The Early Women's Movement in Trinidad and Tobago, 1900–1937," pp. 101–120 in Saskia Wieringa, editor, *Subversive Women: Women's Movements in Africa, Asia, Latin America, and the Caribbean*. London: Zed Books.

Reed, Jean-Pierre and John Foran. 2002. "Political Cultures of Opposition: Exploring Idioms, Ideologies, and Revolutionary Agency in the Case of Nicaragua." *Critical Sociology* 28 (3) (October): 335–370.

Reich, Robert. 1993. *L'économie mondialisée*. Paris: Dunod.

Reinsborough, Patrick. 2004. "Decolonizing the Revolutionary Imagination: Values Crisis, the Politics of Reality, and Why There's Going to Be a Common-Sense Revolution in This Generation," pp. 161–211 in David Solnit, editor, *Globalize Liberation: How to Uproot the System and Build a Better World*. San Francisco: City Lights Books.

Renan, Ernest. [1882] 1997. "What Is a Nation?" pp. 8–22 in Homi K. Bhabha, editor, *Nation and Narration*. New York: Routledge.

Riquer Fernández, Florinda. 2000. "Los Pobres de PROGRESA: Reflexiones," pp. 283–310 in Valencia, Gendreau, and Tepichín, editors, *Los Dilemas de la Política Social: ¿Cómo Combatir la Pobreza?* México: Universidad de Guadalajara, ITESO, Universidad Iberoamericana, planteles Golfo y Santa Fe.

Rizal, José. 1888. Letter to Dr. Adolf B. Meyer, Dresden. Unpublished letters collection. Chicago: Newberry Library.

Robbins, Bruce. 1998. "Actually Existing Cosmopolitanism," pp. 1–19 in Pheng Cheah and Bruce Robbins, editors, *Cosmopolitics*. Minneapolis: University of Minnesota Press.

Roberts, Mere, Brad Haami, Richard Benton, Terre Satterfield, Melissa Finucane, Mark Henare, and Manuka Henare. 2004. "Whakapapa as Maori Mental Construct: Some Implications for the Debate over Genetic Modification of Organisms." *The Contemporary Pacific* 16 (1): 1–28.

Robins, Steven. 2003. "Whose Modernity? Indigenous Modernities and Land Claims after Apartheid." *Development and Change* 34 (2): 265–286.

Rogers-Hayden, Tee. 2004. "Commissioning Genetic Modification: The Marginalization of Dissent in the RCGM." Unpublished Ph.D. thesis. The University of Waikato, Hamilton.

Román, Luis Ignacio. 2000. "Acumulación de la Pobreza y Política Social," pp. 85–94 in Valencia, Gendreau, and Tepichín, editors, *Los Dilemas de la Política*

Social: ¿Cómo Combatir la Pobreza? México: Universidad de Guadalajara, ITESO, Universidad Iberoamericana, planteles Golfo y Santa Fe.

Roosevelt, Elliott. 1946. *As He Saw It*. New York: Duell, Sloan and Pearce.

Root, Maria. 1992. "The Impact of Trauma on Personality: The Second Reconstruction," pp. 229-265 in Laura Brown and Mary Ballou, editors, *Personalities and Psychopathologies: Feminist Reappraisals*. New York: Guilford Press.

Rosca, Ninotchka. 1995. "The Philippines' Shameful Export." *Nation* 260 (15): 522–527.

Rose, Kalima. 1992. *Where Women Are Leaders*. London: Zed Books.

Ross-Larson, Bruce, Meta de Conquereaumont, and Christopher Trott. Editors. 2006. *Human Development Report: Beyond Scarcity: Power, Poverty and the Global Water Crisis*. New York United Nations Development Program (UNDP).

Rossi, Benedetta. 2004. "Revisiting Foucauldian Approaches: Power Dynamics in Development Projects." *The Journal of Development Studies* 40 (6): 1–29.

Rostow, Walt Whitman. 1971. *Stages of Growth: A Non-Communist Manifesto*. Cambridge: Cambridge University Press.

Rowbotham, Sheila and Stephanie Linkogle. Editors. 2001. *Women Resist Globalization: Mobilizing for Livelihood and Rights*. London: Zed Books.

Rowell, Andrew. 1996. *Green Backlash: Global Subversion of the Environmental Movement*. London: Routledge.

Roy, Arundhati. 2004. *An Ordinary Person's Guide to Empire*. Boston: South End Press.

Royal Commission on Genetic Modification (RCGM). 2001. *The Report of the Royal Commission on Genetic Modification*. Wellington.

Rubin, Gayle. 1975. "The Traffic in Women: Notes on the Political Economy of Sex," pp. 157–210 in Rayna Reiter, editor, *Toward an Anthropology of Women*. New York: Monthly Review Press.

Sachs, Wolfgang. Editor. 1992. *The Development Dictionary: A Guide to Knowledge as Power*. London: Zed Books.

Sachs, Wolfgang. 1993. *The Development Dictionary*. London: Zed Books.

Saldaña-Portillo, María Josefina. 2003. *The Revolutionary Imagination in the Americas and the Age of Development*. Durham: Duke University Press.

San Juan, Epifanio. 1992. *Racial Formations/Critical Transformations: Articulations of Power in Ethnic and Racial Studies in the United States*. Atlantic Highlands: Humanities Press.

San Juan, Nina. 1991–1992. "No More Blue Christmas" (in four parts). *Tinig Filipino* (December, January, February, March).

Sarkis, Marianne. 1995. "Female Genital Mutilation: An Introduction." http://www.fgmnetwork.org/intro/fgmintro.html. Accessed February 20, 2008.

Sassen, Saskia. 1998. *Globalization and Its Discontents*. New York: The New Press.

Sassen, Saskia. 2003. "Global Cities and Survival Circuits," pp. 254–274 in Barbara Ehrenreich and Arlie Russell Hochschild, editors, *Global Woman: Nannies, Maids, and Sex Workers in the New Economy*. New York: Metropolitan Books.

Schech, Susanne and Jane Haggis. 2000. *Culture and Development. A Critical Introduction*. Oxford: Blackwell.

Schuurmann, Frans J. 2000. "Paradigms Lost, Paradigms Regained? Development Studies in the Twenty-first Century." *Third World Quarterly* 21 (1): 7–20.

Scott, Catherine V. 1995. *Gender and Development: Rethinking Modernization and Dependency Theory*. Boulder: Lynne Rienner Publishers.

Scott, James C. 1976. *The Moral Economy of the Peasant: Rebellion and Subsistence in Southeast Asia*. New Haven: Yale University Press.

Scott, James C. 1985. *Weapons of the Weak: Everyday Forms of Peasant Resistance.* New Haven: Yale University Press.

Scott, James C. 1990. *Domination and the Arts of Resistance: Hidden Transcripts.* New Haven: Yale University Press.

Secretaría de Desarrollo Social (SEDESOL). 2000. *Reporte Técnico para la Medición de la Pobreza.* Gobierno de México.

Sen, Amartya. 1981. *Poverty and Famines: An Essay on Entitlement and Deprivation.* Oxford: Clarendon Press.

Sen, Amartya. 2006. *Identity and Violence: The Illusion of Destiny.* New York: W. W. Norton.

Sen, Gita and Caren Grown. 1987. *Development, Crisis, and Alternative Visions: Third World Women's Perspectives.* New York: Monthly Review Press.

Shanin, Teodor. 1986. *The Roots of Otherness: Russia's Turn of the Century,* volume 2: *Russia, 1905–07: Revolution as a Moment of Truth.* New Haven: Yale University Press.

Sharoni, Simona. 1995. *Gender and the Israeli-Palestinian Conflict: The Politics of Women's Resistance.* Syracuse: Syracuse University Press.

Sheller, Mimi. 1997. "Quasheba, Mother, Queen: Black Women's Public Leadership and Political Protest in Postemancipation Jamaica." Lancaster University: Department of Sociology. http://www.comp.lancs.ac.uk/sociology/soc049ms.html. Accessed September 22, 2004.

Shepard, Benjamin, and L. A. Kauffman. 2004. "A Short Personal History of the Global Justice Movement: From New York's Community Gardens, to Seattle's Tear Gas, Quebec's Fences, the 9/11 Backlash, and Beyond," pp. 375–388 in Eddie Yuen, Daniel Burton-Rose, and George Katsiaficas, editors, *Confronting Capitalism: Dispatches from a Global Movement.* Brooklyn: Soft Skull Press.

Shepherd, Verene, Bridget Brereton, and Barbara Bailey. Editors. 1995. *Engendering History: Caribbean Women in Historical Perspectives.* London: James Curry.

Sherlock, Phillip and Hazel Bennett. 1998. *The Story of the Jamaican People.* Kingston: Ian Randle Publishers.

Shiva, Vandana. 1988. *Staying Alive: Women, Ecology, and Survival.* New Delhi: Kali for Women.

Shiva, Vandana. 2002. *Water Wars: Privatization, Pollution, and Profit.* Cambridge: South End Press.

Shiva, Vandana. 2005. *Building Water Democracy: People's Victory against Coca-Cola in Plachimada.* New Delhi: Navdanya.

Shohat, Ella and Robert Stam. 1994. *Unthinking Eurocentrism: Multiculturalism and the Media.* London: Routledge.

Shultz, Jim. 2005a. "Launching the Final Battle in Bolivia's Water War." http://www.democracyctr.org/blog/2005/11/launching-final-battle-in-bolivias.html. Accessed November 25, 2007.

Shultz, Jim. 2005b. "The Politics of Water in Bolivia. *The Nation* (January 28). http://www.thenation.com/doc/20050214/shultz. Accessed February 28, 2006.

Simon, David. 2006. "Beyond Antidevelopment: Discourses, Convergences, Practices." *Singapore Journal of Tropical Geography* 28: 205–218.

Sinnott, Megan. 2004. *Toms and Dees in Thailand: Transgender Identity and Female Same-Sex Relationships in Thailand.* Honolulu: University of Hawaii Press.

Sivanandan, A. 1980. "Imperialism in the Silicon Age." *Monthly Review* 32 (3) (July–August): 24–42. First published in *Race and Class* (Autumn 1979.)

Smith, William Gardner. 1963. *The Stone Face.* New York: Farrar, Strauss, and Company.

Solnit, David. Editor. 2004a. *Globalize Liberation: How to Uproot the System and Build a Better World.* San Francisco: City Lights Books.

Solnit, David. 2004b. "Introduction: The New Radicalism: Uprooting the System and Building a Better World," pp. xi–xxiv in David Solnit, editor, *Globalize Liberation: How to Uproot the System and Build a Better World.* San Francisco: City Lights Books.

Sommer, Doris. 1988. "Not Just A Personal Story: Women's Testimonies and the Plural Self," pp. 107–130 in Bella Brodzki and Celeste Schenck, editors, *Life/Lines: Theorizing Women's Autobiography.* Ithaca: Cornell University Press.

Soros, George. 1999. *La Crisis del Capitalismo Global: La Sociedad Abierta en Peligro.* México: Plaza y Janés.

Speed, Shannon. 2007. *Rights in Rebellion: Indigenous Struggle and Human Rights in Chiapas.* Stanford: Stanford University Press.

Speed, Shannon, R. Aída Hernández Castillo, and Lynn M. Stephen. Editors. 2006. *Dissident Women: Gender and Cultural Politics in Chiapas.* Austin: University of Texas Press.

Spivak, Gayatri Chakravorty. 1986. "Three Women's Texts and a Critique of Imperialism," pp. 262–288 Henry Louis Gates, Jr., editor, *"Race," Writing, and Difference.* Chicago: University of Chicago Press.

Spivak, Gayatri C. 1996. *The Spivak Reader: Selected Works of Gayatri Chakraborty Spivak,* edited by Donna Landry and Gerald MacLean. New York: Routledge.

Spivak, Gayatri C. 1999. *A Critique of Postcolonial Reason: Toward a History of the Vanishing Present.* Cambridge: Harvard University Press.

Spoonley, Paul and Andrew Trlin. 2004. "Immigration, Immigrants, and the Media: Making Sense of Multicultural New Zealand." Paper produced as part of the New Settlers Programme Project. Palmerston North, NZ: Massey University. http://masseynews.massey.ac.nz/2004/Clippings/Immigration-paper-July-04.doc. Accessed July 25, 2007.

Spratt, Amanda. 2005. "New Zealand Faces up to a Much More Diverse Future." *The New Zealand Herald,* May 22, p. 22.

Srinivas, Smita. 1997. "Self-Employed Women's Association (SEWA) of India Paving the Way for Women's Economic Progress." *Women and Money,* MicroCredit Section (June).

Starr, Amory. 2005. *Global Revolt: A Guide to the Movements against Globalization.* London: Zed Books.

Statistics New Zealand. 2008. "GDP per capita." http://www.stats.govt.nz/products-and-services/nz-in-the-oecd/gdp-per-capita.htm. Accessed November 24, 2008.

Steinglass, Matt. 2000. "Out of Amsterdam: How a Dutch Company's Batik Textiles Became the Basis of 'Traditional' West African Culture." *Metropolis Magazine* (December). http://www.metropolismag.com. Accessed July 8, 2004.

Stora, Benjamin. 2001. "Les Habitudes Criminelles Françaises," pp. 59–64 in Olivier Le Cour Grandmaison, editor, *Le 17 Octobre 1961: Un crime d'état à Paris.* Paris: La Dispute.

Sturgeon, Noël. 1997. *Ecofeminist Natures.* New York: Routledge.

Swidler, Ann. 1986. "Culture in Action Symbols and Strategies." *American Sociological Review* 51 (2) (April): 273–286.

Sworn Statements from Some Abu Ghraib Detainees. 2005. http://media.washingtonpost.com/wp-srv/world/iraq/abughraib/151362.pdf. Accessed August 14, 2007.

Szulc, Tad. 1962. "Billion in U.S. Aid Stirs Praise and Criticism in Latin America." *New York Times* (March 12), sec. 1:1+.

Tadiar, Neferti Xina M. 2004a. "Domestic Bodies," pp. 113–150 in *Fantasy-Production: Sexual Economies and Other Philippine Consequences for the New World Order.* Hong Kong: Hong Kong University Press.

Tadiar, Neferti Xina. 2004b. *Fantasy-Production: Sexual Economies and Other Philippine Consequences for the New World Order.* Hong Kong: Hong Kong University Press.

Thianthai, Chulanee. 2005. "Growing Up in a Transitional Society: A Study on Gender Differences and Changes in Body Image, Perceptions of the Young Thai Generation." Paper presented at the Thai Studies Association Conference, Dekalb, Illinois, April 4.

This Is What Democracy Looks Like. 2000. Documentary film. www.bignoise-films.com. Seattle: Independent Media Center/Big Noise Films.

Thompson, E. P. [1963] 1966. *The Making of the English Working Class.* New York: Vintage Books.

Thompson, Edward Palmer. 1971. "The Moral Economy of the English Crowd in the Eighteenth Century." *Past & Present* 50: 76–136.

Tinker, Irene. 1995. "The Human Economy of Microentrepreneurs," pp. 25–39 in Louise Dignard and Jose Havet, editors, *Women in Micro- and Small-Scale Enterprise Development.* London: Westview Press.

Tomes, Nancy. 2000. "The Making of a Germ Panic, Then and Now." *American Journal of Public Health* 90 (2): 191–198.

Touraine, Alain. 1984. *El Regreso del Actor.* Buenos Aires: Eudeba.

Trinh, Thi Minh-Ha. 1989. *Woman, Native, Other: Writing Postcoloniality and Feminism.* Bloomington: Indiana University Press.

Trlin, Andrew. 1979. *Now Respected, Once Despised: Yugoslavs in New Zealand.* Palmerston North: Dunmore Press.

Trouillot, Michel-Rolph. 2002. "The Perspective of the World: Globalization Then and Now," pp. 3–20 in Elizabeth Mudimbe-Boyi, editor, *Beyond Dichotomies: Histories, Identities, Cultures and the Challenge of Globalization.* Stony Brook: SUNY Press.

Truman, Harry S. 1994. "Inaugural Address, January 20, 1949," pp. 292–298 in Davis Newton Lott, editor, *The Presidents Speak: The Inaugural Addresses of the American Presidents from Washington to Clinton.* New York: H. Holt and Co.

Tsing, Anna L. 1993. *In the Realm of the Diamond Queen.* Princeton: Princeton University Press.

Tsing, Anna L. 2005. *Friction: An Ethnography of Global Connection.* Princeton: Princeton University Press.

Turlings, Yvette. 2002. "Fashion-Makers of Africa: 'Dutch Wax' in Ghana." Radio Netherlands Wereldomroep. http://www.rnw.nl/special/en/html/ghana020408.html. Accessed July 8, 2004.

Turner, Terence. 1999. "Indigenous Rights, Environmental Protection and the Struggle over Forest Resources in the Amazon: The Case of the Brazilian Kayapo," pp. 145–169 in Jill Kerr-Conway, Kenneth Keniston, and Leo Marx, editors, *Earth, Air, Fire, Water.* Amherst: University of Massachusetts Press.

Ubaldo, Mary. 2002. Urduja Designs. www.urduja.com. Accessed March 1, 2004.

United Nations Development Programme (UNDP). 1999. *Human Development Report.* New York: UNDP and Oxford University Press.

United States Treasury Department. 1945. *Questions and Answers on the Fund and Bank.* Washington, DC: United States Treasury Department.

Valence, Georges. 1992. *Les Maîtres du Monde: Allemagne, États-unis, Japon.* Paris: Flammarion.

Valencia Lomelí, Enrique and Rodolfo Aguirre Reveles. 1998. "Discursos, Acciones y Controversias de la Política Gubernamental Frente a la Pobreza," pp. 27–99 in Luis Rigoberto Gallardo Gómez, and Joaquín Osorio Goicoechea, editors, *Los Rostros de la Pobreza: El Debate.* México D.F.: ITESO y la Universidad Iberoamericana, Tomo I.

Veblen, Thorstein. [1899] 1973. *The Theory of the Leisure Class*. With an introduction by John Kenneth Galbraith. Boston: Houghton Mifflin.

Vidal-Naquet, Pierre. 1963. *Torture: Cancer of Democracy*. London: Penguin.

Villarreal, Magdalena. 1994. *Wielding and Yielding: Power, Subordination and Gender Identity in the Context of a Mexican Development Project*. Wageningen: Wageningen Agricultural University.

Villarreal, Magdalena. 2000. "La Reinvención de las Mujeres y el Poder en los Procesos de Desarrollo Rural Planeado." *Revista de Estudios de Género La Ventana* 11: 7–35.

Villarreal, Magdalena. 2001. "Cashing Identities in the Non-Material World of Money." Unpublished paper.

Villarreal, Magdalena. 2004. "Striving to Make Capital do Economic Things for the Impoverished: On the Issue of Capitalization in Rural Microenterprises," pp. 67–82 in Tiina Kontinen, editor, *Development Intervention: Actor and Activity Perspectives*. Helsinki: University of Helsinki.

Viola, Andreu. 1999. *Antropología del Desarrollo. Teorías y Estudios Etnográficos en América Latina*. Barcelona: Paidós.

Visweswaran, Kamala. 1994. *Fictions of Feminist Ethnography*. Minneapolis: University of Minnesota Press.

Wallerstein, Immanuel. 1979. *The Capitalist World Economy*. Cambridge: Cambridge University Press.

Wallerstein, Immanuel. 1995. *After Liberalism*. New York: The New Press.

Walton, John. 2003. "Globalization and Popular Movements," pp. 217–226 in John Foran, editor, *The Future of Revolutions: Rethinking Radical Change in the Age of Globalization*. London: Zed Books.

Ward, Colleen and Anne-Marie Masgoret. 2004. "Discrimination against Immigrants Seeking Employment: Fact or Fiction?" Paper presented at Annual Meeting of the New Zealand Psychological Society, Wellington, New Zealand.

Weatherford, Jack. 1997. *The History of Money*. New York: Three Rivers Press.

Weismantel, Mary. 1989. *Food, Gender, and Poverty in the Ecuadorian Andes*. Philadelphia: University of Pennsylvania Press.

Wentholt, Wyger. 2000. "The Real Dutch Wax. . ." http://findarticles.com/p/articles/mi_qa5391/is_/ai_n21452672. *New African*. March 2000. Accessed November 20, 2008.

West, Guida, and Rhoda Lois Blumberg. Editors. 1990. *Women and Social Protest*. Oxford: Oxford University Press.

Wikimedia Commons. *Regions of the Philippines, Pangasinan*. http://en.wikipedia.org/wiki/Regions_of_the_Philippines. Accessed May 8, 2008.

Williams, Raymond. 1960. *Culture and Society, 1780–1950*. New York: Columbia University Press.

Williams, Raymond. 1977. *Marxism and Literature*. Oxford: Oxford University Press.

Wilmot, Swithen. 1995. "'Females of Abandoned Character'? Women and Protest in Jamaica, 1838–65," pp. 284–292 in Verene Shepherd, Bridget Brereton, and Barbara Bailey, editors, *Engendering History: Caribbean Women in Historical Perspectives*. London: James Curry.

Wilpert, Gregory. 2006. *Changing Venezuela by Taking Power: The History and Policies of the Chavez Government*. London: Verso.

Wilpert, Gregory. 2007. "Chavez Announces Nationalizations, Constitutional Reform for Socialism in Venezuela." http://www.venezuelanalysis.com/print/2164. Accessed June 29, 2008.

Wilson, Ara. 1999. "The Empire of Direct Sales and the Making of Thai Entrepreneurs." *Critique of Anthropology* 19 (4): 401–422.

Wilson, Ara. 2003. "Bangkok, Bubble City," pp. 203–226 in Jane Schneider and Ida Susser, editors, *Wounded Cities: Destruction and Reconstruction in a Globalized World.* Oxford: Berg Publishers.

Wilson, Ara. 2004. *The Intimate Economies of Bangkok: Tomboys, Tycoons, and Avon Ladies in the Global City.* Berkeley and Los Angeles: University of California Press.

Wilson, Ashleigh. 2005. "Sub-standard of Living." *The Australian*, April 7, 2005, pp. 1, 6.

Womack, John. 1999. *Rebellion in Chiapas: An Historical Reader.* New York: The New Press.

Women in Black. 1993. "Israel Women in Black: End the Occupation." *Women in Black Newsletter* (October).

Wood, Geof. 1985. *Labelling in Development Policy: Essays in Honour of Bernard Schaffer.* London: Sage Publications.

World Bank, n.d. "Book on Culture and Development." http://web.worldbank.org/WBSITE/EXTERNAL/TOPICS/EXTPOVERTY/EXTCP/0,,contentMDK:20222729~pagePK:162100~piPK:159310~theSitePK:463778,00.html. Accessed October 22, 2007.

Wright, Jeanette. 2006. "Science, Politics and Genetic Engineering: A Discourse Analysis of the Worldviews Framing the Environmental Risk Management Authority (ERMA) of New Zealand." Unpublished Master's thesis. The University of Waikato, Hamilton.

Yeoh, Brenda S.A. and Shirlena Huang. 1998. "Negotiating Public Space: Strategies and Styles of Migrant Female Domestic Workers in Singapore." *Urban Studies* 35 (3): 583–602.

Yuen, Eddie, Daniel Burton-Rose, and George Katsiaficas. Editors. 2004. *Confronting Capitalism: Dispatches from a Global Movement.* Brooklyn: Soft Skull Press.

Zafra, Nicolas. 1977. *Jose Rizal, Historical Studies.* Quezon City: University of the Philippines Press.

Zapatista. 1998. Documentary film. www.bignoisefilms.com. Santa Barbara: Big Noise Films.

Ziai, Aram. 2004. "The Ambivalence of Post-Development: Between Reactionary Populism and Radical Democracy." *Third World Quarterly* 25 (6): 1045–1060.

Zuazo, Alvaro. 2006. "Bolivia's president orders army to natural gas fields after declaring nationalization." *Associated Press.* May 1, 2006. http://www.accessmylibrary.com/coms2/summary_0286-15072721_ITM. Accessed July 27, 2008.

Zugman, Kara. 2001. "Mexican Awakening in Postcolonial America: Zapatistas in Urban Spaces in Mexico City." Ph.D. dissertation. University of California, Santa Barbara.

Index

E

F

G

H

For Product Safety Concerns and Information please contact our EU representative GPSR@taylorandfrancis.com Taylor & Francis Verlag GmbH, Kaufingerstraße 24, 80331 München, Germany

T - #0067 - 230425 - C0 - 229/152/16 - PB - 9780415650533 - Gloss Lamination